LULU LINEAR PUNCTATED:
ESSAYS IN HONOR OF GEORGE IRVING QUIMBY

George I. Quimby aboard the Hudson's Bay Company supply ship, the *Fort Churchill*, in Hudson's Bay during the summer of 1939. The archaeological and geological survey that brought Quimby here is discussed in the Introduction.

ANTHROPOLOGICAL PAPERS

MUSEUM OF ANTHROPOLOGY, UNIVERSITY OF MICHIGAN
NO. 72

LULU LINEAR PUNCTATED: ESSAYS IN HONOR OF GEORGE IRVING QUIMBY

edited by
Robert C. Dunnell
and
Donald K. Grayson

ANN ARBOR, MICHIGAN
1983

© The Regents of the University of Michigan
The Museum of Anthropology
All rights reserved
Printed in the
United States of America
ISBN: 0-932206-94-8

CONTENTS

Illustrations vii
Tables ix
Introduction
   Robert C. Dunnell and Donald K. Grayson 1
George Irving Quimby: The Formative Years
   James B. Griffin 7
Archaeological Theory: 1936
   Albert C. Spaulding 19
Long Term Land Use Patterns: Some Implications
for Archaeology
   Lewis R. Binford 27
Artifact Class Richness and Sample Size in Archaeological
Surface Assemblages
   George T. Jones, Donald K. Grayson, and Charlotte Beck 55
A Pan-Continental Perspective on Red Ocher and Glacial
Kame Ceremonialism
   Robert L. Hall 75
Aspects of the Spatial Structure of the Mayo Site (15-JO-14),
Johnson County, Kentucky
   Robert C. Dunnell 109
Mississippian Seen from La Tène: On Comparisons
of Prehistoric Social Disorganizations
   Carl-Axel Moberg 167
A Quantitative Approach to Culture Change:
The Delaware Indians as an Ethnohistoric Case Study
   David A. Baerreis 185
Rethinking the French Presence in the Upper Great Lakes
   David S. Brose 209

The Role of Native Animals in the Food Economy of the
Historic Kickapoo in Central Illinois
  Paul W. Parmalee and Walter E. Klippel 253
The Holly Oak Shell Game: An Historic Archaeological Fraud
  David J. Meltzer and William C. Sturtevant 325
Contributors 353

ILLUSTRATIONS

Frontispiece. George I. Quimby aboard the *Fort Churchill* in Hudson's Bay during the summer of 1939	ii
McKern's 1936 crew at Red Cedar River site by Rice Lake	11
Spring vacation at Serpent Mound, April 1938	14
Idealized Nunamiut economic zonation	35
Territory of one Nunamiut band in relation to annual ranges	37
Annual ranges of Nunamiut Eskimo and G/wi Bushman in relation to Tehuacán reconstructed "territories"	44
Total debitage concentration over time at Sudden Shelter	48
Class frequency structure of an assemblage	57
The relationship between number of artifacts counted and numbers of artifact classes encountered	58
Frequency of stone tool classes at Site 35LK84, Central Oregon	59
The Steens Mountain region, southeastern Oregon	60
Surface survey sampling units, Steens Mountain region	62
The distribution of mapped "sites" in the Steens Mountain region	63
Frequencies of stone tool classes for four Steens Mountain region surface assemblages	66
The relationship between numbers of objects counted and numbers of tool classes present in Steens and Catlow upland samples	67
The relationship between numbers of objects counted and numbers of tool classes present in Catlow lowland and Alvord upland samples	68
The relationship between numbers of sherds counted and number of classes represented in 38 ceramic assemblages from the Lower Yazoo Basin	71
Bull-roarers, buzzers, turkey-tails, and sandal-sole gorgets	74
The turkey-tail as a bull-roarer	77
Orion and its symbolism	91
Paint Creek—Levisa confluence showing the location of the Mayo site and nearby archaeological sites	111
Feature 9, a slanting rock grave	119
A well preserved paired hearth feature	130
Nearly intact house from the northeastern section of the Mayo site	131
Plan of the Woodside component at the Mayo site	134
SYMAP of all prehistoric artifacts	135
SYMAP of all Woodside vessel sherds	137
SYMAP of all lithic material	138
SYMAP of Woodside projectile points	139
SYMAP of bone	140
SYMAP of shell-tempered cordmarked ceramics	142
SYMAP of shell-tempered roughened ceramics	143
SYMAP of shell-tempered plain ceramics	144

Six cluster RELOCATE of functional variables 148
Six cluster GRPING using stylistic variables 150
Six cluster average-link grouping of stylistic variables 151
Radial model of the distribution of functional feature classes 154
T-test values comparing radial distance means for functional feature classes 156
Comparison of mean radial distances of selected functional artifact classes
  and feature classes 158
Map of the northern Lake Michigan basin showing locations mentioned
  in the text 212
Dunn Farm Plateau site (20Lu58) 214
Dunn Farm (20Lu22) and Plateau (20Lu58) sites: topography and
  excavation unit locations 215
Dunn Farm Plateau site aboriginal ceramic and groundstone artifacts 219
Dunn Farm Plateau site rimsherd profiles 220
Dunn Farm Plateau site chipped stone artifacts 224
Dunn Farm Plateau site European trade goods 231
Cast brass "Jesuit" ring from unit 2c 233
Examples of bone and tooth artifacts 274
Examples of bone pathology 282
Bone fragments exhibiting puncture marks from chewing, probably by dogs 288
Examples of cut marks on white-tailed deer antler and skull sections 293
Engraving on the Holly Oak pendant and the La Madeleine engraving 330
The La Madeleine engraving 331
Photograph by F. W. Putnam in 1890 of La Madeleine engraving, Lenape
  stone, Holly Oak pendant drawn and photographed 334
The Holly Oak and La Madeleine mammoths compared with other French
  Paleolithic depictions 335
The assemblage purportedly from the Holly Oak site, as photographed
  in 1889 or 1890 337
Hilborne T. Cresson, April 1868 340
In camp at Turner Group, Ohio, 1890: Ernest Volk, Marshall Saville,
  Hilborne T. Cresson 342

TABLES

Demographic expectations for designated regions assuming a Nunamiut type of system of land use 43
Correlation coefficients (Pearson's r) between tool counts and number of tool classes 65
Fort Ancient house size and shape 133
Radial data for feature classes 154
Radial data for selected artifact classes 157
Variability in the use of La Tène, Western and Central Europe 169
Spatial variability in Mississippian 173
Delaware purchases at trading posts compared with non-Indian purchases at Kaskaskia, Illinois 191
Percentages of purchases according to major categories 202
Seasonal distribution of Delaware purchases from Menard and Vallé at the James Fork, White River, Missouri 203
Sales of furs and skins in 1829–31 by the Delawares to Menard and Vallé on the James Fork of White River, Missouri 206
Aboriginal ceramics from the Dunn Farm Plateau site 218
Lithic debitage from 22Lu58 225
Metric attributes of Dunn Plateau chipped stone projectile points, knives, and bifaces 226
Some summary statistics for contact period upper Great Lakes chipped stone triangular points 228
Dunn Farm Plateau site glass beads 234
Estimated pounds of meat and caloric values for Rhoads site animals 261
Age distribution of deer (percentage of each grouping) from the Rhoads site 289
Rhoads site deer elements, number of pieces, and approximate percentage of each with cuts 291
Species, numbers, and estimated meat weights of Rhoads site freshwater mussels 299

INTRODUCTION

Robert C. Dunnell and Donald K. Grayson[1]

In June 1983, George Irving Quimby retires as the Director of the Thomas Burke Memorial Washington State Museum and as Professor of Anthropology at the University of Washington to become Professor Emeritus. Although "retirement" signals little more than the opportunity for George to return full time to the research that has occupied his attention for nearly 50 years, it is an appropriate time for colleagues and friends to pay tribute to one of American archaeology's most distinguished practitioners. George has uniquely influenced generations of archaeologists, not only as a founder of the profession as we know it today but also as a major contributor to eastern, Arctic, and historical archaeology. The diversity of contributors to this volume is testimony to his influence, but it only scratches the surface of the number of archaeologists whose careers and lives have been touched by George. Of practical necessity, this volume is of modest size. Those colleagues who wished to participate in this volume but, who for one reason or another, were unable to contribute form an impressive list: Junius Bird (deceased), Charles Cleland, Richard Ford, William Haag, Jesse Jennings, Volney Jones (deceased), Moreau Maxwell, Stuart Neitzel (deceased), Christopher Peebles, and Robert Ritzenthaler (deceased).

In choosing the title for this volume, we have tried to express the dual essence of Quimby's impact: solid scholarship tempered by his unique sense of perspective on himself and on the machinations of his fellow archaeologists. Lulu Linear Punctated is probably the only pottery type named after a prostitute. Phillips's (1970:107) presentation captures the essentials:

> Lulu Linear Punctated. Plaquemine phase type roguishly named by Quimby in his Medora site report (1951, pp. 121–122) ... it is not unlike Hollyknowe Ridge Pinched, but I doubt whether we should be justified in making it a variety of that type. We shall have to let it stand as a type in splendid isolation, name and all.

1

The etiology of Lulu Linear Punctated may be unconventional, but so is George, and the type is no less serviceable than Hollyknowe Ridge Pinched and certainly far more memorable.

Griffin's account of "The Quimby Formative" in this volume conveys the same sense of a serious scholar who retains the ability to poke fun at the discipline's foibles. George's appreciation that archaeologists are human beings as well as archaeologists has endeared him to people throughout the profession, and perhaps enraged some as well. Griffin's characterization of George remains as true today as it was during the Quimby formative.

Any career as long and as active as Quimby's necessarily incorporates the occasional curious turn, but George seems to have experienced more than his share. How many of us, for example, have had our field camps treated as archaeological sites in their own right by later students? George has.

During the summer of 1939, Quimby and George M. Stanley canoed along the east coast of Hudson Bay to study the raised beaches and archaeology of the area. On July 12, the weather turned bad ("I am getting my religion back," Quimby [1978a:122] wrote in his diary), and, on July 15, the two found themselves stuck on a then-uncharted piece of rock in the Loon Island group. Without natural shelter, Quimby and Stanley built a wall 4 feet high and 30 feet long to protect themselves from the wind. Unable to leave and extremely bored ("I had already read all of our numerous can labels ... I was tired of not winning at checkers" [Quimby 1978a:123]), Quimby incised messages on two tabular rocks, one in Latin, one in ancient Chinese characters, but both bearing similar themes. "UNA FEMINA NUDA IN LECTULO MELIOR EST QUAM CENTUM IN CAELO" read the Latin message; Quimby, always the gentleman, paraphrased the Chinese message as "a woman with certain specified attributes possessed something of great value" (Quimby 1978a:123). Almost forty years later, Quimby learned that this site had been discovered and had become the target of a research proposal. "An Exotic Campsite in East Hudson Bay" (Quimby 1978a) was written to eliminate the possibility of confusion.

When, in 1965, George left the Field Museum (where he retains a position as Research Associate) to come to the University of Washington, his work already spanned the Late Pleistocene (e.g., Quimby 1958, 1959, 1963a) through the historic period (e.g., Quimby 1937, 1939b, 1942a, 1962, 1963b, 1966b), from the Arctic (e.g., Quimby 1940a, 1945a, 1945b, 1946b, 1948b) to the Gulf of Mexico (e.g., Quimby 1951, 1957) and beyond (e.g., Quimby 1947, 1949). It encompassed descriptive and analytic reports (e.g., Quimby 1938, 1939a, 1941a, 1941b, 1942b, 1943,

1957, 1966a; Binford and Quimby 1963; Ford and Quimby 1945) as well as synthetic and interpretive works of lasting significance (e.g., Quimby 1952, 1954, 1960a, 1960b; Martin, Quimby, and Collier 1947). His work included not only archaeology and ethnohistory, but ethnology as well (e.g., Quimby 1940b, 1944, 1946a). On becoming a resident of the Pacific Northwest, George was able to develop his earlier interest in the Northwest Coast (e.g., Quimby 1948a), now concentrating his efforts on the historic period (e.g., Quimby 1970, 1971, 1972, 1977, 1978b, 1978c). Although George continues to publish on a wide variety of topics and areas (e.g., Quimby 1979; Quimby and Casteel 1975; Holm and Quimby 1980), Northwest Coast ethnohistory and archaeology have increasingly captured his attention.

This interest led to a new area of endeavor—ethnographic film—which George has pursued with his colleague Bill Holm. The consequences have included two excellent films, *In the Land of the War Canoes* (Quimby and Holm 1973) and *The Image Maker and the Indians: Edward Curtis and his 1914 Kwakiutl Movie* (Quimby and Holm 1979), as well as a book about Edward Curtis (Holm and Quimby 1980).

George became Director of the Burke Museum in 1968. The growth of the Museum since that time has been impressive. George inherited a museum that frequently operated in the red and that lacked any significant internal source of funds. He also inherited a museum whose exhibits posed serious fire hazards and whose exhibits rarely changed. The numbers alone tell the story of Quimby's impact. In 1968, the Museum's budget was $175,000, virtually all from outside sources; in 1982, the Museum budget was $985,000 of which approximately 41% was generated from internal programs, including the Museum's gift shop, lecture series, and, above all, extremely successful coffee shop (instituted in 1979). In the years just prior to George's arrival, a new year may or may not have seen a new exhibit; in 1983, there will be ten new exhibits, nearly one a month. Those who know the Burke Museum only from the Quimby years can have little appreciation for the good he has done within its walls.

George also anticipated trends in museum administration, and, during the late 1960s, began to argue for the establishment of a graduate program in museology. His efforts came to fruition in 1973 when the Museology Master's Program admitted its first class of students. The program now enjoys considerable success in attracting students and in placing its graduates in a wide variety of museum positions throughout the country. Although George has given over his administrative and instructional roles in the program to his able Curator of American Ethnology, James D. Nason (a Quimby appointee), the existence of the program and much of its character is a direct result of his insight and initiative.

No brief summary can do justice to George's long and varied career as an archaeologist, ethnohistorian, and administrator. We look forward to seeing the results of his new research, conducted without the burden imposed by administrative duties, and to continued contact long into the future. The essays in this volume are offered not as a reflection of Quimby's career, but rather as a token of respect for Quimby the scholar and with deep appreciation for having known him as a person.

Notes

1. We thank Robert Free (Assistant Director, Burke Museum) and Susan Harshberger (Program Assistant, Burke Museum) for assistance during many stages of preparation for this volume. We also gratefully acknowledge the tireless assistance of Mary D. Dunnell (long-time Quimby friend and admirer) in the editorial process. In the end, our major debt is to George Quimby, whose good name and wide circle of colleagues made our task as editors a simple one.

REFERENCES

Binford, L. R., and G. I. Quimby
    1963   Indian sites and chipped stone materials in the northern Lake Michigan area. *Fieldiana: Anthropology* 36:277–302 (reprinted in *An archaeological perspective*, by L. R. Binford, pp. 346–372, 1972, Seminar Press, New York).

Ford, J. A., and G. I. Quimby
    1945   The Tchefuncte culture, an early occupation of the Lower Mississippi Valley. *Society for American Archaeology, Memoir* 2.

Holm, B., and G. I. Quimby
    1980   *Edward Curtis in the land of the war canoes: a pioneer cinematographer in the Pacific Northwest.* University of Washington Press, Seattle.

Martin, P. S., G. I. Quimby, and D. Collier
    1947   *Indians before Columbus: 20,000 years of North American history revealed by archaeology.* University of Chicago Press, Chicago (paperback ed. 1974, University of Chicago Press, Chicago).

Phillips, P.
    1970   Archaeological survey in the Lower Yazoo Basin, Mississippi, 1949–1955. *Papers of the Peabody Museum of Archaeology and Ethnology* 60.

Quimby, G. I.
    1937   Notes on Indian trade silver ornaments in Michigan. *Papers of the Michigan Academy of Science, Arts, and Letters* 22: 15–24.
    1938   Dated Indian burials in Michigan. *Papers of the Michigan Academy of Science, Arts, and Letters* 23:63–72.
    1939a   Aboriginal camp sites on Isle Royale, Michigan. *American Antiquity* 4:215–223.
    1939b   European trade objects as chronological indicators for the archaeology of the historic period in Michigan. *Papers of the Michigan Academy of Science, Arts, and Letters* 24:25–35.
    1940a   The Manitunik Eskimo culture of east Hudson's Bay. *American Antiquity* 6:148–165.

1940b	Some notes on kinship and kinship terminology among the Potawatomi of the Huron. *Papers of the Michigan Academy of Science, Arts, and Letters* 25:553–563.
1941a	Hopewellian pottery types in Michigan. *Papers of the Michigan Academy of Science, Arts, and Letters* 26:489–495.
1941b	The Goodall Focus, an analysis of ten Hopewellian components in Michigan and Indiana. *Indiana Historical Society Pre-history Research Series* 2(2):63–161.
1942a	Indian trade objects in Michigan and Louisiana. *Papers of the Michigan Academy of Science, Arts, and Letters* 27:543–551.
1942b	The Natchezan culture type. *American Antiquity* 7:255–275.
1943	The ceramic sequence within the Goodall Focus. *Papers of the Michigan Academy of Science, Arts, and Letters* 28:543–548.
1944	Aleutian Islanders, Eskimos of the North Pacific. *Field Museum Anthropology Leaflet* 35.
1945a	Pottery from the Aleutian Islands. *Fieldiana: Anthropology* 36:1–13.
1945b	Periods of prehistoric art in the Aleutian Islands. *American Antiquity* 11:76–79.
1946a	Natchez social structure as an instrument of assimilation. *American Anthropologist* 48:134–136.
1946b	Toggle harpoon heads from the Aleutian Islands. *Fieldiana: Anthropology* 36:14–24.
1947	The prehistory of Kamchatka. *American Antiquity* 12:173–179.
1948a	Culture contact on the northwest coast, 1785–1795. *American Anthropologist* 50:134–136.
1948b	Prehistoric art of the Aleutian Islands. *Fieldiana: Anthropology* 36:77–92.
1949	Cochise and Mogollon sites: excavations. *Fieldiana: Anthropology* 38:26–33.
1951	The Medora site, West Baton Rouge Parish, Louisiana. *Field Museum of Natural History Publication* 664.
1952	The archeology of the Upper Great Lakes area. In *Archeology of the Eastern United States*, edited by J. B. Griffin, pp. 99–107. University of Chicago Press, Chicago.
1954	Cultural and natural areas before Kroeber. *American Antiquity* 19:317–331.
1957	The Bayou Goula site, Iberville Parish, Louisiana. *Field Museum of Natural History Publication* 814.
1958	Fluted points and geochronology of the Lake Michigan basin. *American Antiquity* 23:247–254.
1959	Lanceolate points and fossil beaches in the Upper Great Lakes region. *American Antiquity* 24:424–426.
1960a	Habitat, culture, and archaeology. In *Essays in the science of culture in honor of Leslie A. White*, edited by G. E. Dole and R. L. Carneiro, pp. 380–389. Crowell, New York.
1960b	*Indian life in the Upper Great Lakes 11,000 B.C. to A.D. 1800*. University of Chicago Press, Chicago.
1962	A year with a Chippewa family, 1763–1764. *Ethnohistory* 9:217–239.
1963a	A new look at geochronology in the Upper Great Lakes region. *American Antiquity* 28:558–559.
1963b	The Gros Cap cemetery in Mackinac county, Michigan. *Michigan Archaeologist* 9(4):50–57.
1966a	The Dumaw Creek site: a seventeenth century prehistoric Indian village in Oceana county, Michigan. *Field Museum of Natural History Publication* 1014.
1966b	*Indian culture and European trade goods*. University of Wisconsin Press, Madison.
1967	The Indian tribes of the Upper Great Lakes region. In *The North American Indians: a source book*, edited by R. C. Owen, J. Deetz, and A. Fisher, pp. 576–580. Macmillan, New York.

1970	James Swan among the Indians: the influence of a pioneer from New England on coastal Indian art. *Pacific Northwest Quarterly* 61:212–216.
1971	Humor among the treaty makers and fur traders or Joe Miller's joke book in the Pacific Northwest. *Ethnohistory* 18:267–271.
1972	Hawaiians in the fur trade of north-west America, 1785–1820. *Journal of Pacific History* 7:92–103.
1977	Women on the lower Columbia River in the early nineteenth century. *Anthropological Papers, Museum of Anthropology, University of Michigan* 61:230–241.
1978a	An exotic campsite in east Hudson Bay. *Historical Archaeology* 10:121–123.
1978b	Yankee artist, James Madison Alden in Washington Territory 1854. *Pacific Northwest Quarterly* 69:31–33.
1978c	Trade beads and sunken ships. In *Archaeological essays in honor of Irving B. Rouse*, edited by R. C. Dunnell and E. S. Hall, Jr., pp. 228–243. Mouton, The Hague.
1979	A brief history of WPA archaeology. In *The uses of anthropology*, edited by W. Goldschmidt, pp. 110–123. American Anthropological Association, Washington, D.C.

Quimby, G. I., and R. W. Casteel (editors)
    1975   *Maritime adaptations of the Pacific.* Mouton, The Hague.

Quimby, G. I., and B. Holm (producers)
    1973   *In the land of the war canoes: Kwakiutl life on the Northwest Coast* (film). University of Washington Press, Seattle.
    1979   *The image maker and the Indians: Edward Curtis and his 1914 Kwakiutl movie* (film). University of Washington Press, Seattle.

GEORGE IRVING QUIMBY: THE FORMATIVE YEARS

James B. Griffin

The subject of this essay was born in Grand Rapids, Michigan, on May 4, 1913. This took place in his parents' home, 21 South Union Avenue, which was built in the 1840s or 1850s and is now on the Federal Register of Historic Buildings and is called "The Old Quimby House." This large frame structure was added to, modified and modernized over the years and is a monument whose present fittings cannot be attributed to the age of the foundation timbers. With George's arrival, his parents must have lived an even more eventful life. His mother was an ardent collector of old furniture, glass or almost any items that are regarded as antiques. His father was the proprietor of a book store and was an ardent supporter of the Little Theater group in Grand Rapids. Both were interested in the history of the Grand Rapids area, including Indian groups. This interest is exemplified in the belief that the mark "01" on a very large oak tree, which was on the northwest corner of the Quimby lot, was a blaze mark for the old Kalamazoo trail. Grand Rapids had two groups of Indian mounds. The Converse group was located on the west side of the river on Court Street just south of the Gerald Ford Museum, and the Norton group on the east side of the river in Wyoming Township, Kent County, south of town. This was well known to many residents.

When George was in the second grade he saw an article about the Seminole Indians of Florida in the *National Geographic*. His mother had told him how the Indians of the Grand Rapids area participated in trading activities in the nineteenth century. He put these two experiences together one day after school, gathered up the family soap supply, put it in his cart, and, with several friends, headed south on Union Street with the intention of going to Florida to trade with the Indians. About sundown the young entrepreneurs came to a barn on the southern edge of

Grand Rapids four miles or so from their starting point. They decided to bed down there. By happy coincidence the barn was on the property of Mark Hall, a cousin, who reassured the worried Quimbys and other parents that their offspring were safe. An interest in trading activities was to surface later in other contexts.

Among other activities was marching in the parades of Civil War and Spanish American War veterans. George has written "that in our parade positions we tried to avoid the Civil War soldiers in their splendid blue uniforms of the 'Grand Army of the Republic' because nearly all of them chewed tobacco and were careless, long range spitters." George has also indicated the importance in his youth of the Kent Scientific Institute housed in a three-story Victorian mansion of brick and wood. This was the forerunner of the present Grand Rapids Public Museum. In his words

> This museum was a fascinating mixture of junk and fine artifacts and mounted zoological specimens from all over the world exhibited in unlighted, dusty display cases of infinite sizes and shapes. Labels were hand printed, inadequate in content, and in retrospect loaded with misinformation. But in the first half of the 1920s it was for me a real adventure to explore the Kent Scientific Institute and it was not only the best museum but it was the only museum I had ever seen.
>
> I particularly liked the uncataloged collections of American Indian artifacts, the antique weapons, Egyptian artifacts, and mummies. In the barn-like annex among the other mounted animals there was an impressive stuffed camel leaking a trail of sawdust that manifested an antique state of taxidermy and preservation which I was then too naive to comprehend. By today's standards that museum was a disaster but for me it was an exciting introduction to the world of museums.

It is not really quite accurate to say that the Kent Scientific Institute was the first museum George had ever seen. Perhaps it was in a formal use of the term, but his home, in an informal sense, was a museum in its own right. Since both of his parents were compulsive collectors, the house had many of the attributes of such an institution. His father collected books and paintings. With such a home environment it was natural for George to feel that such activities were normal, and he acquired antique guns and other weaponry.

Another interest of his mother's was sailing, for she had enjoyed that sport as a teenager on Lake Macatawa, Ottawa County, Michigan. She made sure that George learned how to handle a skiff at age eight or nine. This was rented at Partridge's Resort on White Lake near Muskegon, Michigan, and the skiff soon had a spruce sapling stepped in the forward thwart as a mast. Another spruce limb acted as a boom for a bed sheet section which was the mainsail. The Yacht Club at White Lake had an active sailing school, training the youngsters to sail the sloop and other craft of the period. As his sailing skills improved he progressed to being a crew member of a Class A, 38 foot, sloop-rigged skimming dish named the Phantom, which they raced every Saturday. Arriving early, they beached the craft and applied Vaseline to the bottom of the dish to reduce friction. In 1928, the Phantom captured all racing honors. In 1929, George was Fleet Captain of Sail in the Junior Yacht Club. He was intrusted with sailing a 35 foot yawl, the Beaver, whose owners wanted to move it from Manistee to White Lake, and for George this was a high point. While George was learning, one of his mentors was an elderly man who had been a sailor on a British square-rigged ship in the Crimean War (1854–56).

For three years, 1930–32, George was a member of the crew of a 45 foot Alden fore- and aft-rigged wooden schooner called the Aurora of about 25 tons burden, with an auxiliary engine. This vessel, except for the engine, was essentially the same as vessels in use during the eighteenth century. It belonged to two Bissell brothers, neighbors of the Quimbys. The brothers acquired the schooner from their grandfather, who, tiring of sweeping out his wife's china shop, had invented the carpet sweeper. During three summers they sailed some 3000 miles, and visited Indian villages and other lakeside communities on Lake Michigan and Georgian Bay. In 1930, the Aurora won the Chicago–Saugatuck race and was the only boat to finish in a bad storm. The reason, according to George, was that they could not get their sails down and had to keep going. In 1931 they were the youngest crew to sail the Chicago–Mackinac race. Of the 23 boats that finished, they came in twenty-second.

George graduated from Central High School in Grand Rapids in 1932 and entered the University of Michigan that fall. In his first two years he took four courses in English, three courses in Geology, two in Geography, and one course each in Spanish, Journalism, Philosophy, Fine Arts, Forestry, and Anthropology. The latter was "The American Indian" and as a result he decided to enter his junior year as a Concentrate in Anthropology. In his last two years he took three courses in Geology, three in English, one each in Geography, History, and Sociology, and thirteen in Anthropology.

I probably first met George in the fall of 1934, for one of his courses was Advanced Museum Methods for which he was probably qualified because of his training at home. I remember I urged him to take the course in Pleistocene Glaciation from George M. Stanley, for I had taken it the year before and felt that every archaeologist ought to have an exposure to it, particularly in the Great Lakes region. Among his other graduation notations is that he had completed Physical Education—my major surprise in going over his records—and also lectures in Hygiene. Perhaps on the basis of the latter he was given unqualified admission to the Graduate School. In the summer of 1935 George was part of the excavating crew at the Younge site along with H. Holmes Ellis, Norman D. Humphrey, and Alfred K. Guthe, working under Emerson F. Greenman. In the preface of the report George is cited as having cleaned and repaired the skeletal material, bringing it to a condition suitable for measurement and observation.

One of our first trips together was in 1935 when George told me about the Hopewellian material in the Kent Scientific Museum and indicated that I could stay in his home during my visit. The notes and photographs taken at that time became the basis for his Master's Thesis in 1936, and with additions, it was later published as Volume 2, Number 2 of the *Indiana Historical Society Prehistory Research Series* in 1941.

As a result of a meeting with Eli Lilly and his anthropological research team in the fall of 1936 at Lake Wawasee, Indiana, it was decided that an attempt should be made to identify the material culture of early historic tribes believed to have occupied the northern Indiana and southern Michigan area. Glenn A. Black was to work primarily in Indiana with headquarters in South Bend. The Michigan area was to be examined by representatives from the Museum of Anthropology at the University of Michigan. Greenman objected to my working in the state, but he felt it was all right for Quimby to participate. George was to have done fieldwork with the Potawatomie near Athens and was being coached by Leslie A. White and Mischa Titiev for this venture, but the archaeological survey was more enticing. One of the motivations for that summer's work was a reported Iroquois village site which was viewed by some archaeologists as perhaps representing the movement of the Iroquois from the Mississippi Valley to New York. The village site was not found, but others were, including the Mocassin Bluff site. This was called to our attention by George Birdsall, an ardent amateur archaeologist living in South Bend. It was later to be excavated by the Museum of Anthropology and eventually published.

The summer of 1936 found George excavating at Rice Lake, Wisconsin under W. C. McKern. Other members of the crew were George Lidberg, Joffre L. Coe, John Adair, Albert C. Spaulding, and Leland R. Cooper (Fig. 1). That summer provided Quimby with more rigorous experience in field techniques and with McKern's tentative application of the Midwestern Taxonomic Classification for the Wisconsin area. Spaulding and David B. Stout entered the graduate program in the fall of 1936 and received their Master's degrees in the spring of 1937. They were a trio with quite different interests and aptitudes. George had become interested in the fall of his senior year in the trade silver in the Great Lakes Range, and his course paper became "Notes on Indian Trade Silver Ornaments in

Fig. 1. W. C. McKern and crew at Rice Lake, Wisconsin, June 1936. *Left to right*: George Lidberg; Joffre L. Coe; John Adair; W. C. McKern; George I. Quimby; Albert C. Spaulding; and Leland R. Cooper.

Michigan." He presented it at the spring 1936 meeting of the Michigan Academy of Science, Arts, and Letters, and it was then published in Volume 22 of that organization's *Proceedings* in 1937. His interest in intercultural contact, which appeared as early as his desire to trade with the Seminole, was the subject of his first professional paper. This interest has continued throughout his career. His willingness to work on, complete, and publish his ideas has marked his career from this early beginning.

In his museum working hours, he had associations with a number of co-workers. Volney H. Jones was active in the Ethnobotanical Laboratory with Melvin R. Gilmore as his not-very-active mentor. Gilmore was in poor health and walked with short, shuffling steps from the elevator to his office. Early in life, Gilmore had become adapted to the tall grass prairies of the Dakotas and Nebraska. When he lived in the New York area working for the Museum of the American Indian, and also in Ann Arbor, he kept his watch on Central instead of Eastern Time. This enabled him to appear on Nebraska time and leave with a clear conscience on Michigan time. Quimby noticed that the sound of shuffling feet reverberating in the hall would prompt Jones to assiduously apply himself in the laboratory adjoining Gilmore's office. Several times shortly before

Gilmore normally appeared, a shuffling sound could be heard in the hall; Jones would go into his routine, look up and see George standing in the doorway.

In the latter half of the 1930s three Americans were prominent on the radio and in stirring up the populace to right the wrongs of American society. Huey Long organized a "Share the Wealth" group, Gerald K. Smith formed an "America First" group, and Father Coughlan from the Shrine of the Little Flower in Royal Oak, Michigan, called for "Social Justice." We were told in the Museum, by George, that he had formed Ann Arbor chapters for each of these with himself as Secretary. He claimed to send in glowing accounts of the growth and deep interest among the members of the aims and interests of each of the three rabble rousers, receiving in return literature and paraphernalia to promote his nonexistent chapters. Mail was received, he claimed, at his Zeta Psi fraternity house, but I cannot recall at the moment any of the replies to justify his claims.

During his work on the collections in the Museum he came across one of the fish skin raincoats of the Aleut. This inspired George to produce a replica of the long pointed Aleut hats so that he could have his picture taken on the roof of the Museum, dressed as an Aleut and holding an atlatl and spear as though he were in the act of throwing. This was superimposed on a scene of an ice-covered bay, with a ship in the bay, so that it looked like you were seeing an Aleut in his native habitat. A copy was sent to his mother and she wrote back commenting on what strange looking people the Aleut were. About the same time George was writing a paper for one of Carl Guthe's courses on the archaeological methodology of Waldemar Jochelson in his excavation of Aleut sites, which had been published by the Carnegie Institute of Washington.

He received a Graduate Fellowship for 1937/38 and continued to take courses from Guthe, Titiev, and White. The courses that Quimby had from Titiev and White in kinship systems and social organization were beneficial to him for his study of Potawatomie kinship (which was published in the *Papers of the Michigan Academy* in 1940) and to his interpretation of the function of Natchez social structure (which appeared in the 1946 *American Anthropologist*). He is one of relatively few archaeologists who has published contributions in social anthropology.

James A. Ford came to Ann Arbor for a year, receiving an M.A. degree in 1938, writing it under Guthe. During the spring vacation period of 1938, George went to Buffalo for rest and relaxation, and I asked him to see if the Buffalo Museum of Science had a collection from the Fisher site in Illinois that it would be willing to turn over to the Ceramic Repository. When he returned and reported, he had a grin on his face and stated that they had a fair amount that they would send us. It was more than that, for the three large wooden packing cases included not only the Fisher material but Iroquois pottery from the Buffalo area, a large amount of Weeden Island material from Florida, and Middle Mississippi pottery from Missouri and Arkansas. This was piled into the cases and mixed without any data. Much of the Mississippian material had been collected by Riggs, and I believe the Weeden Island sherds were from C. B. Moore's work. In any event, George certainly produced and also participated in sorting the pottery into regional assemblages along with Jim Ford and myself. He also participated in the Ann Arbor meeting where the style of the type descriptions was adopted (Griffin 1976:25-27).

George was also able to associate in the Museum with Georg K. Neumann. Neumann was working on the skeletal material from Fort Ancient sites with Fred R. Matson, who had an undergraduate degree from the University of Illinois in ceramic engineering. Carl Guthe had a long-range plan for the development of a ceramic research center in the Museum of Anthropology, for his involvement in Southwestern archaeology with five years at Pecos had impressed him with the value of systematic ceramic studies. The Ceramic Repository for the Eastern United States had been established in 1928. Its development was accentuated in 1933 by the appointment of Benjamin March in the Oriental Range of the Museum and by Matson's joining the staff in 1934. This meant that there was a strong emphasis on the study of prehistoric ceramics from various viewpoints.

During spring vacation in 1938, Quimby, Neumann, and Jim and Ethel Ford visited sites in southern Ohio where we were joined by John Cotter, John Buckner, Richard Morgan, and William Haag (Fig. 2). Trips such as this enabled Quimby to associate with many of the active archaeologists of the period. He also was involved in Museum activities when the Society for American Archaeology was being formed and was one of its early members.

Quimby's academic year of 1938/39 was spent in the Anthropology graduate program at the University of Chicago, when it still had an outstanding reputation for training in archaeology. During his graduate year at the University of Chicago, George was asked by George Stanley to accompany him on a geological survey of the east side of Hudson Bay in 1938 observing post-glacial changes and beach elevations. This was because of Quimby's training in geology, his ability to navigate, and because he would be a good companion. As a result of his collecting activities on this trip, "The Manitunik Eskimo Culture of East Hudson's Bay" appeared in late 1940 in *American Antiquity*. On this trip George reported that, after some period of time directing the movements of his Eskimo rod

Fig. 2. Spring vacation, April 1938, at Serpent Mound, Adams County, Ohio. *Left to right*: Georg K. Neuman; John L. Cotter; James B. Griffin; George I. Quimby; John Buckner; James A. Ford; Ethel Ford; Richard G. Morgan; and William G. Haag.

man in English, he decided to try out his newly acquired vocabulary. He was gratified to see that his rod man responded equally well to George's instructions in Eskimo. Being a true scientist, he decided to test by giving directions in Spanish. The test indicated that the rod man reacted equally well whether English, Eskimo, or Spanish was spoken. His interpretation of the materials obtained on the Belcher Islands was greatly aided by Diamond Jenness, Frederica De Laguna, and Henry Collins. This was the first of his several papers on sub-Arctic cultures.

> Stanley and I had a rather exciting trip. While he piloted the canoe, I offered up prayers. We finally got to Richmond Gulf without guides, thereby establishing some kind of a record. The archaeological remains were damn slim, except on the Belcher Islands where a Thule-Dorset? culture is plentiful. I have a pile of specimens which were obtained from pothunting eskimos. I intend to write them up during the year with Jenness's dig. Stanley coveted them a bit, mainly for aesthetic reasons, but I made off with them in a very ungentlemanly fashion.

His graduate studies were interrupted by a stint in Louisiana working as laboratory supervisor for the Work Projects Administration archaeological program under Jim Ford's direction. He thus became familiar with Lower Mississippi Valley prehistory, and his work there produced a number of publications. Capitalizing on earlier excavations and reports, Ford and Quimby compiled a manuscript on the Tchefuncte culture, which was completed in the early spring of 1940. Quimby sent it up to Parkin, Arkansas where Phillips, Ford, and I were working on the Central Mississippi Valley survey. My reaction to its form then was that it failed to adequately place Tchefuncte in relation to other eastern complexes and particularly that it could be regarded as a Lower Valley counterpart to Adena in the Ohio Valley. Whereupon Ford took Quimby to task for that omission. War activities intervened to prevent completion of the Tchefuncte report, and George did not provide a "final" draft until early 1944, which was then read by Ford. On June 8, 1944, George wrote:

> A few weeks ago Jim wrote to me a letter stating that he had somewhat modified the Tchefuncte Report in the interests of diction clarity etc. Upon receiving the report I discovered that this modification consisted in removing all references to the probability that Adena and Tchefuncte were contemporary, removing qualifying phrases from statements etc., and removing any reference to cord-marked pottery in any complex which might otherwise be coeval with Tchef. All cord-marking has to be either simple stamped or fabric marked. I was very amused by this. I can correct the factual sections o.k. and where it becomes a matter of Jim's personal interpretation I head the section "conjectures" which I think takes care of the matter. The really important part of the report is the factual account of Tchefuncte. Jim believes that Copena is the earliest limestone tempered horizon and the probable source of the limestone tempering in Adena. This is implied in his handling of the question although he doesn't come right out with it. Apparently he is not familiar with the limestone tempered material in Tennessee. To his credit, however, he ends this statement by stating that more data are needed. I'll try to repair this error.

The revised comparative statement was a much broader statement, and I was happy to later recommend to Douglas Byers that it be published as the first *Memoir* of the Society of American Archaeology.

In Baton Rouge, George was acquired as a husband by Helen Ziehm from Pine Bluff, Arkansas, who was studying art at Louisiana State University. This alliance provided a valuable balance and stability over the years. In late October 1940, after two paragraphs of archaeological problems he wrote:

> In the meantime I got married to a girl from Pine Bluff, Arkansas. She is a teaching fellow in sculpture here, and locally pretty well known for her wood and rock carvings. My only complaint is that she teaches at 8 A.M. We have a nice little apartment, eat out since we both are working, altho she cooks breakfast. I am learning not to shove her out of the way and go thru doors ahead of her etc. etc. Surprising amount of adjustment to this marriage business. I am getting so I don't jump out of the window when somebody knocks on the door. We had the approval of both our families, and I was married at Pine Bluff Oct. 13 in the Presbyterian Church with a medium high Episcopal ceremony. Retreated from Arkansas over to Miss., took her on a tour of Indian Mounds on Hy. 61, also thru Vicksburg monument. She doesn't mind at all. In the swamps she always goes first to scare away the snakes and

Frenchmen. All in all we seem to be an ideal combination, both of us too lazy to ever fight. She won't let me throw my clothes on the floor, have to hang them up, but I forgive her. ... Also she is dead against any drinking except beer and wine in moderate quantitites. This is a money saver. I sure like it a lot and am sorry I didn't begin sooner. If we have any children we can name them Exemption, Class II, etc. and at the same time I will sue a couple of Drug companies and that ex-archaeologist, Dr. J. T. Lewis. But all in all she is a swell person whom you and Ruby would like very much.

We did.

With the end of the relief labor support in Louisiana, George became the Director of the Muskegon, Michigan Museum in 1941/42 and then accepted a position as a Curator in the Department of Anthropology in the Field Museum of Natural History in Chicago in 1942, where he remained until 1965. He had a major role in the revitalization of a number of exhibits in Anthropology, particularly those dealing with the prehistory of the eastern United States. These were lively, colorful, and emphasized some of the major developments of the prehistory societies, with a minimum of specimens. These were readily understandable to the average museum visitor.

A major project of his first five years was his collaboration with Paul S. Martin and Donald Collier in writing *Indians Before Columbus: 20,000 Years of North American History Revealed by Archaeology*, published by the University of Chicago Press in 1947. This became the first effective textbook in North American archaeology. Among his curatorial duties was that of care for the superb Northwest Coast collection at the Field Museum, which helped to prepare him for his later position at the Washington State Museum.

In the summer of 1947, George had his introduction to field work in the Southwest as director of the daily activities for Paul S. Martin's program near Glenwood, New Mexico. On January 16, 1948, he wrote "Now that I have seen the Southwest there is no further incentive to work in that area although I must confess that I would like to spend my winters in Tucson. I wouldn't mind working on my own, but this being field director for someone else gets to be a bit complicated at times." His ability to handle some of the situations was shown when Joe Brew came to visit the excavation. George took Joe up to the tent where Martin was listening to classical records. Leaving Joe outside, George went in to announce Joe's arrival. The resulting comments from Martin indicated in no uncertain terms that he was not pleased, and his remarks were quite audible outside the tent. Whereupon George came out and told Joe that Paul had said how pleased he was to have him visit and could he stay for supper. The disinclination to work in the Southwest, I believe, was influenced by his association with the Great Lakes climate. In the East you don't have to bite snakes in the summer in order to get rain.

When the Festschrift for Fay-Cooper Cole was being planned, George was an obvious choice for a presentation of "The Archaeology of the Upper Great Lakes Area," but he could have prepared a chapter on a number of other areas such as the lower Mississippi Valley. His interest in the interrelationship of the early Americans and their environment led to his "Cultural and Natural Areas Before Kroeber" published in *American Antiquity* in 1954. These interests he continued in later papers. His background of 25 years provided his popular volume on *Indian Life in the Upper Great Lakes 11,000 B.C. to A.D. 1880* published by the University of Chicago Press in 1960, and his *Indian Culture and European Trade Goods* volume in 1966, published by the University of Wisconsin Press.

My correspondence file with George is fairly thick with an exchange of our ideas about various facets of archaeology. In addition, he made numerous trips to Ann Arbor on a semi-annual basis for years, and quite often I visited Chicago for one reason or another. We worked together on many projects with both good will and good results. His removal to Seattle resulted in much less intimate contacts.

Even with this short and incomplete summary of some of his activities preceding and during his early years in anthropology, it is evident that a considerable part of his contributions to anthropology and museum activities were strongly influenced by his early interests, training, fieldwork and associations with many different professionals. It is appropriate that this volume in honor of his career be published by the Museum of Anthropology at the University of Michigan. His contributions have given prestige to the anthropology program at the University. He has been for many years one of its most successful and prominent products.

REFERENCES

Griffin, J. B.
    1976   A commentary on some archaeological activities in the mid-continent 1925–1975. *Midcontinental Journal of Archaeology* 1:5–38.

ARCHAEOLOGICAL THEORY: 1936

Albert C. Spaulding

The announcements of the impending retirements of George Quimby and Joffre Coe came as no surprise to me because of my own situation. Both are intimately connected with my introduction to archaeology, which occurred in the summer of 1936 at the excavations conducted by Will C. McKern for a joint Milwaukee Public Museum—University of Wisconsin program. In subsequent years, all of us were intimately associated with James B. Griffin and the University of Michigan. Quimby had received his undergraduate training there, and both of us worked on and acquired our M.A. degrees from Michigan in the 1936/37 academic year. Coe came to Michigan as a graduate student after his military service in World War II and completed his Ph.D. degree while I was a faculty member there. All of this presents a strong temptation to indulge in gaffer reminiscences extending over 45 years under the pretense that the world is eagerly awaiting valuable historical insights from a seminal period in American archaeology as exemplified by our activities. I cannot resist this temptation altogether, but I will compromise by confining myself pretty much to the topic of archaeology as viewed from Rice Lake and Spencer Lake, Wisconsin, in the summer of 1936.

From my point of view, both Quimby and Coe were enviably sophisticated. My knowledge of archaeology was the product of reading in the University of Montana library, so I knew much more about the palace of Minos at Knossos and the dawn of European civilization as expounded by Childe than I did about the archaeology of the eastern United States. Quimby had actually participated in archaeological excavations under Emerson Greenman and worked in the Museum of Anthropology at Michigan; he could also allude knowingly to the Michigan excavations in the Near East. Coe had excavated in North Carolina and with the University of Chicago. Our leader, McKern, had worked in California anthropology, Polynesian (Tonga) archaeology, Colorado archaeology, and the archaeology of Wisconsin from 1925 on as an assistant curator and later as head of the Department of Anthropology and finally as Director of the Milwaukee Public Museum. Ralph Linton visited the excavations for some time as the representative of the University of Wisconsin. In addition to the archaeologists in the strict sense, the party included University of Wisconsin anthropology majors, of whom I recall John Adair, William Bascom, and David Stout, several other university students of various origins and interests, and a professional photographer, George Waite, who had earlier participated in the Beloit College field work in North Africa. This was an impressive assemblage as viewed from Montana, and I paid close attention to the formal and informal instruction and discussions that were a more or less continuous part of our working and evening activities.

Formal instruction was provided by McKern. It included, of course, our daily directives on what to do and how to do it in the excavating. The basic pattern of these instructions was essentially modern in form. For the most part, we were excavating burial mounds, a Hopewell group at Rice Lake and a late prehistoric or protohistoric mound at Spencer Lake. We cleared brush and turf from the surface of the mound to be excavated, McKern laid out a 5- or 10-foot grid with the aid of a surveyor's level and compass, staked the grid intersections and read elevations (arbitrary datum, I think) at each intersection, and we proceeded to excavate. The basic excavation unit was a rectangle 5 or 10 feet wide and long enough to extend a short distance beyond the mound edges at either end; we excavated 5- or 10- foot slices. The vertical section was carefully preserved for a final cleaning and mapping, and the horizontal floor of the excavation was cleaned and inspected at frequent intervals. The features we encountered (mostly burials) were excavated as units. Photographs, maps, and verbal descriptions were provided for vertical and horizontal sections and for features. Prepared looseleaf forms were used for the feature descriptions. The material collected was labeled, sometimes repaired, and packed for transport to the Museum. In brief, the excavating and recording techniques were systematic and carefully controlled; they were the basic methods that we still use.

According to my best recollection, these methods were no novelty to Quimby as he had worked in much the same fashion with Greenman in Michigan, nor can I recall any special comments from Coe on the basis of his previous experience with the University of Chicago and in North Carolina. There was good communication among the middlewestern archaeologists. In fact there had been a more or less official attempt to propagandize for adequate field methods by the Committee on State

Archaeological Surveys under the sponsorship of the National Research Council with Carl Guthe as a moving spirit, and the need for close regional cooperation and coordination was generally recognized. Indeed, the need for better cooperation and communication on a continental level had very recently led to the formation of the Society for American Archaeology and the establishment of *American Antiquity* with McKern as its editor. American archaeology had become a professional discipline in the general sense of interrelating the already professional activities of such centers as the Smithsonian Institution and the Universities of Chicago, Harvard, Michigan, California, and Nebraska with other institutions having respectable but ancillary research programs, exemplified by the University of Kentucky.

McKern's instruction did not stop with field techniques. He was a firm supporter of the ecumenical movement, and he lectured to us in the evenings on the integrating Midwestern Taxonomic System (called the McKern system by everyone but McKern) as a device for improving the accuracy of communication in a regional context. He also lectured on the archaeological cultures of Wisconsin, and he commented on the information and concepts coming to him as editor of *American Antiquity*. Quimby, Coe, and I, the dedicated archaeologists of the group, listened respectfully, but I cannot recall much in the way of spirited below-stairs discussions inspired by McKern's remarks. My present interpretation is that we were still too naive intellectually to be anything but cautiously noncommital on the value of the McKern system. In fact, we probably did not have any very clear grasp of just what the system was.

The points emphasized by McKern according to my partial total recall included (1) the need to supplement the vague term "culture" or "a culture" with a more precise set of graded terms expressing the degree of similarity between or among two or more archaeological entities, (2) the need to provide an objective measure of degree of similarity, and (3) the desirability of concentrating on a single region with its generally similar archaeological materials and freely interacting archaeologists to insure the necessary uniformity and comparability in trait recognition and description. McKern had a nice sense of dimensional homogeneity: the system was concerned only with physical similarity as one essential aspect of the study of archaeological materials. The result of classification was not to be considered an end product of archaeological research; rather, it was to be interrelated with chronology and geographical locus in the production of a full culture history of the region.

At this point, introspection tells me that I cannot disentangle precisely what McKern told us in 1936 from information acquired elsewhere and slightly later, so I supplement my memory by referring to two nearly contemporaneous documents, McKern's "The Midwestern Taxonomic Method as an Aid to Archaeological Culture Study" (1939) and James B. Griffin's *The Fort Ancient Aspect* (1943). I am quite sure that we were told that the proper measure for degree of similarity between two entities was "percentage of traits in common"; this is the similarity measure now called Jaccard's Coefficient. Its calculation is simple: divide the number of traits common to the two entities by the total number of traits exhibited by both. McKern had second thoughts on this coefficient that are expressed in the 1939 paper: "Experience seems to demonstrate that absolute mathematical percentages in trait similarity can not be successfully employed to establish the class relationship between two compared manifestations" (McKern 1939:311). The difficulties were that fully comparable and complete information for both entities would be an unlikely circumstance and that all traits could not be assumed to have equal weight (for example, presence of corn or simple bone awls at both entities does not have the same implication for the cultural typology of a region as does the common presence of a complex decorative motif for pottery). Nevertheless, quantitative similarity could be helpful in the right circumstances, notably in the case of determining finer relationships in a set of generally quite similar entities. McKern recognized clearly that the concept "trait" was itself vague and that this vagueness could be reduced by consideration of "trait elements," for example shell tempering, loop handles, or cord-imprinted decoration within the general trait of pottery. As best I can remember, he did not pursue this concept to the point of attempting to define a minimal unit of culturally significant behavior, a behaviorally generalized extension of the linguists' concept of phoneme. Neither can I recall any discussion of increasing the sensitivity of the similarity measure by taking into account relative quantities of traits in addition to simple presence or absence information.

One source of confusion lay in the term "component." It is clear that McKern (1939:308) defined the entities to be classified, the field of classification, as manifestations of a single community at a single site. Since a given site might have two or more such manifestations present, it was necessary to establish the validity of the entity—to avoid trying to classify a mixture of discrete manifestations—by showing that the assemblage of traits characterizing it recurred "in characteristic purity and practical completeness at other sites. . . ." The recurrence demonstrated the cultural reality of the manifestation in question and also defined the set of manifestations comprising a focus, the bottom set in the classificatory hierarchy. The individual manifestation was a component of a focus; it would be unrecognizable if were not. On the other hand, it was also a component of the total cultural manifestations of a mixed site. This double sense of "component" led to confusion; to some it implied that the field of classification was the focus, and I can recall later spirited arguments on just what it was that was being classified in the McKern system. The concept of recurrence further implied that a distinctive manifestation occurring at a single site was either a theoretical impossibility or at least unclassifiable. The solution, of course, is simply to recognize that two separate problems are being conflated. The first is defining a set of traits that are the products of a single community at a site (by implication, produced over a time period short enough so that there was little internal change). The second is, granted that such a definition has been accomplished, does the set so defined resemble very closely other sets of traits from other sites? Although McKern was undoubtedly right to emphasize recurrence as an important technique for recognizing community-specific sets of traits, one can easily visualize a stratigraphically validated set of traits so distinctive as to constitute a single-member focus. There can be single-component foci as well as single-component sites. Perhaps one should speak of components of a site and members or elements of a focus to avoid ambiguity. I have devoted so much space to this confusion to illustrate the character of the discussion of the later 1930s; analytical sophistication is a hard-bought thing, and the first steps are the hardest.

The graded set of terms emerging in McKern's 1939 paper were focus, aspect, phase, pattern, and base. The members of a focus should exhibit near identity, the set of foci comprising an aspect should share a "preponderating majority of the traits and trait elements" but would differ "in fine cultural detail," for example in patterns of pottery decoration. The set of aspects making up a phase resembled one another in the "general character" of the traits in common, examples of the level of generalization being incised pottery decoration, burial practices, or house types; quantitatively, "a near majority of traits shared in common by compared aspects determine the phase, and these traits comprise the phase complex." Patterns were sets of phases sharing a "small complex of broadly general traits," for example shell-tempered *versus* grit-tempered pottery; Mississippi and Woodland were obvious patterns. The final and most general class was the base, "characterized by a few fundamentals, such as relate in the most general way to the food quest (horticulture, hunting, seed gathering), community order (camps, permanent villages), or possession of classes of products of outstanding cultural import (pottery, basketry)." McKern did not offer specific examples of the base, but presumably the potteryless Archaic cultures would be distinguished from the Woodland-Mississippi at the level of bases. (In fact, the Archaic cultures were grouped together at the pattern level by most authors.)

The McKern system was used effectively by a number of researchers.

As a prime example, Griffin (1943) defined and described the Fort Ancient aspect with its several foci and discussed its position in the Upper Mississippi phase. The graded labels served his purpose well; archaeological nature did cleave at McKernian joints, so to speak. Nevertheless, there was an undercurrent of resistance, a feeling that something was wrong. This reservation was often expressed by pointing out that the system did not deal with chronology, a vital archaeological concern. Here the critics were forestalled by McKern, who plainly stated that the system was explicitly undimensional and intended to elucidate physical resemblances only. This argument was simply too sophisticated for the state of the art: many could not rid themselves of the notion that the McKernian classification must be thought of as the end product of archaeological analysis rather than one ingredient or aspect of archaeological analysis. But even if one rose above this elementary misconception, there was still a vague sense of uneasiness.

I cannot recall any profound or profitable discussions about the McKern system among Quimby, Griffin, and myself in the 1936/37 year at Michigan, although we certainly talked about it and other matters. It seems to me on reflection that we had a dim awareness of the complexities of numerical taxonomy (a term that had not yet come into use) and a feeling that the system incorporated some problems that nobody was talking about plainly. The vagueness of the concept of trait was one of the problems. Still more basic was an inchoate sense of the clustering implications of the graded terms. A focus was a group of components, an aspect was a group of foci, a phase was a group of aspects, and a pattern was a group of phases. But how would one deal with a group of components that obstinately refused to cluster? The group might be evenly spaced on a linear scale, for example: the distance between A and B could be (on a 0 to 1 scale) .05, between B and C also .05, and so on, but the distance between A and U would be 1 (with a similarity measure of 0). How could this continuum be chopped into foci or aspects? Or there might be weak clustering such that the maximum distance between adjacent components in the group A-D was .05, the maximum distance between neighbors within the group E-H was also .05, and the distance between component D and component E was .10. This seems to define two groups, say two foci; any member of the A-D focus is closer to another member of the focus than it is to any member of the E-H focus and similarly for the members of the E-H focus. But component D is more similar to component E, a member of another focus, than it is to component A, a member of its own focus, and a dilemma rears its horns. Problems of this kind could not be (at any rate, were not) dealt with effectively at the level of analytical and mathematical sophistication available to us at the time.

More generally, nobody stated clearly enough that the problem was, given a group of archaeological manifestations of interest, to devise an archaeologically meaningful quantitative measure of similarity between all pairs of manifestations, to analyze the resulting square matrix of scores to detect and characterize any kinds of systematic relationships that might be present in the matrix, and to interpret the patterning (or lack of it) plausibly in terms of culturally patterned human behavior operating over time and in various social and natural environmental circumstances. McKern himself had a keener appreciation of the broad problem than most: he understood the need for a formal and dimensionally independent classification, and he recommended the regional approach because, among other reasons, the factor of environmental variability was reduced in importance.

I am not sure what moral is to be drawn from this episode in the intellectual history of archaeology. Quimby and I were very busy learning the most basic tools of the trade, and we were not in a position to concentrate on this level of abstraction. I was reading about Hopewell and Middle Mississippi and looking at (and washing) pottery in the Ceramic Repository, not studying the mathematics of matrices. The same thing was true of our instructors, I think; their primary concern was still the augmentation of the corpus of reliable data and analysis and comprehension on a broad basis. I am not at all sure that they were wrong on this ordering of values.

REFERENCES

Griffin, J. B.
    1943   *The Fort Ancient Aspect*. University of Michigan Press, Ann Arbor.
McKern, W. C.
    1939   The Midwestern Taxonomic System as an aid to archaeological culture study. *American Antiquity* 4:301–313.

LONG TERM LAND USE PATTERNS: SOME IMPLICATIONS FOR ARCHAEOLOGY

Lewis R. Binford

Almost anyone who has studied or analyzed stratigraphic sequences has noted that there are periodicities or "punctuations" in the intensity with which a given place has been used. Commonly one might observe a period of intense use followed by relatively minimal use not uncommonly of a slightly different kind, and then another period of intense use, etc. This pattern is well represented and monitored by the excavators at Sudden Shelter (Jennings et al. 1980), Rodger's Shelter (McMillan 1976), Hogup Cave (Aikens 1970), and many others. The purpose of this paper is to explore at least one set of conditions which, when operative, brings into being occupational periodicities at archaeological sites. In addition I will explore the possibility of developing methods for using this understanding to infer past conditions from changing patterns of occupational intensity at sites.

Most archaeologists are comfortable with the idea of seasonal mobility as a characteristic of at least some hunter-gatherer adaptations. There is even an increasing acknowledgement of variations in site function generated somewhat independently of seasonal patterns of mobility. There has, however, been essentially no discussion of long term patterns of change in the disposition of a complete system in space.

Most of the information which can be gathered from contemporary hunter-gatherers regarding long term systems dynamics is anecdotal in character and is frequently woven into an idiom of folklore, since that is the way in which informants tend to recall the characteristics of the "extended range" as I will discuss it here. I will draw primarily upon my experiences with hunter-gatherer systems, particularly the Nunamiut Eskimo for relevant materials.[1] In addition to direct experiences, I have, over a very long period of research and teaching, studied the ethnographic and historical literature treating hunting-gathering adaptations. Out of these experiences I have gradually developed a view of hunter-gatherer land use. I think I know something about what the world of hunter-gatherers was like with regard to long term patterns of economic geography. The purpose of this paper is to share with the reader something of this viewpoint. I will then use this understanding to discuss some of the patterned variability which the archaeologist might expect to occur as a consequence of the long term mobility patterns examined.

Obviously long term patterns of land use are not something that an observer resident with a group of people for the normal tenure of ethnographic field work would have the opportunity to observe. In fact it is my impression that most ethnographers view the situation of the peoples they study in a normative manner and expect that the way they were at the time of study reflects a stable system state. My research forced me to reject such an idea and to seek ways of gaining at least some temporal perceptions of the Nunamiut system. Clues to the dynamic character of their land use came through questioning aimed at understanding the composition of, and in turn their conceptualizations of, local groups or "bands." Since my views of long term mobility grew out of investigations of local groups or "identity" groups, it is perhaps best to begin this discussion with a brief summary of the Nunamiut concepts of "band" and local group.

NUNAMIUT "LOCAL GROUP" CONCEPTS AND TERRITORIALITY

It is interesting that anthropologists have given much attention to the cultural conventions and frameworks in terms of which persons relate to one another (kinship studies) but have given little attention to the cultural conventions whereby persons are articulated to resources and economic space. We may speculate that part of the reason is that a very different type of field observation is called for in the latter type of investigation and secondly because it involves a difficult empirical question. The difficulty arises because all entities, either social or individual, by virtue of their simple existence have some spatial properties. Spatial properties such as aggregation, independent distribution, and association are frequently the criteria used by the investigator for the recognition of social units. Upon recognition it is generally assumed that such recognized social units have culturally specified spatial attributes. It is true that they must have spatial properties by virtue of their existence, but it is very important to point out that these attributes may not be cultural or dependent upon any culturally specified relationships between social units and economic space *per se*.

I previously suggested that culturally organized social systems are dependent upon the expedient assignment of meaning to experience (Binford 1977:3). Just because humans experience geographical reality, there is no necessary reason to expect this experience to be culturally organized. The cultural organization of experience arises in the context of evolution driven by selection.

In comparing hunting and gathering adaptations, one is struck by the variability in the culturally organized behavior with respect to resources and hence economic space. For instance, it would appear that among some groups it is possible to understand their particular patterns of distribution in space simply as a by-product of the organizational properties of the environment and the culturally specified roles for interpersonal interaction. In such a situation there are *no* culturally specified relationships between social persons and economic space *per se*. For instance, a frequently noted condition is to find an aggregate of persons localized in a camp or settlement. We may ask how these associated persons are related one to another and find that they may be all related through cultural conventions of "kinship," and it is these conventions which serve to facilitate the social association. We may find a similar localization some distance away. Inquiry as to "why" the people are independently distributed and why they are differentially associated may yield a variety of responses: "I am here because this is where my brother is living," "I am not living there because I have no relatives there," etc. Further questioning may reveal persons in one place with relatives in the other. Inquiry as to why the person is associated spatially with one relative and not the other may range from "I am here because there were too many people over there," "I am here because hunting is better here," or "I am here because my relative here needs my help," "I am here because there is not enough firewood for us all to be together and besides I don't get along as well with my uncle over there as I do with my uncle here." These examples should point out that the two dimensions cited are: (1) the relative distribution of resources, and (2) the social relationships between people. Contrast these statements with what one might encounter interviewing persons in a contemporary urban setting. Why do you live here and not over in the next house with your brother. "Because I own my own house." Why do you always walk along on the path around the field during your afternoon walks? "Because I might be arrested for trespassing if I walked across that field; it belongs to Mr. X." In these answers clearly a third dimension has been added, the culturally specified relationship between social persons and geographical space or resources *per se*.

Research and investigation of ethnographically-documented groups of hunters and gatherers with regard to the degree and character of culturally specified relationships between person, social units, and economic space are rendered difficult by a third factor, the cognitive idiom in terms of which people express relationships. Allow me to make this point clear from some of my recent field experiences.

Working with the Nunamiut Eskimos it was important for me to obtain information about their distribution and numbers as far back in time as the living informants could speak with accuracy. The method was simply to question about prior distributions of people and "what happened to them."

Informant statements obtained at Anaktuvuk Pass are generally in agreement that the "Nunamiut" as conceived of by the people themselves is somewhat different from the way they have been characterized by explorers, other coastal Eskimos, or anthropologists. Informants relate that "their people," the Nunamiut proper, consist of four major regional localizations of people. These were (1) a population centered on the Upper Colville River above the mouth of the Killik River referred to as the *Kangianirmiut*, (2) a population centered in the Killik River basin with range extensions into the mountains, referred to as the *Killikmiut*, (3) a population centered in the Upper John River–Anaktuvuk Pass area referred to as the *Kajalikmiut*, and (4) a population centered in the Upper Itkillik River drainage and the Ulu Lake area, referred to as the *Itkilermiut*.

Informants agreed that there were other localized populations in the interior which were collectively referred to by the Coastal peoples as "Nunatakmiut" along with the four populations mentioned above. These were the *Utukok*, *Noatak*, and *Kobuk* Eskimo, all inland populations roughly equivalent to the "Nunamiut" as they conceived of themselves. Thus among the "inland" people four regional populations were recognized and distingushed, while the coastal population referred to all under a single term simply meaning "inland people."[2]

Further questioning revealed that within any one of the previously named regional populations of the "Nunamiut" there were small named units which appeared to represent localized groups. At least I made that initial assumption. Further questioning also revealed that these "local" units were generally specified by reference to some feature of geography or folkloristic event occurring in a specified geographic setting. These microunits could be considered to be composed of persons who shared a similar "homeland" identity. Further questioning revealed that this was an incorrect assumption. Actual tabulation and census data on persons associated at given camps demonstrated that the "on the ground groups" were not necessarily made up of persons or even family heads who shared a common "homeland identity." Similarly, interviewing individuals on their life histories revealed that the actual patterns of association in concrete settlement contexts bore very little relation to the "homeland identity" of the person being interviewed. For instance, four old informants, all over 70 years of age, are very specific in their personal identities. One considers himself an "Ulu-Lake man." Another informant considers himself a "Noatak man" while two others consider themselves "Tulugak men." Tulugak Lake (Raven Lake) is in the vicinity of the contemporary village. Further investigation revealed that the "Ulu-Lake man" was born at Tulugak Lake in 1896. His mother was considered a "Tulugakmiut" and was related as mother's elder brother's daughter to one of the old men who considers himself "Tulugakmiut." In addition, the grandfathers of both men were stepbrothers and both of them had considered themselves "Tulugakmiut." The informant's father had considered himself a "Killikmiut man." Thus it is clear that the "identity group" of the informant was not inherited from either the mother or the father and had nothing necessarily to do with the place of birth.

Why then does an individual consider himself an "Ulu-Lake man"? Further investigation revealed that the "identity unit" of a person was established in terms of where and with whom the person was associated during the period of life when he was learning his adult role. During late childhood and into his postpubescent but premarital years a child learns in great detail the local terrain. This is accomplished and conceptually mapped in terms of stories and experiences of earlier generations in that particular environmental setting and by the accumulation of his personal experiences, some of which may take on folkloristic significance. In this context an individual begins to develop his identity as well as contributing his experiences to the oral traditions of the area. The repertoire of stories accumulated during early life is therefore largely related to the people who have lived in the area where the young man is resident during this critical period.

In short, folklore has a strong environmental reference. In turn this folklore makes up a large part of a person's social identity. A man's "band" identity is developed by both his expression of sentiment and knowledge of a geographically based oral tradition. A man may change his residence, yet he maintains his "social identity" largely through his manner of expression and conversation regarding the habitat where he learned his adult role and through the members of past generations whose experiences in the same area are known to him through oral tradition. These "identity units" are egocentric in their composition. For instance, any one man considers all other persons who shared this period of his life as constituting the socially defined "identity reference group." At the same time the persons of an older generation who are considered by the young man to be, for instance, "Ulu-Lake people" may conceive of themselves as members of other reference groups such as "Noatak people" etc. The core of such a reference group is the other young people who shared parallel experiences while growing up. We can see that any given person may consider himself a Tulugak man, while the other younger persons may consider the same person as a Killik man, or as a Ulu-Lake man, depending upon each individual's association with others.

It should be clear by now that "band" identity is an egocentric phenomenon and may at any given point in time bear little, if any, relationship to the composition of "on the ground" co-residentially associated persons. For instance, I have had the experience of interviewing an older informant and asking his "band identity" and being told he considered himself a "Itkillik man." I might then ask how many "Itkillik men" there were in 1900. The informant might think and give an answer of around thirty-five. I would then ask where they were camped in 1900 and receive a very puzzled look from the informant. Further questioning would reveal that all thirty-five were resident in different places in association with Eskimos whom the informant considered to be non-Itkillik people.

Thus, investigation into the problem of named "bands" at the local level reveals that statements of group affiliation turn out to be statements describing lasting affiliation between persons rather than statements of any lasting association between persons and geographical space. However, informants all agree that in the past as well as during the period after 1935 these named "identity units" may have had some lasting significance in terms of the spatial distribution of persons, but this arose from the relative stability of the settlement pattern and not from any change in the cultural significance of the named units.

What then is an "Ulu-Lake man"? It is a person who shares certain *social* bonds with others who were coresident with him at Ulu-Lake. It is not a man who is culturally related to Ulu-Lake, territorially speaking. The "identity groups" which are phrased in a geographical idiom are social categories which have no necessary spatial significance. These are what might have been termed "sodalities" (Service 1962:22) based on association rather than on criteria of kinship *per se*.

There are many cases in which a social unit is expressed in a geographical idiom and therefore may be mistaken by the observer for a unit sharing common relationships to land rather than sharing exclusively social bonds deriving from some conventions of association. Repeated questioning of informants regarding the cultural specification of relationships between persons and geographic or economic space failed to yield any indications that territory or resources were culturally assimilated to social roles. A typical statement was, "Anyone is free to hunt or fish anywhere, but you must be polite about it if other people are there." In short, if you are placed in social juxtaposition with others, there are cultural means for associating and accommodating persons one to another, but there is no cultural means of accommodation necessary between persons and resources if there is not a physical juxtapositioning of persons around those resources.

My conclusions regarding the Nunamiut was that there was *no cultural specification of territoriality*. Any Nunamiut was free to go anywhere and to use any resource. The only constraints were social in character, the particular manner in which a person could articulate with ease with persons he might encounter. If, then, there is *no territoriality*, does this mean that there is no regular patterning to the distribution of persons spatially? Certainly not. There are no cultural specifications regarding resources or geographical space among oak trees, deer, or any other species, yet we find regular patterns among hunters and gatherers who have no culturally specified territoriality. *The patterns derive from the interaction of culturally organized social dimensions and the non-culturally organized distribution of resources and life space.*

While this conclusion is interesting and casts some light on a number of problems which have been widely discussed in anthropology regarding "band" structure and territoriality, the research lead which struck me most was that the Eskimo expected to be living in one place for a substantial period of time—at least long enough for the young men to learn a regionally specific body of folklore—but acknowledge that they would most likely be living elsewhere during much of their life. *That is, the Eskimo expected that a given association between persons and a place would last for a considerable time, yet they did not expect it to last anywhere near as long as a person's lifetime.*

In order to follow out this hint of a potentially interesting situation, I devised a scheme for interviewing elderly Eskimo men regarding the patterns of land use which their parents had trained them to expect during their lifetime. This approach worked very well with five old Nunamiut men who had been essentially reared to carry on the traditional mode of adaptation. This mode was interrupted by a major crash in the caribou population during the early years of this century, and more importantly by the replacement of traditional technology with the modern "mail order" technology of the near-contemporary Nunamiut (Binford 1979). The important thing was that the parents of the old men had not anticipated the drastic changes which were to occur. By interviewing these men as to what their parents expected life to be like for them, I hoped to gain a small glimpse of mobile big game hunters prior to the changes related to the intrusions of modern life.

REGIONAL PATTERNING IN SYSTEMS POSITIONING

In recognition that the Nunamiut case is probably neither unique nor wholly representative of all hunters and gatherers (among whom we find a wide range of variability in the degree that spatial relationships are culturally specified), I will refer to the economic space of an aggregate of persons as their *range* in cases where their economic space is not culturally specified. In general, non-territorially organized groups differentially exploit their range so that more intense use is made of some parts than of others. The intensively utilized segments of non-territorial groups' *ranges* will be referred to as their residential *core areas*.

I have previously described the Nunamiut system as logistically organized (Binford 1978, 1980). That is, resources are commonly obtained by task groups moving considerable distances beyond a normal foraging radius where temporary camps may be established during the several days the groups are away from the residential camp. Given such an organization, there is a pattern of economic zonation to the range surrounding any given residential site. This generalized pattern is shown in Figure 1. We may think of this zonation in terms of an immediate area surrounding the camp where resources are very quickly exhausted. This area, designated the foraging radius, rarely provides much in the way of foodstuffs unless there is a highly aggregated, renewable or unearned resource adjacent to the site. This area is frequently the "campground" for visitors and the "play" zone for children. Beyond the play zone is the area searched and exploited by parties which leave the camp and return home in a single day. This zone rarely extends beyond 6 miles of the residential camp.

Archaeological sites produced in this zone are commonly what I have called *locations* (Binford 1980), although in some circumstances there may be trapping sites, hunting blinds, and some special-use sites within the foraging radius. Beyond the *foraging radius* is the *logistical radius*. This is the zone which is exploited by parties who stay away from the residential camp at least one night before returning. Beyond the logistical radius are lands unoccupied in the residential sense, here termed the *extended range*. In recognition that most hunter and gatherers are annually mobile (that is they move their residential sites from one place to another during the year), the area regularly used residentially and logistically during an annual seasonal cycle is referred to as the *annual*

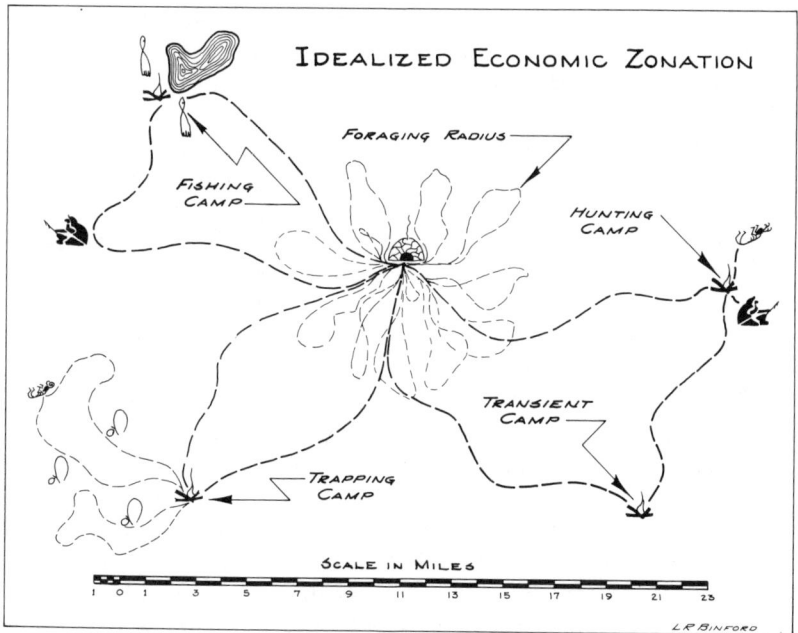

Fig. 1. Idealized Nunamiut economic zonation.

range. Under the ideas of "territorial groups" common in anthropological descriptions, most observers have tended to interview informants regarding their annual range and equate this with their territory. The implication has been that annual ranges did not vary greatly from one year to the next.

Systems which are not demographically "packed," that are bounded by neighboring systems immediately beyond the logistical zone of their annual range, enjoy a peripheral zone termed here the "extended range"—an uninhabited area surrounding the "annual range" of the system viewed at any one time. In my opinion this is the most important zone conditioning the long term change that may characterize the history of a system. This is the zone which is technically "no-man's land" relative to the annual range of a system and is therefore the area which may be taken up by excess population manifest as "new groups" in the region. In so far as this occurs, the original group has ever *decreasing long term mobility options*.

In my experience with the Nunamiut, it was clear that the placement of the *annual range* was not stable over long periods of time. During the mid-1930s their annual range was centered in the Killik River basin; during the early 1940s another range was centered in the Chandlar Lake area. In the late 1940s and early 1950s the annual range was centered in Anaktuvuk Valley. In the Nunamiut case, the "hub" of an annual range appears to be the *location of summer settlements*. Summer was the period of the year when subsistence *insecurity* was apt to be most common on a year-to-year basis. This stems from (1) the low food value of nutritionally poor spring-killed caribou, (2) the dispersed nature of caribou herds during summer, making supplementary hunting difficult and unpredictable, and (3) the relative uncertainty of storage techniques during the warm months. Summer strategies were to seek a placement so as to enable the taking of fish and Dall sheep. A site on a lake or substantial river within logistical range of sheep country was an ideal summer location. There were relatively few such locations. In the east there were Itkillik Lake, Tulugak Lake, and Chandlar Lake, each serving as the "summer hub" of an annual range. In the west, the middle Killik River served as a similar summer hub for an annual range during recent Nunamiut history.

The average size of known annual ranges was about 1650 square miles (4275 km^2) for a band of approximately 35 people. There was some tendency for there to be overlapping use of areas depending upon which summer "hub" an annual range was centered. For instance, I have records of a band with summer sites regularly located at Chandlar Lake. However, for one period of time (approximately 3 years) the fall and winter sites were in the Okomilaga and Upper Alatena-Nigu valleys, while during another 2 year period, the fall and winter sites were on the middle Killik River area. In short, given a hub, which among the Nunamiut tends to be a summer site, the distribution of sites during the more "flexible" seasons of the year may tend to radiate out much as the loops of different foraging trips radiate out from a base camp. This is one type of "drift" in site placement within an annual range which might be termed short term. *Long term range drift* (Hill 1969) *is a pattern in which a group relocates in space so that there is little if any overlap in area with previous annual ranges.* Among the Nunamiut this generally took the form of shifting the summer hub of the annual range. During the course of my records one band of approximately 35 people utilized 2.5 annual ranges during the course of 22 years or almost 9 years per "annual range." Viewing my data historically, the gross range of the Nunamiut for which I have documentation (excluding the years of stress during the caribou population crash of 1910-15) represents 4.46 annual ranges per band. During the period of record, each band of inland Nunamiut had available an *extended territory* equal to approximately 4.5 annual ranges. If a band remains centered in a given annual range for approximately 9 years and moves through 4.46 or realistically 5.0 such ranges without competing with another band, this cycle takes between 40 to 45 years or essentially the active life of a male hunter and the reproductive life of a female.

Figure 2 displays the summary information on land use which I recovered from five old Eskimo men regarding what they had "expected" to happen if their lives had not changed drastically from the "traditional" life of inland caribou hunters. The old men all started their "model" of expected land use in the home range where they were born—this they called their "birth country." There they expected to live until they were approximately 6–10 years of age. Within this range they expected to move through normal annual rounds of residential movement camping at different places and generally "being mobile" but within a generalized range. The size of the annual ranges sketched by the men varied between 2400 and 1500 square miles (6215 and 3885 km²) with an average of 2007 square miles (5198 km²). That is the area bounded by a perimeter drawn approximately 12 miles (1610 km²) out from identified *residential sites*. This area includes many of the special purpose sites used by hunting,

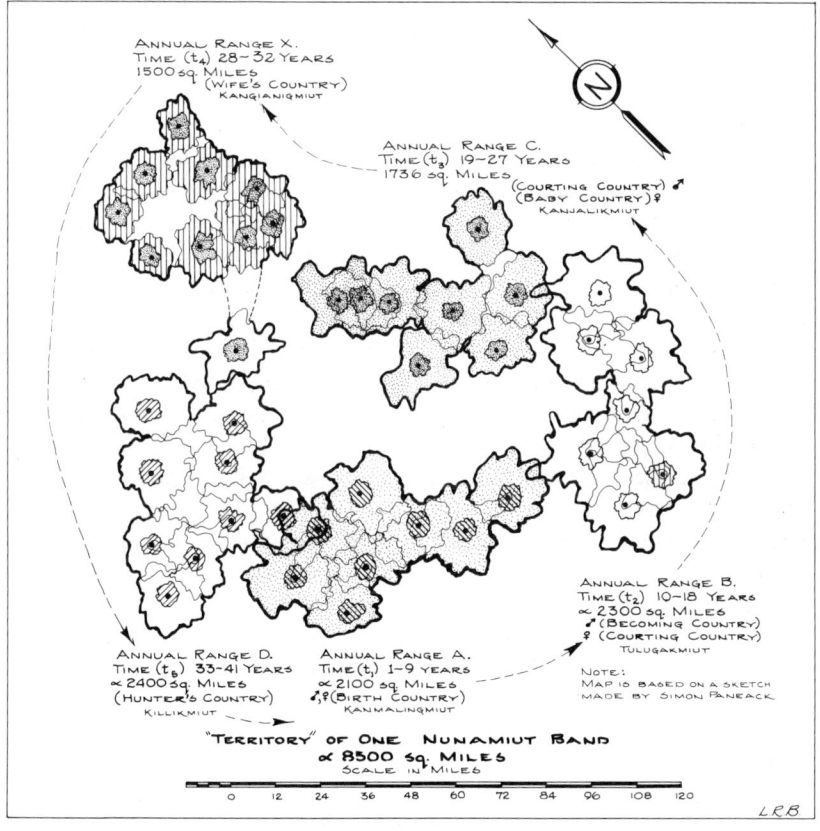

Fig. 2. Territory of one Nunamiut band in relation to annual ranges.

trapping, or other types of logistically organized task groups (but not all such sites by any means).

After the *annual range* has been positioned in an area, typically a river valley, for a number of years, the willows—the major and in most cases the only source of firewood—begin to be depleted in the favorable places for winter houses. Similarly local sheep populations may well be depressed in number since under normal conditions they were heavily hunted during the mid- to late-summer months (see Binford and Chasko 1976; Campbell 1978). In like fashion the local populations of ground squirrel—particularly around summer residential camping locations—would be diminished and snares would be set at ever-increasing distances from the optimal spots for summer camps. In addition to the unrelenting depletion of the local area around camping spots, there would be a general increase in what might be called commensal vermin. As use of locations as residential camps intensifies over time, there is an inevitable increase in debris from both human as well as dog consumption and excretion. Associated with this buildup of organic by-products is an inevitable increase in the population of flies. The latter are the biggest threat to the successful storage of dried meat during the summer months (Binford 1978)—an insecure time for the Nunamiut (Campbell 1970). Camping in a single area gradually depletes the usable resources around camping spots and improves the environment for flies and other vermin.

These conditions were frequently verbalized by the old men in terms of changing attitudes among the people. "When we first move into a valley everything is good, people want visitors, people want to see friends, people want to share, but as time goes on, things get used up and the place gets full of flies, then people start to fight. When that happens it's time to move to a place where nobody has lived for a long time." The old men all agreed that between six and ten years was about the duration of occupation in any given annual range.

In short, the sustained use of a given annual range results in (1) reduction in the number of locational options for the placement of residential camps as the willows and local populations of supplementary food species are depleted around residential camps and (2) this tends to intensify the localization of camp groups into the fewer larger and more productive patches in the habitat, where as group sizes tended to increase in camps, the effect of impact is stepped up. The overall result was to increase tension and competition among "band units" and as tension builds the decision to move to a "new area" becomes increasingly inevitable.

As young men, the Nunamiut elders expected to move into what they refer to as "becoming country" not more than ten years after they were born (Fig. 2*B*). The new annual range into which they moved between the ages of 6 to 12 was the area in which they expected to be living when they were learning the adult roles of a hunter. They would be making long trips to other uninhabited regions as well as to areas occupied by adjacent groups since they must have detailed knowledge of the "lifetime range" or the area over which they can expect to live during their lifetime. This was the area which provided their "group identity." From a girl's perspective the "learning country" of the boy was the "courting country" of the girl. The average age at marriage for boys was 28 years while for girls it was only 17 years (see Binford and Chasko 1976). Hence while boys were learning the cultural geography of their "lifetime range" girls were courting boys of other bands who visited the girls' camps as part of their travels for learning the landscape.

After seven to ten years living in this core residential area the "band" would move on to another core residential area, which normally coincided with a major valley or watershed area. This third residential area was called by boys their "courting country" while for the girls it was called "birthing country." Boys were seriously courting girls living in areas which they visited in terms of their "learning travels." On the other hand, girls were generally married and their husbands were living matrilocally, and the girls could expect to be giving birth. It should be pointed out that it was not uncommon for a marriage to precipitate the move from one residential core area to another since it was considered "impolite" for the resident male to "know too much about the area when the new husband moved in, much better for all the men to learn the details of the area together, then they always respect each other."

On marriage the male leaves his "courting country" (Fig. 2*C*) and moves into the area occupied by his wife's people (Fig. 2*X*). There he may stay for anywhere between five and six years. The stay of the male in his "wife's country" is generally shorter than the normal stay of a "band" in a given annual range. This is not a jural "rule," only a behavioral tendency noted by informants. The next move by a male is commonly back to his "band" after his period of "bride service." By this time he expects his "band" to have moved into a new annual range (Fig. 2*D*). It is this area in which he will achieve his maximum notoriety as a hunter ("hunter's country") and as an expert at performing male roles. My data on the life histories of male Nunamiut show that their hunting proficiency tends to increase and reach a peak at about age 32. There is something of a plateau between 32 and 39 when a man achieves his maximum successes as a hunter. Beginning at around age 40 this success begins to decline and in general the rate of decline is a function of individual variability in what appears to be age-correlated changes in eyesight. Most Eskimo men become increasingly nearsighted after the age of 40. This obviously reduces their hunting effectiveness as such vision change progresses. If the man does not suffer from myopia his hunting fitness may decline at a slower rate until his early fifties when even "exceptional hunters'" achievements rapidly decline.

After living the average of nine years in "hunter's country" the band moves back into the annual range occupied at the time the man was born. In this setting he becomes a respected elder in the country in which he had been born. There he had learned his earliest folklore about the past and the people who had preceded him. He had his first memorable experiences in a culturally described landscape. These experiences he passes on fondly and takes the young men out to examine the places of importance of their forebears and to him as a young person.

While from the perspective of any given year or even a series of years the "territory" of a group may appear to coincide with an annual range, the members of the local group identify with the extended range. The entire expanse of the extended range is where the "history" of a local group has unfolded. Folklore is rich in stories relating events and exploits and deaths of relatives which occurred over the entire extended range. After all, any single adult man would have lived over most of the extended range during the course of his active live. One's life history is played out on the spatial stage of the extended range.

Part of the education of the youth consists of introducing young men to this vast area. While a local group may be using a given "annual range," a traveling party made up of older relatives and young men may commonly set out to visit places of particular importance over the extended range. The composition of such a "walkabout" group among the Nunamiut is not uncommonly a young man (12–16 years of age) and a male cousin guided by his mother's brother. The duration of such a trip is frequently from about April until the following October. The party will leave a "settlement" in spring when sled travel is still possible and move rather rapidly before melt (generally in late May and early June) to a distant "hub" area of a previously used annual range. All along the way the young men are being instructed in the "crossing spots," the denning areas of wolves, the trails frequently followed by caribou, the location of salt licks where sheep can be taken, and places where firewood is concentrated. Places where underground springs release water during winter resulting in the availability of "unfrozen" water as well as the dangerous potential of getting wet are regularly noted. Locations where traps are successfully placed for fur bearers and where hibernation spots of bears have tended to be located, all are noted. Such a "walkabout" party may camp at the summer "hub" location during the summer while making frequent trips to points of importance within the "annual range" commonly utilized by the local group occupying that particular annual range. The return trip to the then-occupied "annual range" would be commonly made in fall after sled travel was possible. The return trip may be circuitous, involving travel through other annual ranges, observing evidence of caribou movement, and in general monitoring the dynamics of the habitat.

The return of such a walkabout party to a residential camp is an important event. Several days may be spent in conversation and detailed descriptions of the area covered, terrain, evidence of game densities, and the overall discussion of the specific places visited. Older men who had once lived in the area visited will ask seemingly endless questions of the young boys regarding their experiences. All of this information may be applied in the following several years to a decision about moving the annual range and exploiting another segment of the extended territory.

Walkabouts or educational trips are not the only use made of the extended range during the tenure of any given annual range. There are conscious attempts made to monitor the character of the habitat over the total extended range. This may be done incidentally while passing through on the way to visit relatives in other ranges. There also may be specific information-gathering trips made into an area if incidental trips have not yielded a picture of conditions in the area and if hunting of low-density resources (such as predators) generally requires that hunting parties cover much greater areas than normal for procuring food. Thus under certain conditions the logistical range of a system is periodically greatly extended, resulting in logistical parties covering major parts of the extended range. Predator hunting, educational travel, and specific monitoring probes maintain the informational levels needed to make decisions as to where to move next if pressure seems to be mounting for a move.

Most often the decision to move is not a corporate phenomenon such that the entire local group picks up and moves to another segment of the extended range. More commonly a single family or a pair of families may judge the area occupied to be increasingly "unlucky" for finding game. The final motive for moving away may be in fact some "social affront" one group considers it has suffered at the hands of another local family or set of families. This type of situation frequently arises with regard to stored food. For instance, the "unlucky" family may advertise that it has been "unlucky" to relatives believed to have "plenty" of stored food. The latter relatives may not respond with gifts or invitations to use their stores. The "unlucky" family may then decide that they do not want to be associated with such low, unworthy persons who refuse to share their "wealth" of food with deserving relatives. More commonly however, the "unlucky," food-seeking family may actually confront the relatives that have stores. If requests for food are refused, there is an overt social rift and the "unlucky" family can only save face by moving away from such "stingy" relatives, the reason for moving being a disagreement with relatives. Later, if word is received that the families that moved are having "good luck" other families gradually drift their way, finally resulting in a move from one annual range to another during the course of several seasons.

The picture which I obtained of long term mobility among the Nunamiut implies a number of things relative to patterns of site production, histories of "place" utilization, and the scale of land use which might characterize at least some members of hunter and gatherer groups.

SCALE OF LAND USE

In the case discussed here, it should be clear that the subsistence security of the Nunamiut is achieved by having a number of alternative annual ranges available for use. This type of land use pattern means that the "population density" when viewed from a regional perspective is very small. On the other hand the "effective" density is considerably higher and may approach something of a constant over substantial periods of time in spite of the fact that there may be a change in regional density brought on by the formation of more groups. This pattern of land use results in some rather surprising values for regional densities. It has attendant implications for the scale of the geographical distribution of a single sociocultural system as manifest archaeologically over a considerable period of time.

In the Nunamiut case, there was a 45 year cycle with an average of 9 years spent in each of the annual ranges in which a man expected to have lived during his active life. Each annual range covered approximately 2000 square miles (5180 km^2), which means that approximately 10,000 squre miles (25,900 km^2) were used as one's *lifetime range* or the *band range* for the group with whom a person tended to remain associated most of his life. The size of such a local band was between 25 and 35 people in the Nunamiut case. This yields a population density of 0.003 persons per square mile for the lifetime or "band range," while one would see a population density of 0.015 persons per square mile in any given annual range. Perhaps the best way to illustrate the relative characteristics of this land use pattern is to project the Nunamiut case against some well known areas of the world and see how they would appear demographically if they were occupied by populations similar to the Nunamiut.

TABLE 1
DEMOGRAPHIC EXPECTATIONS FOR DESIGNATED REGIONS
ASSUMING A NUNAMIUT TYPE OF SYSTEM OF LAND USE

Place	Area in Sq. Miles	No. of Minimal Bands Expected	No. of Persons	No. of Breed. Units
New Mexico	121,666	12.20	365	0.73
Arizona	113,909	11.39	342	0.68
California	158,693	15.87	476	0.95
Utah	84,916	8.49	255	0.51
Nevada	110,540	11.05	331	0.66
New York (state)	49,576	4.96	149	0.30
Missouri	69,686	6.97	209	0.42
South Carolina	31,055	3.11	94	0.19
France	212,841	21.28	638	1.28
Great Britain	94,214	9.42	282	0.56
Italy	116,303	11.63	349	0.70
Israel	7,993	0.80	24	0.05

Almost certainly, anyone examining Table 1 would be "shocked" and perhaps mildly amused by the suggestion that there would be only 24 people in the entire country of Israel, or that there would be only 638 people in all of France! When phrased in this manner the "past" is hard to imagine, but the fact is that the scale at which many archaeologists tend to think of land use by hunter and gatherer populations is not just amusing, it is totally misleading. For instance, Figure 3 illustrates the documented annual range for the Nunamiut Eskimo over a five-year period when they were living in the Anaktuvuk Valley area during the late 1940s. On the left is the annual range of the G/wi Bushman as documented by Tanaka (1971) over one seasonal cycle. These two ethnographically documented areas are shown to the same scale as the entire region surveyed by the Tehuacán project, within which MacNeish (1972:497–498) pictures multiple territorial bands moving about by at least El Riego times. While this caution regarding the "scale" of the archaeologist's view of land use versus the hunter-gatherer's view of land use is of considerable interest, my purpose here is to discuss patterns of archaeological accumulation in sites as they might be conditioned by long term patterns of mobility.

While this caution is of some interest, the Nunamiut data should not be taken as a "normative" statement on hunter-gatherer land use patterning as is commonly done by those who see the aim of ethnographic research as the production of empirical generalizations. (See, for instance, the generalization by Hayden [1981] that hunter-gatherer annual ranges are equal to approximately 2500 km^2 coupled with the implication that these annual range units are equal to the "lifetime ranges" or at least to band territories.)

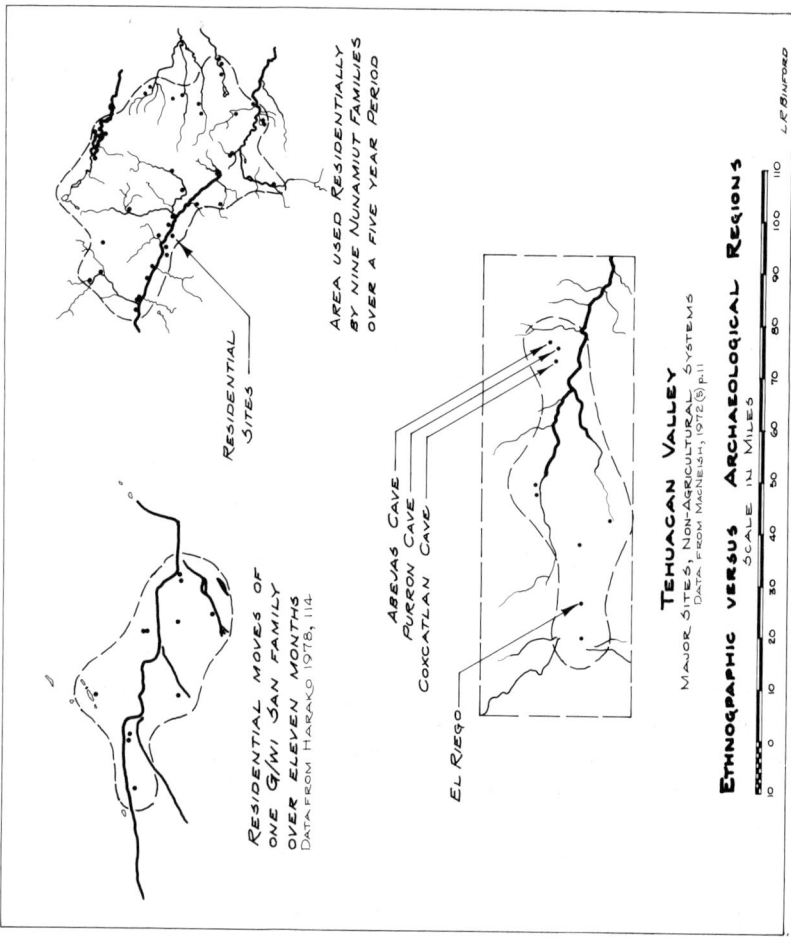

Fig. 3. Annual ranges of Nunamiut Eskimo and G/wi Bushman in relation to Tehuacán reconstructed "territories."

I could imagine that the pattern of "nesting" a series of annual ranges into a "lifetime" or "extended range" as illustrated here might well vary considerably among hunters and gatherers living in different environments. For instance, in "quick recovery" environments with high primary production, there may well be less use of multiple annual ranges, although the ethnographic information suggests that the "mobility metabolism" may be higher with at least multiple circuits or "passes" being made through a territory during a single year (see Harrison 1949:135). That there are different patterns of both mobility and land use among tropical hunter-gatherers is suggested by the provocative observation by Kloos (1977:120). He notes that long term mobility among the Akuriyo of Surinam was not arranged primarily in terms of food but was a series of "treks" along known paths between places of procurement for non-food resources such as fiber for hammocks, reeds for arrows, and stone for axes.

We must stop using inaccurate empirical generalizations and realize that our task is the understanding of variability. We cannot glibly assume that annual ranges are equivalent to territories and therefore are stable over long periods. We cannot assume that a given pattern of long term land use as illustrated here for the Nunamiut is common to all hunter-gatherers. This case serves to alert us that our common ideas of equivalence between an annual range and band territories are not generally justified. We must therefore stop "interpreting" site patterning in terms of questionable ideas as MacNeish has done (MacNeish 1972). In addition, we must strive to develop methods which will permit us to "see" in more realistic terms different patterns of long term land use characteristic of past systems. One such approach might be to increase our understanding of the consequences of long term mobility patterning on archaeological site formation.

LONG TERM MOBILITY AS A CONDITIONER OF SITE CONTENT

The first clear consequence of these long term patterns of land use for site formation is an expectation of periodicities in site use. During times in which a given site is incorporated in the normal use pattern within a lifetime range and as long as the "band" is occupying the annual range in which the site is located, we might expect the site to be used relatively frequently. It is also true that some "functional" variability in site use will arise in response to movement of residential sites from place to place within the annual range.[3] Nevertheless, we may expect maximum intensity of use during the period of time in which the site is actually incorporated in the active annual range of the group.

On the other hand, when a group shifts annual ranges, the places within the previously occupied area generally change radically in their pattern of utilization. I have shown (Binford 1982) that a shift in the position of a residential site correlates with a shift in the "use potential" of other places in the region. When a residential site is in one place, another site within the range may be regularly used as a temporary camp or a logistically organized extractive camp. On the other hand, a move in the residential site sets up a new set of spatial relationships relative to the new residence, and the use potential of the old sites may be radically altered. The same place may now be inappropriate for its former use because of its changed position relative to the new residential site. The same principle applies to shifting or positioning of the entire system within the macroregion. Given a change in the annual range of the system, sites which were previously residential in function may now become logistical in character. Similarly, favorite hunting camps regularly used from the perspective of one annual range may now be only used as transient camping spots, once the annual range is shifted to another segment of the lifetime range.

Given variable durations of the use of annual ranges, one can appreciate that the repetitious use of a place may vary considerably between one phase of regional positioning for the system and another. With such shifts in annual range, the tempo of site use almost certainly changes, as do at least some functional characteristics of site utilization. This alone is probably sufficient to result in a recognizable difference in the character of a deposit accumulated over a substantial period of time.

We might see a considerable buildup of archaeological material at a site relating to its use during the tenure of one annual range. When the annual range shifts, the same site most likely would be used in a different way and in a different tempo of occupational reuse. This shift would show up as differences between the "assemblages" of material accumulated while the site was within an annual range versus when it was part of the extended range of an annual range centered elsewhere. The magnitude of the contrast might well be considerable. The fidelity of use at a place occupied as a component of one annual range is apt to be high with a corresponding likelihood of considerable internal homogeneity among the remains deposited. On the other hand, the same place utilized by the same people living on a different annual range is quite likely to have served different functions and hence to exhibit considerable assemblage contrast with the material deposited earlier. This means that "strata" that are recognizable because of differing anthropogenic conditions would also tend to be more internally homogeneous and exhibit marked contrasts with adjacent superimposed strata. Archaeologically, such a shift could give the appearance of considerable change. *It would occur, however, not as a consequence of change in the organization of the system, but only in its positioning within the region.*

Associated with such a change in site function, and hence assemblage content, may be a correlated change in the occupational tempo and/or intensity of utilization at a site. This would result in changed rates of archaeological accumulation per unit of time and/or natural depositional episodes at the site. This would have the effect of producing a "punctuated" curve of use intensity at the site over time as has been illustrated for Sudden Shelter by Jennings and his associates (1980) (Fig. 4). We might well expect there to be some correlated shifts in assemblage composition and use intensity. Such patterning should be investigated for clues to systems functioning rather than assuming that superpositional changes in the character of archaeological deposits necessarily indicate organizational changes in cultural systems. In the case of the dynamics I have described, such a change could occur depositionally at a given archaeological site *in the absence of system change.* All that would be needed to produce it is a repositioning of the system in space. With this there would be formal changes in both content and use intensity chronologically arranged within the deposits at some (if not most) sites within the geographical area of the systems' repositioning. Thus, there might be stratigraphic or at least superpositioned archaeological deposits differing in content and use intensity; these would not be a measure of culture change, only systems positioning. Archaeologists have not generally considered this possibility; in fact, the equation of a change in a deposit with culture change is almost a "basic tenet" of archaeological interpretation:

> ... because ... peoples were accustomed to take shelter in the mouths of caves, kept coming back to the same caves ... and hence built up a more or less complete series of assemblages in stratigraphic order ... one can use this sequence to date the other remains in the local area. [Rouse 1972:123]

SUMMARY

It is suggested here that at least some, if not most, hunter-gatherer systems practice a pattern of extensive space use. The equivalence between a social group and a "territory" as well as the equivalence between "territory" and annual range as might be observed by an ethnographer have been brought into question. I have illustrated how a single group may utilize a series of annual ranges sequentially, and I have suggested that this is likely to have been a much more common condition in the past when human populations were small.

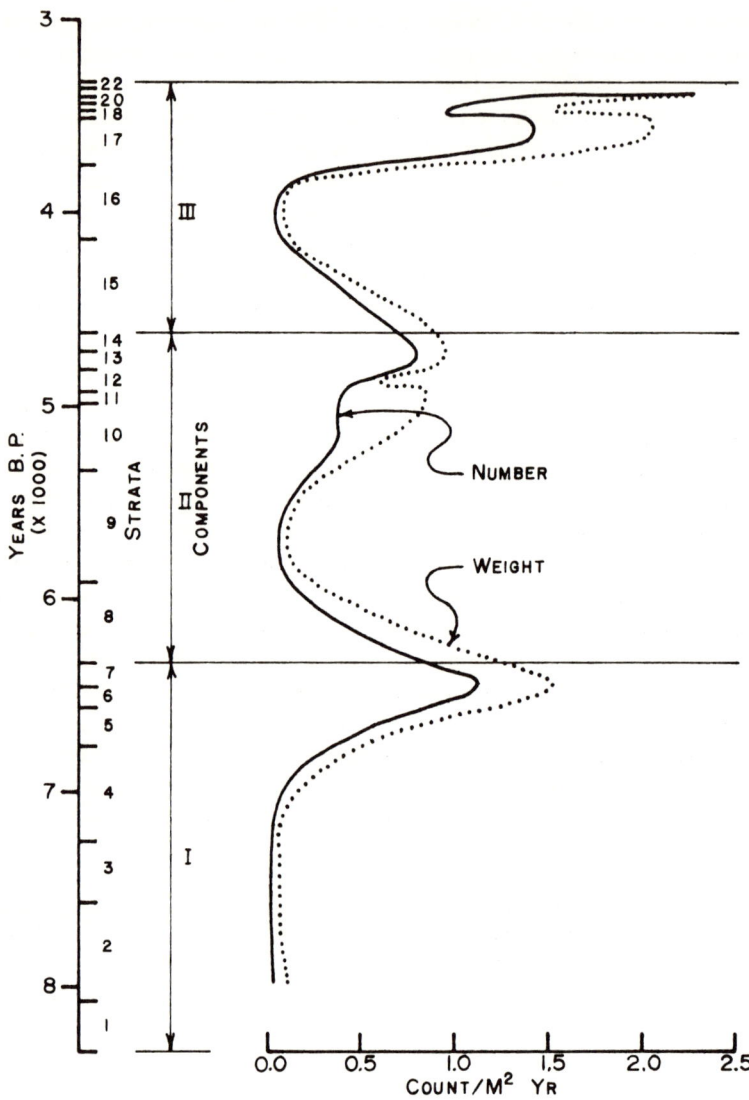

Fig. 4. Total debitage concentration over time at Sudden Shelter.

Extensive land use reduces the impact of human presence on resources and on the biosphere in general. Given the failure of a set of exploitative tactics at a particular place, it also insures that one can move to another place and execute similar or alternative tactics. Such systems are both land extensive and information extensive. As I have suggested, much continuous monitoring of the extended range is, at least in temperate and northern settings, a common phenomenon of hunter-gatherer adaptations. It is the information gathered in places where the group is not living that makes possible optimal movement decisions and the adoption of alternative tactics. These may have a good chance of working given some failures in the tactics used where one is located.

It is fully recognized that we do not know the factors conditioning such extensive land use among hunters and gatherers in general. However, the recognition of multiple annual ranges as one form of land use signals the need for archaeologists to develop techniques for investigating possible variability in long term mobility strategies and how these might be conditioned ecologically.

A knowledge of the Nunamiut settlement system has made it possible to anticipate some of the patterning which might result from long term mobility in the depositional histories of particular sites. We can expect changed patterns of utilization for particular places as the position of the system changes through a series of annual ranges. We may anticipate that not only are given places apt to be used somewhat differentially depending upon the placement of a given group in an annual range, but also that the intensity of utilization is apt to vary with such shifts in the position of the socio-cultural system within the region. This can have the effect of producing stratigraphically or at least superpositioned deposits which may differ in content and occupational intensity per unit of time at particular sites. Such variability does not necessarily monitor any culture change whatsoever.

One can readily appreciate that much less intense use of locations occurs when sites are within the extended range of a system. With a system like the Nunamiut, where the annual range shifts through roughly a 45- to 50-year cycle, most places are within the extended range for most of the time, and only during a relatively short 6- to 10-year period will any one place be part of an annual range. *This means that the larger the extended range, the less frequent and the shorter will be periods of intense use of particular sites or places in a given region.* It is also quite likely that the larger the extended or lifetime range of a system, the less similarity can be expected between occupations generated outside the annual range. *This means that greater micro-stratigraphic diversity may be expected among recognizable depositional units produced within the extended range of large-scale systems.* While these observations are of some interest and at least point to the inadequacy in the assumptive meanings routinely ascribed to chrono-stratigraphic variability in archaeological sites, there are other positive and provocative implications of these observations.

IMPLICATIONS

Imagine for a moment the implications of population growth occurring among populations practicing a pattern of long term mobility as outlined for the Nunamiut. It would be likely that daughter communities would increasingly establish annual ranges in areas that had previously been the extended range of the parent group. With each successive establishment of a new group, the long term mobility options of each group are diminished. This inevitably leads to intensification of subsistence strategies within less space. Intensification means using smaller animals, a greater diversity of species, storage of resources with limited access windows but abundant during the period of availability, etc. It is my view that it is the long term mobility options which are affected by population growth. These in turn force intensification options of which agriculture is only one (see Athens 1977; Osborn 1977), although, as it turned out, one with greater intensification potential than most.

This is not the proper place to develop my current ideas regarding the origins of agriculture, although I note that intensification forced by regional packing is a condition favoring such developments. Of greater importance here, however, is the realization that some changes should be expected in the chronological patterning manifest in the archaeological record as long term mobility strategies are disrupted by virtue of packing, with a resulting reduction in the scale of movement, and an increasing localization of systems. When regional packing is extreme, "micro-bands" may occupy a lifetime range equal in area to an annual range under less closely packed conditions. Obviously such changes should result in more intense use of fewer places. This in turn tends to increase rates of cultural deposition at fixed locations where occupations are increasingly concentrated. Residential sites may exhibit an increasing breadth of species and a general trend toward increased use of smaller and smaller animals as the overall range is reduced for any given system. *The "broad-spectrum" trend noted by Flannery (1968) should be correlated with increasing occupational intensity at residentially used sites.* On the other hand, for logistically utilized sites there may be an increase in intensity of occupation but a reduction in species diversity and a trend toward increased numbers of larger animals. As the residential core of the system becomes more localized, there will be an increase in the exclusive logistical use of some specific locations such as hunting camps (see Binford 1982; Vierra 1975).

I am fairly convinced that evolutionary changes which ultimately operated to favor the beginnings of food production were processes which operated at the organizational level of long term mobility strategies comparable to those described here. My purpose has been to describe what I know about one system's long term strategies. I think I have been able not only to suggest the importance of this level of tactical organization among hunter-gatherers but also to suggest how some patterned consequences of both the long term patterns and changes within them might be manifest in the archaeological record. Scaling such properties as intensity, periodicities, and within- and between-period variability in archaeological deposits has not been an endeavor of archeologists thinking in more traditional ways. If we are going to seek links between general theoretically grounded explanations (see Dunnell 1980) for long term historical trends or major events such as the beginnings of food production, we must begin to investigate the static consequences of such processes for details of the archaeological record not previously observed or regularly discussed. This paper has been a probe in that direction.

Notes

1. For additional works on the Nunamiut see Amsden [1977], Binford [1978, 1980], Gubser [1965], and Ingstad [1954].
2. For a slightly different view on this issue see Burch [1976].
3. See Binford [1982] for a more detailed discussion of these processes.

REFERENCES

Aikens, C. M.
    1970   Hogup Cave. *University of Utah Anthropological Papers* 93.
Amsden, C. W.
    1977   A quantitative analysis of Nunamiut Eskimo settlement dynamics: 1898–1969. Ph.D. dissertation, Department of Anthropology, University of New Mexico, Albuquerque.
Athens, J. S.
    1977   Theory building and the study of evolutionary process in complex societies. In *For theory building in archaeology*, edited by L. R. Binford, pp. 353–384. Academic Press, New York.
Binford, L. R.
    1977   General introduction. In *For theory building in archaeology*, edited by L. R. Binford, pp. 1–10. Academic Press, New York.
    1978   *Nunamiut ethnoarchaeology*. Academic Press, New York.
    1979   Organization and formation processes: looking at curated technologies. *Journal of Anthropological Research* 35:255–273.

1980 Willow smoke and dog's tails: hunter-gatherer settlement systems and archaeological site formation. *American Antiquity* 45:4-20.
1982 Mobility, economic zonation, and site histories. *Journal of Anthropological Archaeology* 1:5-31.

Binford, L. R., and W. J. Chasko
1976 Nunamiut demographic history: a provocative case. In *Demographic Anthropology*, edited by E. B. W. Zubrow, pp. 63-143. University of New Mexico Press, Albuquerque.

Burch, E. S.
1976 The "Nunamiut" concept and the standardization of error. In *Contributions to anthropology: the interior peoples of northern Alaska (Archaeological Survey of Canada, Paper 49, Mercury Series)*, edited by E. S. Hall, Jr., pp. 52-97. National Museums of Canada, Ottawa.

Campbell, J. M.
1970 The hungry summer. In *Culture shock: a reader in modern cultural anthropology*, edited by P. K. Bock, pp. 165-170. Alfred A. Knopf, New York.
1978 Aboriginal human overkill of some game populations: examples from northern Alaska. In *Archaeological essays in honor of Irving B. Rouse*, edited by R. C. Dunnell and E. S. Hall, Jr., pp. 179-208. Mouton Publishers, The Hague.

Dunnell, R. C.
1980 Evolutionary theory and archaeology. *Advances in Archaeological Method and Theory* 3:35-99.

Flannery, K. V.
1968 Archeological systems theory and early Mesoamerica. In *Anthropological archeology in the Americas*, edited by B. J. Meggers, pp. 67-87. The Anthropological Society of Washington, Washington, D.C.

Gubser, N. J.
1965 *The Nunamiut Eskimos: hunters of caribou*. Yale University Press, New Haven.

Harrison, T.
1949 Notes on some nomadic Punans. *The Sarawak Museum Journal* 5:130-146.

Hayden, B.
1981 Research and development in the Stone Age: technological transitions among hunter-gatherers. *Current Anthropology* 22:519-548.

Hill, J. N.
1969 A processual analysis of non-seasonal population movement in man and other terrestrial mammals. *Anthropology UCLA* 1:49-60.

Ingstad, H.
1954 *Nunamiut: among Alaska's inland Eskimos*. G. Allen and Unwin, London.

Jennings, J. D., A. R. Schroedl, and R. N. Holmer
1980 Sudden Shelter. *University of Utah Anthropology Papers* 103.

Kloos, P.
1977 The Akuriyo way of death. In *Carib-speaking Indians. Culture, society, and language*, edited by E. B. Basso, pp. 114-122. University of Arizona Press, Tucson.

MacNeish, R. S., F. A. Peterson, and J. A. Neely
1972 The archaeological reconnaissance. In *The prehistory of the Tehuacan Valley, Volume 5*, edited by R. S. MacNeish, pp. 341-495. University of Texas Press, Austin.

McMillan, R. B.
1976 Rodgers shelter: a record of cultural and environmental change. In *Prehistoric man and his environments: a case study in the Ozark highland*, edited by W. R. Wood and R. B. McMillan, pp. 111-112. Academic Press, New York.

Osborn, A. J.
1977 Strandloopers, mermaids, and other fairy tales: ecological determinants of marine resource utilization—the Peruvian case. In *For theory building in archaeology*, edited by L. R. Binford, pp. 117-205. Academic Press, New York.

Rouse, I. B.
    1972   *Introduction to prehistory.* McGraw-Hill, New York.

Service, E. R.
    1962   *Primitive social organization: an evolutionary perspective.* Random House, New York.

Tanaka, J.
    1971   *Bushman—a study of ecological anthropology.* Shisaku-sha Publisher, Tokyo (In Japanese).

Vierra, R. K.
    1975   Structure versus function in the archaeological record. Ph.D. dissertation, Department of Anthropology, University of New Mexico, Albuquerque.

ARTIFACT CLASS RICHNESS AND SAMPLE SIZE IN ARCHAEOLOGICAL SURFACE ASSEMBLAGES[1]

George T. Jones, Donald K. Grayson, and Charlotte Beck

Artifact class richness, or the number of artifact classes represented in a given archaeological assemblage, is a common interpretive tool in archaeology. Functional class richness is frequently used to infer the diversity of activities carried out at a given site, it often serves as a basic datum in constructing regional settlement patterns, and it is commonly used to track cultural change through time. "The three most productive sites, due to the large numbers of artifacts present and the variety of implements included, suggested a more intensive occupation relative to the other sites and were therefore labelled 'base camps,'" wrote Judge (1973:199) of Folsom sites in the central Rio Grande Valley of New Mexico. At Hogup Cave, Aikens (1970:191) noted that settlement units I and II differed dramatically, a difference that could be seen "most strikingly as a decline in number and variety of artifacts, which appears to signify adoption of a new pattern of resource use and probably a decline in frequency of visits to the site." Stylistic class richness also plays a major role in archaeological interpretation, used to infer, for example, the length of time represented by an assemblage, episodes of culture contact, and the possibility that a given assemblage is mixed. The ethnoarchaeological literature (e.g., Yellen 1977) agrees that there is much meaning to be extracted from patterns of artifact richness across space and through time.

Research in ecological and paleontological settings, however, has shown that class richness can be a treacherous measure because of its dependence on sample size (e.g., Grayson 1981; Pielou 1975; Raup 1975). In this paper, we argue that artifact class richness may be largely determined by the size of the retrieved sample, and that sample size effects must be understood before meaningful statements about assemblage richness may be made. We explore this issue using the data base provided by the Steens Mountain Prehistory Project (Aikens, Grayson, and Mehringer 1983).

ARTIFACT CLASS RICHNESS AND ASSEMBLAGE SIZE: SOME GENERAL CONSIDERATIONS

Paleontologists are rarely surprised when the number of classes—taxa—they encounter in a faunal assemblage can be shown to be highly correlated with the absolute number of remains of organisms they have retrieved from a given set of faunas (e.g., Raup 1975). Archaeological faunal analysts are also becoming aware of interrelationships between various measures of taxonomic abundance and sample size (e.g., Grayson 1978, 1981). Archaeologists, of course, also realize that very small assemblages of artifacts are not likely to be rich in artifact classes. However, the frequency with which one encounters statements in the archaeological literature that compare values of artifact richness, without taking into account the sizes of assemblages that have provided those classes, suggests that the tight and continuous interrelationship between class richness and sample size has not been adequately recognized.

The nature of this relationship, and the bounds within which it must vary, are easy to establish. On the one hand, one can conceive of an assemblage in which all the objects belong to the same class. Such an assemblage might, for instance, be produced by an isolated class of bifaces. An assemblage of this sort would have the class frequency structure displayed in Figure 1*A*. In sampling a distribution of this kind, only the first object counted would add a new artifact class, all additional objects counted belonging to the same class. On the other hand, one can also conceive of an assemblage in which each object belongs to a different class. Such an assemblage might be produced by the grave goods in an isolated burial, and would have the class frequency structure illustrated in Figure 1*B*. In sampling a distribution of this kind, each object counted would add a new artifact class. The upper and lower boundaries to the relationship between numbers of objects counted and number of artifact classes encountered are produced by these very different kinds of assemblages, and are displayed in Figure 2 (lines A and C).

While assemblages of the kind depicted in Figure 1 certainly exist, most archaeological assemblages show a very different kind of class frequency structure, one in which a few classes are very abundant, but most occupy a mid-range position. Figure 3, which displays the frequency of stone tool classes in an assemblage collected from a small surface site in central

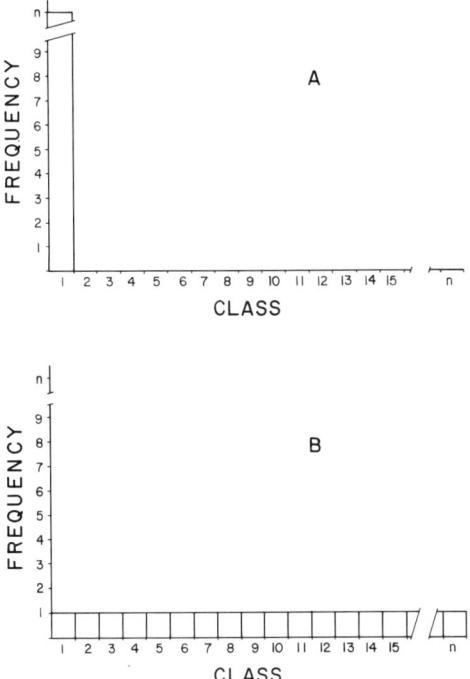

Fig. 1. Class frequency structure of an assemblage in which: *A*, all objects belong to the same class, and, *B*, all objects belong to different classes.

Oregon (Aikens and Minor 1977), illustrates such a distribution. If one were to repeatedly sample a distribution of this form, with replacement and at varying sample sizes, the relationship between number of objects counted and number of classes encountered would be well described by an equation of the form $Y = aX^b$ (Fig. 2, line B), in which:

Y = number of artifact classes encountered
X = number of objects counted
a = Y intercept
b = slope of the relationship between X and Y.

The same relationship would result if a series of assemblages marked by this structure were sampled at different sample sizes.

In short, there is a predictable relationship between sample size and artifact class richness, the exact nature of which depends on the structure of the frequency distribution of the artifact classes themselves. For most

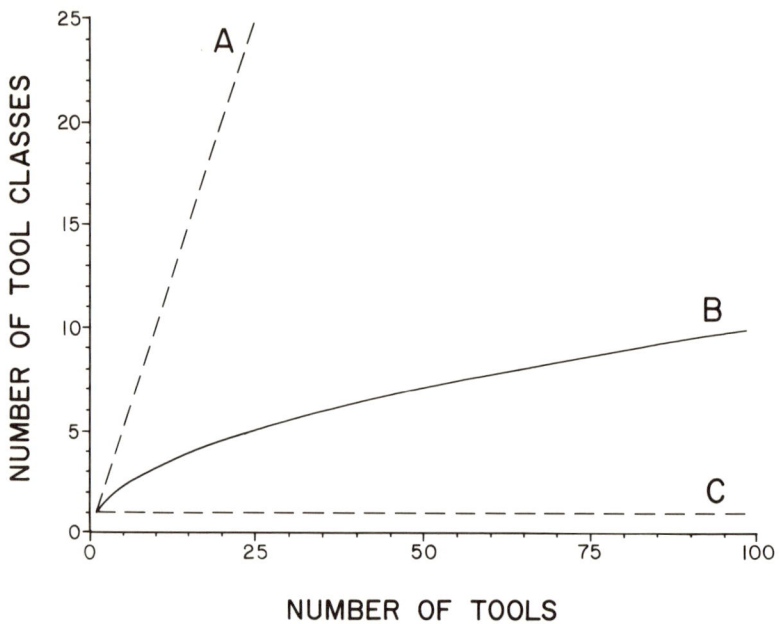

Fig. 2. The relationship between number of artifacts counted and numbers of artifact classes encountered: lines A and C display the bounds between which this relationship must vary; line B displays the general form of the usual relationship between these two variables.

sets of assemblages, it would appear that this relationship will be well characterized by an equation of the form $Y = aX^b$, linear in log–log form.

THE STEENS MOUNTAIN PREHISTORY PROJECT

The Steens Mountain Prehistory Project has been guided by three main goals: (1) to document the nature of human adaptation in a large region of southeastern Oregon, across the entire time span of human occupation in that region; (2) to document independently the nature of prehistoric environments in that region during the same time span; and (3) to integrate the cultural and paleoenvironmental records in order to explore the relationship between cultural and environmental change in the Steens Mountain area. Begun in 1977 and developed as an interdisciplinary research program, the Steens project was directed by C. M. Aikens, D. K. Grayson, and P. J. Mehringer, Jr. and was funded by a series of grants from the National Science Foundation. Completion of the analysis of the surface archaeology of the Steens area has, in addition, been funded by a grant from a private foundation.

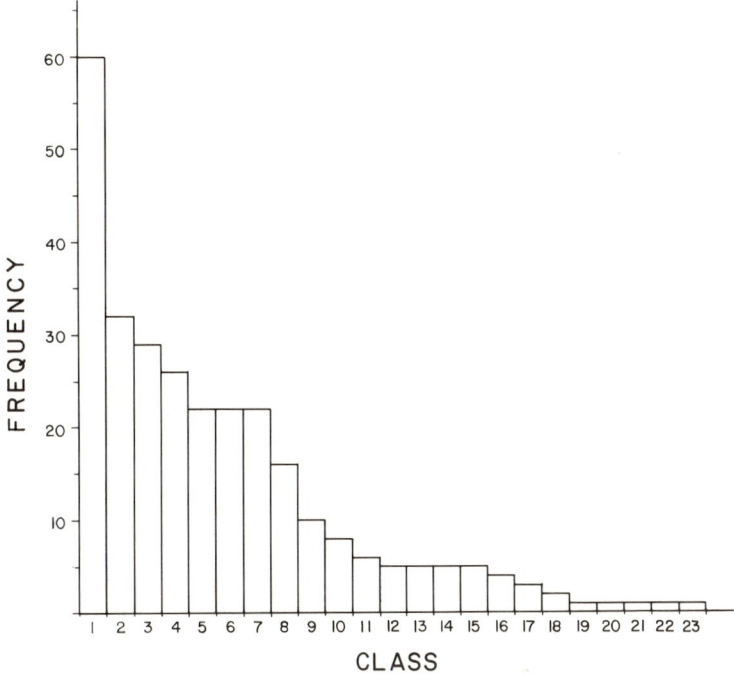

Fig. 3. Frequency of stone tool classes at Site 35LK84, central Oregon (from Aikens and Minor 1977).

The Steens Mountain region encompasses an area of approximately 2000 km^2 that centers on the Steens Mountain Range in southeastern Oregon, and includes the western half of the Alvord Valley to the east and the eastern half of the Catlow Valley to the west (Fig. 4). Elevations in the area range from about 1200 m on the floor of the Alvord Desert to over 2900 m at the crest of Steens Mountain, with vegetation ranging from scattered desert shrubs and grasses in the lowlands to arctic–alpine tundra in the higher reaches of Steens Mountain.

The Steens region was chosen as the focus of research because the area clearly held the potential of providing detailed information on Late Pleistocene and Holocene environments, because the area is characterized by markedly diverse environments, and because the region was known to be archaeologically productive. Paleoenvironmental research for the project was directed by Mehringer, while the archaeological program was planned as two separate but tightly interrelated parts. Excavations were conducted under the direction of Aikens and focused on a series of open

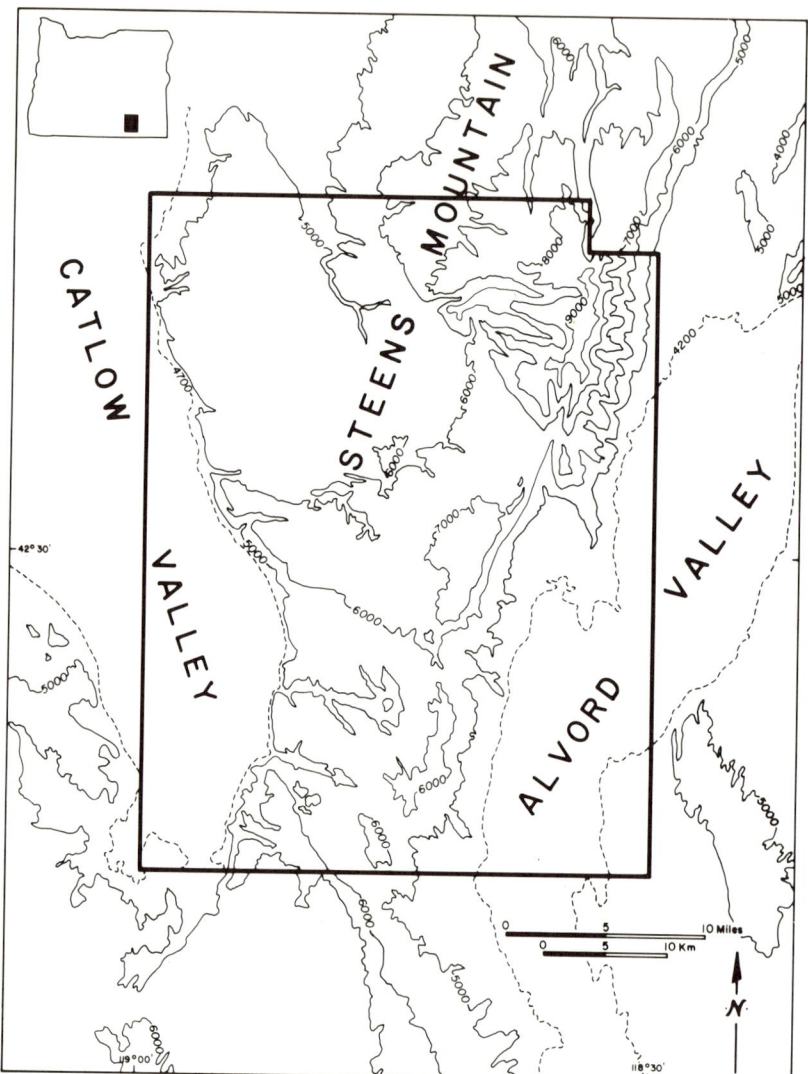

Fig. 4. The Steens Mountain region, southeastern Oregon.

sites and rockshelters. The surface survey was directed by Grayson and provided the data to be discussed below (see Aikens, Grayson, and Mehringer [1983] for a summary of the Steens project as a whole).

THE STEENS PROJECT SURFACE SURVEY

Although a detailed account of the goals and procedures of the Steens project surface survey cannot be presented here, it is essential to note that the questions we were asking demanded that we gather detailed information on the distribution of artifacts across space within the Steens area. Our sampling design and collection procedures were constructed with this requirement in mind. Here, we present only enough information concerning our approach to provide background for our discussion of artifact richness and sample size.

To draw the sample of areas to be surveyed, the project area was first stratified according to the major drainage systems of which it is composed (Alvord, Catlow, Malheur); each of these was then subdivided into upland (Steens Mountain) and lowland (basin) sections. The upland sections were then divided into the separate, smaller drainages of which they are composed, and a 10% sample of each drainage type was drawn randomly for inspection. Because no comparable physiographic units exist in the lowlands, the basins were sampled using one-eighth mile (.20 km) wide, east–west transects placed three miles (4.6 km) apart. To ensure that the equally spaced transects had not coincided with any similarly spaced cycles in the archaeological record, north–south transects one-fourth mile (.40 km) wide and one mile (1.61 km) long were randomly placed between the east–west transects. For a number of reasons, only the Alvord and Catlow uplands were examined during the course of the survey. The location of all survey units is shown in Figure 5; the justification of this sampling design, and the results of our statistical tests for sample adequacy, will be presented elsewhere.

All sampling units were surveyed and collected during the 1978, 1979, and 1980 field seasons. Artifacts were gathered from sampling units in two ways. First, survey crews consisting of individuals spaced 15 m apart walked each unit under the direction of a single crew leader. Whenever an artifact was encountered, the survey crew stopped while the crew leader assigned that artifact a number and recorded its location on a scaled enlargement of a USGS topographic map. When artifact densities were too great to allow the accurate recording of artifact locations on the enlarged maps, these dense scatters of artifacts, now termed "sites," were mapped by separate crews using plane table and alidade or tape and compass.

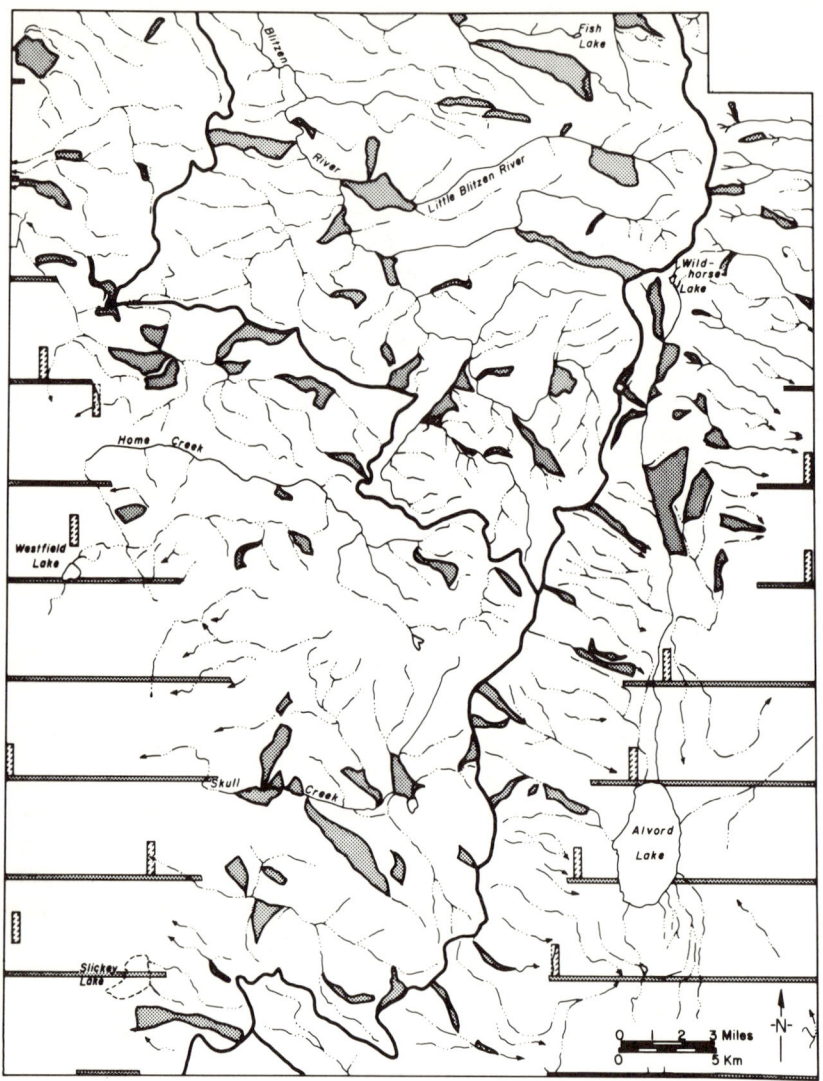

Fig. 5. Surface survey sampling units, Steens Mountain region.

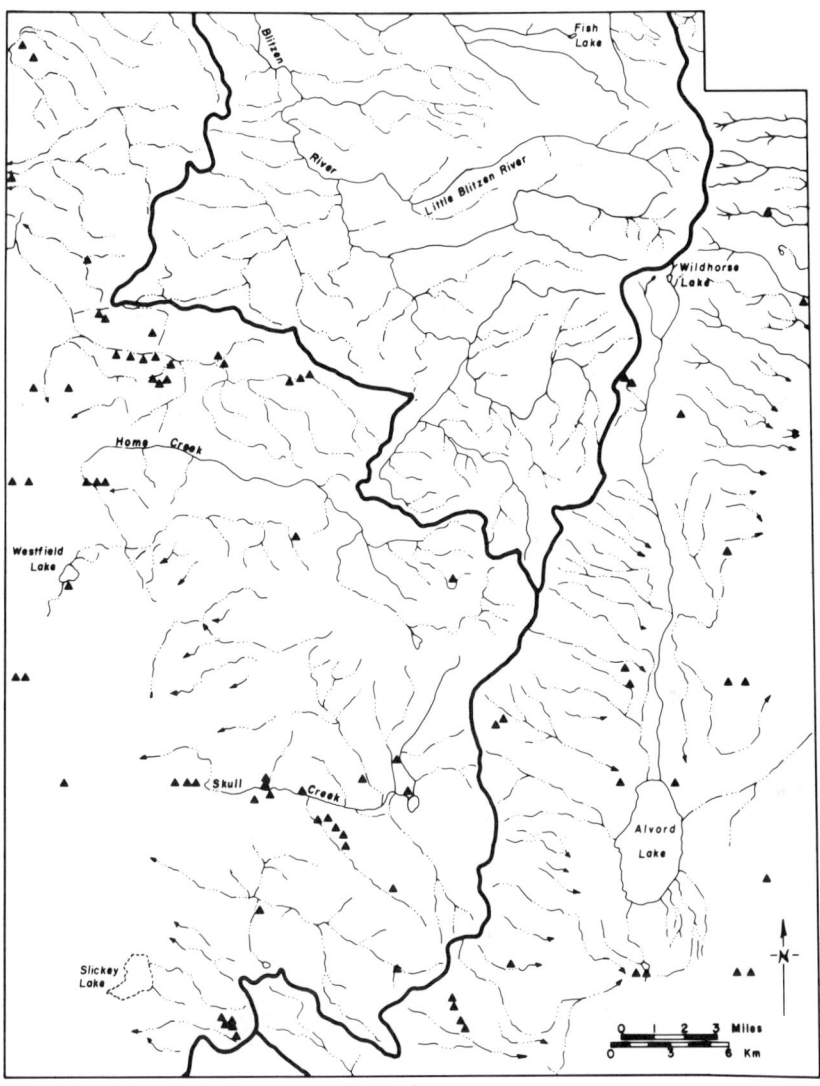

Fig. 6. The distribution of mapped "sites" in the Steens Mountain region.

The surface survey was completed by the end of the 1980 field season, at the cost of 2550 person-days in the field. The artifacts from 19 transects and 71 drainages had been recorded, mapped, and catalogued, including the preparation of detailed distribution maps for the 81 high artifact density "sites" (Fig. 6).

The amount of information generated by these procedures was immense. Approximately 160,000 artifacts, each with precise provenience, were recovered during the course of the survey and have now been analyzed. Some 1300 of these artifacts represent temporally diagnostic projectile points. Approximately 92% of the objects came from sites; the remaining artifacts came from lower density portions of sampling units (termed "offsite" samples). Judging from projectile point styles, the entire known time span of human occupation in the Great Basin is represented in the sample. Our sequence begins with fluted points that are presumably Late Pleistocene or Early Holocene in age, and ends with Desert Side-notched points. All temporally intervening Northern Great Basin point styles are represented, as are the Late Pleistocene/Early Holocene crescents.

Description and analysis of this collection began in 1978 and has continued since. The first goal of this work has been the functional classification of all used (worn) artifacts, a classification that follows the approach formulated by Dunnell (e.g., Dunnell and Campbell 1977; Dunnell and Beck 1979). This approach identifies objects according to the nature and position of wear on those objects, and produces a functional classification without requiring any knowledge of the specific functions that produced a given wear pattern. The functional classification of the artifacts recovered during the Steens project surface survey was conducted by Jones and Beck, and forms the basis of the following discussion.

ARTIFACT CLASS RICHNESS AND ASSEMBLAGE SIZE IN THE STEENS MOUNTAIN AREA

We have argued that for most artifact assemblages, the relationship between artifact class richness and assemblage size will be well described by equations of the form $Y = aX^b$. The artifact assemblages from the Steens region illustrate this relationship well. Histograms of functional class frequencies for "site" and "offsite" samples are of the form displayed in Figure 3; representative Steens examples are provided in Figure 7. Table 1 presents the correlation coefficients (Pearson's r) between numbers of objects counted and numbers of classes encountered for all

TABLE 1
CORRELATION COEFFICIENTS (PEARSON'S r) BETWEEN TOOL
COUNTS AND NUMBER OF TOOL CLASSES[1]

Assemblage Set	r	p
Alvord Upland Offsite	0.95	<.001
Alvord Upland Site	0.91	<.001
Catlow Upland Offsite	0.93	<.001
Catlow Upland Site	0.87	<.001
Alvord Lowland Offsite	0.93	<.004
Alvord Lowland Site	0.82	<.001
Catlow Lowland Offsite	0.92	<.001
Catlow Lowland Site	0.91	<.001
All Offsite Samples	0.94	<.001
All Site Samples	0.87	<.001
All Surface Samples	0.92	<.001

[1] Both variables were transformed using common logarithms.

site and offsite samples, and for three composite samples. Four representative examples of these relationships are illustrated in Figures 8 and 9. Clearly, tool class richness is strongly correlated with assemblage size in the Steens setting.

These correlations are impressively high, ranging from 0.82 (Alvord Lowland Sites) to 0.95 (Alvord Upland Offsite), corresponding to a range of from 68% to 90% of the variance in stone tool functional class richness that is statistically accounted for by sample size alone. For all Steens area surface samples, the correlation coefficient between tool counts and number of tool classes is 0.91; 83% of the variance in stone tool functional class richness may be statistically accounted for by sample size across all of these assemblages.

It should not be thought that the nature of these relationships is somehow a function of the kind of tool classification we have employed. Provided that the frequency structure of the classes involved is of the sort displayed in Figures 3 and 7, richness and sample size will be highly correlated. Thus, it is not surprising that when all Steens offsite artifacts are reclassified according to stages of stone tool manufacture and retouch, there is a markedly high correlation between the numbers of objects counted and the number of classes encountered ($r = 0.89$, $p < .001$). Here, sample size can account for 79% of the variance in technological class richness in the Steens offsite samples. This is not to say that the exact nature of this relationship will remain unaffected when different classificatory schemes are applied to a set of assemblages. Different classifications change the underlying class frequency structure of archaeological assemblages by expanding or contracting the number of classes that may have members. To take an obvious example, were the

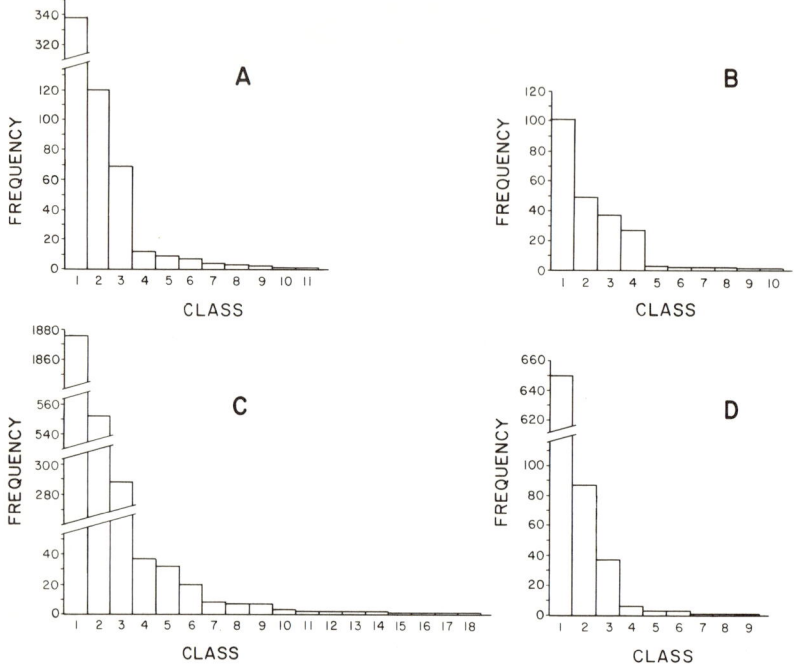

Fig. 7. Frequencies of stone tool classes for four Steens Mountain region surface assemblages: *A*, Catlow Drainage 1-56, offsite sample; *B*, Alvord Transect 4; *C*, Catlow Transect 6, site 6/1; and, *D*, Catlow Drainage 1-33, site 1-33/1.

artifacts that comprise each Steens assemblage to be classified according to whether they are "lithic" or "non-lithic," a relationship of the sort shown in Figure 1*A* would result, since virtually all objects would fall into a single class, "lithic." Such effects are reflected in changes in the amount of variance statistically explained by assemblage size, and by changes in the slope of the relationship between numbers of objects and numbers of classes.

We do not claim to have demonstrated that the size of the samples retrieved from the Steens area has determined the richness of the assemblages involved in all cases. It is reasonable to suppose that assemblage size and class richness are correlated within the artifact populations in the Steens area. The relationships we have discovered at least in part reflect this fact. Small assemblages representing a restricted set of activities and marked by few artifact classes certainly exist here, as do large assemblages characterized by many artifact classes. We do claim, however, that the presence of sample size–class richness correlations that

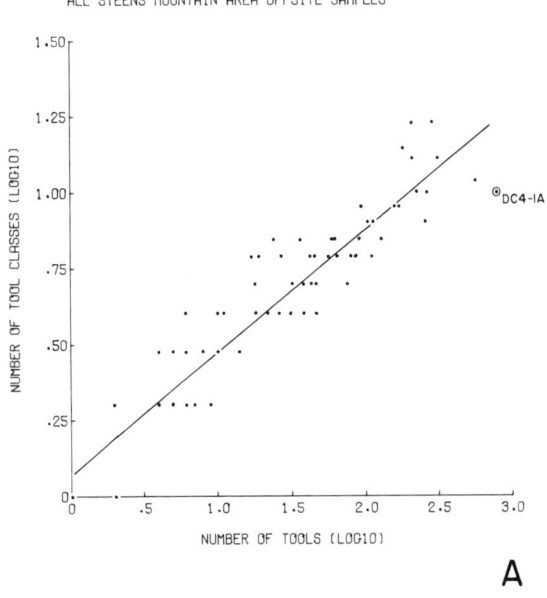

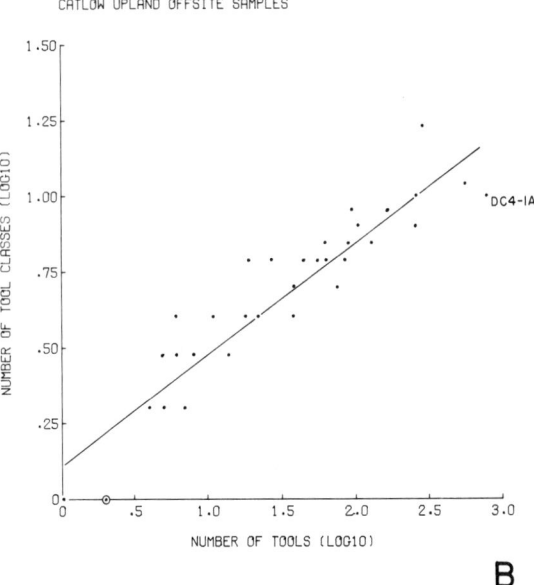

Fig. 8. The relationship between numbers of objects counted and numbers of tool classes present in: *A*, all Steens area offsite samples, and, *B*, all Catlow upland offsite samples.

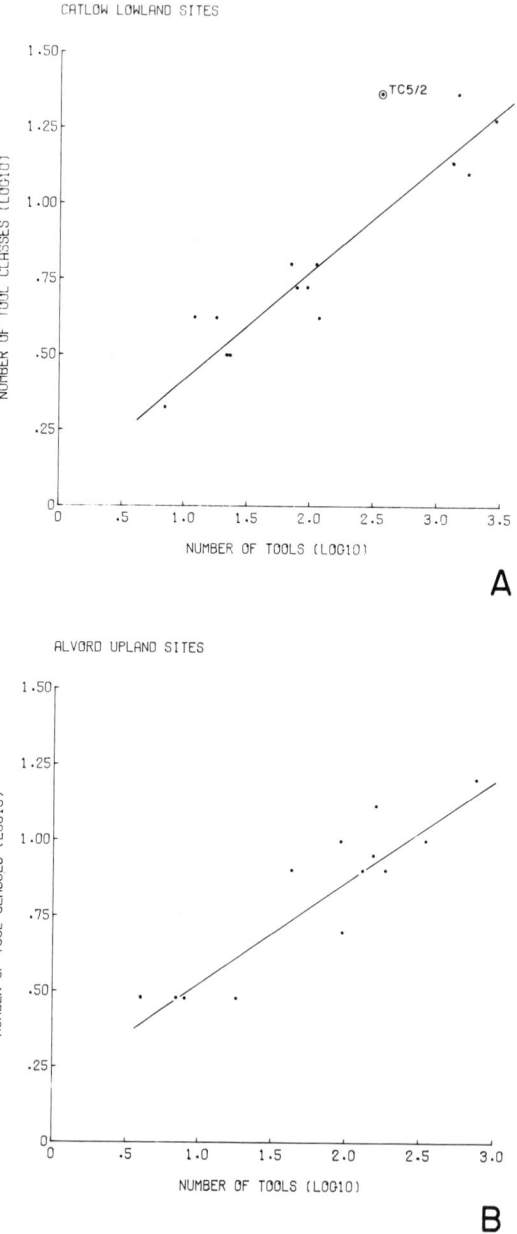

Fig. 9. The relationship between numbers of objects counted and numbers of tool classes present in: *A*, all Catlow lowland site samples, and, *B*, all Alvord upland site samples.

can be predicted on the basis of changing sample sizes alone provides a strong caution against a straightforward archaeological interpretation of differences in assemblage richness.

We conclude that unless sample size effects are taken into account, interpretations of changing artifact class richness across space and through time may be little more than interpretations of differing numbers of artifacts collected. If sample size effects are determining richness values, those effects can be controlled. Once the relationship between number of objects and numbers of classes across a series of assemblages is known, whether a given assemblage is richer or poorer in artifact classes than would be predicted from the number of artifacts it contains can be determined directly from the regression itself. Those assemblages that contain more classes than would be expected for samples of their size will lie above the regression line; those with fewer classes than expected will lie below it. The vertical distance between the regression line and a given assemblage is, of course, a measure of the failure of sample size alone to predict class richness. Thus, the residuals, the amount of unexplained variance, become the target of detailed analysis as regards artifact class richness (see Grayson 1978 and 1981 for a similar approach in the analysis of archaeological and paleontological faunas).

In the Steens artifact samples, for instance, Catlow drainage DC4-1A is a two standard deviation outlier among all Steens area offsite samples. While the sample of artifacts from this drainage is large (757 objects), with a high proportion of worn items (60%), artifact richness is low: 10 tool classes as compared to the 18 classes predicted by the regression (Fig. 8A). We note that when compared only to other offsite samples from the Catlow uplands (Fig. 8B), the number of tool classes contained by DC4-1A is close to the predicted value. In this setting, DC4-1A conforms more closely to the predicted relationship because of the constraint that such a large sample places on the regression. In the company of more cases, with a larger proportion of comparably-sized assemblages, the control of DC4-1A on the regression is less substantial, and it emerges as a true outlier (see Draper and Smith [1966] for a discussion of this effect; an introductory discussion is provided by Lewis-Beck [1980]). There are other examples of assemblages, such as Catlow Lowlands Site TC5/2, that always fall far from the regression lines, and whose artifact class richness is thus poorly explained in terms of assemblage size alone (see Fig. 9A). Such residuals must become a focus of further research.

In addition to directing attention to residuals, the relationship between sample size and class richness also focuses interest on assemblage size itself. Why, it must be asked are different assemblages characterized by differing numbers of artifacts, and thus by differing numbers of artifact classes? One obvious possibility relates to the sizes of the sampling units: the larger the units, the greater may be the number of objects retrieved, and thus the richer the composition of the assemblage. A detailed consideration of why artifact density varies across space, however, goes well beyond the scope of this paper. Similarly, the slopes of the regression lines that characterize the relationship between numbers of tools and numbers of tool classes across assemblages invite further study. In the Steens assemblages, for instance, the slope of the Catlow Lowland Offsite tool class regression line differs significantly (at $p < .10$) from the slopes of all other tool class regression lines, except for those of the Alvord Upland Site and Alvord Lowland Offsite assemblages. This raises the question as to why classes are added at a significantly slower rate to the Catlow Lowland Offsite assemblages, a question we are now exploring.

The relationship between the number of tools counted and the number of tool classes they represent in the Steens area assemblages points to more questions than we can now answer. We have examined only the expected number of tool classes for assemblages of given sizes but, in so doing, have posed additional questions that concern two related yet different issues. The first of these involves artifact diversity, or the nature of the distribution of artifact numbers across artifact classes. While a given regression for a set of assemblages might predict, for instance, that an assemblage of 50 objects will be composed of five artifact classes, it does not directly predict how those artifacts will be distributed among the classes. The second issue concerns artifact class composition, or the kinds of classes represented in a given assemblage or set of assemblages. Assemblages whose total number of artifact classes is accurately predicted by numbers of artifacts counted may, of course, also be composed of tool classes that are totally dissimilar in kind. Some aspects of diversity and composition are likely to depend on artifact class richness and sample size, and the relationship between richness and sample size thus may be important in exploring these dependencies. However, assemblage diversity and composition will be of crucial importance in understanding such issues as variation in assemblage size, variation in regression coefficients across assemblages, and the role of sample size in the interpretation of class richness.

CONCLUSIONS

It should be clear that artifact class richness may be heavily dependent on the number of objects counted in any given assemblage and across sets of assemblages. While few archaeologists are likely to be surprised by this

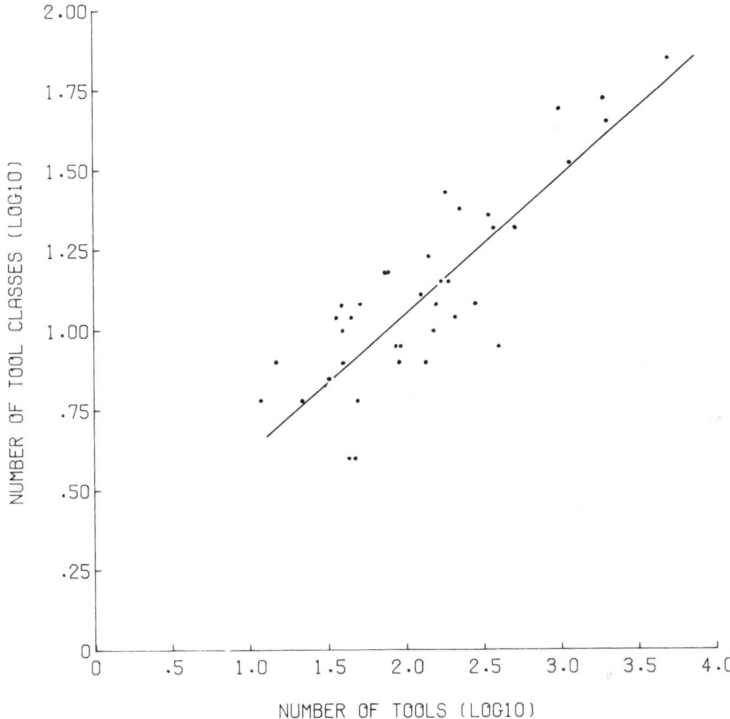

Fig. 10. The relationship between numbers of sherds counted and number of classes represented in 38 ceramic assemblages from the Lower Yazoo Basin, Mississippi (from Phillips 1970).

argument, and some might even find it trivial, it is nonetheless true that the relationship between class richness and sample size is pervasive, and that it is easy to be unaware of the fact that changes in artifact class numbers across space or through time may be tracking little more than changing sample sizes.

Although we have used functional class richness in the Steens Mountain surface assemblages to illustrate the relationship between numbers of objects counted and numbers of classes encountered, our arguments could have been made just as well using any number of examples from the archaeological literature. Ceramic assemblages, for instance, show the effect well. Figure 10 illustrates the relationship between number of sherds counted and number of classes represented in a series of 38 assemblages reported by Phillips (1970) from the Lower Yazoo Basin, Mississippi. Numbers of sherds and numbers of classes per assemblage are highly correlated ($r = 0.85$, $p < .001$), clouding Phillips's use of both numbers and kinds of classes represented to infer the length of occupation registered by each assemblage. Here, stylistic classes show the effect demonstrated by functional classes in the Steens area.

It would serve little purpose to expand our list of empirical examples. Artifact class richness may depend heavily on the number of objects counted in any given assemblage. Any interpretation of class richness requires that the relationship between these two variables be established and explored prior to the use of class richness in archaeological interpretation. Only in this way can the effects of sample size on richness be taken into account. To fail to do so runs the risk of interpreting as meaningful differences in class richness those aspects of archaeological assemblages that are best explained in terms of differing sample sizes.

Notes

1. The Steens Mountain Prehistory Project was funded by National Science Foundation Grants BNS-77-12556 and BNS-80-06277 to C. M. Aikens, D. K. Grayson, and P. J. Mehringer, Jr., and by a grant from Mr. Bingham's Trust for Charity to D. K. Grayson. We gratefully acknowledge the support of these organizations. This paper benefited substantially from critiques presented by R. C. Dunnell and D. H. Thomas.

REFERENCES

Aikens, C. M.
   1970   Hogup Cave. *University of Utah Anthropological Papers* 93.
Aikens, C. M., and R. Minor
   1977   The archaeology of Coffeepot Flat, south-central Oregon. *University of Oregon Anthropological Papers* 11.
Aikens, C. M., D. K. Grayson, and P. J. Mehringer, Jr.
   1983   Final report to the National Science Foundation on the Steens Mountain Prehistory Project. Manuscript on file, Anthropology Program, National Science Foundation, Washington, D.C.
Draper, N. R., and H. Smith
   1966   *Applied regression analysis*. Wiley, New York.
Dunnell, R. C., and C. Beck
   1979   The Caples site, 45-SA-45, Skamania County, Washington. *University of Washington Reports in Archaeology* 6.
Dunnell, R. C., and S. K. Campbell
   1977   Aboriginal occupation of Hamilton Island, Washington. *University of Washington Reports in Archaeology* 4.
Grayson, D. K.
   1978   Reconstructing mammalian communities: a discussion of Shotwell's method of paleoecological analysis. *Paleobiology* 4:77-81.
   1981   The effects of sample size on some derived measures in vertebrate faunal analysis. *Journal of Archaeological Science* 8:77-88.
Judge, W. J.
   1973   *Paleoindian occupation of the central Rio Grande Valley in New Mexico*. University of New Mexico Press, Albuquerque.

Lewis-Beck, M. S.
   1980   *Applied regression: an introduction.* Sage Publications, Beverly Hills.
Pielou, E. C.
   1975   *Ecological Diversity.* Wiley, New York.
Phillips, P.
   1970   Archaeological survey in the Lower Yazoo Basin, Mississippi, 1949–1955. *Papers of the Peabody Museum of Archaeology and Ethnology* 60.
Raup, D.
   1975   Taxonomic diversity estimation using rarefaction. *Paleobiology* 1:333–342.
Yellen, J.
   1977   *Archaeological approaches to the present: models for reconstructing the past.* Academic Press, New York.

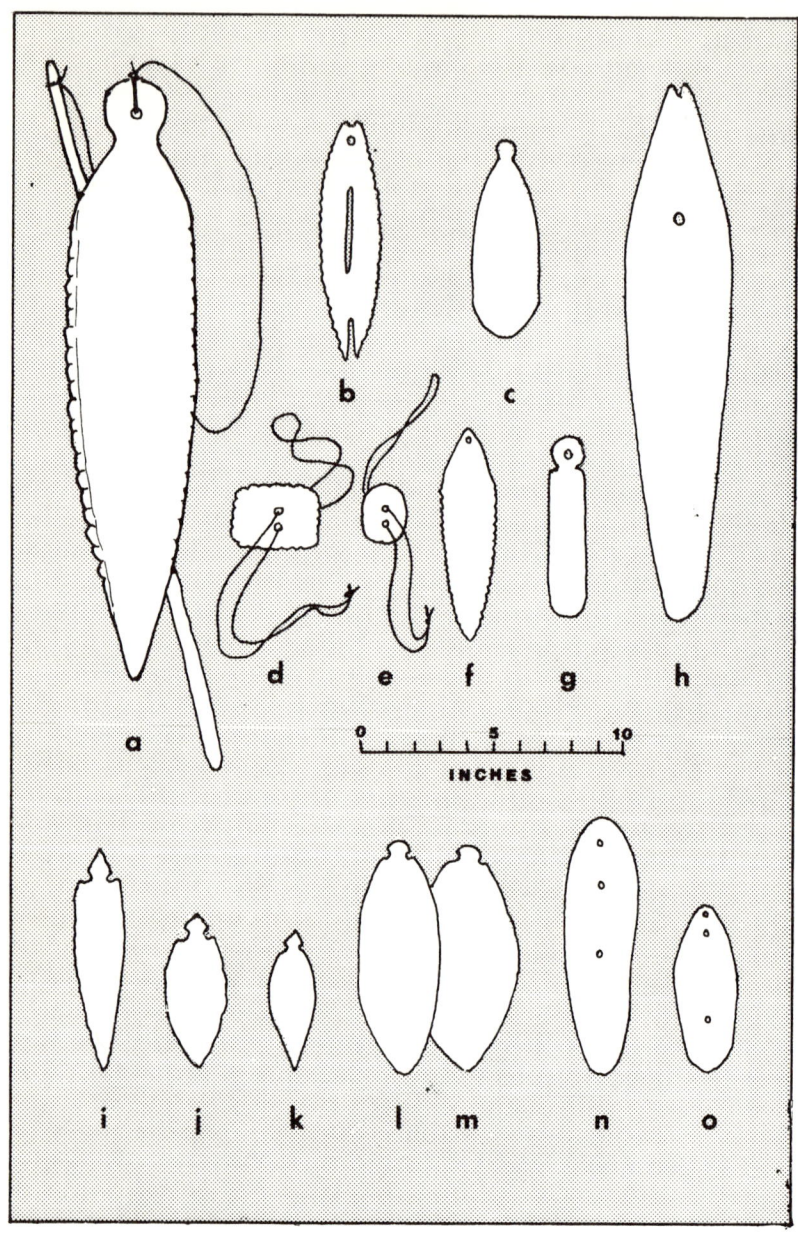

Fig. 1

A PAN-CONTINENTAL PERSPECTIVE ON RED OCHER AND GLACIAL KAME CEREMONIALISM[1]

Robert L. Hall

THE "RED OCHER" CULTURE

The "Red Ocher Culture" is an archaeological complex which bridges the Late Archaic and Early Woodland periods of Midwestern prehistory. The taxonomic unit known as "Red Ocher" was first defined by Fay-Cooper Cole and Thorne Deuel in their book *Rediscovering Illinois* in 1937. Twenty-five years later Robert E. Ritzenthaler and George I. Quimby (1962) published a monograph in which they drew together the additional information which a generation of field work and study had added to the knowledge of the Red Ocher culture. Many problems could not yet be resolved, such as the exact relationship between the coeval Red Ocher and Glacial Kame cultures. Red Ocher extended into Ohio but was

Fig. 1. Bull-roarers, buzzers, turkey-tails, and sandal-sole gorgets: *a*, wooden bull-roarer, Gros Ventre (after Kroeber 1908:Fig. 26); *b*, wooden bull roarer, "old type," Powhatan (after Speck 1928:Fig. 134a); *c*, wooden bull-roarer, "new type," Powhatan (after Speck 1928:Fig. 134b); *d*, wooden buzzer, Point Barrow Eskimo (after Murdoch 1892:Fig. 376), decoration not shown; *e*, stone buzzer, Hopi (after Culin 1975 [1907]:Fig. 1016), decoration not shown; *f*, wooden bull-roarer, Point Barrow Eskimo (after Murdoch 1892:Fig. 377); *g*, wooden bull-roarer, Apache (after Bourke 1892:Fig. 431), decoration not shown; *h*, wooden bull-roarer, Bororo, Brazil (after Lowie 1946:Fig. 52), decoration not shown and size estimated; *i*, flint turkey-tail, Wisconsin (after Ritzenthaler and Niehoff 1958:Fig. 2); *j*, flint turkey-tail, Indiana (after Ritzenthaler and Quimby 1962:Fig. 116); *k*, flint turkey-tail, Illinois (after Cole and Deuel 1937:Fig. 19); *l*, flint "tanged knife" resembling turkey-tails of Binford's Fulton type *var.* Knox (see Didier 1967:Fig. 1g), provenience uncertain, possibly Kentucky (after Perino 1972:Fig. 68b); *m*, flint "tanged knife" resembling turkey-tails of Binford's Fulton type *var.* Knox, Illinois (after Perino 1972:Fig. 68c); *n*, marine shell sandal-sole gorget, Ohio (after Cunningham 1948:Pl.VI-3); *o*, stone sandal-sole gorget, Illinois (after photo in personal files).

centered in northern Illinois, southern Wisconsin, northern Indiana, and the southern half of Lower Michigan. The Glacial Kame distribution overlapped much of the area in which Red Ocher was found but was centered slightly to the east in the Indiana, Michigan, and Ohio area (Cunningham 1948:36; Tuck 1978:Fig. 1). Ritzenthaler and Quimby placed Early Red Ocher around 1500–1200 B.C. and in the Late Archaic; they placed Late Red Ocher around 500–100 B.C. and in the Woodland period, though this terminal date would now be regarded as too late. There are no dates for Glacial Kame, but "dates older than 1000 B.C. are suspected" (Tuck 1978:39).

The distinction between Red Ocher and Glacier Kame is tied to certain distinctive ceremonial objects, notably the so-called "turkey-tail" knives or points for Red Ocher and the "sandal-sole" gorget for Glacial Kame (Fig. 1). In their summary paper on the Red Ocher Culture, Ritzenthaler and Quimby go so far as to say:

> If, in the future, sites are found in which sandal-sole gorgets and the diagnostic Red Ocher traits are in direct association, then we shall be forced to conclude that Red Ocher and Glacial Kame were identical; but until that time we have two closely related but distinguishable cultures manifested primarily by their burial customs. [Ritzenthaler and Quimby 1962:255–256.]

In this paper I propose to investigate the taxonomic problem which Ritzenthaler and Quimby defined, but from the perspective of cognitive archaeology. What exactly is it that we are comparing or contrasting? What meaning may the turkey-tail blades and sandal-sole gorgets have had for the people that made them? I will attempt to demonstrate an approach or method for looking beyond the turkey-tail and sandal-sole as objects in inventories of culture traits. I will try to show that the utilitarian appearance of the turkey-tail may conceal unsuspected ritual or symbolic functions which could be important for understanding the relationship of the turkey-tail to the sandal-sole gorget, which from its form and material (normally marine shell) is more understandable as a non-technological artifact.

Because turkey-tails are made of chipped "flint" (chert) they have the appearance of being practical tools. Many of them probably were practical tools. But, some just do not have the form of efficient knives or points. The name "turkey-tail" is derived from the similarity of the notched base of the blade to the tail of a turkey when plucked of its feathers. Often the size of the base is quite small in proportion to the great length and width of the blade, indicating that the notched base was not intended to be hafted on a wooden handle or shaft. The form of the

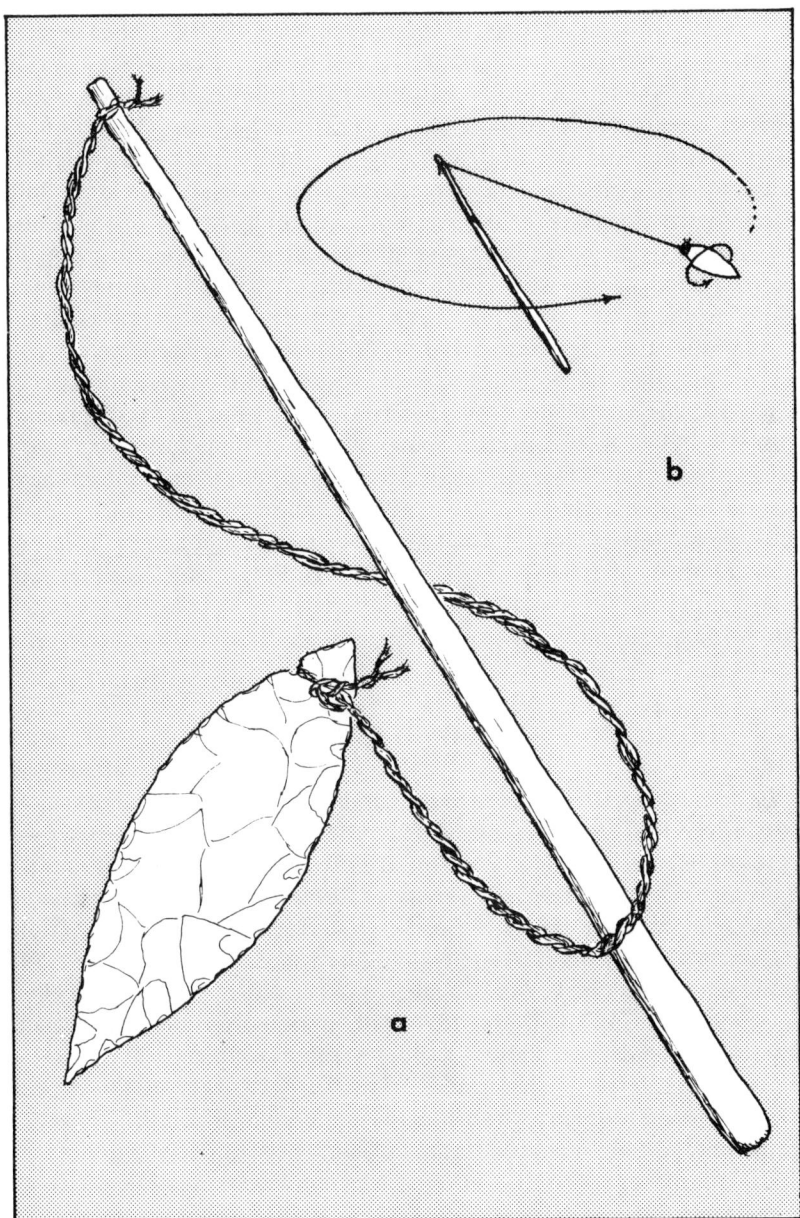

Fig. 2. The turkey-tail as a bull-roarer: *a*, the author's interpretation of the way in which a turkey-tail may have been mounted for use as a bull-roarer; *b*, the manner in which a bull-roarer rotates on its axis to produce a humming noise as it is swung.

turkey-tails with the very small bases reminds me of a bull-roarer, an object which was suspended on the end of a twisted cord (Figs. 1a, 2).

In North America bull-roarers were used (1) in weather magic, (2) to generate a sound which represented a spirit in initiations, (3) as amulets for protection, and were (4) probably viewed by some individuals as vision tokens. These are magico-religious and social functions. Bull-roarers were normally made of wood, but bull-roarers of stone are known. One of the principles I have used repeatedly in trying to probe the cognitive core of prehistoric cultures is that of resolving possible composite artifacts into their constituent parts and seeking the multiple associations of those parts (cf. Hall 1977). If some turkey-tails were in fact bull-roarers, then the components would be the bull-roarer, normally of wood, and the flint blade, not normally a bull-roarer. These components ordinarily relate to two distinct semantic sets. If some turkey-tails were actually used as bull-roarers, in what ways could those semantic sets have intersected in thought to suggest the innovation of a bull-roarer from flint? We are talking here of a cultural process based upon the principle of "bisociation" as defined by Koestler (1964; Hall 1977:505). If an area of intersection can be found, then the inference of a composite artifact obtains some support as a hypothesis.

COGNITIVE ASPECTS OF FLINT

As defined by Ritzenthaler and Quimby (1962:246-249), the nuclear traits of the Red Ocher Culture include the use of red ocher to cover the graves of burials in a flexed position, the presence of tubular marine shell beads and worked copper in a variety of forms, commonly as beads, and the presence of three classes of flint bifaces. The latter include (1) certain large "whitish-flint blades," some knife-like and as large as 19 inches (48 cm) in length, (2) "turkey-tail" blades of "hornstone, a bluish-gray chert from southern Indiana," and (3) small, unnotched, somewhat crude, ovate-trianguloid chert knives or points, often asymmetrical and often occurring in caches of fifty or more examples. The turkey-tails have been of special interest because the distinctive material of which they are made occurs only in certain parts of southern Indiana and Illinois, although the turkey-tail blades themselves have been found widely in the Upper Great Lakes area.

Even a cursory reading of the literature on the religious life and mythology of the Indians of Mesoamerica and North America brings out the fact that a flint blade and the material from which it was made could have a meaning for aboriginal peoples quite different than any an archaeologist might imagine if the flint blade were only considered from a technological point of view. What exactly might the symbolic value of flint have been?

In Aztec mythology, Citlalinicue, Star Skirt, was also identified as Teteoinnan, Mother of Gods. This was a goddess associated with the night sky, where she lived alone with a consort, Citlallatonac, Starshine (Brundage 1979:35, 155, 165, 227n.). Here she gave birth to *tecpatl*, the flint knife of sacrifice. The flint knife fell from the sky and landed in the ancestral homeland of the Aztecs, where 1600 gods emerged from the knife, led by their leader Xolotl. To provide human beings to serve these 1600 gods, Xolotl was commissioned to enter the underworld to recover the bones of human beings killed by the flood which concluded the previous creation, the era of the fourth sun. In some versions of the story this role was attributed to a twin, Quetzalcoatl, or to both jointly (Brundage 1979:120; León-Portilla 1963:107-111). The bones recovered by Quetzalcoatl and/or his double Xolotl were eventually ground in a mortar and given life by being sprinkled with blood drawn from the sexual organs of the gods:

> The Great Mother took the bones, ground them up, and placed them in an earthen tub. Over this Quetzalcoatl drew blood from his genitals, allowing the precious fluid to flow into the dust. The other gods followed suit, and out of the paste came a man and then a woman, the first created humans of the fifth sun. [Brundage 1979:123]

If we examine this myth we can see that the original flint knife, *tecpatl*, was actually in effect an ancestral figure for all the Aztecs of the Fifth Sun, the fifth era of creation current at the time of the Spanish conquest, according to this myth. By extension, particular flint knives in later years could also have been regarded as the symbolic equivalents of the original and ancestral Tecpatl. In another Aztec myth the knife of sacrifice was derived from one of five fragments into which the goddess Itzpapalotl (Obsidian Knife Butterfly) shattered when she was thrown into a fire. The goddess broke into five pieces, each of a different color, but the knife of sacrifice was derived from a white sliver which was recovered by the god Mixcoatl (Brundage 1979:171). The white knife was effectively a transformation of the goddess.

In the Vienna Codex, a Mixtec record, the god Nine Wind is shown being born from a personified stone blade of the shape and character of the Aztec flint knife of sacrifice (Furst 1978:56, 95, 100, 106, 316-317). The calendrical name Nine Wind was associated with the central Mexican god Quetzalcoatl as Ehecatl, god of the wind, but Nine Wind was also the ritual name of the prismatic blade of obsidian (Caso 1967:191). Wind was a fertilizing element, the breath of life, equatable with the soul, but the wind was apparently itself born of stone. Moreover, one of the hazards to the departing souls of the Aztec dead was *itzchecava*, the "wind of knives," a barrier of cold and strong wind which they must endure (Sahagún 1971:191). In New Mexico the Zuñi thought of the whirlwind as a god with flinty wings (Cushing 1979:210).

In Mesoamerica, years in the solar calendar were identified in part by the names of particular days within the year which are referred to as year-bearers. The day signs were also associated with particular geographical directions. Thus, Reed years were associated with the east, Flint years with the north, House years with the west, the Rabbit years with the south (cf. Durán 1971:359–393):

> This is what was believed regarding the North: in that direction lay the underworld. It was called Mictlampa, which means the Infernal Region. A Flint Knife symbolized these years, and it stood for the cold, the ice, and the thin airs of those parts .... [Durán 1971:392]

In Winnebago myths of the Hare cycle, Hare killed his grandfather Flint to avail himself of the material of which Flint was made:

> Finally [Hare] jumped toward [Flint] and chased him all over the earth, clubbing him and forcing him to scatter his flint arrow-points all over the earth. Then he killed him. Thereupon he picked up some of the flint arrow-points that he found. The best ones were blue. [Radin 1948:96]

In Cherokee belief it was Rabbit who opposed Flint and shattered his body with a wooden wedge and a mallet (Mooney 1900:274–275). The Ojibwa culture hero Nanabozho had an identity as a rabbit at birth and in some accounts killed a brother, Flint, whose remains he scattered over the land to produce the flint we know (Barnouw 1977: 15, 74–75, 82n., 83, 92; Brinton 1976:181; Fisher 1946:232). In the mythology of the northern Iroquois, Flint was one of a pair of twins who was also killed by his brother. "Fleeing for life, the blood gushed from him at every step, and as it fell turned into flint-stones" (Brinton 1976:184). Flint's brother in the Iroquois versions did not have an identity as Rabbit or Hare. He was known variously as Sapling, Maple Sprout, Creator, Sky-Holder, Good Minded, and Thrown Away (Fenton 1962:292–293). The Algonquian name Nanabozho (or Manabozho, Wenebojo, Manabush, Nanabush, Manapus, Michapaux, Michabo) translates literally as Great Rabbit (e.g., Menominee *masha* "great" + *wabus* "rabbit"; Ojibwa *misha* "great" + *wabus* "rabbit," cf. Hoffman 1896:87, 114). As a creator figure, Nanbozho corresponds to Iroquois Sapling.

In the Potawatomi version, Nanabozho was the eldest of four brothers born as quadruplets (cf. Fisher 1946:232; Hewitt 1910a:20-21). Nanabozho was a human, although his name translates as "great rabbit." The fourth brother was Chakekenapok, whose birth caused the death of their mother, which Nanabozho resented and resolved to avenge:

> Chakekenapok finally turned and fled, but Nanabozho pursued him all over the world, finally overtaking and striking him with a deerhorn or a chert, fracturing or chipping pieces from various parts of his body, and destroying him by tearing out his entrails. The fragments from Chakekenapok's body became huge rocks, and the masses of flint or chert found in various part of the world show where the conflicts between the two brothers took place, while his entrails became vines. [Hewitt 1910a:20]

The rabbit brother of the quadruplets was the third, Wabosso, who traveled north and became a "white hare." The second brother was Chipiapoos, who was drowned by spirits who plotted against Nanabozho and Chipiapoos. This brother corresponds to the wolf brother of Nanabozho in the Cree and Menominee versions (cf. Fisher 1946:231; Hoffman 1896:87, 115). The name Chipiapoos does not translate as wolf, however. Chipiapoos translates as "corpse rabbit" (Paul Proulx, pers. comm.). Among the Algonquian Potomacs of the Atlantic Coast it was the Great Hare who was not only creator and "chief god" but also lord of the afterworld, dwelling at the place of "the rising of the sun" (Swanton 1946:749). It was Chipiapoos, Corpse Rabbit, who became lord of the land of souls in the Potawatomi version and who corresponded to the wolf brother in the Menominee version who after death traveled to the land of the setting sun and became master of the Menominee afterworld (Hewitt 1910a:20; Hoffman 1896:88). If there is a thread of continuity between the Great Hare personator represented in Hopewell Mound 25 in Ohio (Willoughby 1935) and the historic Algonquian Nanabozho as Great Hare, it could well be one relating to the Great Hare as a lord of the afterworld or underworld.

The identity of Flint is also variable. In northern Iroquois versions and some Algonquian versions of the hero myth, Flint was a twin whose birth resulted in the death of the mother. The good twin revenged the death by killing his brother Flint. In one untypical Menominee version Manabush (the Menominee Nanabozho) was the grandson of Nokomis (Earth) and Manabush's *mother* was Flint:

> The Flint grew up out of Nokomis [Earth], and was alone. Then the Flint made a bowl and dipped into the earth; slowly the bowlful of earth became blood, and it began to change form. So the blood was changed into Wabus, the Rabbit. The Rabbit grew into human form, and in time became a man, and thus was Manabush formed. [Hoffman 1896:87]

The relationship of this particular Menominee Nanabozho to Flint was somewhat like that of the Mixtec god Nine Wind to the stone knife from which he was born, or the Aztec god Xolotl to the flint knife from which he was derived. The northern Iroquois Flint was a male and not noted as an ancestor figure, but he was conceived by a flint-tipped arrow. The objective of the variant cited of the Menominee myth on the birth of Manabush seems to have been to relate Manabush to his mother as fire was related to flint, since we have the prefatory statement, "The daughter of Nakomis, the Earth, is the mother of Manabush, who is also the Fire" (Hoffman 1896:87). The relationship of flint to fire is paralleled in the Winnebago myth of Hare's defeat of Flint, for after obtaining flint arrowpoints from Flint, Hare made some arrows, and "whenever he pressed one very tightly the lodge would be filled with lightning" (Radin 1948:96).

The Iroquois Flint had a sharp comb or ridge of flint on the top of his head (Hewitt 1903:274). It was with this weapon that he forced his way through his mother's armpit at birth, killing her (Fenton 1962:292). This sharp ridge of flint can be compared to the ridge "shaped like a rooster's crest" which is shown on the hood of the person impersonating the Aztec god Centeotl, the maize god. This hood was called *itzlacoliuhqui*, which means "curved obsidian knife," the name of the Aztec god of frost and cold (Brundage 1979:69, 231n.; Sahagún 1971:115; Vaillant 1948:184, 192–193). Iroquois Flint is also the personification of ice, cold, and winter. The Mexican parallel shows the wide area over which ice and stone, particularly flint, were cognitively associated in North America, extending from the sub-arctic to the sub-tropics.

The actual name of Iroquois Flint, the dark force in Iroquois cosmology, was Tawiskaron. This name is based on a northern Iroquois noun root to which Hewitt (1910b) attributes the meanings "ice, hail, sleet," and in historical times "glass." The name Tawiskaron actually translates as "He is arrayed in ice in a double degree" and is glossed "Flint" because the Iroquois word for flint is based on the same nominal root. The Cherokee cognate of northern Iroquois Tawiskaron is Tawiskala. Lounsbury (1982) has observed that this name is almost homophonic with the first half of the name Tlahuizcalpantecuhtli, the central Mexican lord (*tecuhtli*) of the dawn (*tlahuizcalli*), who was essentially the same at Itzlacoliuhqui, the Aztec god of frost (Thompson 1971:173, 220). Itzlacoliuhqui resembled Tawiskaron in appearance as well as in associations, as mentioned above. Hewitt noted that in some Algonquian languages the words "ice" and "flint" were cognate, as were "flint" and "wolf," and he went on to equate as mythical characters the Iroquois "Flint," the Algonguian wolf and flint brothers of Nanabozho, and the northern Algonquian cannibal cold north giant "Windigo" (1910b:708-709). The southern Iroquoian language Cherokee preserves reflexes of the same Iroquoian root with the meaning "smooth, crystal, slippery, slick, and flint," suggesting that the basic semantic association of the root was "smooth, slick" (Hewitt 1910b:708). Flint, ice, and glass all share the properties of slickness, but the idea of "crystal" mediates two opposed associations of flint. Flint was associated in thought both with fire and with ice. Flint could be an ice metaphor, but flint was also a source of fire and could be associated with lightning (above). Flint, ice and glass all share the properties of slickness, but the idea of "crystal" mediates two opposed associations of flint. Clear crystals, whether of ice or stone, refract sunlight and appear to have captured a spark of light or fire.

Aside from crystals, at least one other substance mediates the ideas of ice and stone. Patty Jo Watson (personal communication) has pointed out that cave drip formations like stalactites and stalagmites closely resemble icicles but were made of calcite. Fogelson (1980) details the relationships between the northern Algonquian Windigo with his heart of ice, the Cherokee Stoneclad with heart of rock crystal, the Iroquois Flint or Tawiskaron with his heart of flint, and certain Iroquois stone giants who came to their end by being buried under rocks in a "narrow defile." Since in one version this narrow "defile" or canyon was described as a cave or caves sundered by an earthquake (Fogelson 1980:142), the myth is a remarkable description of caves where Indians could and did mine calcite, gypsum, and other minerals from the walls of passages sometimes filled with enormous blocks of breakdown rock:

> Upper Salts Cave consisted of a series of large walking passages and big rooms . . . which are littered with boulders of every size fallen from walls and ceiling at some time in the past. Such debris is called "breakdown" by speleologists . . . . It is clear from the distribution of the remains that much of the massive Upper Salts breakdown occurred before the prehistoric people began coming into the cave. However, there are also places where rocks have fallen on top of Indian material. This is also true in the non-commericalized parts of Mammoth Cave seen by Hall and P. Watson . . . . [Watson 1969:3-4]

> Middle Salts is a series of canyon-like passages . . . . In places passages are nearly choked with breakdown debris, and often one must crawl for considerable distances through narrow spaces between boulders . . . . [Watson 1969:4]

Wyandotte Cave in southern Indiana was a source of calcite utilized by prehistoric Indians and was also a source of the Bluish "flint" or "hornstone" (chert) used for the manufacture of turkey-tail points (Patrick Munson, personal communication; cf. Watson 1969:74). Salts Cave

Kentucky, was extensively mined in the Early Woodland period for gypsum crystals and other materials (Watson 1969:57-64, Pl. 13).

The flint-, stone-, and ice-associated supernaturals that appear in the oral literature of eastern North America are almost always malevolent, but it is to this group of beings that one can look for the mythical originator of the Iroquois False Face Society, a curing society (Fogelson 1980:142-143). In a Seneca myth the origin of this society was traced to the experiences of a hunter who was given the patronage of Genonsgwa, the last of the race of ancient Stone Giants buried under boulders in the manner already described. The hunter secured the wisdom of Genonsgwa in the giant's cave (Fogelson 1980:142; Parker n.d.:397-400). The Cherokee especially valued the magical qualities of quartz crystals, which were sometimes said to have been derived from the heart of Stoneclad (Fogelson 1980:140).

COGNITIVE ASPECTS OF THE BULL-ROARER

As a technomic artifact the bull-roarer is a musical instrument and is usually found under that listing in book indexes. In his paper on musical instruments in the prehistoric southwestern United States, Brown (1967:78-79) classifies the bull-roarer as a "whirling aerophone." Bull-roarers were used principally as ceremonial objects and for magical purposes, but they sometimes came to lose their sacred and magical associations and became mere toys (Culin 1975 [1907]:750). Bull-roarers were once in use on all continents and constitute one of the oldest categories of ceremonial objects known to anthropology. They figured importantly in initiation ceremonies and often represented ancestors or the spirit patron of the ceremony.

While all bull-roarers make a humming, whirring noise, the symbolism and ritual uses varied with the geographical situations and world views of the peoples using them. Hough (1907:171) noted that in North America bull-roarers were used in semi-arid areas to invoke clouds, lightning, and rain, and in humid areas to bring fair weather. They were also used in far northern areas to summon the north wind and snow (see below). The Navajo and Apache used bull-roarers to drive away evil influences in curing and purification rites and as protective charms (Reichard 1974:261, 531, 620, 733). The Navajo, Apache, and Hopi made bull-roarers from the wood of lightning-struck trees; wind and lightning symbolism prevailed in the decoration of Apache, Navajo, Hopi, and Zuñi bull-roarers (Bourke 1892:477-478; Hough 1907; Mails 1974:29; Matthews 1887:436). The storm theme was often personified by making the bull-roarer anthropomorphic. Navajo bull-roarers came in both male and female sizes. According to John Bourke (1892:587), nineteenth-century Apache wore amulets which were made of the same form and decoration as bull-roarers but miniature in size. These were said to have been placed on the necks of children or on their cradles.

The Navajo and Apache are southwestern peoples of the Athapascan language family. Far to the north in the Canadian sub-arctic, the northern Athapascan linguistic relatives of the Navajo and Apache used bull-roarers for weather magic. A north wind bringing snow was something desirable for northern hunters. The north wind could be lured with the aid of a bull-roarer or a related noise-maker we call a buzzer (e.g., Fig. 1d–e) and by making a figure of a man or rabbit of snow set to face the north wind (Cooper 1946:297). This practice was found, in fact, across the whole sub-arctic—among the Athapascans of western Canada and the Algonquians of eastern Canada (Flannery 1946:266):

> The buzzer is made of a bark or wooden disc or of moose bone, to which two strings are attached parallel. The disc or bone is then revolved with a twirling motion and the strings are alternatively loosened and held taut, causing the disc or bone to rotate rapidly with a loud buzzing, whirring, droning noise . . . . The bull roarer is made of a flat almond-shaped or lozenge-shaped bit of wood with a string attached to it, and is whirled around the head . . . . Both the buzzer and the bull roarer are now more commonly used as children's toys, but are sometimes used, and were formerly used habitually, particularly after the first thaw of late winter, to bring the cold north wind to form a crust on the ice so that travel by snowshoe and transportation by toboggan would be less laborious. . . . At Lake of the Woods and Rainy Lake, a rabbit skin is sometimes thrown on the fire to bring the cold weather. . . . At Obidjuan, a snow man, the figure of *Kimucwuminaw*, as they call North Wind being, is made, if cold weather is desired. Skinner reports this practice, too, from the Eastern Cree. [Cooper 1930:515]

Kroeber (1908) reports the presence of the bull-roarer as a child's toy among the Gros Ventre, a Plains Algonquian group related to the Arapaho (Fig. 1a). The name given this "toy" betrays the possibility of an earlier association with weather magic, however. The name translates as "making cold," a name used also by the Gros Ventre for the thermometer, "probably from the widespread Indian idea that the bull-roarer breeds wind" (Kroeber 1908:191).

The thunderstorm and north wind associations of bull-roarers are found combined in the beliefs of the northern Ojibwa with material tokens of the power granted by visions from guardian spirits which have blessed a hunter. As Ruth Landes relates:

> In hunting . . . the great powers came through revelations from, or of, some animal or bird manito. The Thunderbird gave his protege powers over the weather, usually working in conjunction with the North Wind manito. Invoking them, the favored

Indian could raise a wind that formed a crust on the February snow, or froze the thawing March waters, or made snow fall thickly, or cleared stormy skies. Simultaneously, the same Indian used a kind of bull-roarer or cedar horn whose noise evoked rushing winds by sympathetic magic. Bull-roarer and horn weather-influencer were widely distributed among northeastern American Indians: individual Ojibwa may have regarded them as vision tokens. [Landes 1968:33]

The Koskimo division of the Kwakiutl Indians of Vancouver Island, western Canada, used the bull-roarer to simulate the sound of the voice of a spirit believed to carry off and initiate young people during the winter ceremonials. This spirit was Winalagilis, the Warrior-of-the World, who lived in the far north (Boas 1966:172-173):

> About midnight of this day a number of men secretly climb the roof of the houses of the village and begin to whirl the whirring sticks.... The noise of these sticks is supposed to be the voice of Haialilagas or Winalagilis, who comes to take away another novice. [Boas 1897:610]

The Nootka of Vancouver Island used bull-roarers to represent the sound of the tails of supernatural wolves which initiated novices into the Lokoala, a secret society which celebrated its festivals in winter:

> The Lokoala is believed to have been instituted by the wolves, the tradition being that a chief's son was taken away by the wolves, who tried to kill him, but, being unsuccessful in their attempts, became his friends and taught him the Lakoala. They ordered him to teach his people the ceremonies on his return home.... Every new member of the Lokoala must be initiated by the wolves. At night a pack of wolves— that is, Indians dressed in wolf skins and wearing wolf masks—make their appearance, seize the novice, and carry him into the woods.... On the following day the wolves return the novice dead. Then the Lokoala must revive him. The wolves are supposed to have put the magic stone haina into his body, which must be removed in order to restore him.... It seems that this stone is quartz. The idea is the same as that found among the Kwakiutl, where the Matem is initiated by means of quartz, which is put into his body by the spirit of his dance (Boas 1897:632-633). [Drucker 1951:106, 388]

The mode of restoring to normalcy the novices initiated by the wolves reminds us of the manner in which the Iroquois Tawiskaron lost his power to his older brother, by yielding the flint which was inside his body, an act which Hewitt likens to the snapping off of an icicle (Fogelson 1980:144; Hewitt 1910b:709-710). It reminds us also that in the myths and folktales associated with Cherokee Stonecoat and the Algonquian Windigo the heart of the supernatural being is always found to be made of ice or rock crystal. In the case of the Windigo, it was also believed that mortal Indians could become possessed of the spirit of the Windigo and become cannibals, often eating their own family. This is the Indian explanation of the familiar Windigo psychosis (e.g., Hay 1971). Both the concept of a heart of ice and a heart of stone are found in a folktale of the Plains Cree:

> Then they melted bear's grease. They made her drink it. In this way they made her vomit repeatedly. They kept her vomiting a long time. Presently she threw up some ice. Then she came back to her natural self. When she regained her memory, she spoke thus: "I have eaten my children and my husband. I cannot bear it; please slay me," she said . . . . And so she was slain. Then she was burned up. When in time she had burned up, a search was made. There a beautiful little stone was found. Then they went and placed it in a pit. [Bloomfield 1934:155]

THE TURKEY-TAIL AS BULL-ROARER

The ideas "flint" and "bull-roarer" had many thought associations which were shared. Flint was associated with ice and cold from Mexico to Canada, but was also associated with fire and lightning in the Midwest and presumably more widely. The bull-roarer was used for weather magic associated with rain and lightning in temperate areas and with north wind and cold in more northern areas. Flint and the bull-roarer were both directly or indirectly associated in North America with the origin of shamanistic societies based upon learnings acquired from mythical supernatural beings in the wilderness—wolves and stone men—categories which were also conceptually related. "Wolf" and "Flint" were sometimes cognate as words and were sometimes the names of structurally equivalent characters in myths. Bull-roarers were found to represent the sounds of approaching wolves and north-associated supernaturals and by imitative magic to be capable of summoning the Thunderers and North Wind. Amulets of bull-roarer form were found in the Southwest, and objects of bull-roarer form were found as items of ritual costume decoration among the Kwakiutl (Boas 1897:Fig. 165). In Iroquoian languages, words for flint were found to be cognate with those for ice and rock crystal, and the Cherokee were found to have believed in the magical powers of rock crystals often thought to have been derived from mythical monsters such as Stonecoat.

The cognitive associations of flint and bull-roarers overlap sufficiently, and the form of bull-roarers so closely approaches that of some leaf-shaped flint points and knives, that it is reasonable to expect to find this intersection of idea-sets manifested in material form as a composite artifact—a bull-roarer chipped of flint. This was my initial inference from the form of the turkey-tail points so distinctive of the Late Archaic Red Ocher culture. I am indebted to George Hamell for also bringing to my attention a reference to the actual use of stone blades as bull-roarers by the Navaho:

> Further evidence as to the association, in the Apache mind, of the magic-working bull-roarer with lightning, and the association of lightning with obsolete stone implements, seems to be afforded by the bull-roarers of the Navajo, a people closely related both in blood and culture to the Apache, for "The Navajo chanters say that the sacred groaning stick may be made only of the wood of a pine tree which has been struck by lightning," and the Navajo use large ancient stone blades which they find, particularly those made from a greenish silicious stone, as bull-roarers in some of their curative ceremonies [a practice observed and communicated by E. H. Morris]. [Hildburgh 1919:85]

Ritzenthaler and Niehoff recognized that the very small notched base of the turkey-tail was impractical as a shaft or handle haft and suggested "a non-utilitarian function" such as "suspension from the neck as an ornament" (Ritzenthaler and Niehoff 1958:117). The Apache did attach flint implements to cords for use as protective amulets (Hildburgh 1919). Most turkey-tails are rather large for personal charms to be worn regularly, and I consider them much too uniform over very large areas to have been tokens of highly personalized vision experiences.

Benedict (1973 [1923]:56) has said that the guardian-spirit concept did exhibit "an almost constant tendency to externalize or perpetuate itself in some sort of social group," that is, to become the basis for societies of individuals who shared a common spirit-guardian or patron, groups of individuals blessed by the same spirit power, whose adoptive children they were thought to have been:

> Neighboring tribes cultivated visions similar to the Ojibwa's (see Benedict 1974 [1923]) but often externalized them in artifacts serving as amulets and as sizable bundles which were often portable altars. [Then, far from being secret and personal] one such "dream" could serve generations, possibly centuries, through its materialization; the original experience of dreaming then became a sacred tale explaining the origin and powers of the bundle. [Landes 1968:38]

Binford (1963:180) has noted that turkey-tails from the Pomranky site in Michigan exhibited polish on the high ridges of the flake scars on the blade but had no polish on the base or at the tip, suggesting to him that the specimens may have been carried around, acquiring the polish while rubbing together. This would have been the case if the turkey-tails had been parts of a sacred bundle. Binford said that "in view of the context in which they are normally found some social function rather than technoeconomic function is suggested . . . a ritual function" (Binford 1963:187–188).

Turkey-tails could have been used in the Midwest during Terminal Archaic and Early Woodland times as condensed symbols combining various means of representing a tribal or society supernatural patron related to the mythical Flint, or Stonecoat, or the icy Windigo. As such they could have been kept in bundles and periodically used as bull-roarers or worn as amulets or simply kept as tokens of "spirit patronage" (e.g.,

Benedict 1974 [1923]:14, 16; Landes 1968:33, 38). They could have been used in puberty rites or initiations into shamanistic societies under the patronage of the supernatural. Sacred bundles are often buried with the persons who owned them. Some prototype of Windigo could have once filled the role of the patron, in which case the modern folkloristic concept of Windigo could be viewed as the survival of the idea of such a patron stripped of his ritual associations. The use of bull-roarers and ice figures by northern hunters to attract the north wind could be another survival of the magico-religious system in which Windigo once figured, or one from which Windigo emerged. This would make Windigo akin to the Kwakiutl Cannibal-at-the-North-End-of-World, one of the principal spirits who initiated novices during the winter ceremonials (Boas 1966:173).

I have learned through Raymond Fogelson that the Plains Cree, in fact, have a masked curing and clown society known as the Windigokan or Cannibal Cult (Mails 1973:354-355; Skinner 1914). The functions of the Windigokan resembled somewhat those of the Iroquois False Face Society, which has its origin within the prehistoric magico-religious milieu to which Windigo related. Archaeology affirms that in the Early Woodland Adena culture there existed persons committed to impersonate wolves, because their upper incisors were removed to accommodate certain wolf masks which have also been found (Webb and Baby 1957:61-67).

In her study of turkey-tail points, Didier (1967:35) suggested that the explanation for the midwestern distribution pattern of turkey-tails "must be sought not just in terms of the circulation and dispersion of Harrison County [Indiana] 'flint', but in the exchange of flint for copper—this is basically a flint-copper exchange system." Glacial Kame culture shell gorgets were made from marine univalves, which necessarily implies prehistoric exchanges with areas far outside the midwestern distribution of Glacial Kame culture. Objects of marine shell occur in the Red Ocher culture (e.g., Cole and Deuel 1937:66, 225), but there are no co-occurrences of turkey-tails and shell gorgets of sandal-sole shape. A review of the literature on historic Indian religion and mythology in midcontinental North America will reveal that in many contexts relevant to this paper, shell was the symbolic equivalent of stone, crystal, or flint (cf. Barnouw 1977:76, 92).

THE SANDAL-SOLE GORGET

When sandal-sole gorgets have been observed *in situ* with burials, these gorgets were said to be located on or near the head or chest. In Cunningham's *Study of Glacial Kame Culture*, the approximate locations of 32 sandal-sole gorgets were given. Two were found on the head, 5 near the head, 13 around head and shoulders, 1 on the chest, and 11 "on the front of the skeletons about the middle" (1948:7, 11–12, 16, 25–26). Of the two gorgets found on the top of the head, one was said to have been located with the larger end toward the front of the skull, the other with the larger end toward the rear. There was no consistent occurrence specifically on the head to permit arguing for an exclusive function such as that of the bone roach-spreader of historic times. Nor was there a consistent occurrence on the chest to suggest a use only as a pendant.

Holes drilled in the sandal-sole gorgets are sometimes said to show signs of wear. In fact, there was no real pattern of use which could be inferred from the wear. One gorget exhibited wear which suggested that the gorget had been secured to another object on its convex side (Holmes 1883:266). It is hard to imagine what this use may have been. There is possibly more information to be obtained from the spacing and physical relationships of the holes than from the wear.

In the true sandal-sole gorgets, those which look more like sandal-soles than generalized pendants, the holes have a specific pattern. There are three holes, two clustered more closely and near the "toe" or larger end, a third separated from the first two and near the middle of the gorget, and the holes are always in a straight line. There are, however, other shell gorgets found in Glacial Kame contexts that are not sandal-sole in shape, other sandal-soles which are made of stone rather than shell, and stone gorgets with three holes that are not sandal-soles. In some of these more aberrant types the holes differ in not being in a straight line (Fig. 3; Cunningham 1948:Pls. II-3, VI-7, X-3). This may not seem an important point, but I will argue that it is not accidental and has to be explained. Craftsmen making gorgets from shells transported in trade for 700, 800, or 900 miles into Michigan or Illinois from the Gulf Coast are not likely to have just accidentally displaced one of the holes quite obviously out of alignment with the other two.

Fig. 3. Orion and its symbolism. Scale variable: *a*, Shell sandal-sole gorget, Glacial Kame complex, Ohio (after Cunningham 1948:Pl.VI-6); *b*, Shell gorget, Illinois (after Cunningham 1948:Pl.VI-7, reversed); *c*, Shell gorget, Glacial Kame complex, Burch site, Michigan (after Cunningham 1948:Pl.II-3, reversed); *d*, Slate gorget, Michigan (after Cunningham 1948:Pl.X-3, reversed); *e*, Stone gorget, Meadowood phase, Oberlander No. 2 site, New York (after Ritchie 1965:Pl. 60, No. 19, reversed); *f*, Shell gorget, Glacial Kame complex, Isle La Motte site, Vermont (after Ritchie 1965:Pl.48, No. 5, reversed); *g*, Stone gorget, Baumer focus, Illinois (after Griffin 1952:Fig. 96, No. 14); *h*, Constellation Orion, ascendent (after Mayall and Mayall 1954:279,281); *i*, Copper reel-shaped gorget, Copena complex, Alabama (Griffin 1952:Fig. 150, No. 6); *j*, Stone gorget, Point Peninsula focus, New York (Griffin 1952:Fig. 16–p); *k*, Protective design called "spiderweb" from a painted skin robe, Teton or Yankton Dakota (after Wissler 1907:Fig. 23); *l*, Bead-bordered cloth gorget, Winnebago, A.D. 1828 (after Horan 1972:293).

RED OCHER AND GLACIAL KAME CEREMONIALISM

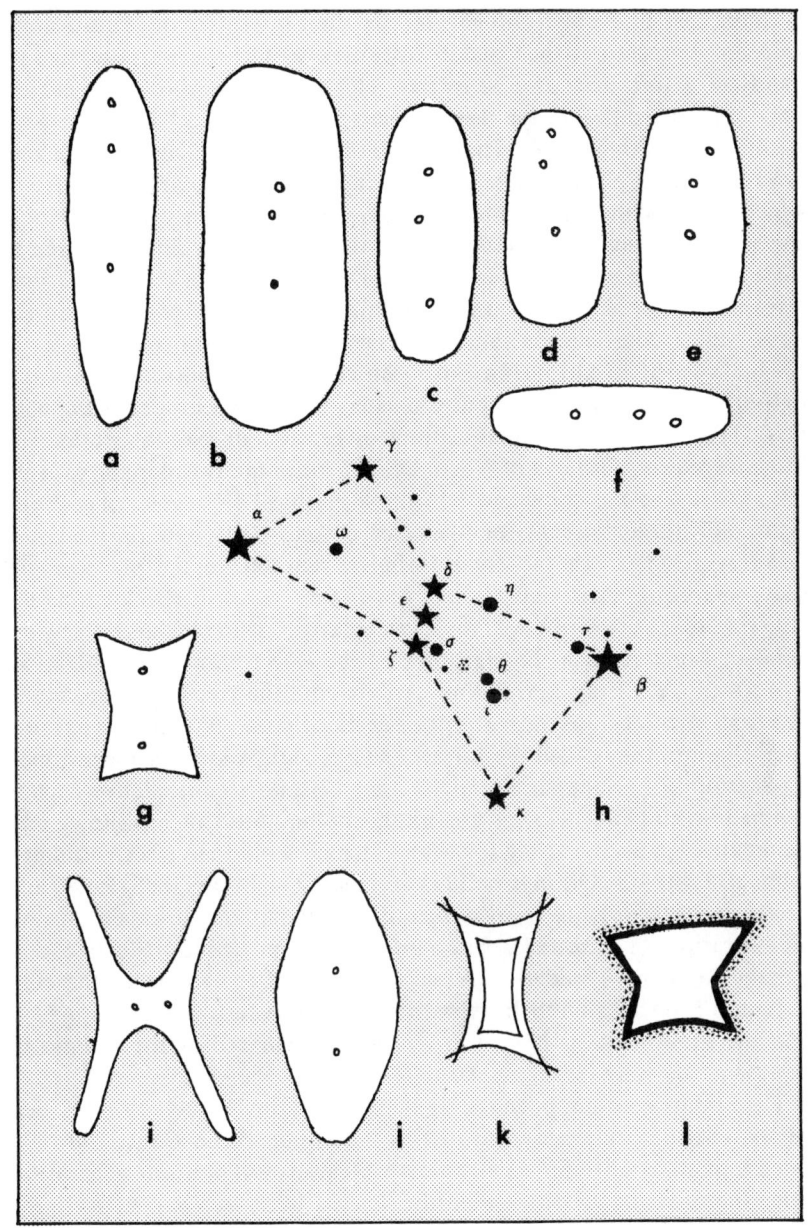

Fig. 3.

In the case of the aberrant gorgets, the three holes form an obtuse angle with one arm shorter than the other, somewhat like the hour and minute hands of a timepiece at 1:30 or 7:00. This arrangement of holes corresponds closely to that of the three principal stars which define the "sword" in the constellation Orion. These are the stars known as *sigma, theta*, and *iota Orionis* (Fig. 3h). There are so many millions of stars, any three of which could be imagined to form the same shape, that it would be highly speculative to suggest a relationship of those particular three in Orion to the holes in the aberrant Glacial Kame gorgets, except that those three also have a special mythical relationship to the Big Dipper seen in the Ursa Major constellation, and this becomes important.

The "sword" of Orion is a European concept, of course. Orion was a figure in Greek mythology, but the asterism which Europeans know as Orion has figured in the imaginations of peoples all over the world. The Siouan speaking Hidatsa of North Dakota knew the sword in the constellation Orion as the hand severed from a mythical character called Long Arm. The three stars of the "belt" of Orion—*delta, epsilon*, and *zeta Orionis*—from which the "sword" hung, represented the place on the wrist of Long Arm where the hand was severed (Beckwith 1969 [1937]:41-42). The Crow Indians, close relatives of the Hidatsa, knew the hand of Long Arm in the night sky as the Hand Star (Lowie 1918:93).

According to Fray Bernardino de Sahagún, the Aztecs recognized an asterism of three stars near the Pleiades as a constellation (or part of a constellation) they called the Firesticks (1953:60). Anderson and Dibble's translation of Sahagún renders the Nahuatl constellation name Mamalhuaztli (Firesticks) as Castor and Pollux, but Coe has shown that Sahagún's Spanish glossing for Mamalhuaztli would have been rendered more accurately as Orion (Coe 1975:26). Orozco y Berra (1880, 1:499) and Chavero (1900:451) have also identified Mamalhuaztli as Orion. An identification of Firesticks with Orion is supported by the fact that Sahagún (1953:62) said that Aztec men burned the figure of the constellation Firesticks on their wrists, star by star, a custom that reminds us that the three stars of the belt of Orion were believed by the Hidatsa to represent the wrist of Long Arm.

The Hidatsa did not burn the figure of the Hand constellation on their wrists, but the principal performer in the Hidatsa Sun Dance did tie a dried human hand to his wrist, an act which was symbolically equivalent, since the dried hand represented the severed hand of Long Arm. In the Mayan Dresden Codex the lower firestick, the hearth board, is sometimes represented by the glyph of the day Manik (Gates 1978:191). Manik corresponds to days known elsewhere in Mesoamerica by names which translate as "Deer" (cf. Caso 1967:10-11). The Mayan glyph Manik is a hand cupped upward, and the lower firestick which receives the phallic fire drill is commonly regarded as female, so we have the symbolic equation: Manik = hand = deer = female firestick (hearth board).

The Siouan-speaking Osage knew the three stars of the belt of Orion as Three Deer—not as three animals which were deer, but as one man named Three Deer (La Flesche 1932:138). The stars *theta* and *iota Orionis* in the sword of Orion were known to the Osage as *Double-star* and *Stars-strung-together* (La Flesche 1932:91, 138, 395). *Theta* and *iota* in *Orion* would correspond to the two adjacent holes in the "toe" end of the sandal-sole gorget, if the holes represent stars in Orion at all. In Cunningham's study of sandal-sole gorgets, only three gorgets were mentioned as having holes which showed evidence of wear. In all three examples it was the pair of holes near the "toe" which showed wear (Cunningham 1948:8, 20). On one of these gorgets the evidence was of wear on the holes themselves as well as a groove between the holes, indicating that a cord had passed between them (cf. Holmes 1883:266). It is these two adjacent holes which I am suggesting correspond to the stars in Orion which the Osage called Stars-Strung-Together and Double Star and to two of the stars in the Hand Star of the Crow and Hidatsa.

The Hand Star, the stars forming the sword of Orion, represented the hand cut from the arm of Long Arm in Hidatsa myth (above). I have suggested (Hall 1977:510–513) that Long Arm was once a personification of the constellation Ursa Major. This is logical for two reasons. First, the Hidatsa and Crow formerly were a single people, and the most detailed origin myth of the Crow Sun Dance related by Lowie (1956:302–304) attributes the beginning of that ceremony to instructions given by the moon and seven men. Lowie himself considered the seven men represented either the Pleiades or the Dipper. Second, Long Arm was supposed to have had an arm so long that he was able to reach down from the sky and snatch up a twin known as Spring Boy while Spring Boy was sleeping, during the day according to some versions and during the night according to others (Beckwith 1969 [1937]:38; Lowie 1918:66, 83, 91, 97). The Big Dipper in Ursa Major has a long handle resembling an arm which does, in fact, reach all the way to the earth during the winter at latitudes south of Nebraska and central Illinois.

Representational art is not common on sandal-sole gorgets. The two best defined art forms found on sandal-soles are a cross and a bear. An elaborate cross appears engraved upon a conch shell sandal-sole from the Mulen site, a Late Archaic Glacial Kame site in Randolph County, Indiana, and a bear upon a gorget from Hardin County, Ohio (Cunningham 1948:Pls. VI-2, VII-1). The cross looks at first glance like a Christian emblem, but the cross was present in Mesoamerica before the

Spanish and Christ and was probably as early in North America as well. The cross was a stylized world tree or cosmic axis and in ritual often took the form of a trimmed tree with a short cross-piece toward the top, as in some versions of the Plains Sun Dance. In the Teton Sun Dance, it was to this cross-piece that the ropes were tied from which warriors suspended themselves (Densmore 1918:118).

The bear and world tree are actually cognitively related, as we learn from an account of the symbolism of an (eastern Algonquian) Munsee-Mahican bear sacrifice ceremony:

> [The Creator's] abode is high above the clouds at the crown of the firmament, near the summit of the invisible mythical tree that rises from the earth-dome and reaches to the sky. So the center-post, as its symbol, *extends from the Big House to the hand of the Creator in the sky* .... It is the ancient concept of the world-tree, a most important and outstanding symbol of Delaware religion throughout. The phantom tree was visualized in the center-post .... Each year when the skin of the sacrificed bear was brought into the Big House it was hung on the east side of the center-post after the old skin which had hung there during the year was taken down .... The allegory of the sky-tree, the sky-bear, the earth-bear, and earth tree is thus carried out. [Speck and Moses 1945:40; emphasis theirs]

> The Munsee-Mahican Big House is a sky projection upon earth, specifically the constellation Ursa Major [Great Bear] projected upon the floor of the Big House sanctuary. The interior furnishings of the sanctuary and the stations formally occupied by the ceremonial officials correspond to the position of the stars forming the constellation. The acts and movements of the ritual performers parallel the movements of Ursa Major as the events of the annual life cycle of the earth-bear *symbolically rotate with those of the Sky Bear*. [Speck and Moses 1945:32; emphasis added]

A sky bear wheeling through the northern night sky around a mythical world tree would also have been duplicated symbolically by a bull-roarer engraved with a bear, circling around its wooden handle. It would have been anticlimatic to have said earlier that the turkey-tail form and the sandal-sole form are each ideally suited to use as bull-roarers. I have made working bull-roarers of oak wood in the form of the turkey-tail and of heavy gauge aluminum in the form of the sandal-soles. The aerophonic properties of these substitutes are probably quite close to those of the original (albeit hypothetical) articles. I am not arguing that when one looks at a turkey-tail point that one is always looking at a point which was used as a bull-roarer, since we know that there were protective amulets in the form of bull-roarers and that flint points were used as amulets without any bull-roarer associations. I am likewise not arguing that a shell sandal-sole gorget was necessarily used as a bull-roarer, only that the form could have been based upon that of a bull-roarer. The use of drilled holes in sandal-sole gorgets to represent certain stars in the constellation Orion could have been suggested subliminally by the identification of stars in Orion with the holes in the hearth board in which the fire drill turns to produce fire by friction.

TURKEY-TAIL EQUALS SANDAL-SOLE

In a previous paper I identified Long Arm as a northern Plains equivalent of the Aztec god Tezcatlipoca, a god who was transformed into a jaguar and placed in the northern night sky as the long-tailed constellation Ursa Major, the Big Dipper (Hall 1977:510–513). I would now identify Long Arm as a possible Hidatsa equivalent of Mixcoatl, a patron deity of the nomadic Chichimecs who occupied the northern frontier of Mesoamerica. There is no real contradiction here, because in Mexican belief Tezcatlipoca transformed himself into Mixcoatl before drilling the first fire of the fifth sun, the fifth era of creation in Aztec cosmology (Brundage 1979:133).

The Big Dipper had another important identity in central Mexico. Sahagún quite specifically said that the Big Dipper was also visualized as a scorpion, an insect which carries its sting at the end of a long curved tail (Sahagún 1953:66). A scorpion tail was an occasional attribute of two Mayan gods illustrated in black—the gods known as God L and God M (Kelley 1976:72). God L was a Mayan god of traveling merchants whose Aztec equivalent was Yacatecuhtli, the god of the *pochteca*, the class of Aztec long-distance traders. Mayan God M has been equated with Aztec Mixcoatl (Kelley 1980:22–24).

In Mayan iconography the stinger on the scorpion's tail was shown as a claw or as a human hand (Kelley 1980:25; Thompson 1971:76–77, Fig. 13, nos. 23–24). There is thus no contradiction in seeing the handle of the Big Dipper as an arm, such as that of Long Arm, or as a tail, such as that of the scorpion. Whether arm or tail, there was potentially an imagined hand to be cut off to produce that seen by the Hidatsa in the constellation Orion as the Hand Star. In the Munsee-Mahican bear sacrifice ceremony, the center-post of the Big House was an *axis mundi* imagined to extend "*to the hand of the Creator in the sky,*" as previously noted. The "hand of the Creator" would thus have been located on the end of the handle of the Little Dipper in the position of the Pole Star. In Mesoamerica the human hand would have been seen at the same location if God L were seen in the sky as a scorpion and as the Little Dipper.

The associations above indicate a cognitive relationship between the human hand and the stinger of a scorpion in the minds of ancient Mesoamericans. Thompson (1971:77, 132) noted a perceived relationship between the human hand and the stone knife of sacrifice in Mexico and puzzled at the lack of a pictured association of the stone knife and the scorpion tail. If hand can symbolize stinger and knife as well, then knife should also be able to represent stinger. There does seem to be another association between the stinger and the stone knife which is not obvious.

In the *Ritual of the Bacabs* of the Yucatec Maya there was an "Incantation for the placenta" in which the placenta was given attributes of "biting" and "stinging" and was called a "stinger" (Roys 1965:59). Labor in childbirth is a great cause of pain, but if the placenta were to be regarded as flint, then this would be an indirect association of a "stinger" and the bifacial flint knife, and there are reasons to associate the placenta and the stone knife. It can be argued that the process of producing a prismatic blade from a stone core was the cognitive parallel of the history of the placenta and fetus. It will be remembered that prismatic blades of obsidian were known in Mexico by the calendric name Nine Wind and that in the Vienna Codex the Mixtec god Nine Wind was born from a bifacial stone knife (see above). An illustration shows the the god Nine Wind attached by an umbilical cord to the stone knife (Furst 1978:56, 100, 106, Pl. II).

In the aboriginal mythology of the United States, the younger and wilder of twin brothers was sometimes said to have grown from the afterbirth. This relates to a belief, once probably worldwide, that the afterbirth was the twin of a child (cf. Budge 1973, 2:95; Frazer 1935, 2:162, 224). In Iroquois tradition the younger twin was Flint or Tawiskaron. Pawnee Long Tooth Boy grew from the afterbirth of his brother (Dorsey 1969 [1904]:89–90). Long Tooth Boy was tamed by the snapping off of his long tooth or tusk, just as Tawiskaron was tamed by the snapping off of the "flint" within him, an object which Hewitt saw also as an icicle (Hewitt 1910b:709–710). In the mythology of the Hidatsa and Crow, Spring Boy was the equivalent of Pawnee Long Tooth Boy and was tamed by the cutting off of his long teeth (Crow) or the reduction of his tusk while in a sweat bath (Hidatsa), or by inducing Spring Boy to vomit up shells he had swallowed while in the spring (Hidatsa) (Beckwith 1969 [1937]:33–34); Bowers 1965:305; Lowie 1918:77). Monster Slayer and Child-of-the-water were heroic twins who figured in much Navajo mythology, but each had an alter ego or counterpart which grew from the afterbirth of the two children, afterbirth which had been buried in the ground (Reichard 1974:483). In Arapaho, Creek, and Seminole myths a wild twin grew from the afterbirth of a boy (Dorsey and Kroeber 1903:387n.; Greenlee 1945:142; Swanton 1929:4), and in a Natchez myth a wild twin grew from the navel string of his brother (Swanton 1929: 222–223).

The relationship of the placental twin to the other twin was necessarily that of younger twin, because the afterbirth follows the child born second. When the afterbirth was thrown into a spring, the wild character of the twin was associated with shells and water. The contemporary Yucatec Maya bury the placenta under the hearth stones of their homes (Redfield and Villa Rojas 1934:359, in Roys 1965:59), and the placenta was inferentially associated with flint. In the *Ritual of the Bacabs* the "Incantation for the placenta" immediately preceded "The word for the cooling of a pit-oven," and this second incantation immediately preceded that for "The birth of the flint" (Roys 1965:58-63). In the incantation for the birth of flint it is obvious that the calendrical name One Ahau was given to flint blades struck from a core:

> This rock is its mother. Her offspring are you, small fragments of flint . . . 1 Ahau was its day. Split off, it comes. . . . On 1 Ahau was the birth of the flint . . . . [Roys 1965:61-63]

The incantation for the cooling of a pit oven does not specifically mention either flint or food, but Tozzer does mention that in his day the Lacandones of Mexico heated their flint in a fire before flaking it (1907:60). The clinching evidence is the name One Ahau for the prismatic flint blade or flake knife. At the beginning of this paper I commented on an observed similarity between Iroquois Tawiskaron/Tawiskala (Flint) and Tlahuizcalpantecuhtli, the morning star as the Aztec god of the dawn. One Ahau was the calendrical name of Venus after heliacal rising following inferior conjunction with the sun (Thompson 1971:219, 224). Inferior conjunction was the time when the planet Venus as the evening star disappeared into the fire of the sun at dusk. When Venus moved ahead of the sun after several days it reappeared as the morning star. This "heliacal rising" was also regarded as an emergence from the earth (cf. Roys 1965:62). There is a parallel to be seen here between the heat-treating of flint cores, buried in an earth oven, the transformation of food, buried in an earth oven, the period of gestation of the fetus in the womb, and the experience of the afterbirth buried under the hearth. Hidatsa Spring Boy was "tamed" in a sweat lodge, which can be seen both as a metaphorical oven and a metaphorical womb.

Seler refers to an affinity which "undoubtedly exists" between the Mexican gods Mixcoatl and Tlahuizcalpantecuhtli as the god of the planet Venus (1963:194-195). Since I have related Mixcoatl to Hidatsa Long Arm and Tlahuizcalpantecuhtli to Iroquois Flint, I must also relate Long Arm to Flint. This is a logical comparison, but it does create the paradox (1) of Flint capturing himself, since Spring Boy also can be related to flint, and (2) that of Long Arm being both Ursa Major and Venus. These seeming paradoxes are partly due to the reconvergence of similar mythical elements from parallel mythical traditions, as will be explained in a later paper.

The Cuicatecs of Mexico see the three stones of their hearths as the skulls of three goddesses of sustenance. The Cuicatecs also identify these three hearth stones with the three stars in Orion's belt (Hunt 1977:158-159). Since the Yucatec Maya bury the placenta beneath their hearth stones, there is a potential association here between the placenta and the three stars in Orion's belt, stars which we have previously identified with part of the Crow-Hidatsa Hand Star constellation and with part of the Aztec constellation Firesticks.

Let us imagine a placenta buried beneath a celestial hearth and then substitute a bifacial flint knife for the placenta. We have thereby placed a flint knife at the point in the asterism which the Hidatsa say was the Point at which Long Arm's hand was cut off. But, if we consider that the human hand was regarded by the Maya as a metaphor of the hearth board in drilling fire, then we should consider the flint knife to be a metaphor of the hand itself. Thompson (1971:132) makes this exact equation and adds that the name for the stone knife of sacrifice was "the hand of god." If we think of the flint knife in this example as a turkey-tail knife of the Red Ocher complex, and if we think of the celestial hand as the Hand Star of the Crow and Hidatsa, visualized as the sword rather than the belt of Orion, then we have in effect made a symbolic equation of the turkey-tail with the sandal-sole gorget of the Glacial Kame complex, because we have previously seen the way in which the stars in the sword of Orion may be represented by the drilled holes in the sandal-sole gorget. The implications of the above are that the most distinctive ceremonial objects of the Red Ocher and Glacial Kame complexes differed in their material form but could have symbolized much the same thing.

THE PLACENTA AS A TALISMAN FOR VISIONS

Among the Twana of Washington State, a tribe located on the west side of Puget Sound, a newborn child was believed to have an especially close relationship to the afterworld. The Twana believed in two lands of the dead. The soul of the deceased went to a first land of the dead, where it remained until it died a second death. The soul then went to the second land of the dead, from which it was reborn eventually as a human infant in this world (Elmendorf 1960:517). The newborn baby was "a point of contact with the supernatural." The afterbirth was also regarded as supernaturally potent and was called "the one who brings (the child)." The afterbirth was buried or placed in a fork in a tree:

> [An] infant might remain in this world and grant his father guardian-spirit power if he died soon after birth. To receive this the father had to take the infant's corpse into the forest, place it in a tree, and remain in the vicinity bathing and fasting. The same ritual was gone through with a prematurely delivered fetus or with the placenta in a normal birth. [Elmendorf 1960:518]

> The spot for "hiding" the afterbirth or infant corpse was supposed to be one favorable for spirit encounters, preferably near a stream or lake in which the husband could swim, bathe, and scrub his body. While thus engaged he might expect a guardian-spirit encounter . . . . A spirit vision gained in this way was not from the placenta or dead baby; neither could function as or confer guardian-spirit power. Apparently the afterbirth, fetus, or infant corpse, ritually handled, created a favorable situation for attaining a spirit vision. [Elmendorf 1960:415–416]

For the Twana, the placenta (as afterbirth) thus functioned much like the medicine doll in the Crow Sun Dance. The pledger in the Crow Sun Dance was aided by the magic of the doll to obtain a vision (Lowie 1956:298). I see a structural parallel between the use of an actual placenta in a vision quest and the agency of an initiator representing the personified placenta as younger twin. This homology would presumably extend to a flint biface with placental or uterine associations or one used as a token of a younger mythical twin. The turkey-tail point could thus have mediated the acquisition of visions and spiritual power in much the same way as the placenta did for the Twana.

Turkey-tail points could once possibly have been included in ceremonial bundles such as those of the Crow and Hidatsa sun dances. Robert Lowie (1915:Fig. 5b–c) illustrated the contents of a Crow Sun Dance medicine doll bundle which contained (in addition to the doll) two armless, legless human figures with triangular bodies cut from rawhide. These rawhide figures bear a provocative resemblance to the spearpoint-shaped Gros Ventre bull-roarer illustrated in Figure 1*a* (this paper). Sandal-sole gorgets could similarly have functioned as talismans to aid in the acquisition of visions or spirit powers.

TWO-HOLE GORGETS AS VISION TOKENS

The pattern of three stars which I see in the holes of some Glacial Kame gorgets as the sword of Orion occurs as far east as the Isle La Motte site in Grand Isle County, Vermont (Ritchie 1965:Pl. 48, No. 5). This occurrence is on a shell bar gorget within a Glacial Kame assemblage which also included parts of broken sandal-sole gorgets. The same pattern of holes occurs on a stone gorget of the Meadowood culture of New York State (Ritchie 1965:Pl. 60, No. 19; Tuck 1978:Fig. 9d). Meadowood is a culture believed to have been an "eastern equivalent of the late Old Copper and Glacial Kame cultures" and "perhaps a slightly later variant" (Tuck 1978:Fig. 9d). These gorgets each have the displaced third hole to which I have called attention earlier, a hole which I believe represented the star *iota Orionis*. I see these gorgets as links between the Archaic three-hole sandal-sole gorgets and the later two-hole Woodland gorgets. The Meadowood gorget was from the site Oberlander No. 2, which also produced a turkey-tail point (Ritchie 1965:Pl. 60, No. 8).

The non-displaced holes on the Meadowood gorget are in the same relationship to the gorget as a whole as the holes which normally appeared on two-hole stone gorgets in the Woodland period of the eastern United States (Fig. 3). The only way I can interpret this is to suggest that the two-hole gorgets carried much the same symbolic load as the shell sandal-sole gorgets. There is the additional parallel that two-hole gorgets resembled the noise-makers known as buzzers (Fig. 1*d,e*), which functioned much like bull-roarers. Sandal-sole gorgets were probably not used as bull-roarers but they were shaped like some bull-roarers and could have represented bull-roarers. Buzzers were used in weather magic, much as bull-roarers were (Cooper 1930:515; see above). Orion symbolism for the holes in two-hole gorgets would relate such gorgets to the constellation Orion as a whole, which can be seen as an hourglass or butterfly form (Fig. 3*h*). This may help to explain the tendency of two-hole gorgets to evolve into or assume hourglass shapes.

The hourglass form is one which the Teton Dakota in historic times regarded as a protective device when drawn on a shield or Ghost Dance shirt (Wissler 1907:35, 49–50, Figs. 11–12, 23–24). The hourglass form was called a spiderweb (cf. Culin 1975 [1907]:777, 779) and was said to represent the heavens. The design also figures in a ceremony related to a dream experience:

> *Women often receive power by dreaming of this* [*design*]. Some such women are supposed to perform a kind of ceremony, somewhat secret, in which a child is taken out to a lonely place, where a swing or hammocklike structure is made in the form of the spider-web design, supported by the four corners, and the child is placed upon it. This is to bring good fortune to the child. A design of the spider-web might then be placed upon the robe of the child as a *symbol of its having experienced the ceremony* (Fig. 23). [Wissler 1907:50 emphasis added]

The hourglass form can be related to the spiderweb design and through the spiderweb to the placenta and womb (cf. Dorsey 1969 [1904]:84–85, 343–344), and we have already related the placenta to the bifacial flint knife and to the younger of twin heroes in mythology. The hourglass figure was painted on the body of the personator of the younger of the twin War Gods of the Navajo, for whom it represented a war trophy taken by the twins (Matthews 1969 [1897]:253-254, Pl. VII, Fig. 42). A hand representing that of Long Arm was similarly worn by a Hidatsa representing the younger of twin heroes, a hand which was a trophy of combat with Long Arm and which was also seen in the sky as the Hand Star asterism within the hourglass-shaped constellation Orion. The hand worn by the Hidatsa figured in a rite in which a young Hidatsa acquired a medicine bundle and the powers it offered to obtain a vision. The two-hole gorgets may have served as tokens of an initiation or vision experience, much as bull-roarers may have been regarded as personal vision tokens by individual Ojibwa, as Landes (1968:33) suggests.

CONCLUSIONS

The significance of flint turkey-tail points and shell sandal-sole gorgets may not be buried with the Indians who used them. The archaeological record is not mute when examined in a pan-continental, deep-time perspective drawing on the full resources of both ethnology and archaeology. The success of this approach shows the importance of looking at prehistory as George Quimby has done—with eyes which can see North America as it existed before the culture areas of Kroeber.

The overlapping associations of flint and bull-roarers could have easily led to the innovation of a bull-roarer in the form of a flint turkey-tail knife, and bull-roarers made of stone knives were, in fact, used by the Navajo. Both in Mesoamerica and in the Southwest, the wind was closely identified with cutting edges of stone. Flint was also closely associated with ice and cold, as was the bull-roarer in Canada. The concept of the *windigo* as a mythical personification of winter can be related both to mythical characters identified with flint and to weather magic involving bull-roarers. The idea of *windigo* may be a survival from a time when such a mythical character was personified in puberty rites as an initiator of adolescents.

The sandal-sole gorget has cognitive associations less positively defined than the turkey-tail of flint, but compatible with those of the turkey-tail. They point to the proposition that turkey-tail knives and sandal-sole gorgets can be related to certain stars in the constellation Orion and in myth those stars can be derived from the constellation Ursa Major as a celestial manifestation of a supernatural such as Long Arm, who introduced the Hidatsa Sun Dance. Long Arm can be related to Iroquois

Tawiskaron or Flint, as can Spring Boy, the first Hidatsa initiated into the rites of the Sun Dance.

Both flint knives and sandal-sole gorgets are shown to have uterine associations, and the heat-treating of flint among the Maya is shown to relate metaphorically to gestation and to the treatment of the placenta after birth. The concept of the mythical character Flint is shown to relate to the afterbirth as a spiritual twin of a newborn infant.

Turkey-tail knives/points and sandal-sole gorgets are seen to have been talismans used in the acquisitions of visions or spirit powers or as material tokens of the powers, blessings, or patronage of mythical supernaturals as ancestors or ancestresses of descent groups, originators of tribal or lineage rituals, and/or initiators of youths in puberty rites. It is suggested that turkey-tails and sandal-sole gorgets were condensed symbols with similar referents within a magico-religious milieu of a kind still existing in historic times. The three-hole shell sandal-sole gorget of the Late Archaic is seen as a forerunner of the more abundant two-hole stone gorget of the following Woodland period, which could have been an individual vision token and protective charm.

The symbolic referents of turkey-tails and gorgets, three-hole and two-hole, were similar, but the material symbols themselves were quite different in appearance. This may mean that these ceremonial objects served some social strategy for maintaining a group boundary between the prehistoric Indian groups who were the bearers of the Red Ocher and Glacial Kame complexes (cf. Hodder 1982:185–186). In other words, there may have been two different orders of symbolic meaning, only one of which has been considered up until now. To the extent that Red Ocher and Glacial Kame were adjacent, contemporary complexes (and the time factor is not clearly known), the choice of flint bifaces or shell gorgets as symbolic artifacts can have related to a need to symbolize the solidarity of competing social groups or competing segments of society (cf. Hodder 1982:85). The purpose of this paper has been to consider the possible meanings of turkey-tails and sandal-sole gorgets to the people who made them, concentrating on the possible symbolic content. The social use made of the symbols is another aspect of the study which must be considered separately.

Notes

1. Throughout this paper I have benefited from the wisdom of many colleagues, but I would like especially to thank George Hamell of the New York State Museum, Albany, who for several years has generously shared with me his thoughts on Iroquois cosmology and the symbolism of flint, shell, and crystal.

REFERENCES

Barnouw, V.
    1977   *Wisconsin Chippewa myths and tales*. University of Wisconsin Press, Madison.

Beckwith, M.
    1969   *Mandan-Hidatsa myths and ceremonies* (reprint of 1937 ed.). Kraus Reprint
    [1937] Co., Millwood, New York.

Benedict, R.
    1974   *The concept of the guardian spirit in North America* (reprint of 1923 ed.). Kraus
    [1923] Reprint Co., Millwood, New York.

Binford, L.
    1963   The Pomranky site, a Late Archaic burial station. In Miscellaneous studies in typology and classification, edited by A. M. White et al., pp. 149–192. *Anthropological Papers, Museum of Anthropology, University of Michigan* 19.

Bloomfield, L.
    1934   Plains Cree texts. *Publications of the American Ethnological Society* 26. G. E. Stechert, New York.

Boas, F.
    1897   The social organization and the secret societies of the Kwakiutl Indians. *Annual Report of the U.S. National Museum for 1895*:311–738.
    1966   *Kwakiutl ethnology*. University of Chicago Press, Chicago.

Bourke, J. G.
    1892   The medicine-men of the Apache. *Ninth Annual Report of the Bureau of Ethnology (1887–88)*:443–603.

Bowers, A. W.
    1965   Hidatsa social and ceremonial organization. *Bureau of American Ethnology, Bulletin* 195.

Brinton, D. G.
    1976   *Myths of the Americas*. Multimedia Publishing, Blauvelt, N.Y.

Brown, D. N.
    1967   The distribution of sound instruments in the prehistoric Southwestern United States. *Ethnomusicology* 11:71–90.

Brundage, B. C.
    1979   *The fifth sun*. University of Texas Press, Austin.

Budge, E. A.
    1973   *Osiris and the Egyptian resurrection*. Vol. 2. Dover, New York.

Caso, A.
    1967   *Los calendarios prehispánicos*. Universidad Nacional Autónoma de México, México.

Chavero, A.
    1900   Los dioses astronómicos de los antiguos mexicanos. In *Códice Borgiano, interpretación del códice*, by J. L. Fábrega. México.

Coe, M.
    1975   Native astronomy in Mesoamerica. In *Archaeoastronomy in pre-Columbian America*, edited by A. F. Aveni, pp. 3–32. University of Texas Press, Austin.

Cole, F. C., and T. Deuel
    1937   *Rediscovering Illinois*. University of Chicago Press, Chicago.

Cooper, J. M.
    1930   Field notes on Northern Algonkian magic. *Proceedings of the Twenty-third International Congress of Americanists*, pp. 513–518. New York.
    1946   The culture of the northeastern Indian hunters: a reconstructive interpretation. In Man in northeastern North America, edited by F. Johnson, pp. 272–305. *Papers of the R. S. Peabody Foundation for Archaeology* 3.

Culin, S.
    1975   *Games of the North American Indian* (reprint of 1907 ed.). Dover, New
    [1907] York.

Cunningham, W. M.
   1948   A study of the Glacial Kame culture. *Occasional Contributions from the Museum of Anthropology of the University of Michigan* 12.
Cushing, F. H.
   1979   Zuñi. University of Nebraska Press, Lincoln.
Densmore, F.
   1918   Teton Sioux music. *Bureau of American Ethnology, Bulletin* 61.
Didier, M. E.
   1967   A distributional study of the turkey-tail point. *Wisconsin Archeologist* 48:3–73.
Dorsey, G.
   1969   *Traditions of the Skidi Pawnee* (reprint of 1904 ed.). Kraus Reprint Co.,
   [1904] New York.
Dorsey, G. A., and A. L. Kroeber
   1903   Traditions of the Arapaho. *Field Columbian Museum Publication* 81. *Anthropological Series* 5. Chicago.
Drucker, P.
   1951   The Northern and Central Nootkan Tribes. *Bureau of American Ethnology, Bulletin* 144.
Durán, D.
   1971   *Book of the gods and rites and the ancient calendar.* University of Oklahoma Press, Norman.
Elmendorf, W. W.
   1960   The structure of Twana culture. *Washington State University Research Studies* 28, *Monographic Supplement* 2.
Fenton, W.
   1962   This island, the world on the turtle's back. *Journal of American Folklore* 75:283–300.
Fisher, M. W.
   1946   The mythology of the Northern and Northeastern Algonkians in reference to Algonkian mythology as a whole. In Man in northeastern North America, edited by F. Johnson, pp. 226–262. *Papers of the R. S. Peabody Foundation for Archaeology* 3.
Flannery, R.
   1946   The culture of the northeastern Indian hunters: a descriptive survey. In Man in northeastern North America, edited by F. Johnson, pp. 263–271. *Papers of the R. S. Peabody Foundation for Archaeology* 3.
Fogelson, R.
   1980   Windigo goes south: Stoneclad among the Cherokees. In *Manlike monsters on trial*, edited by M. Halpin and M. M. Ames, pp. 132–151. University of British Columbia Press, Vancouver.
Frazer, J. G.
   1935   *Balder the Beautiful.* Vol. 2. Macmillan, New York.
Furst, J. L.
   1978   Codex vindobonensis mexicanus 1: a commentary. *Institute for Mesoamerican Studies*, Pub. 4. State University of New York, Albany.
Gates, W.
   1978   *An outline dictionary of Maya glyphs.* Dover, New York.
Greenlee, R.
   1945   Folktales of the Florida Seminole. *Journal of American Folklore* 58:138–144.
Griffin, J. B. (editor)
   1952   *Archeology of eastern United States.* University of Chicago Press, Chicago.
Hall, R. L.
   1977   An anthropocentric perspective for eastern United States prehistory. *American Antiquity* 42:499–518.

Hay, T.
 1971 The Windigo psychosis: psychodynamic, cultural, and social factors in aberrant behavior. *American Anthropologist* 73:1–19.
Hewitt, J. N. B.
 1903 Iroquoian cosomology, first part. *Bureau of American Ethnology, Annual Report* 21 (1899-1900):127–339.
 1910a Nanabozho. *Bureau of American Ethnology, Bulletin* 30, Pt. 1:11–23.
 1910b Tawiskaron. *Bureau of American Ethnology, Bulletin* 30, Pt. 2:707–711.
Hildburgh, W. L.
 1919 On the flint implements attached to some Apache "medicine cords." *Man* (June):81–87.
Hodder, I.
 1982 *Symbols in action.* Cambridge University Press, Cambridge.
Hoffman, W. J.
 1896 The Menomini Indians. *Bureau of American Ethnology, Annual Report* 14, Pt. 1.
Holmes, W. H.
 1883 Art in shell of the ancient Americans. *Second Annual Report of the Bureau of Ethnology (1880-81)*:179–305.
Horan, J. D.
 1972 *The McKenney-Hall portrait gallery of American Indians.* Crown, New York.
Hough, W.
 1907 Bullroarer. *Bureau of American Ethnology, Bulletin* 30, Pt.1:170–171.
Hunt, E.
 1977 *The transformation of the hummingbird: cultural roots of a Zinacantan myth.* Cornell University Press, Ithaca.
Kelley, D. H.
 1976 *Deciphering the Maya script.* University of Texas Press, Austin.
 1980 Astronomical identities of Mesoamerican gods. *Archaeoastronomy* 2:S1–S53.
Koestler, A.
 1964 *The act of creation.* Macmillan, New York.
Kroeber, A. L.
 1908 Ethnology of the Gros Ventre. *Anthropological Papers of the American Museum of Natural History* 1(4).
La Flesche, F.
 1932 A dictionary of the Osage language. *Bureau of American Ethnology, Bulletin* 109.
Landes, R.
 1968 *Ojibwa religion and the Midewiwin.* University of Wisconsin Press, Madison.
León-Portilla, M.
 1963 *Aztec thought and culture.* University of Oklahoma Press, Norman.
Lounsbury, F.
 1982 Tawiskala. Paper delivered at the Annual Conference on Iroquoian Research, Rensselaerville, New York, October 9.
Lowie, R. H.
 1915 Crow sun dance. *Anthropological Papers of the American Museum of Natural History* 16:1–50.
 1918 Myths and traditions of the Crow Indians. *Anthropological Papers of the American Museum of Natural History* 25(1).
 1946 The Bororo. In Handbook of South American Indians, edited by J. H. Steward, *Bureau of American Ethnology, Bulletin* 143:419–434.
 1956 *The Crow Indians.* Rinehart, New York.
Mails, T. E.
 1973 *Dog soldiers, bear men and buffalo women.* Prentice-Hall, Englewood Cliffs, New Jersey.

 1974 *The people called Apache*. Prentice-Hall, Englewood Cliffs, New Jersey.
Matthews, W.
 1887 The mountain chant: a Navajo ceremony. *Bureau of Ethnology, Fifth Annual Report* (1883–84):379–467.
 1969 *Navaho legends* (reprint of 1897 ed.). Kraus Reprint Co.,
 [1897] New York.
Mayall, R. N. and M. W. Mayall (revisers)
 1954 *Olcott's field book of the skies* (fourth ed.). G. P. Putnam's Sons, New York.
Mooney, J.
 1900 Myths of the Cherokee. *Bureau of American Ethnology, Nineteenth Annual Report*.
Murdoch, H.
 1892 The Point Barrow Eskimo. *Bureau of American Ethnology, Ninth Annual Report*.
Orozco y Berra, M.
 1880 *Historia antigua y de la conquista de México* (4 Vols. and Atlas). México.
Parker, A. C.
 n.d. Seneca myths and folktales. *Buffalo Historical Society Publication* 27.
Perino, G.
 1972 A little about ovoid and tanged knives. *Central States Archaeological Journal* (July):100–105.
Radin, P.
 1948 Winnebago hero cycles: a study in aboriginal literature. *Indiana University Publications in Anthropology and Linguistics Memoir* 1.
Redfield, R., and A. Villa Rojas
 1934 Chan Kom, a Maya village. *Carnegie Institution of Washington Publication* 448.
Reichard, G. A.
 1974 *Navaho religion*. Bollingen Series 18. Princeton University Press, Princeton.
Ritchie, W. A.
 1965 *The archaeology of New York State*. Natural History Press, Garden City, New York.
Ritzenthaler, R., and A. Niehoff
 1958 A Red Ochre burial in Ozaukee County. *Wisconsin Archeologist* 39:115–19.
Ritzenthaler, R., and G. Quimby
 1962 The Red Ocher Culture of the Upper Great Lakes and adjacent areas. *Fieldiana, Anthropology* 36(11):243–75.
Roys, R.
 1965 *Ritual of the Bacabs*. University of Oklahoma Press, Norman.
Sahagún, B. de
 1953 General history of the things of New Spain, book 7—the sun, moon, and stars, and the binding of the years, translated by Arthur J. O. Anderson and C. E. Dibble as *Florentine Codex*, Pt. 8. *School of American Research Monographs*, 14, Pt. 8. Santa Fe.
 1971 *A history of ancient Mexico*. Blaine Ethridge Books, Detroit.
Seler, E.
 1963 *Comentarios al Códice Borgia*. Vol. 2. Fondo de Cultura Económica, México.
Skinner, A.
 1914 Political organizations, cults, and ceremonies of the Plains-Ojibway and Plains-Cree Indians. *Anthropological Papers of the American Museum of Natural History* 11(6).
Speck, F. G.
 1928 Chapters on the ethnology of the Powhatan tribes of Virginia. *Indian Notes and Monographs* 1(5). Museum of the American Indian, New York.

Speck, F. G., and J. Moses
    1945   The celestial bear comes down to earth. *Scientific Publications* 7. Reading Public Museum and Art Gallery, Reading.
Swanton, J. R.
    1929   Myths and tales of the Southeastern Indians. *Bureau of American Ethnology, Bulletin* 88.
    1946   The Indians of the southeastern United States. *Bureau of American Ethnology, Bulletin* 137.
Thompson, J. E. S.
    1971   *Maya hieroglyphic writing.* University of Oklahoma Press, Norman.
Tozzer, A. M.
    1907   *A comparative study of the Mayas and the Lacandones.* Macmillan, New York.
Tuck, J. A.
    1978   Regional cultural development 3000 to 300 B.C. In *Handbook of North American Indians*, edited by B. G. Trigger, 15:28–43. Smithsonian Institution, Washington, D.C.
Vaillant, G. C.
    1948   *Aztecs of Mexico.* Doubleday, Garden City, New York.
Watson, P. J.
    1969   The prehistory of Salts Cave, Kentucky. *Illinois State Museum Reports of Investigations* 16.
Webb, W. S., and R. S. Baby
    1957   *The Adena people. No. 2.* Ohio State University Press, Columbus.
Willoughby, C. C.
    1935   Michabo the Great Hare: a patron of the Hopewell mound settlement. *American Anthropologist* 37:280–286.
Wissler, C.
    1907   Some protective designs of the Dakota. *Anthropological Papers of the American Museum of Natural History* 1(2).

ASPECTS OF THE SPATIAL STRUCTURE OF THE MAYO SITE (15-JO-14) JOHNSON COUNTY, KENTUCKY

Robert C. Dunnell

INTRODUCTION

In the fall of 1939 and winter of 1940, the Works Progress Administration archaeological program excavated a small "Fort Ancient" settlement in Johnson County, Kentucky (Fig. 1). The WPA program in Kentucky was under the general direction of William S. Webb; J. C. Greenacre supervised the excavation of the Mayo site, 15-JO-14. The excavation of a Fort Ancient site was highly unusual for the Kentucky WPA program (cf. Hanson 1966:1) since priority was typically given to burial mounds and other topographically visible sites. From Greenacre's notes it appears that the Mayo site may have been dug largely by accident. The major excavation at the nearby C & O Mounds, 15-JO-2 and 15-JO-9 (Webb, Haag, and Snow 1942), was gradually being terminated and its work force transferred to Mayo. The only hint that any archaeological problem may have motivated the decision to excavate the Mayo site lies in Greenacre's comments on the stratigraphic relationship between shell- and grit-tempered ceramics. Grit-tempered ceramics were typical of the C & O Mounds. At one point in his notes Greenacre remarks that the Mayo site demonstrates the stratigraphic priority of the grit-tempered series. This statement, unfortunately typical of many of Greenacre's interpretive remarks, is inaccurate. Both grit- and shell-tempered ceramics occur at Mayo but they are stratigraphically undifferentiated. Nevertheless, the fact that Greenacre singles out this issue for comment suggests that the demonstration of such a relationship may have been an objective of the project.

Given the priorities of the Kentucky WPA program and Webb's disinclination for the analysis of ceramic collections (Schwartz 1967:109), it is not at all surprising that the Mayo site was never analyzed or reported. It was not until 1962, as part of a survey of Fort Ancient remains in Kentucky, that the material and records were relocated and the magnitude and composition of the collection known (Dunnell 1962). At that time, my examination was limited to a random sample of excavation units for which I tabulated ceramic attributes. Even this limited examination demonstrated, however, that the late prehistoric occupation of the eastern mountain region of Kentucky differed in significant ways from Fort Ancient in the middle Ohio Valley, so much so that material from this region was assigned to a new tentative focus/phase, termed the Mayo focus. Until the middle 1960s, the Mayo site constituted the only professionally acquired data pertinent to the late prehistoric period in the entire eastern mountain region of Kentucky.

The picture changed dramatically with the investigations conducted in conjunction with the construction of Fishtrap Reservoir, located approximately 35 airline miles southwest of the Mayo site. Here 11 sites representing two distinct functional types were identified as late prehistoric (Dunnell 1967, 1972). Most of these were small, circular town sites closely affiliated with the Mayo site in their ceramics. One of these, the Slone site, 15-PI-11, was excavated almost in its entirety (Dunnell, Hanson, and Hardesty 1971) and several of the others were tested (Dunnell 1966a). Because the Fishtrap data were far more extensive, when a new phase was formally defined for this material, it was termed the Woodside phase after one of the Fishtrap sites (Dunnell 1967).

The relation between the late prehistoric occupation of the eastern mountains of Kentucky and the Fort Ancient known from the Ohio Valley proper was regarded with some suspicion from the beginning (e.g., Dunnell 1962; Schwartz 1962). The more complete information from the Fishtrap reservoir served to reinforce these concerns. On the one hand, *in the Fishtrap area* Woodside clearly appears as the product of a migration from further downstream in the Levisa drainage. On the other hand, the ceramic affinities are not with Fort Ancient proper, but with Appalachian assemblages (e.g., Evans 1955; Johnson, Adovasio, and Marwitt 1980; Solecki 1949). Whether the Woodside phase and similar Appalachian assemblages should be regarded as Fort Ancient depends less upon their content and structure than it does upon the nature of Fort Ancient. If Fort Ancient is to designate an homologous historical entity, then there is little reason to regard any of these assemblages as Fort Ancient. On the other hand if Fort Ancient is interpreted as a particular kind of adaptation associated with simply organized cultural systems, then these assemblages, and many others as well, might be properly included within it.

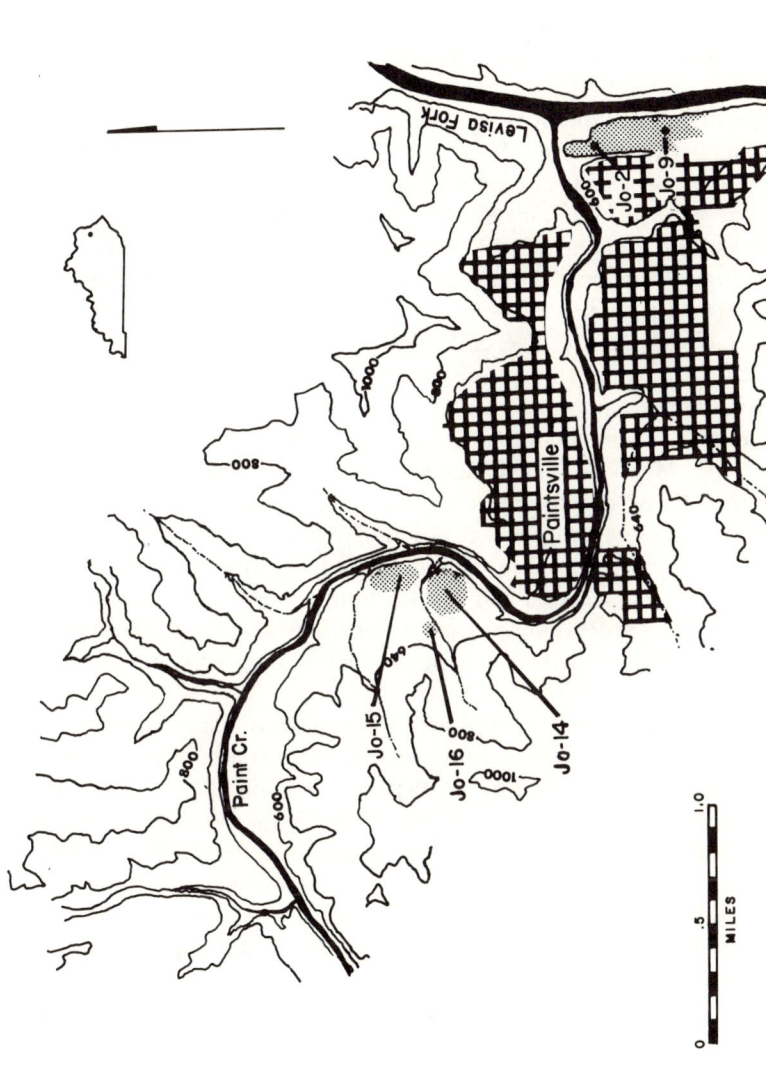

Fig. 1. Paint Creek – Levisa confluence showing the location of the Mayo site and nearby archaeological sites. The 600-foot contour approximates the scarp of the 10 m terrace; the 840-foot contour approximates the edge of floodplain deposits.

Upon completion of the Fishtrap investigations, the Mayo site assumed increased significance. Lying halfway between Fishtrap and the Ohio Valley in the Levisa Fork river system, it seemingly offered the possibility of resolving the origins of the Woodside phase. Seriations suggested that it was earlier than any of the Fishtrap Woodside sites. Further, a well-developed Woodland occupation was documented for this portion of the Levisa system (e.g., Webb, Haag, and Snow 1942), something that is entirely lacking in the Fishtrap area. In short, it appeared that the Mayo site might represent a locality where Woodside was developmental rather than intrusive. For this reason, I went to the University of Kentucky in the summer of 1970 to duplicate the extant records for the site and to analyze the collection, comprising approximately 28,000 items. I also spent one week in the Paint Creek valley attempting to relocate the site and to acquire a better idea of the physical environment and associated archaeological materials than could be obtained from the existing records. Unfortunately, the Mayo site, although earlier than any of the Fishtrap Woodside sites (RL-322, 1060±90, A.D. 890; RL-311, 800±100, A.D. 1150), is ceramically Woodside and does not itself directly bear on the origins of the phase.

Although a few methodological papers derived from the ongoing analysis of the Mayo site have appeared (Jermann 1973; Jermann and Dunnell 1979) no descriptive report has been prepared. The time separating the analysis from the excavation as well as defective records have made the analysis a complicated undertaking in which far more time has been devoted to correction and rectification of the records than to analysis proper. This process has proceeded sufficiently far to allow the spatial structure of the site to be outlined in some detail. That outline is the object of this paper.

The Mayo site locality was repeatedly occupied for many centuries; this analysis is strictly concerned with the Woodside component. Two large contiguous blocks were opened by WPA crews; only the larger of these, the western block excavation, contains significant Woodside material. The eastern block, about one-third the area of the western block, lacked any subsurface features, contained only scattered artifacts, and even these relate to a Woodland occupancy of the region. The eastern block, the test trench connecting the two blocks, and all of the outlying trenches and individual tests units are ignored in this analysis.

THE DATA

The extant data pertinent to the WPA excavation of the Mayo site consist of the original level bags and their contents and a small series of contemporary paper records relating selected aspects of the excavation and its results. The tedious process of rectifying the existing records into a single, internally consistent data source is still incomplete; however those data fields critical to an analysis of spatial structure are sufficiently reconstructed that the results reported here will not be materially altered when the process is complete.

Artifacts

Almost all of the artifacts are contained in the original collection sacks stored since completion of the excavation. Provenience information is written on the outside of each container. Only a handful of bags had defective information (i.e., missing information or impossible designations) and a few appeared to duplicate other units (due to mislabeling?). For the most part the contents had been washed in the field but they had not been sorted, "culled," or otherwise analyzed. The frequent inclusion of bits of coal, crop residue, and other debris attest to both the thoroughness of the original collection and the absence of any post-excavation analysis.

There are only two exceptions to these generalizations. First, a small amount of material, mostly stone but including other materials as well, had been catalogued prior to 1960 in a system no longer in use at the University of Kentucky. Unfortunately, the catalogue cards for this material could not be located. Undoubtedly this material accounts for some of the missing data (i.e., units almost certainly dug but for which no artifacts with provenience could be found), but probably it involves no more than four or five units. Secondly, a few dozen stone artifacts, mostly projectile points, had been catalogued in the 1970s by Lee H. Hanson, Jr. The bags from which the catalogued items had been taken had not been otherwise sorted, and thus it was easy to associate the two. My own random sampling of the site (Dunnell 1962) and that of Purrington (1967) involved only a few bags and all the materials were returned to their original containers.

The material had been stored in large boxes, and the paper bags had generally protected the material from serious damage during the several moves the collection endured over 40 years. There are two exceptions to this general statement—shell and uncalcined bone. Neither is well preserved at 15-JO-14 and once these materials dried, virtually any movement caused them to crumble into dust. Consequently, bags containing either of these materials usually revealed a mass of crumbs unless there were large bones. Even these were severely eroded and rounded. As a result, no serious faunal studies of the site can be undertaken, even though a considerable quantity of both bone and shell were originally collected.

Records

The site records are quite limited. They consist of a site survey form completed by Greenacre after termination of the excavation, a schematic map of the excavations, a three section, detailed ground plan of the western block excavation at a scale of 1:60; a field specimen record including 66 entries; 3 burial forms; 54 feature forms; 83 photographs; and 6 pages of field notes. The field notes, site survey form, and general plan of the site are all of limited value, mostly contributing a set of possible parameters within which all of the records could be interpreted. None contained sufficient specific information to be treated as a data source by itself. The field specimen record, with the exception of three entries, was used to designate material recovered from features and thus duplicates the feature forms. The photographs and detailed ground plans are the most valuable parts of the record. With one exception, there is a photograph of each feature. There are 8 photographs of house plans after excavation, 3 pictures of burials, 3 pictures of groups of *in situ* artifacts, and 16 general site pictures. All are high quality, large format photographs (5 × 7 inches). In 1970, the original negatives could not be located and a new set of 4 × 5 inch negatives were made from the prints. Since then, the original negatives have been found (Duffield, personal communication); however, the photographs reproduced here are from the 4 × 5 negatives. For the main excavation area the ground plan records all features and postmolds. The last are numbered consecutively. As no features or postmolds were found outside the main excavation and the Woodside town is contained in it, the absence of ground plans for the remainder of the excavation is of little consequence. The ground plans do *not* include the boundaries of the excavated area.

The records for features and burials are similar, being more or less completed forms that were widely used by the WPA and TVA excavations under Webb's direction. The forms always include a 1:12 horizontal plan of the feature and show one or more grid stakes. Profiles are only occasionally present. Plans and profiles are highly schematic with respect to feature contents and boundaries as demonstrated by the photographs. Maximum length and width were almost always recorded; less frequently the thickness or internal depth of the feature is given. The Cartesian location of each feature is also given, though usually inaccurately, beneath the level of the 5-foot square. Nonetheless, all features recorded could be accurately located by combining the photographs, ground plan, field specimen record, and plan on the feature form with data given. Each feature was also assigned a "functional" name (e.g., "fireplace," "fire basin," "rock pile in a pit," etc.) but the use of these names is highly inconsistent. Additional comments occur on only some forms and are not consistent from form to form. They provide, however, the only means of determining feature characteristics, apart from the drawings and photographs, and played a major role in ascertaining how the naming was done. The three burial forms are similar except that they also include judgments on the age and sex of the body and comments on its position.

Some critical records are absent. There is no extant postmold record giving Cartesian locations though the fact that they are numbered on the ground plans strongly suggests that such a record was made at the time of the excavation. As all of the plotted postmolds constitute a complete numerical sequence, it appears that *all recorded postmolds* were actually plotted. There is no general map which precisely locates the site. The site location had to be obtained by matching the general site photographs with the distant topography and the alignment of the excavation units. The brief field examination in 1970 confirmed the inferred location. The most deleterious absence is that of any listing of the excavated units or even an accurate map of the boundaries of the excavations. The basic information was obtained from bag proveniences coupled with the schematic plan of the excavation and the ground plans. Although the boundaries of the main excavation area are now known with some confidence, there are still some areas of imprecision. Although the excavation boundaries used in this analysis are undoubtedly quite close to the actual boundaries in 1940, the total area excavated will always be strictly unknown. The depth to which various parts of the site was excavated is also problematic in minor respects. The photographs and bag records both agree in suggesting that with the exception of the eastern margin of the site, it was uniformly excavated to a depth of 1 foot. In the eastern area, however, the deposits included a small ravine fill. Here bag proveniences alone provided information on depth of excavation as the photographs do not show this area after excavation was complete. In this analysis, only the upper foot of the excavation is considered so that the slight imprecision concerning the depth of excavation along the eastern periphery is of no import.

Biases

All of the records are substantially biased. That biases exist is readily determined by reference to the photographic record and by comparison with other closely related sites such as Slone. It was possible to ascertain the nature of many of the biases and the kinds of criteria employed by Greenacre in making excavation/recording decisions. While this information is insufficient to correct the majority of the existing records, it does indicate the manner in which various data fields are not representative. Since postmolds and features play an important role in this analysis, a brief outline of these biases and their calibration is important.

Three criteria led Greenacre to designate something as a feature: the presence of ash and/or burned earth; the presence of large quantities of artifacts and/or debris; and the presence of structurally significant rock. All of the recorded features have one or more of these characteristics. The most common kind of feature at similar sites, empty pits, are completely unrecorded for the Mayo site except where the density of artifacts in the soil which ultimately came to fill the pit was heavy enough to attract attention. Inspection of the general area photographs reveals many unrecorded features of this sort. While the locations and horizontal dimensions of these unrecorded features can be extracted from the photographs, the photographs themselves do not cover the entirety of the site and therefore the bias cannot be uniformly corrected. None of these features has been included in the present analysis. Consequently, this particular class of feature is grossly underrepresented at the Mayo site. Features involving fire in any form, however, are probably quite accurately enumerated in the record.

There are further biases in the information provided for those features that were recognized. With but a single exception, all features are designated "pits" without the slightest regard for whether there is any empirical evidence of a subsurface structure. Fortunately, the excellent photographs resolve this problem in every case so that it has been possible to differentiate unambiguously surface and subsurface features throughout the site. Greenacre's treatment of features which I herein designate sheet middens is typical of the problem faced in using his records and illustrates the interaction of his criteria for feature recognition and his preoccupation with fire and pits. All of these deposits are recorded as "fireplaces" or "fire pits" with "quantities of burned bone." While their dimensions are generally much larger than those of other features similarly designated, there is no recognition on Greenacre's part that they are a different kind of feature. The photographs fail to reveal any evidence of a pit; on the contrary all of the material lies in a single horizontal plane with the long axes of the larger items parallel to the ground surface. Examination of the feature contents does show that these deposits are largely comprised of bone; however, invariably none or only a small fraction of the bone is calcined as Greenacre reported. Ash was the marker used by Greenacre to designate these features as fires; in no case did he note the presence of burned earth. Consequently, it is clear that ash and bone have separate origins and the ash is not the product of a fire at this locality. The association between bone and ash is not obscure. The soil matrix of the Mayo site is sufficiently acid that bone and shell readily disintegrate unless calcined, even when protected as in graves. The quantities of ash, however, locally alter the pH in a basic direction providing conditions that led to modest bone preservation.

The particular "pit" bias of Greenacre renders many of his measurements rather meaningless. The thickness measurement supplied on the feature forms variously records the thickness or internal depth of subsurface features, the depth to which a surface showed evidence of burning or staining, or the thickness of objects lying on a surface. In some cases, it led to the excavation of pits where none existed as in the case of surface fires and sheet middens. The heat altered or stained soil under the feature would be excavated and this excavation constituted the "pit." On occasion Greenacre would note that these excavations encountered no artifacts. In digging a pit under one such fire, Greenacre reports that no artifacts were found in the burned earth, except where a few objects had moved downward in cracks. Further, his presumption that he was dealing with pits led him to ascribe discrete boundaries to surface features where none existed. Invariably they are irregular ovals of a highly schematic nature. Here again, the photographs identify the problem and provide a means of resolution. The maximum measurements given on the feature forms, however, bear little relation to the size of the entity that they purport to describe.

A second kind of bias occurs in the treatment of features that occur in close proximity. If discovered simultaneously, Greenacre invariably recorded the two features as a single entity with the measurements and description pertaining only to the larger of the two. The presence of a second feature is evident only from the photographs, occasionally in the plans, and sometimes in the additional notes. Unfortunately, features do occur in pairs throughout the site. Toward the end of the excavation Greenacre recognized this paired aspect and began to record both elements separately, though still on the same form. The precise location and dimensions of the second element of these paired features had to be laboriously extracted from the photographic record. Artifacts found in the two features were usually mixed as a single unit and this could not be corrected.

One of the most striking contrasts between Mayo and other similar sites is the near absence of graves. While it is possible that different burial practices are involved, every bit of evidence points to this aspect of the record being the product of Greenacre's biases in feature recognition and recording. The three graves identified as such by Greenacre are all simple pits; each contained an *adult* body in a poor state of preservation and the fill of the pit contained significant quantities of artifacts from the general midden. They were all relatively shallow. Given Greenacre's biases in the recognition of features, one must presume that it was the presence of artifacts in the fill of these pits that led him to recognize them as features and thus to excavate them. An untold number of graves are probably represented by the unrecorded pits evident in the photographs. Because they are the only rectangular pits that occur on the site and in fact were the only rectangular pits to occur at Slone, estimating the number of unreported graves from the area photographs may be possible. This has not been done here, however, since it cannot be uniformly done for the whole of the excavated area.

Two rectangular pits that are undoubtedly graves were not so recorded by Greenacre. One was a small rectangular pit, again containing artifacts in the fill but lacking any bones. Pits of similar size and shape at Slone were graves of infants and children. Even with the better preservation at that site, the osseous material was often very limited, sometimes little more than tooth enamel. Since this pit lies adjacent to two of the three identified graves, its identification as a grave is virtually certain. The second unrecognized grave is also a rectangular pit with significant numbers of artifacts in the fill. Excavation revealed a series of large stone slabs resting against one wall, a classic example of the "slanting rock" grave type from Slone (Dunnell, Hanson, and Hardesty 1971:37-38). No bones were encountered and Greenacre did not identify the pit's function. In every other case, the feature photographs were made after the excavation of the feature was complete. It must be presumed that the photograph of this feature was similarly made after excavation had been completed (Fig. 2). It thus appears that Greenacre did not encounter any bones because he did not remove the rocks resting against the wall. Bodies in this grave type lie behind the rocks and are not in the main body of the pit (Dunnell, Hanson, and Hardesty 1971:37-38). Graves are probably quite numerous at the Mayo site but they were systematically unrecorded and sometimes were not even recognized as graves when they were "accidentally" excavated. Because of the serious nature of the biases affecting this class of data, no use is made of graves in the analysis.

The treatment of postmolds seems to have been typical for WPA excavations. Once identified, they were dug out and measurements taken of the mold. Without a postmold record, the internal depth of the postmolds has been lost. Good estimates of the diameters were obtained from the 1:60 ground plans, as comparison with the photographs showed variation in size on the ground plans to be closely correlated with apparent size variation in the photographs. There is no question that Greenacre knew how to recognize postmolds. He did not record them uniformly, however. In areas in which there were no obvious house patterns, he was apparently a faithful recorder to judge from the ground plan and photographs. Where there were obvious house patterns, however, Greenacre was considerably less faithful to reality. He carefully

Fig. 2. Feature 9, a slanting rock grave. Although not reported as a grave, the form is identical with the slanting rock grave type at Slone.

recorded all the postmolds that comprised the house walls and all of the interior posts, but he frequently omitted postmolds that were not directly associated with the apparent structures. These omissions occur in spite of the fact that the photographs reveal that these postmolds had been excavated. Because excavated postmolds are easily recognized in the photographs, it has been possible to reconstruct their locations in almost every case. Less than a dozen postmolds which occur in photographs with poor reference points have yet to be reduced to their Cartesian coordinates. Because of their small number, their absence here is of little consequence.

This brief sketch of the complexities that arise from the nature of the Mayo site records may make the data appear quite deficient when, in fact, many modern excavations, if analyzed by someone other than the original excavators, would have many of the same biases. Nonetheless, the presence of such biases has limited the kinds of analyses possible and the significance that can be accorded to fine-scale distinctions. Even more importantly, these biases severely limit the range of comparisons that can be drawn with other, better documented and more recently excavated sites.

PHYSICAL STRUCTURE

As the foregoing indicates, the available records provide little information on the nature of the physical deposits or their vertical structure. Fortunately, the site is not complex stratigraphically. If it were, no meaningful spatial analysis could have been undertaken.

Geomorphology

The Mayo site is situated on a high (ca. 10 m) alluvial terrace in the first bottom of Paint Creek above its confluence with Levisa Fork of the Big Sandy River (Fig. 1). Landform features and stratigraphy within the Lower Paint Creek valley are identical with those of the Levisa valley proper. As is the case in the Fishtrap reservoir area (Dunnell 1972), the 10 m terrace is a Holocene depositional feature, the tread of which became depositionally stable between 1000 and 2000 years ago. In the Paint Creek area, this is well attested by the fact that Early Woodland and later materials are widely encountered on the surface of the 10 m terrace; preceramic materials are virtually never exposed by plowing. In postcontact times severe downcutting has been initiated in the major streams, perhaps because of increased water volume due to deforestation. The effects have included accelerated lateral channel movement such that the 10 m terrace has an actively eroding scarp in many places and a complex series of unpaired erosional terraces have been produced at lower elevations. These lower terraces are, of course, devoid of prehistoric material on their surfaces.

At the Mayo site locality, the recent downcutting phase has consumed nearly one-third of the archaeological site. Since the topographic situation is uniform for all known Woodside phase settlements in the Levisa valley, all of these settlements have suffered similar erosional loss to a greater (e.g., 15-PI-13) or lesser (e.g., 15-PI-11) extent. Although historic floods have occasionally covered the 10 m terrace, very little deposition has taken place because maximum sedimentation occurs before overbank conditions are reached (Ritter 1978:266). As a consequence, the Woodside occupation at Mayo took place on a surface within a few inches of the modern surface. It is essentially a two-dimensional site.

Under these conditions, plowing is the major determinant of the site's vertical structure. For most of the site, plowing has meant that the actual living surfaces have been destroyed along with the upper portions of deeper subsurface features. Many shallow subsurface features disappeared completely. On the northeastern margin of the site and to a lesser extent in the northwestern section, the living surface was further beneath the surface or plowing somewhat shallower than typical. Fragments of the living surface, sometimes fairly extensive, were encountered directly beneath the plowzone. The distribution of surficial features and the frequency of shallow subsurface features is rather directly a function of this post occupational process and not of the occupation itself. The metric attributes of the surviving features have been seriously affected.

The excavators of the Mayo site thus encountered "sterile" deposits at the base of the plowzone or slightly beneath it in nearly every area excavated. Consequently, only two half-foot (15.25 cm) arbitrary levels were removed from most of the site. This procedure removed all the general midden and left exposed the deeper foundation structures for easy excavation. There is one area, the entire western margin of the site, which is a clear exception. The western margin of the site abutted a "drain," or small ravine eroded into the 10 m terrace in prehistoric times. While the drain was still evident in 1939, its eastern edge had been filled with occupational debris. Excavation in this area often extended to a depth of 4 feet in half-foot artibrary levels. Greenacre recognized it as a fill but vascillates in his notes between regarding it as an ancient anthropogenic fill originating from the Woodside occupation and a modern fill in which parts of the site adjacent to the ravine had been dumped in the ravine to make the field more suitable for cultivation. It is not possible to resolve this quesion definitively from the extant records. Indeed both processes were probably involved. As discussed below, the best evidence for a modern origin of the fill comes from the southwestern edge of the site; the northwestern ravine fill is most likely of aboriginal origin.

Occupational History

In many respects the essentially two-dimensional character of the site is ideal for spatial analysis. It also creates a number of problems. First, all occupations of the terrace surface, since it became geomorphologically stable, have the same stratigraphic origin, and the artifacts have been thoroughly mixed by agricultural manipulation. Occupation of the present terrace surface began at approximately the same time as the occupation of nearby 15-JO-2 and 15-JO-9, so there are small but significant quantities of Adena-like material at Mayo as well as material of intermediate age. For the most part, separation of the assemblage into Woodside and non-Woodside components is not difficult. The earlier occupations occur as scattered clusters, quite unlike the "town" form associated with Woodside. The 1970 surface survey of the intact portions of the 10 m terrace in the vicinity of Mayo (the site itself has been destroyed by a subdivision) revealed numerous Woodland age settlement clusters on nearly every topographic high near the front margin of the terrace. Ceramics, and to only a slightly lesser extent projectile points, can be readily separated on typological grounds. The only major classes of artifacts that could not be assigned accurately to one or the other occupations are debitage and utilized flakes. For the spatial analysis, only Woodside material has been used where the distinction was possible. In the case of the unmarked classes, the entirety of each class has been used assuming that the numerical superiority of Woodside material swamps any pattern that might have been discernible in the early material.

Features present similar problems. For the most part, Woodside features are distinctive. In the case of "earth oven"-like structures, however, reliance had to be placed upon accidental inclusions of distinctive artifacts, usually ceramics. Features which contained *only* pre-Woodside artifacts have been eliminated from the analysis. In one case, a feature lacking any distinctive artifacts, but similar in form to identified Woodland types and spatially associated with Woodland artifacts, was attributed to a pre-Woodside occupation.

A small Anglo-American occupation occurs in the northwestern quarter of the site. The occupation is limited to what appears to have been a nineteenth century chicken coop to judge from the datable objects, the presence of chicken eggshell fragments, and the general size and outline of the small associated structure. Artifacts originating in this occupation were readily separable on typological grounds.

Once the non-Woodside occupations are eliminated insofar as possible, the physical structure of the deposit suggests that it can be analyzed as a single vertical unit. There are, of course, differences between the zero to one-half foot level and the one-half to one foot level. The uppermost unit was everywhere wholly within the plowzone; the second level always included some portion of the plowzone but in some places encountered sterile deposits near its base, while in other locations it encountered undisturbed occupational material. Consequently the relative composition of the two levels is slightly different because of preservation factors, and the deeper of the two levels has a lower average density of artifacts through attenuation effects. Our concern lies with whether these differences have an impact on spatial patterning. To examine this problem, two procedures were employed. First, SYMAPs were made of the principal variables independently for each level. The distributions of all of the mapped variables were sufficiently similar that maps of the same variable could not be distinguished without labels. Second, using the 308 provenience units as paired cases, product moment correlations were run for ceramics, lithics, and a combination of the two, accounting for the bulk of the assemblage. Bone was not examined as it would have been most influenced by differential preservation of all the variables. Product moment correlation coefficients of 0.76, 0.63, and 0.70 respectively were obtained which further suggest that the combination of the two levels is reasonably justified.

Because it was not possible to resolve the origin and depositional history of the deeper deposits along the western margin of the site, none of the units excavated beneath 1 foot are used in the analysis. In fact, incorporation of the upper two levels from this area may have been spurious. As will be evident in the density maps presented later, nearly all the "anomolous" compositions are limited to this area and may be the product of entirely different and perhaps not wholly aboriginal formation processes.

Soil Chemistry

The 10 m terrace surface is occupied by Pope silt loam (McDonald and Blevins 1965), a highly acid, well drained to excessively drained soil. The published pH range for this soil is 4.0–5.0; a single soil sample taken in 1970 from an adjacent portion of this 10 m terrace has a pH of 4.1. Under these conditions, only charcoal, ceramics, and stone remain chemically unaltered. Materials such as bone and shell (Watanabe 1950) persist only when calcined. With very few exceptions, mostly limited to the interiors of thick sherds, the temper had been leached from all of the Woodside pottery making it structurally weak and accounting for the highly fragmentary condition of the collection.

Woodside town-type settlements on the Pope silt loam have a marked effect on the local pH, in some cases raising the reaction to as much as 8.2 (Dunnell 1972:59). This effect, however, is not uniform, and soil reaction even within the densest parts of such settlements varies quite substantially. The source of this particular change in hydrogen ion concentration is undoubtedly the digestion of large quantities of calcareous material. As a consequence, the distribution of uncalcined shell and bone is, to a certain extent, a function of the original densities of these materials but obviously not in any simple way. Bone and shell are both less frequent and more poorly preserved at Mayo than at most of the Fishtrap Woodside sites, suggesting that either smaller quantities of these materials were involved initially, or that the Pope silt loam has a more acid reaction in this area, or a combination of both. Greenacre took no soil samples and since the site no longer exists, resolution of this matter is impossible. Unburned bone and shell do have wider distributions than their calcined counterparts indicating that pH alterations had proceeded in some places far enough to allow for modest bone and shell preservation. Nonetheless, the distribution of these two materials is undoubtedly in part a function of extraneous conditions. Bone has been mapped, but it is not included in most of the analyses in which the preservation bias might have an interpretive influence. Shell is not employed at all. Although small quantities are present in approximately one-fifth of the collection units, its fragmentary condition precluded meaningful quantification.

SPATIAL ANALYSIS

Broadly speaking, there are two potentially contrastive spatial structures that can be described at various scales for most archaeological assemblages. A spatial analysis of an assemblage that has been described in functional terms yields, in a general way, activity patterns. A spatial analysis utilizing a stylistic description of the same material yields, in a general sense, a description of interaction frequency (e.g., Hodder 1979; Stiles 1979), often rather uncritically identified with social structure. At the intrasite scale, both functional (e.g., Binford et al. 1970; Brose and Scarry 1976; Dacey 1973; Whallon 1973a, 1973b, 1974) and stylistic (e.g., Hill 1966, 1970; Longacre 1964, 1970) analyses have been attempted for some time. Functional approaches, because they are most similar to the efforts of the quantitative geographers who invented most of the analytic techniques, have tended to dominate. Albeit rather primitively, both kinds of analyses were integrated into the study of Woodside settlements as early as 1964 (Hanson, Dunnell, and Hardesty 1964).

Most spatial analyses at the intrasite scale involve considerable interpretive ambiguity. In part, this is surely due to an overestimation of the cultural significance of provenience data (e.g., Schiffer 1972, 1976). Although means for identifying the scale of significant patterning have been developed (Whallon 1973b), the structure of the method limits it to the rather infrequent archaeological circumstances in which no pattern superposition or mixing has taken place (Hanley, personal communication). Just as surely, another source of ambiguity resides in the classes used to describe the assemblage (cf., Matson and True 1974). Systematic separation of stylistic and functional criteria (e.g., Dunnell 1978a; Jelinek 1976) has not characterized such descriptive systems. Since spatial patterns associated with each will commonly be contrastive, their mixture in variable definitions can only randomize variable distributions. Even in the case of functional analysis, which has been the object of much recent discussion (Dunnell 1978b; Holley and Del Bene 1981; Keeley 1980; Keeley and Newcomer 1977; Odel and Odel-Vereecken 1980), the means of variable definition is still debated.

The Mayo site data are subject to all of these problems and are further constrained by the recording biases and deficiencies already enumerated. Detailed analysis cannot be sustained by these data. The most optimistic expectation is that gross patterning may be detected in data fields that are dominantly functional or dominantly stylistic.

Two kinds of data are available for analysis, each of which must be treated in somewhat different ways. Features and postmolds present a limited array of functional attributes and none that are reasonably construed as stylistic. Many observations that can be made pertain to their post-occupational history. On the other hand, their physical nature precludes transportation since their deposition and/or creation. For this reason, the locations of features and postmolds play a critical role in spatial analysis. They are recorded as presence/absence data with point proveniences.

The other set of data is comprised by discrete objects collected in 5 foot units by half-foot levels. These data have been subject to lateral transportation both during occupation and later by Anglo-American land use practices. The former is likely to have been the more significant as plowing has been repeatedly demonstrated to have limited capacity to transport artifacts on flat surfaces such as obtain at Mayo (e.g., Lewarch and O'Brien 1981). The effect is mainly in spreading distributions rather than disrupting them, and even this effect is limited as a dynamic equilibrium is reached quite rapidly after initial plowing. Nonetheless features and discrete objects are subject to different sets of c- and n-transforms (Schiffer 1976); direct correlations between the two cannot be expected except at the grossest scales. In terms of analysis, the discrete objects are frequency or density data with aggregate provenience. Point provenience data can be transformed to aggregate by imposing an arbitrary grid system and recording the data as counts; aggregate data similarly can be reduced to point provenience by attributing all objects to the grid unit centroid producing a large number of provenience "ties." The transformation from point to aggregate provenience is not generally useful and is not employed here; the transformation from aggregate to point provenience is more useful and has been employed in examining the relation between selected artifact classes and feature classes.

Counting Units

For aggregate data, frequencies are determined by the size of the counting units employed and this in turn influences the number of data points (the principal determinant of pattern resolution) and the accuracy of relative frequencies. Further aggregation increases the accuracy of relative frequencies but it reduces the number of data points. Thus there is a relatively narrow range of counting units that can be used for any given set of data. For the Mayo data, the aggregation of the half-foot and 1 foot levels increased unit counts considerably without any reduction in the number of data points in a spatial frame. Problems arising from missing data and the desirability of meaningful incorporation of low density areas—either functional or stylistic patterns might be correlated with density—necessitated additional spatial aggregation to increase unit counts and smooth the vagaries introduced by missing data. The compromise employed with the Mayo data was to perform a single aggregation from 5-foot (1.52 m) spatial units to 10-foot (3.05 m) spatial units. This arrangement provides 308 data points with centroids on 10-foot centers, quite adequate for pattern recognition at a site the size of Mayo. The procedure simultaneously quadruples unit counts. The reduction of the number of data points from over 1200 units greatly reduced data processing costs. All analyses of discrete objects use the 10×10×1-foot units.

Since the original excavation was not carried out in even multiples of 5-foot units, aggregation to 10-foot units changes the outline of the excavation to a slight degree. In those cases in which only one or two of the included 5-foot units had actually been excavated, these units were deleted from the analysis. When three of the included 5-foot units had been excavated, it was assumed that the relative frequency of the several variables was accurately represented by the combined counts and were corrected by multiplication for a 10-foot unit. Since the Woodside portion of the Mayo site was excavated as a contiguous block, these aggregation effects are limited to the edges of the area that could be mapped.

Data Description

Discrete objects have been described using two sets of variables, one functional and incorporating all of the discrete objects, and a second set that is stylistic, encompassing only the Woodside ceramics. The stylistic description of ceramics employs a simple three dimensional classification of temper, surface treatment, and decoration. Style of decoration, while an attractive dimension, could not be used because decorated ceramics are quite uncommon in the assemblage (44 sherds). While incision, the only technique of decoration present, occurs on all three surface treatments, the small sample made it necessary to combine the decorated combinations into a single variable. Thus only four variables are used: shell-tempered cordmarked undecorated, shell-tempered plain undecorated, shell-tempered roughened undecorated, and shell-tempered incised. These types, roughly analogous to the more or less widely used culture historical types, have been demonstrated to be sensitive to spatial change at Slone (Dunnell, Hanson, and Hardesty 1971) and their behavior in seriation studies (Dunnell 1972) argues that they are dominantly, if not exclusively, stylistic. Projectile point styles have similar potential (Dunnell 1972); however, they are too infrequent at Mayo and display too little variation to be useful here.

Functional categorization of the discrete objects is even more primitive. Over 50 potentially functionally significant variables were used in the initial tabulation of the assemblage. These were collapsed to 29 variables when the data were coded for analysis, eliminating most of the one-member classes. Five of these are limited to Anglo-American materials so that 24 classes potentially can be mapped. Many of them, however, have total frequencies much smaller than the number of data points making their value problematic even in iconographic models. Consequently, for the bulk of the analyses, these 29 variables were further collapsed to 5: vessel fragments, projectile points, utilized flakes, debitage, and all other stone tools. Except for the last variable, all of these classes can reasonably be expected to have played differing roles in the functioning cultural system and each is numerous enough to have a meaningful spatial distribution. Bone, the second largest category of material at Mayo, was excluded because of the preservation biases noted earlier.

Functional classification of the features, given their importance in spatial analysis, was undertaken more carefully. Four attribute dimensions were employed in their classification and were applied in the order of certainty with which the diagnosis could be made from the existing records. The most readily determined distinction is whether or not the feature is a surface or subsurface deposit; next most reliable is the presence of *in situ* firing, followed by categorization of the plan as circular, rectangular, irregular, or compound. Least reliable is the presence of *in situ* contemporary contents. The original excavators did not distinguish between contemporary contents and subsequent and unrelated fill. The photographs and drawings often made it possible to draw such a distinction (e.g., object orientation and arrangement); however, even when there is no observational ambiguity, differences in *in situ* contemporary contents may relate to the condition of the feature at the time the site was abandoned rather than the feature function. For example, storage pits in active use when occupation was terminated might be expected to retain some portion of the stored commodity and/or the vessel in which they were stored. Features having the same function but abandoned long before termination of occupation would appear in the record as empty pits having no functionally relevant contents. The abundance of "empty pits" in most archaeological sites is probably a reflection of just these processes (e.g., Dunnell 1966b). Greenacre's tendency to ignore such features simplifies the situation at Mayo insofar as identification is concerned, though it greatly impairs the value of feature counts.

A more complicated circumstance obtains with pits showing evidence of firing simply because Greenacre faithfully recorded these structures regardless of their artifact content. All of the subsurface fired structures are circular in plan. Although the dimensions vary considerably, these metric properties are not interpretable since all have potentially been influenced by plowing. Fire-cracked rock is present in large quantities in some, small quantities in others, and absent in many. Such differences might be functional or they may simply represent the state of the feature at the time of abandonment, in which case all the fired subsurface features may have had the same function. In this interpretation empty "hearths" are simply ones that had been cleaned before abandonment; partially filled examples are ones in which cleaning had been imperfect; and, the completely filled examples are ones in which the feature had been abandoned while in active use. In this case, the relevance of the contents had to be treated as an hypothesis rather than as simple identification. Four different combinations were carried through the entire analysis: (1) (empty + partially filled + filled); (2) (empty + partially filled), (filled); (3) (empty) (partially filled + filled); and (4) (empty), (partially filled), and (filled). The expectation is that if spatially distinct distributions are found for any set of classes, distinct functions are represented. The reverse, failure to find any spatial distinctions, is not symmetrical. It does not imply that distinct functions are not represented, only that there is no empirical evidence by which they can be separated *if* functional differences exist. As was pointed out in the discussion of graves, preservation also affects the detectability of *in situ* contemporary contents. The presence or absence of bone has as much to do with the age of the buried individual and whether the excavation was complete as it is related to actual presence of bone. Because the shape of graves is unique at Mayo, when reported, they can be identified independently of contents; however, since there is a pronounced bias in detection and reporting, graves were not included in any of the spatial analyses.

Nine classes were ultimately identified in addition to "houses."

1) Surficial, fired, irregular features with *in situ* contents, SURFACE FIRES. These features lack discrete boundaries and were identified in the field by the presence of fired earth. Contents include ash and various calcined materials. As surficial features, their distribution is in part a function of the relation between the living surface and the plowzone.

2) Surficial, unfired, irregular features with *in situ* contents, SHEET MIDDENS. These features lack discrete boundaries and were recognized by the occurrence of dense debris, mainly bone and ceramics, on a horizontal plane. Ash was a frequent constituent; however, the other contents are not burned nor is the surface on which they rest fire altered. Like surface fires, their distribution is in part a function of the relation between living surface and plowzone.

3) Subsurface, fired, circular features without *in situ* contents, CIRCULAR HEARTHS. All have discrete boundaries; where the living surface is present, most have puddled clay "rims" in addition to being marked by fire altered earth. All have varying amounts of ash; none include any fire-cracked rock. In one case where the living surface is intact, a pile of ash was found resting on the surface nearby indicating that they were cleaned out and suggesting that rock is not part of their functional contents. Further, their spatial distribution differentiates them from the partially rock-filled and rock-filled features that are otherwise similar. All of the hearths that occur in the centers of houses belong to this class although they have a much broader occurrence than this context.

4) Subsurface, fired, circular features with *in situ* contemporary contents, PARTIALLY FILLED CIRCULAR HEARTHS. These are identical to Class 3 features save for the presence of small quantities of fire-cracked rock without any identifiable spatial arrangement. They have a distinctive distribution at the periphery of the site and it is their distribution that distinguishes them from Class 5.

5) Subsurface, fired, circular features with *in situ* contemporary contents, EARTH OVENS. Similar in all respect to Classes 3 and 4 except for the presence of a coherent mass of fire-cracked rock occupying most of the pit. These features occur near the center of the site and thus contrast with the otherwise similar Classes 3 and 4.

6) Subsurface, fired, compound features with *in situ* contemporary contents, PAIRED HEARTHS. These features have discrete boundaries and are otherwise similar to the circular hearths and earth ovens in their individual physical properties. Each feature, however, is comprised by two separate circular pits joined at the rim where the living surface is preserved. In each pair, one pit is significantly larger and deeper than the other and one always contains a substantial rock fill (Fig. 3).

7) Subsurface, unfired, circular features with *in situ* contemporary contents, STORAGE PITS. These features have discrete boundaries, appear to have been relatively deeper than most other pits, and were

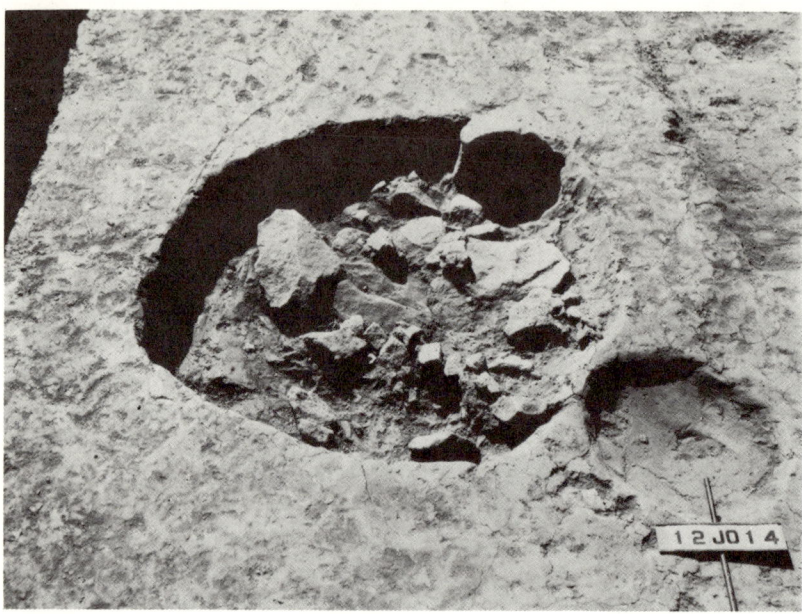

Fig. 3. Well preserved paired hearth feature. Note the difference in diameter and apparent depth between the two components.

uniformly described as having a "kettle-shaped" cross-section, meaning that the mouth of the pit was of smaller diameter than the base. This cross-section, though apparently distinctive, cannot be used as a criterion because profiles were not usually made for features. Most if not all other pit features are simple hemispherical basins or, in the case of graves, straight sided, flat bottomed pits. All examples contained "restorable vessels" or "large group of sherds from the same pot," again unique among the Mayo features. Identical "storage pits" occurred at Slone (Dunnell, Hanson, and Hardesty 1971:20–21).

8) Subsurface, unfired, irregular features without *in situ* contemporary contents, PITS. Apparently considerably larger and deeper than other subsurface features, distinctly not round like other pits or rectangular like graves, these features may be grossly underrepresented by excavation biases.

9) Subsurface, unfired, rectangular features with *in situ* contemporary contents, GRAVES. When preserved or discovered, these roughly rectangular, flat bottomed pits contain a burial. Apparently, both the simple pit and slanting-rock types of Slone (Dunnell, Hanson, and Hardesty 1971:37–38) are represented although the reporting bi-

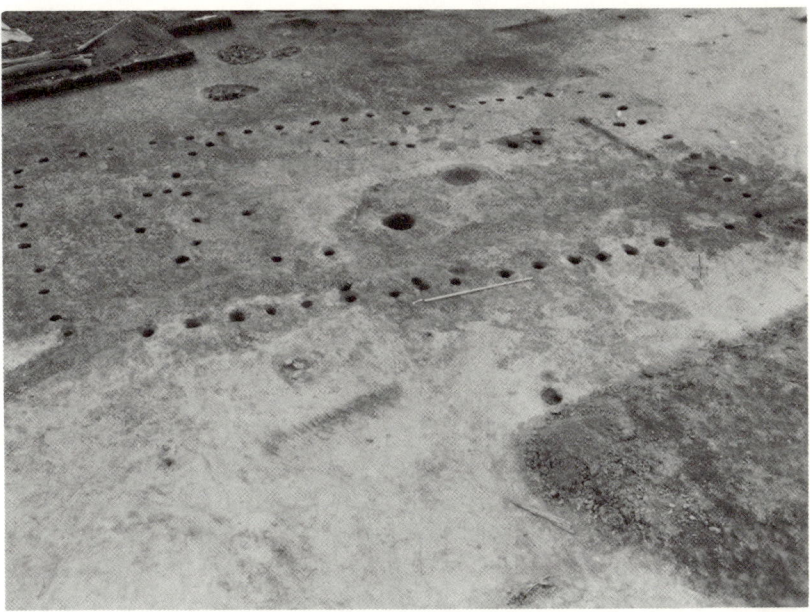

Fig. 4. Nearly intact house from the northeastern section of the site. This is the only complete postmold pattern that is not affected by superposition. Note the remnants of the clay floor near the central hearths. The attached portico shown in Figure 5 was cut off when the photograph was taken.

ases make it impossible to rule out the possibility that other forms occur. As at Slone, the only artifacts in direct association are personal ornaments. One body had a triangular projectile point in the lower abdomen.

In addition, there are eight readily identifiable rectangular houses. They are surface structures with simple pole walls, compact clay floors (where preserved), and apparently included some internal partitions or benches and one or more hearths (Fig. 4). With a single exception they are arrayed in a circular pattern around the central plaza. Plowing has all but eliminated house patterns from the western side of the site. The isolated posts in this area as well as fragmentary but identifiable houses follow a broad band, consistent with the better preserved arrangement in the eastern half of the site. The exception occurs in the southeastern corner of the site. This house is later than the rest of the buildings as its construction destroyed parts of two other houses. It does not share the same alignment as the others. It has been included in considerations of house form, but it has not been included in the spatial analysis.

Where identifiable, each building appears to have an attached structure, probably identical with the "porticos" identified by Hardesty for Slone (Dunnell, Hanson, and Hardesty 1971:11–12). At Slone, however, they were not attached to buildings. At Mayo, while one or more freestanding porticos may be present, the majority are attached to the houses near one of the corners facing the plaza.

Plowing has undoubtedly destroyed many houses; however, when they persist, the vertical nature of the postmolds insures that their metric properties are largely unaffected. Table 1 presents summary data on house size and shape for Mayo and four other Fort Ancient sites. In terms of shape (L/W), the two Woodside sites are highly similar (t = .514, p $\gg$ .5) and contrast with all other Fort Ancient sites which also contrast significantly among themselves. In terms of size (LW) however, the Woodside sites are not significantly different than the Anderson phase Incinerator site and this group contrasts with the much larger Clover phase sites. If much weight can be given to Naroll's generalizations about roofed area and population (LeBlanc 1971; Naroll 1962; Watson 1979:294–297), this pattern may simply reflect nuclear family domestic units in Woodside and at Incinerator and extended family or some other domestic aggregate in the Clover phase. The close similarity with Slone and contrast with other sites bolsters the ceramic argument for the distinctiveness of Woodside with respect to other Fort Ancient phases and perhaps with respect to Fort Ancient as a whole.

It seems likely that the bulk of the isolated postmolds are remnants of houses and porticos in that they tend to have complementary distributions. Under these conditions, no special analysis was made of the isolated posts.

LOCATION AND DENSITY MODELS

There is much current fascination with quantitative pattern recognition; however, the human brain is by far the most effective detector of patterns, especially when geometric shapes and complex patterns are involved. Quantitative methods are of most assistance when data approach uniform or random distributions and thus lack "obvious" pattern. The first step in this spatial analysis was to construct simple iconic models of the two sets of data. For features and postmolds, this amounted to a coded plan as shown in Figure 5. The overall pattern is readily discerned. The site is a doughnut shaped affair, truncated in the north by recent erosion, slightly constrained in the west by the erosional drain, and broken on the south by the edge of the excavation. All classes of features

TABLE 1
FORT ANCIENT HOUSE SIZE AND SHAPE

Phase	Size		Length[1]	Width[1]	LW[1]	L/W
Anderson	33-MY-57[2]	$\bar{X}$	6.60	5.86	39.21	1.12
	n = 14	MAX	8.99	7.01	63.02	1.28
		MIN	5.49	5.18	29.99	1.02
		s	1.08	.58	10.48	.09
Clover	15-GP-22[3]	$\bar{X}$	18.26	7.25	134.21	2.60
	n = 5	MAX	21.49	9.14	196.42	3.23
		MIN	15.53	5.49	92.01	1.93
		s	2.20	1.51	38.70	.47
	45-PU-31[4]	$\bar{X}$	13.96	6.82	97.90	2.04
	n = 11	MAX	19.20	8.54	163.97	2.67
		MIN	10.06	5.49	58.25	1.57
		s	3.00	.99	36.28	.32
Woodside	15-PI-11[5]	$\bar{X}$	8.51	5.90	51.06	1.44
	n = 8	MAX	12.30	6.80	83.64	1.90
		MIN	5.50	4.50	24.75	1.60
		s	1.98	.73	16.02	.27
	15-JO-14	$\bar{X}$	8.52	5.58	47.86	1.55
	n = 6	MAX	10.06	7.16	67.66	1.83
		MIN	7.62	4.72	35.97	1.32
		s	.92	.80	10.58	.47

[1] All measurements in meters.
[2] Original measurements from ground plan supplied by J. M. Heilman.
[3] Hanson 1966.
[4] Hanson 1975.
[5] Dunnell, Hanson, and Hardesty 1971.

and postmolds, whether part of house patterns or not, follow this general pattern with the features having a somewhat broader distribution than the postmolds. The differential effects of plowing are likewise evident in the changing density of both features and postmolds around the ring with the southwestern section being the most impoverished.

To examine the discrete objects in this mode, density maps were prepared using SYMAP (Dougenik and Sheehan 1975). Since the 10-foot analytic units were corrected for uniform area in the preliminary stages of analysis, counts per analytic unit are density measures. Interval structure is a critical matter (Jermann and Dunnell 1979) and markedly influences the appearance of the resulting maps. It has already been shown that all of

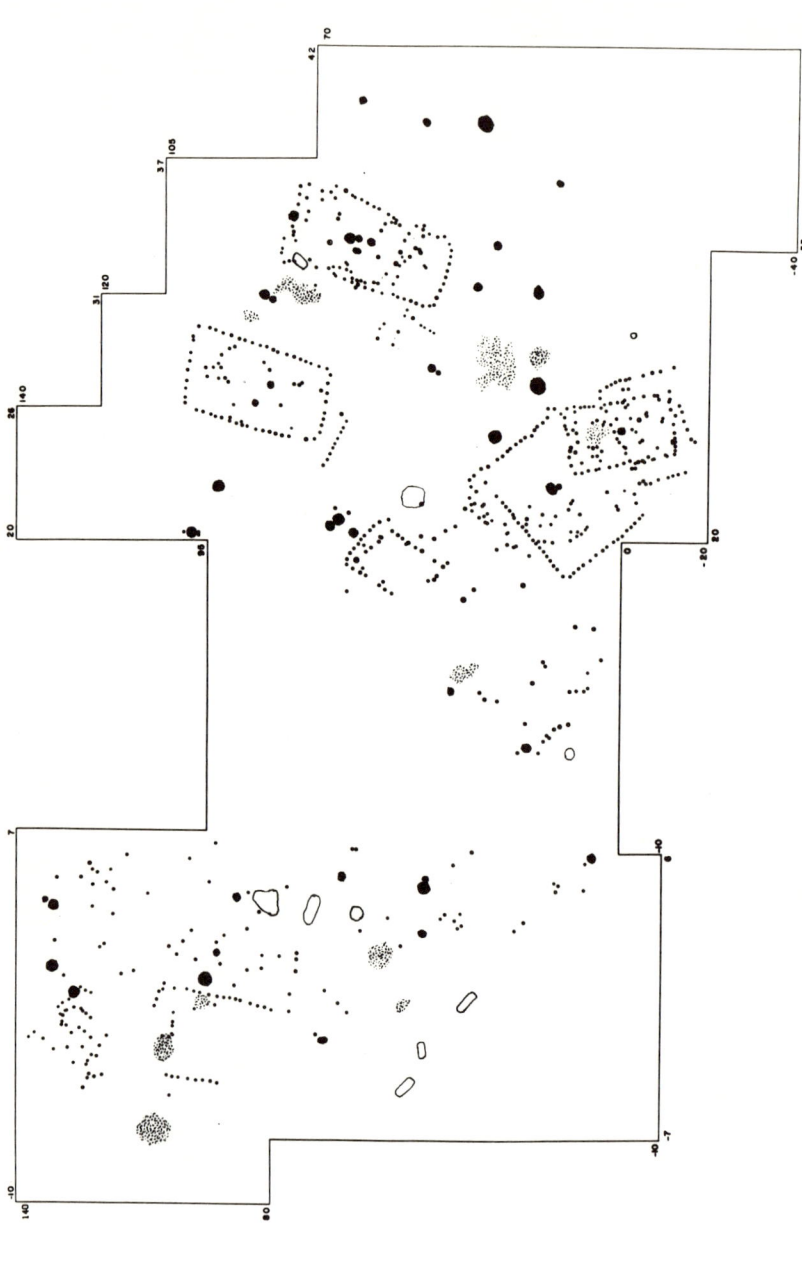

Fig. 5. Plan of the Woodside component at the Mayo site. Solid features represent hearths as a group; stippled areas, surficial features (sheet middens and surface fires); open figures denote all other pits (rectangular shapes are graves, circular shapes are storage pits).

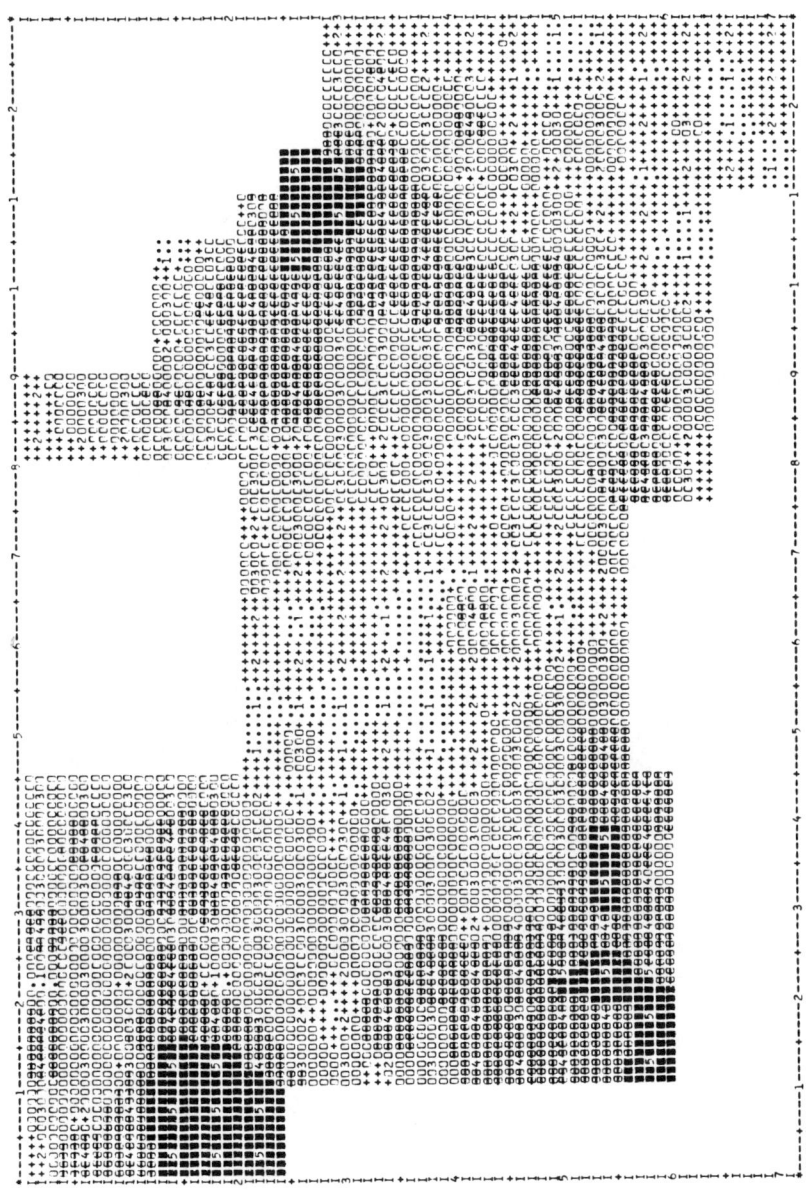

Fig. 6. SYMAP of all prehistoric artifacts. Intervals are as follows: 1 = 0.00-4.17; 2 = 4.17-17.38; 3 = 17.38-72.45; 4 = 72.45-302.01; and 5 = 302.01-1259.00. The small amount of Woodland material is swamped by the numerically superior Woodside component.

the numerically important variables at Mayo conform to a geometric distribution. Consequently, the interval structure employed in mapping all but the smallest classes was geometric. For rare classes (maximum value of 5 or less) intervals were made equal to counts per unit. Since there are 58 coded variables, approximately 70 single variable maps could have been made (e.g., bone was recorded as calcined bone and uncalcined bone so that in addition to these variables, burning as a mode and bone as a unit could be mapped). The possible number of multiple variable maps is astronomical. Figure 6 shows the density of prehistoric material as a unit. Included is a small number (137) of Woodland artifacts. They exert no influence on the map given the numerical superiority (27,813) of the Woodside occupation. Discrete objects as a whole have the same spatial structure as the features—the Mayo site is a doughnut-shaped ring surrounding a vacant center. The distribution of all of the individual variables making up the total assemblage displays the same fundamental spatial pattern. Differences among variables are limited to absolute density, the diameter and width of the ring, and the location of the highest and lowest densities within the ring.

Figures 7 through 10 show variability among functional classes. Vessel fragments (Fig. 7) closely resemble the distribution of all prehistoric material since they are the major constituent of the assemblage (19,299 items). Vessel fragments are rather evenly distributed around the ring with the highest densities occurring just to the outside of the houses. As the most numerous class, vessel fragments have the broadest distribution. Potential functionally significant variables that make up this class (e.g., rim sherds, body sherds, handles) all display the same distribution. Because all of these variables, with the exception of body sherds, are represented by much smaller numbers of objects, the width of their rings is smaller, but the location of the ring and the high densities occur in the same places. Lithics, including chipped stone tools, debitage, projectile points, and utilized flakes (Fig. 8), are similarly distributed in a ring, somewhat more peripherally than vessel fragments. About the only noticeable difference lies in the prominence of lithics in the southwestern corner of the site, on the ravine fill. Again, the included variables all show precisely the same distribution with allowances for smaller numbers of items so that such things as unworked stone, chipped stone tools, projectile points (Fig. 9), utilized flakes, and cores all have essentially the same distribution. Bone (Fig. 10), as an aggregate, likewise displays a ring-shaped distribution differing in only minor ways from lithics and vessel fragments, tending to be slightly peripheral to vessel fragments and with a prominent high in the northwestern corner, again over ravine fill. Visual inspection quickly lends the impression that the location of dis-

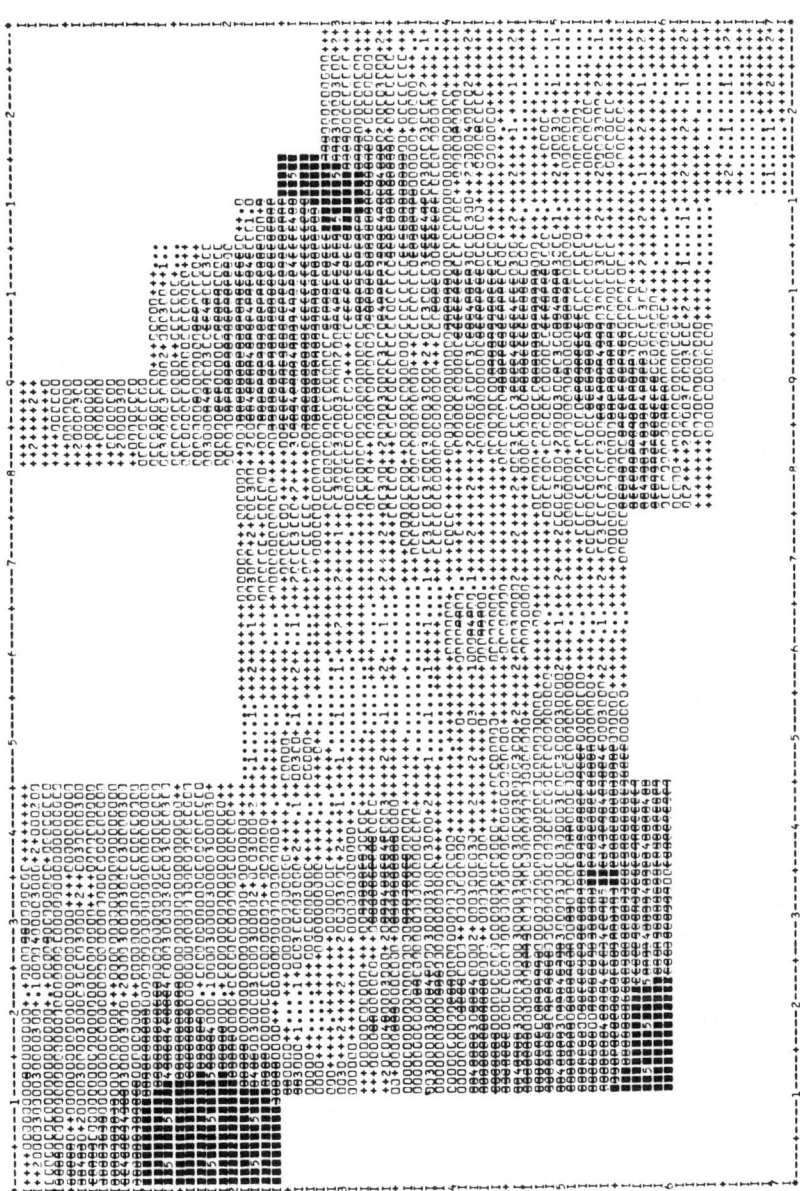

Fig. 7. SYMAP of all Woodside vessel sherds. Intervals are as follows: 1 = 0.00–4.01; 2 = 4.01–16.05; 3 = 16.05–64.30; 4 = 64.30–257.60; 5 = 257.60–1032.00. Composite variables such as rims, body sherds, and appendages all show similar distributions when mapped independently.

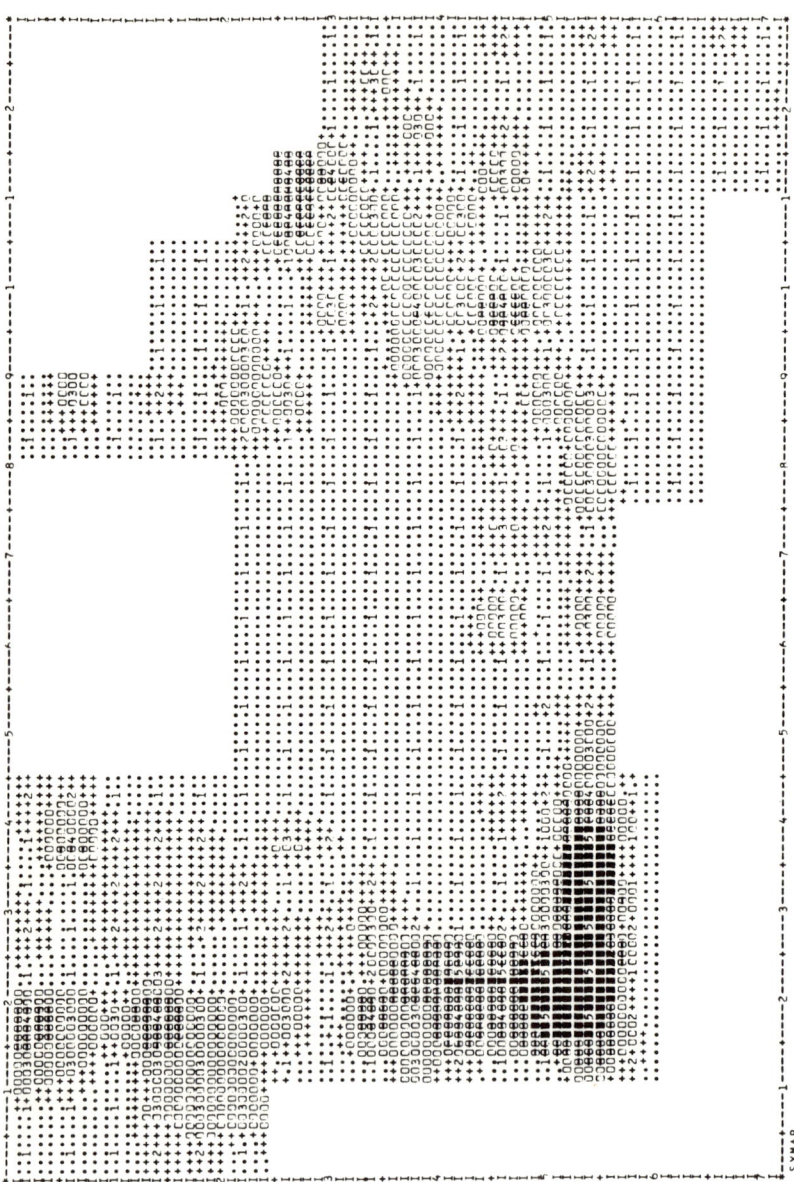

Fig. 8. SYMAP of all lithic material. Intervals are as follows: 1 = 0.00–3.06; 2 = 3.06–9.39; 3 = 9.39–28.76; 4 = 28.76–88.12; and 5 = 88.12–270.00. This map is a composite of many coded variables, all of which have highly similar distributions when mapped independently.

SPATIAL STRUCTURE OF THE MAYO SITE 139

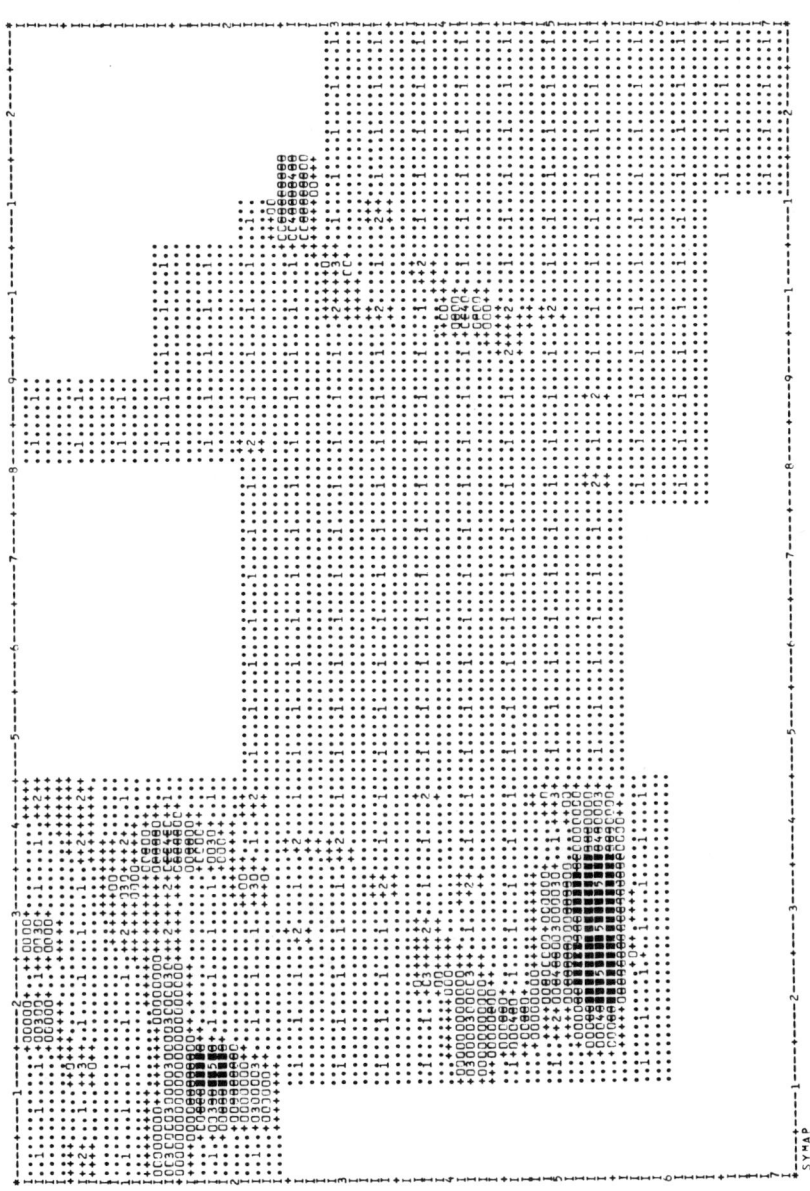

Fig. 9. SYMAP of Woodside projectile points. Intervals are as follows: 1 = 0.00–1.64; 2 = 1.64–2.70; 3 = 2.70–4.44; 4 = 4.44–7.30; 5 = 7.30–12.00. Compare this density distribution with that of total lithics in Figure 8. Projectile points have the most contrastive distribution of all of the component variables making up total lithics.

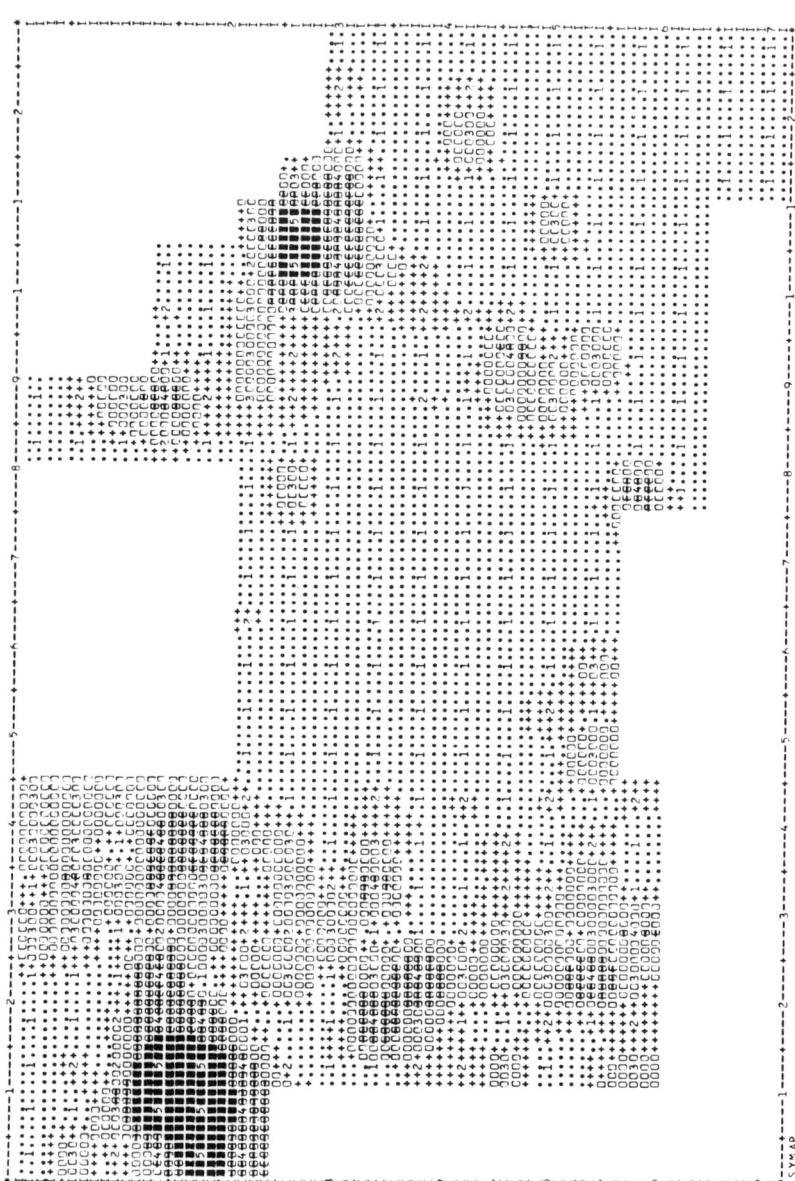

Fig. 10. SYMAP of bone. Intervals are as follows: 1 = 0.00–3.28; 2 = 3.28–10.77; 3 = 10.77–35.36; 4 = 35.36–116.08; 5 = 116.08–381.00. Bone included variables BURNED BONE and UNBURNED BONE which have similar distributions when mapped separately.

crete objects categorized in functional terms is probably a matter of garbage transportation, constituting secondary refuse in Schiffer's (1972) terms, or that there was little spatial differentiation of activities within the ring of occupation activity. Only in the slight tendency for the several classes to be distributed at varying distance from the center of the town is there a suggestion of radial differentiation of activities.

Figures 11, 12, and 13 show the distribution of the three principal pottery types in which stylistic variation is presumably dominant. Again the overriding structure is that of the ring. Within the ring, however, there is little variation that can be detected that is not a direct function of the absolute frequency of ceramics. In short, such stylistic variation as there may be is clearly embedded in small frequency changes, not in major frequencies differences or complimentary distributions.

Iconic modeling clearly reveals the overall structure of the site in terms of the immobile features and the potentially mobile artifacts. There is good agreement between the two sets of data such that if the site were known only from a systematic surface collection, its basic spatial structure would be accurately represented. In terms of features, the ring is comprised by two rows of houses accompanied by smaller features which have a somewhat less restricted field of spatial occurrence. While the absence of a stockade makes it difficult to determine if both rows of houses are contemporaneous, the near superposition of the two rows in the southeastern corner suggests that they are not. Slone, which did have stockades, is clearly the product of multiple occupations (Dunnell, Hanson, and Hardesty 1971), and there is no good reason to suppose that Mayo is different in this regard. The settlement apparently contracted or expanded between at least two occupations.

The ring itself is rather homogenous in terms of discrete objects. There is a slight suggestion of a radial structure in functional categories, a structure that would tend to be erased by expansion or contraction of the settlement over time. A radial structure to activities, is of course, rather directly implied by the ring structure itself and is not inconsistent with feature locations. The limited stylistic variables that can be examined show no structure at all, indicating the town was a homogenous unit stylistically or that variation is more subtle than can be grasped in a simple iconic rendering.

CLUSTER ANALYSIS

Iconic modeling clearly identifies the gross structure of the site. It does not provide a reasonable basis for comparison as the apparent structure

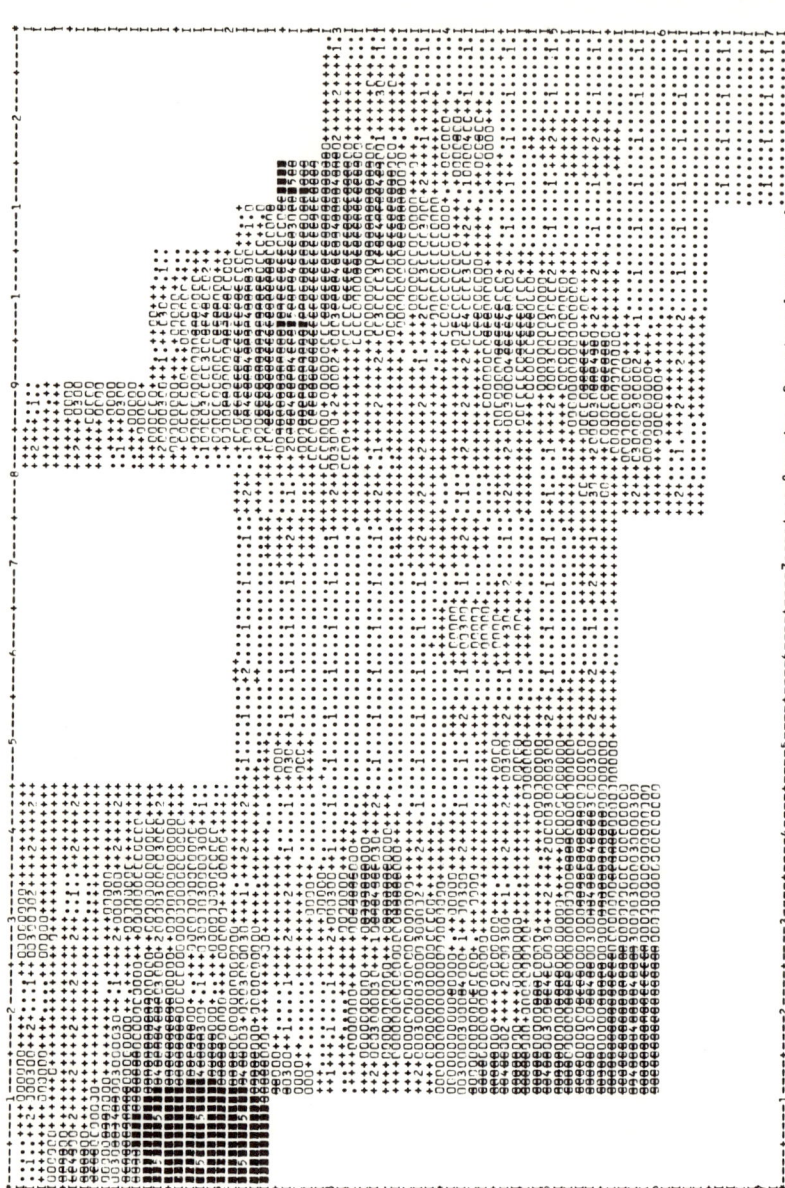

Fig. 11. SYMAP of shell-tempered cordmarked ceramics. Intervals are as follows: 1 = 0.00–3.06; 2 = 3.06–9.39; 3 = 9.39–28.76; 4 = 28.76–88.12; 5 = 88.12–270.00.

SPATIAL STRUCTURE OF THE MAYO SITE 143

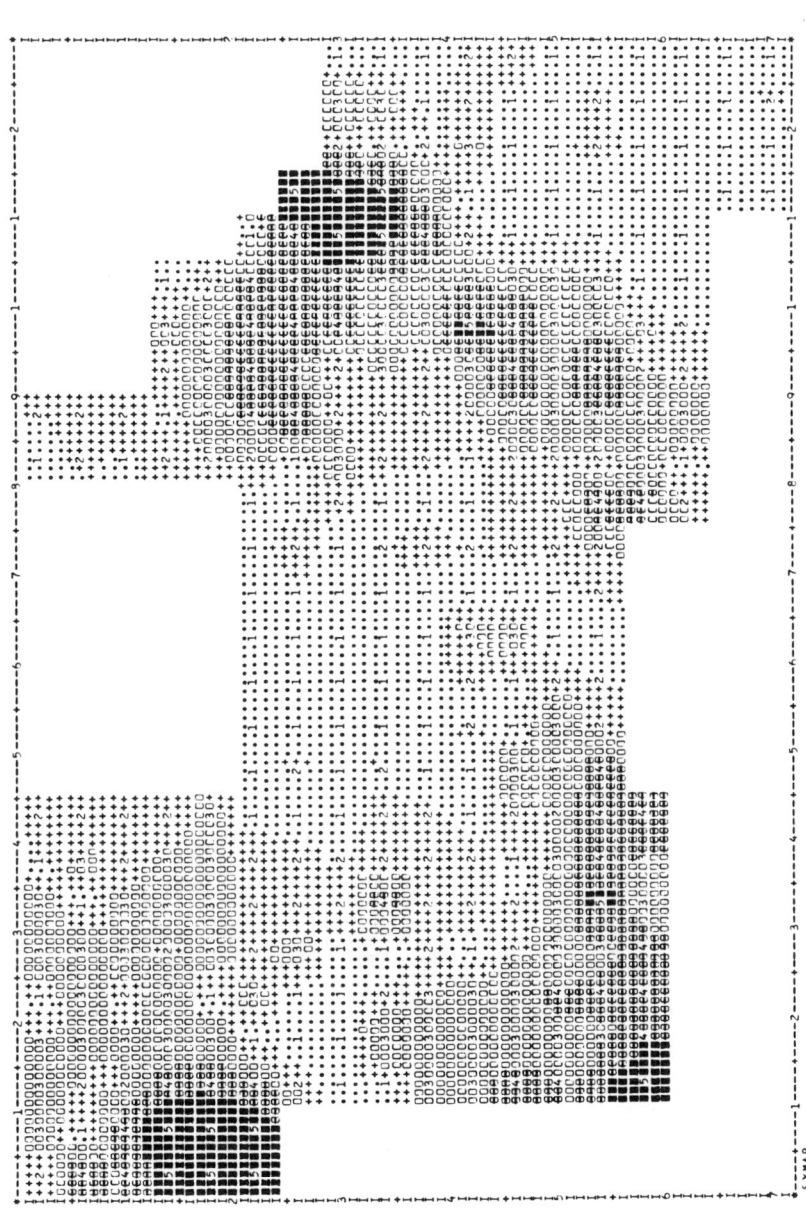

Fig. 12. SYMAP of shell-tempered roughened ceramics. Intervals are as follows: 1 = 0.00–2.88; 2 = 2.88–8.29; 3 = 8.29–23.88; 4 = 23.88–68.76; 5 = 68.76–198.00.

Fig. 13. SYMAP of shell-tempered plain ceramics. Intervals are as follows: 1 = 0.00–2.25; 2 = 2.25–5.07; 3 = 5.07–11.43; 4 = 11.43–25.75; 5 = 25.75–58.00.

derives from a visual impression nor does it provide a means to identify subtle frequency changes within a relatively homogenous mass of features and artifacts. Archaeologists have employed many different means to identify finer structure (e.g., Brose and Scarry 1976; Hietala and Stevens 1977; Hodder and Orton 1976; Whallon 1973b, 1974). None of these procedures are particularly well suited for analysis of the Mayo site. The presence of a vacant area in the middle of the site, truncation of the occupation area by erosion and excavation, and the multiplicity of overlapping patterns violate the assumptions and/or algorithms of most methods of analysis. Further, it is not useful to know that the distribution of artifacts is "clustered" or "non-random" when it is already apparent from iconic modeling that the site has a distinct geometric shape.

For these reasons, it was decided to employ cluster analysis to construct analog models of the functional and stylistic spatial patterns. The principal advantage to this family of methods is that the data or operational taxonomic units are purely formal entities without spatial coordinates and thus are relatively immune to the complexities introduced by incomplete excavation or the vacant plaza. The strategy is simple. The initial step is to calculate the relative frequencies independently for both functional and stylistic variables for each provenience unit. Relative frequencies are used since the iconic models show the ring to be homogenous in terms of density. A similarity matrix is then calculated which compares each unit with every other unit; using these measures, the units are clustered in accord with one of the several clustering algorithms available. Clusters of provenience units, which are purely formal entities at this point, can then be plotted by their spatial coordinates to ascertain whether clustering is correlated with location and if it is, what pattern obtains in the correlation.

Cluster analysis is not without significant problems (e.g., Matson and True 1974; Thomas 1972), not the least of which is the inability to identify a "correct" solution since cluster analysis always produces a solution (e.g., Aldenderfer 1982). This problem is not serious when cluster analysis is used in a deductive mode (e.g., Thompson 1978), i.e., testing whether a given set of variables has an expected structure. Used in an inductive or descriptive mode, as it is here, the problem of identifying a correct solution is paramount and largely insoluble internal to cluster analysis itself. In fact, correctness is usually assessed by the interpretability of the solution rather than with any extrinsic criteria (cf. Whallon 1979). This is compounded by the fact that if different algorithms are employed, markedly different data structuring may result (Aldenderfer and Blashfield 1978).

The solution employed here is to use a number of different clustering algorithms. Only those clusters which arise independently in different analyses are considered descriptively accurate (cf. Lukesh 1981; Sokal and Sneath 1963:166). This means, of course, that one is limited to differences of such magnitude that the various clustering algorithms, irrespective of their particular biases, detect them. In this manner, one can determine the value of clustering without recourse to the interpretability of the clusters themselves. A random spatial distribution of cluster members is just as interpretable as one in which there is perfect spatial correlation among cluster members. Given that secondary refuse is probably always a significant fraction of any assemblage (e.g., DeBoer and Lathrap 1979), the interpretability of random spatial distributions is essential. Some pattern detail is certainly lost; however, there is no real way to determine which of the algorithms has produced the "correct" structure at smaller scales.

There are a number of archaeological factors that will act to prevent anything approaching perfect spatial correlation. First, there is the matter of obtaining accurate relative frequencies over a set of samples that range in total density of zero to several hundreds. Obviously, in the lower density units, sampling error plays an increasingly large role in the input frequencies. To control this, an arbitrary minimum sample size criterion was imposed to exclude the lowest density units, 15 items per unit in the case of stylistic analyses where similarity was calculated on the basis of four variables and 20 items per unit in the case of functional analyses where five and six variables were used. Second, since almost all variables are represented by fragments (e.g., sherds, bones) of much larger entities, there will be "founder effects" where larger objects have been broken and sets of related objects deposited without subsequent spatial dispersion. The use of 10-foot units in averaging counts over a larger area minimizes these effects. They cannot be presumed to have been completely eliminated, however. For this reason, single units or small groups of units added to major clusters at relatively low levels of similarity must be regarded as suspect unless their particular composition is not consistent with the founder-effect hypothesis.

Since the iconic modeling suggested that the ring *might* be internally undifferentiated, the effect of such a structure or lack of structure, had to be considered on clustering results. The net effect of such homogeneity should have been the creation of one relatively large, coherent cluster encompassing the bulk of the provenience units followed by the addition, one by one or in small sets, of the remainder of the provenience units due to founder effects. This "no structure" solution also provides an expectation for algorithms and measures that are insensitive to structure detected by other methods. Thus identification of correct description requires that the spatial distributions generated by two or more clustering methods be coincident in space *and* that any contrasting solution be of the chained, no-structure kind *or* that all solutions be of the chained, no-structure type. These requirements effectively prevent sorting through a pile of dendrograms until one finds a solution that coincides with predetermined notions of structure or is simply understandable.

Three gross kinds of internal patterns might be expected to characterize the ring: radial patterns, that is, a set of overlapping rings of different diameters; circumferential, that is, segmentation of the ring into a variable number of pie-like wedges; or some complex combination of the two. Superposition of patterns, such as would be implied if the town had contracted or expanded, has a differential effect on the detectability of radial and circumferential structure. Radial patterns will be badly disrupted since expansion/contraction is radial. Circumferential patterns are not so effected provided there is no rotation of the pattern accompanying expansion/contraction. Small amounts of rotation, especially if the number of wedges is small, will blur only the edges of patterns.

Over the past seven years as the data were being assembled a wide variety of different clustering methods have been applied, including SERIATE (Craytor and Johnson 1968), GRPING (University of Washington, Department of Geography), CLUST3 (Bonham-Carter 1967), Ward's Error Sum of Squares method (Ward 1963), and RELOCATE from the CLUSTAN package (Wishart 1978). For those methods requiring input as a similarity coefficient, the Brainerd and Robinson Coefficient was used (Robinson 1951); for the others (GRPING and RELOCATE) the percentage composition of the spatial units was used. SERIATE is a cumbersome, expensive procedure with output that is difficult to interpret. It was abandoned early in the analysis. CLUST3's average linkage method was superseded by a similar, more efficient procedure in CLUSTAN although some analyses based on CLUST3 have been published (Jermann 1973; Jermann and Dunnell 1979). GRPING, although it required that a separate program be written to generate a dendrogram output (Jermann 1973), was retained because, though an average link method, it employs the Mahalanobis distance statistic (Mahalanobis 1936) and minimizes intragroup variance in making cluster decisions. Thus it represents a contrastive approach to cluster formation.

Clustering of functional variables is rather disappointing (Fig. 14). Five variables, vessel fragments, projectile points, flake tools, lithic debitage, and other tools, were used. For GRPING a sixth variable, bone, was added, but this does not materially alter the result because of its high correlation with vessel fragments. In general the "no structure" solution

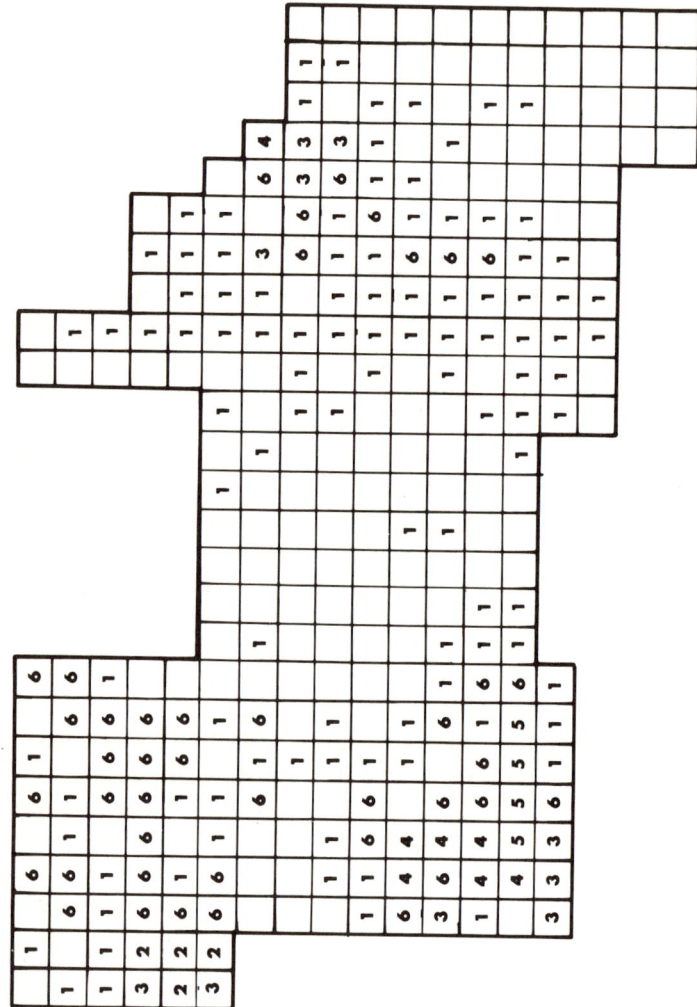

Fig. 14. Six cluster RELOCATE of functional variables. The numbers identify the individual clusters. Empty grid units are those with less than the minimum number of artifacts.

characterized all clustering attempts. The bulk of the site is assigned to a single cluster, irrespective of the number of clusters distinguished, and the remainder of the site is added in small groups of units. Only two pattern observations are repeated through all solutions: (1) three areas, one in the northwest ravine fill, one in the southwest ravine fill, and one on the extreme northeast corner of the site are consistently distinguished from adjacent area and linked together; (2) the western half of the site is more heterogenous than the eastern half, probably as a consequence of the first observation. The one cluster with spatial correlates is distinguished by the high frequency of vessel sherds (and in the case of GRPING, bone) and appears to represent secondary deposition of trash. These same areas also have the highest overall density of artifacts on the site, consistent with trash disposal areas.

To a certain extent this result could have been anticipated from the iconic models. The only visually apparent structure is radial, the very kind of structure that expansion/contraction would seriously modify. This interpretation is consistent with the differential homogeneity from east to west. In the east, there is no physical constraint on the outer limits of the site and a second row of houses is distinct from the inner row; in the west, the ravine constrains the outer limits, and as best as can be judged, there is less radial displacement. Nonetheless the results of functional clustering are meager—a plaza surrounded by a ring of more or less undifferentiated activity, terminating on the outer edge in a few areas with large scale trash dumping.

The stylistic analysis is considerably more informative as consistent results were obtained in all clusterings without regard to the number of clusters distinguished. The analyses employed four variables, shell-tempered cordmarked ceramics, shell-tempered roughened ceramics, shell-tempered plain ceramics, and shell-tempered decorated ceramics. In each case (Figs. 15 and 16, representing the average link clustering from CLUSTAN and GRPING, are typical), the clusters distinguished at various levels show a strong tendency to sort on either side of an axis bisecting the site roughly from the northeast to southwest. In effect there are northern and southern stylistic precincts within the town, and there is modest overlap or mixture where they abut along the axis. The only significant exception to the general pattern is the appearance of a small set of units in the extreme northwest that belongs to the southern assemblage of clusters. But even this exception is consistent over all of the clustering solutions. It seems, therefore, quite reasonable to conclude that in terms of frequency of interaction, the ring at Mayo is not homogenous. Frequency of interaction is not strictly a distance function but rather is

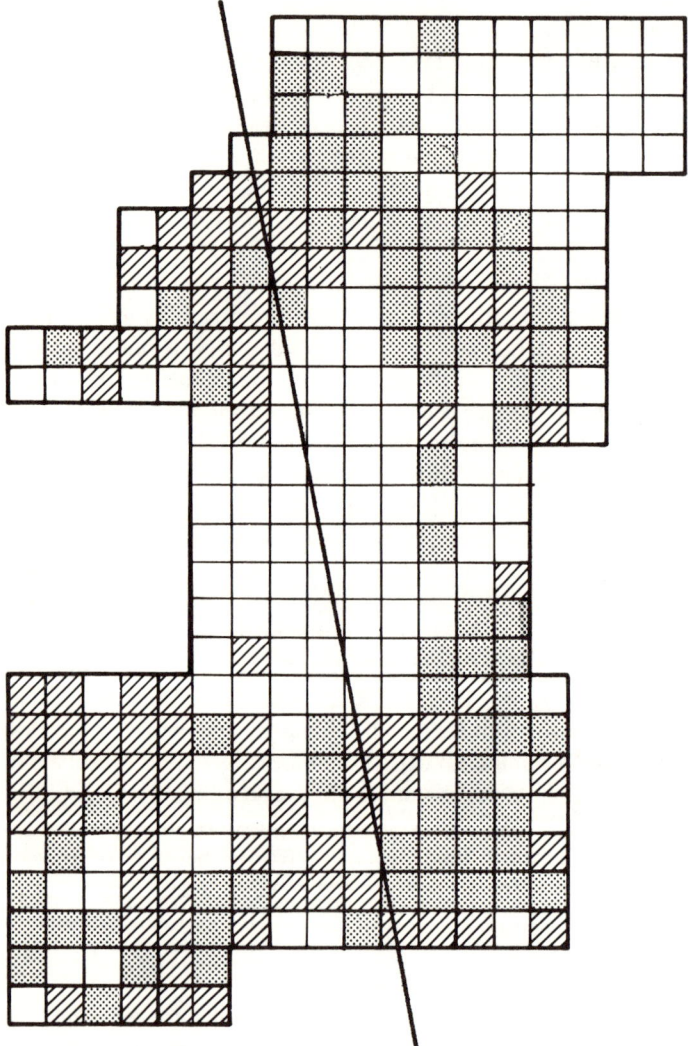

Fig. 15. Six cluster GRPING using stylistic variables. Clusters whose members occur primarily in the northern half of the site are striped; clusters with a southern distribution are stippled.

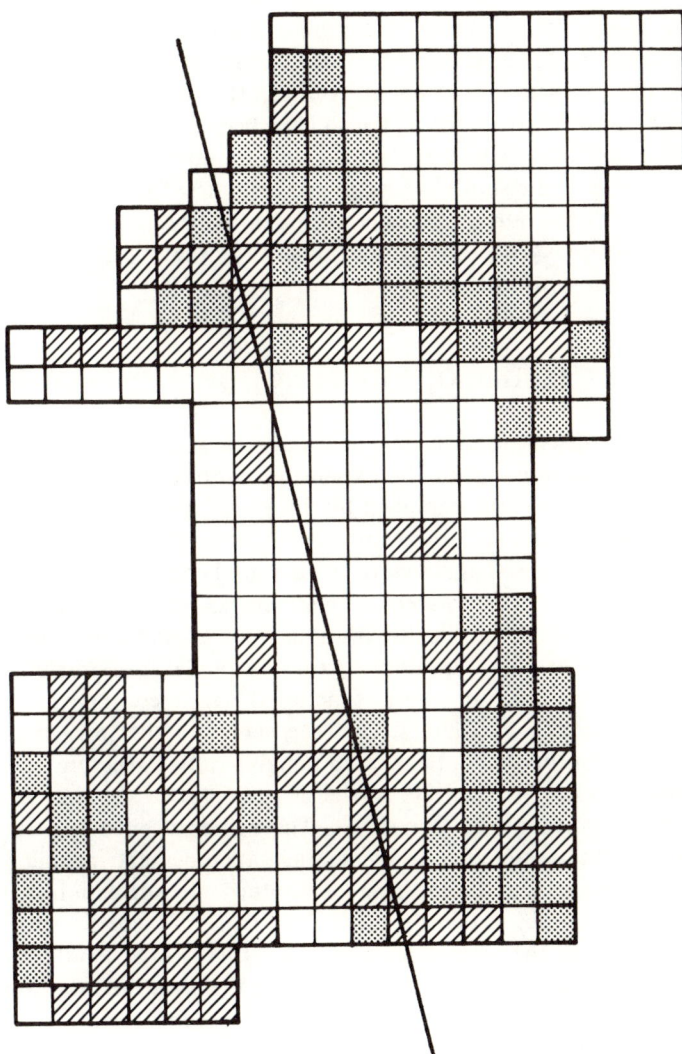

Fig. 16. Six cluster average-link grouping of stylistic variables. Clusters whose members occur primarily in the northern half of the site are striped; clusters with a southern distribution are stippled.

structured by some set of social constraints or patterns that result in the division of the town into two roughly equivalent sections.

The spatial breaks between sets of clusters *do not* correspond with the truncations of the ring by erosion and excavation limits. Both clusters appear on both sides of these breaks. This is important to note in that the effect of missing data in clustering a more or less continuously variable set of data would be to cluster on either side of such breaks. The differences between the two sets of clusters are sufficiently great and their internal similarities sufficiently strong as not to have been affected by the missing data. The northern clusters tend to be dominated by cordmarked ceramics; those in the south by roughened ceramics. Decorated pottery is associated with the northern cluster although its occurrence is too infrequent to have played a direct role in any of the methods using the Brainerd-Robinson Coefficient.

A RADIAL MODEL OF THE FUNCTIONAL STRUCTURE

The lack of discrimination of functional structure by clustering techniques seems attributable to the expansion/contraction of the town in view of the radial structure implied by the plaza/ring of occupation and by the suggestion of the iconic models that there are at least minor functional differences that correlate with radial location in the ring.

In an attempt to further discern such structure, a model was created on a radial principle such that its distributional expectations could be identified in the kind of data available. Again, the model is a simple one. If there is a radial structure to the functional variables, then the mean distance of functional variables from the center of the town ought to differ. If on the other hand, there is no tangible radial structure, then the mean distances ought to all fall in the densest part of the ring and not differ significantly among themselves. The principal advantage of this approach is that it is not affected by missing data unless the missing pieces are skewed to one side of the ring or another. The detection of trash disposal on both sides of the site in the cluster analysis suggests this is not a problem as does the plan of features and structures. Secondly, expansion/contraction of the town, while changing the absolute magnitude of mean distances and increasing dispersion statistics (e.g., s) will not change the rank ordering of the mean distances and will affect their statistical significance only through dispersion.

The initial problem is to identify the center of the town from incomplete data. Incomplete data preclude using any method which requires measurements of individual features or artifacts since this would skew the center in the direction of completeness, or the largest number of measurements. The approach taken was to fit manually the largest possible circle into the plaza such that it intersected no structural elements of the site. The center of the circle was then taken to be the center of the site. This was a relatively easy process since the plaza-ring boundary is intact for over three-quarters of the circle. Even so, since it was a manual procedure, alternative centers of slightly different diameter circles were examined as potential centers by calculating the mean distances for the functional feature classes and selecting the center which minimized the standard deviations (in this case increasing with elliptical deviation from a true circle). A center situated at 87N, 63E satisfied this condition in that the standard deviations for the means of all feature classes were smaller than the corresponding values for alternative centers. The differences were small, so small that a fairly large linear error in locating the center is of minor significance in the measurement of mean distance. The center at 87N, 63E is associated with a 40-foot (12.0 m) diameter circle which is the largest that could be fitted into the plaza.

Provenience data for features and houses were obtained from the feature form plans as the geometric center of the structure. For discrete objects collected by 5-foot units, the original provenience designations (number of blocks east and west of 0 and number of feet north and south of 0 to the north corner) had to be converted to a uniform system (feet) designating the center of the unit rather than a corner. All these coordinates were then transformed to the new grid origin at 63E (X), 87N (Y) and radial distances calculated trigonometrically:

$$\text{radial distance} = \sqrt{(X-63)^2 + (5Y-87)^2}$$

where X and Y are the original coordinates. One house, graves as a class, and four features which could not be identified with the functional classes because of record deficiencies were excluded from the analysis. The mean radial distances for each class are given in Table 2. The same information is displayed in Figure 17. Standard deviations are not shown for classes near the center of the ring to simplify the diagram.

The null hypothesis, that there is no radial differentiation among feature classes and therefore no significant differences between their radial distance means, is clearly not realized in these data. There is marked variation in the location of functional feature classes, so marked that in one instance the standard deviations of adjacent classes do not overlap. Inspection suggests four bands of activities: (1) at the very periphery of the site are partially rock-filled hearths; (2) interior to this ring lies a band

TABLE 2
RADIAL DATA FOR FEATURE CLASSES

Class	n	$\bar{X}$ (ft.)	s	CV
Partially filled hearths	3	129.2	15.1	11.69
Sheet middens	6	91.5	12.4	13.55
Houses	7	87.0	21.8	25.06
Circular hearths	14	84.1	21.8	25.92
Surface fires	6	77.6	16.6	21.39
Paired hearths	6	76.4	21.3	27.88
Storage pits	2	65.2	11.0	16.87
Earth ovens	5	57.5	10.6	18.43
Pits	2	53.5	8.0	14.95

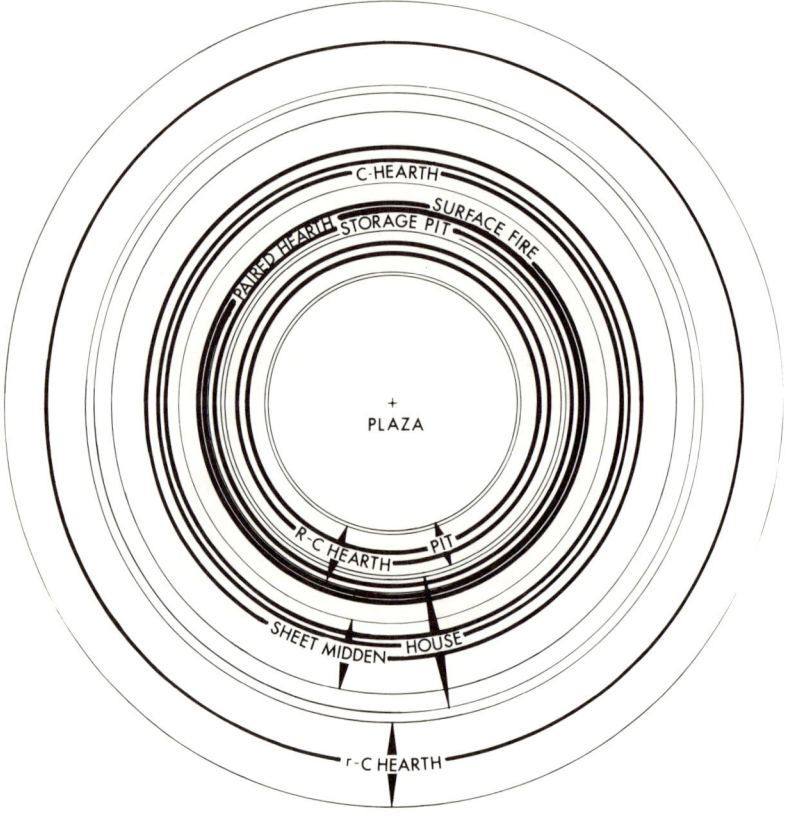

Fig. 17. Radial model of the distribution of functional feature classes. The heavy lines indicate the mean distance of each class from the center of the town; fine lines represent the standard deviations for the classes identified in the lower segment of the model.

comprised by houses, sheet middens (slightly rearward of the houses), and circular hearths; (3) interior to the houses is another band comprised by surface fires, paired hearths, and storage pits which may merge on its interior edge with (4) earth ovens and irregular pits. The relationships implied by this model are in fact realized in the physical relationships among individual features in well preserved areas of the site. Circular hearths are, for example, found in and around houses; earth ovens always appear inside houses.

Figure 18 presents a matrix of t-test scores assessing the different means. The t-test employed is a conservative one which assumes samples with unequal variances (Sokal and Rohlf 1969:374). The arrangement of the matrix is in the order of mean distance so that any radial pattern will be expressed as a regularity in the structure of significant values. The pattern of significant values for both .10 and .05 probability levels indicates a radial structure in the data. It is difficult to give the t-test results a more precise interpretation, however. The specific test, the small number of cases for many variables, and the departure from a true circle all act to underestimate significant differences. The results in Figure 15 are thus a conservative estimate of significant differences among class means. Nonetheless, Figure 18 does provide some sense of the degree to which the radial distance means are legitimately interpretable. It does seem appropriate to regard the three- or four-band structure as an accurate descriptor of functional pattern at Mayo. Whether the relative order of mean distances within bands is meaningful or not will depend more upon comparison with other sites of a similar sort than further elaboration of these data. The absolute magnitude of the radial distances is a describer of the Mayo site itself; the relative order is the comparative measure.

Since the standard deviation is a function of the absolute magnitude of the mean, Coefficients of Variation (Sokal and Rohlf 1969:62–63) are also shown in Table 2. As is evident, they are not randomly distributed either and might, given larger samples, prove to be a useful descriptive tool as well in that they should reflect the degree to which a particular kind of feature is localized in a more readily interpreted fashion than the standard deviations. Certainly, the Coefficient of Variation is more appropriate in site to site comparisons.

Many of the artifact classes that seemingly have the greatest functional import (e.g., manos and projectile points) occur in such small frequencies that they have virtually no impact in the clustering programs or even in the isopleth maps. Seven classes were examined within the radial model. The classes chosen had two features in common: (1) they did not tend to correlate in any obvious way with the trash deposition areas and thus might represent primary refuse of significance for spatial structure; (2)

	8	6	1	7	2	5	4	9	3
6	3.652	-----				——— .10 probability			
1	3.320	0.417	-----			- - - .05 probability			
7	4.769	1.114	0.291	-----					
2	4.676	1.589	0.820	0.844	-----				
5	4.285	1.463	0.834	0.814	0.109	-----			
4	6.106	3.273	1.994	2.744	1.388	1.068	-----		
9	7.221	4.657	2.835	4.422	2.428	1.904	1.023	-----	
3	7.501	4.817	3.094	4.556	2.738	2.209	1.445	0.543	-----

Fig. 18. T-test values comparing radial distance means for functional feature classes. Class 1 = houses; Class 2 = surface fires; Class 3 = pits; Class 4 = storage pits; Class 5 = paired hearths; Class 6 = sheet middens; Class 7 = circular hearths; Class 8 = partially filled circular hearths; Class 9 = earth ovens. The matrix is arranged in order of decreasing mean distance.

they were, with two exceptions, kinds of artifacts that could reasonably be assumed to have different functions. The exceptions are (1) preforms and projectile points to the extent that preforms might simply be "crude" projectile points rather than a manufacturing stage, and (2) stone and ceramic discs which, while they are contrastive in many attributes, are sufficiently similar (and enigmatic) to have conceivably functioned in the same way. The inclusion of these two pairs was an attempt to resolve these questions, again presuming that if they differed in their functions, they would enter the archaeological record in different places barring secondary deposition. Ornaments were especially included because it was presumed that they did not have a particular function and thus might display an anomolous distribution that would record simply the "traffic" within the site. Projectile points, too, were not included strictly for functional reasons because it can be safely presumed that most hunting did not take place within the confines of the town. Rather, it was expected that they should associate with places where they were stored, repaired, or discarded.

Table 3 presents these results. Because of the small sample size and fairly narrow range of radial distances, none of the means are significantly different at the .05 probability level; only one pair, projectile points and ornaments are significantly different at the .10 level. Although with larger sample sizes, such assessments might be of significance in associating particular tool types with each other or with particular feature classes, this approach cannot be pursued here. Of special note, however, is the

TABLE 3
RADIAL DATA FOR SELECTED ARTIFACT CLASSES

Class	n	$\overline{X}$	s	CV
Projectile points	269	87.54	22.67	25.90
Ceramic discs	7	85.60	21.93	25.62
Preforms	10	85.23	28.35	33.26
Drills	12	75.35	33.41	44.34
Mano/metates	5	73.73	21.23	28.03
Stone discs	7	72.70	27.08	37.18
Ornaments	8	64.29	36.91	57.41

tendency for the means to fall in two rather tight groups, one associated with houses (Fig. 19) or perhaps sheet middens and the other with the feature cluster immediately in front of the houses. Projectile points, ceramic discs, and preforms are quite nearly coincident with the house locations and with each other. The pairing of preforms and projectile points argues against the preform designation unless the different functions they represent are localized in the houses. Drills, mano/metates, and stone discs are almost as tightly clustered and occur roughly coincident with surface fires and paired hearths. The different means for ceramic and stone discs suggest they do indeed have different functions and thus enter the archaeological record at different points in space. Ornaments, comprised by isolated beads and pendants, have a mean much closer to the plaza than any of the other groups but, as expected, have the largest coefficient of variation of any group.

The grouping, of means and the apparent association with particular suites of features, while only suggestive of specific spatial associations does at a high scale confirm the nature of functional patterning as radial and suggests the value of this approach at other sites with larger inventories arrayed in a circular fashion.

SUMMARY AND CONCLUSIONS

Late prehistoric settlements in the eastern United States are sufficiently large that relatively few are ever completely excavated. Understanding intrasite spatial patterning is largely dependent upon such large exposures and thus the Mayo site, despite the limitations imposed by data quality, can make an important contribution in this respect. Refinement of analytic methods and further improvement of data quality may enhance our understanding of the site's internal structure, however, the major spatial patterns can be discerned at this juncture.

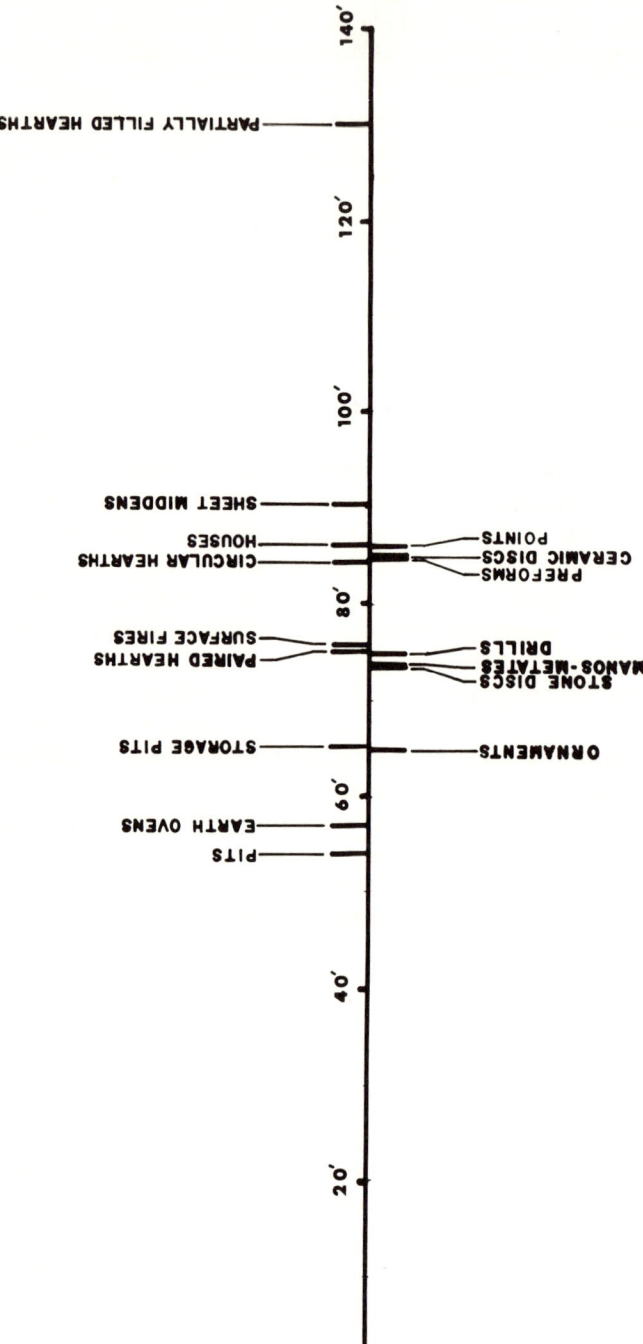

Fig. 19. Comparison of mean radial distances of selected functional artifact classes and feature classes.

The most important pattern, and one which is held in common by many otherwise dissimilar settlements throughout the eastern United States, is the circular arrangement of occupational debris about a vacant plaza. All tabulated variables follow this general pattern, be they structural elements or artifact categories. Finer structure within the ring is detectable.

In stylistic terms, patterning is circumferential. There are two, more or less homogenous, stylistic precincts with relatively sharp boundaries evident in the ceramic types. Style sharing is not a strict function of distance, nor is it random within the community.

Functional patterning, on the other hand, displays a radial patterning recognizable as series of concentric rings in both feature and artifact distributions. Small sample sizes combine with changes in size of the town over time to preclude anything more than suggestive associations of artifacts and features into activity zones; however, it does seem reasonable to describe the functional structure in terms of three major zones or bands. At the periphery of the site and well separated from any other zones is an area of limited primary activity, producing little in the way of debris but apparently associated with a distinctive type of hearth. The cluster analyses also suggest that secondary trash deposition takes place at the site periphery. This activity, mainly involving ceramics and bone, does not take the form of a continuous ring but is clumped, at least in the western part of the site, to take advantage of topographic features.

To the interior of this zone is what might be termed the domestic activity zone. Houses, some kinds of fires, and sheet middens comprise the structural components in this zone. Many different activities took place in this space as the bulk of the artifacts, both in number and kind, originate in this area. Deposition is both primary (e.g., projectile points, ceramic discs, etc.), and secondary (sheet middens).

Immediately in front of the domestic zone, perhaps overlapping it in part, is a third band representing a diverse, but somewhat different set of activities as indicated by the feature types and artifact distributions. With better data, this zone might prove divisible into two distinct bands, the innermost reflecting a limited set of activities lacking distinctive artifacts and associated with the earth ovens and the outermost representing a diverse set of activities associated with several kinds of fires. The plaza itself might be considered an activity zone as well, distinguished by the absence of both structures and artifactual debris of any sort.

It is tempting to accord these patterns a sociological interpretation. Unfortunately, such interpretation is not warranted. The patterns identified relate to entry of the various items into the archaeological record and thus only indirectly to the social partitioning and activity patterning in space (Schiffer 1972, 1976). Both primary and secondary deposition are demonstrably involved at Mayo. Further, it is quite impossible to know if particular spatial associations arise because the variables participate in the same activity or because several unrelated activities take place in the same space simultaneously or cyclically. Finally, there is no testable means of converting functional classes, be they rigorously or intuitively defined, into their sociological counterparts. Sociological terminology may be convenient for discussion, but comparison should be based on the empirical distributions and not their inferential and untested meanings.

Looking beyond the confines of the Mayo site itself, there are some observations of value to be made. Perhaps the most striking of these is the close similarity with the spatial structure described for the Slone site (Dunnell, Hanson, and Hardesty 1971). Like Mayo, Slone has a radial activity pattern optimistically described in terms of four zones—refuse zone, dwelling zone, culinary zone, and plaza (Dunnell, Hanson, and Hardesty 1971:42). Also like Mayo, Slone displays a circumferential stylistic pattern that divides the site into two more or less equivalent precincts (Dunnell, Hanson, and Hardesty 1971:74-80). These similarities are all the more striking since the physical appearance of the two sites is quite different. The presence of a stockade at Slone produces a much more regular arrangement of features and sharper site boundaries. Mayo is much more diffuse, sufficiently so that there is nothing to indicate that the excavators realized they were excavating a circular town. Yet the presence of a stockade seems to have little effect on the basic spatial organization of the communities. Certainly, the plaza/ring arrangement of Woodside communities is not simply a function of the economics of stockade construction. The pattern is present whether or not the site is surrounded by a wall.

The Incinerator site provides another useful source of comparisons with Fort Ancient proper (Heilman 1975; Heilman and Hoefer 1980). Again the basic arrangement is of the plaza/ring type and site surrounded by a stockade. The site plan of Incinerator indicates a remarkably discrete radial patterning of structural elements—a nearly empty plaza surrounded by a ring of burials, in turn surrounded by a band of pits lying in front of houses. While radial, the specific elements of the pattern are quite different, indicative of a different pattern of activities at that site. The location of graves around the outer edge of the plaza contrasts directly with the pattern at Slone, where graves were invariably located in the trash disposal zone at the periphery of the site. At Mayo, graves may follow the Slone pattern or they may be associated with the houses. The deficiencies in locating and recording graves at Mayo make it impossible to incorporate them into the pattern with certainty; however, it is clear that their location is not consistent with the Incinerator site pattern.

Similarly, the house zone at Incinerator is remarkably free of other kinds of structural remains whereas at both Slone and Mayo, this area is a complex of activities and features.

The stylistic structure of the Incinerator site is similar to that evident in the Woodside sites in that it is circumferential; however, it appears to be more complex in that at least three and possibly four style areas can be identified (Heilman 1975, personal communication). Comparable data from the Hardin Village site and Buffalo are lacking.

It is not possible at this point to identify those elements of spatial patterning that are unique to particular phases apart from those elements which may characterize Fort Ancient settlements in general and those which may accompany ring/plaza community organizations everywhere they occur. As interest in intrasite spatial patterning increases, this deficiency may be remedied and spatial pattern contribute much to understanding Fort Ancient in both organizational and taxonomic terms.

One final comment might be made on the analytic methods employed. The techniques for spatial analysis that have entered archaeology from plant ecology and geography, while having many virtues, do not take advantage of the most obvious and overriding geometric patterns that characterize Fort Ancient communities. The application of these techniques to Fort Ancient communities is likely to produce highly unsatisfying results simply because pattern is so evident in these settlements. Visually "evident" pattern, however, is exceedingly difficult to compare from case to case in any rigorous way. Cluster analysis, and most particularly the radial model offered here, appears to offer ways to capitalize on the obvious structure of these settlements in a fashion that can ultimately lead to rigorous intersite comparisons of intrasite patterns. Unfortunately, the Mayo site data are not ideal for developing these approaches to their fullest and it is hoped that others might pursue their development with better controlled data.[1]

Notes

1. In the course of ten years, numerous people have assisted with the Mayo site analysis. Glen E. Rice coded the original data for computer analysis. Jerry V. Jermann did many of the analyses while employed as a research assistant supported by a University of Washington, Graduate School Research Fund grant to the writer. Dennis E. Lewarch, Hella McIntosh, Sarah Studenmund, and Elizabeth Vance also assisted with aspects of the computer analysis. Donald K. Grayson provided valuable statistical advice. J. M. Heilman graciously shared unpublished data from the Incinerator site. Mary D. Dunnell, Donald K. Grayson, Jan F. Simek, Julie K.Stein, and Robert Whallon read the manuscript in draft and provided valuable criticisms.

Lathel F. Duffield and Phillip Drucker of the University of Kentucky deserve special thanks for making the Mayo site available for study and providing space for analysis in Lexington. The original analysis was supported by a University of Washington, Graduate

School Research Fund, Summer Salary Award. To all of these individuals and any I may have inadvertantly overlooked, I express my sincere gratitude.

REFERENCES

Aldenderfer, M. S.
    1982   Methods of cluster validation for archaeology. *World Archaeology* 14:61–70.

Aldenderfer, M. S., and R. K. Blashfield
    1978   Cluster analysis and archaeological classification. *American Antiquity* 43:502–505.

Binford, L. R., S. R. Binford, R. Whallon, and M. A. Hardin
    1970   Archaeology at Hatchery West. *Society for American Archaeology, Memoir* 24.

Bonham-Carter, G. F.
    1967   Fortran IV program for q-mode cluster analysis of nonquantitative data using IBM 7090/7094 computers. *University of Kansas State Geological Survey, Computer Contributions* 17.

Brose, D. S., and J. F. Scarry
    1976   The Boston Ledges shelter: comparative spatial analyses of early Late Woodland occupations in Summit County, Ohio. *Midcontinental Journal of Archaeology* 1:179–228.

Craytor, W. B., and L. R. Johnson
    1968   Refinements in computerized item seriation. *Museum of Natural History, University of Oregon, Bulletin* 10.

Dacey, M.
    1973   Statistical tests of spatial association in the location of tool types. *American Antiquity* 38:320–328.

DeBoer, W. S., and D. W. Lathrap
    1979   The making and breaking of Shipibo-Conibo ceramics. In *Ethnoarchaeology: implications of ethnography for archaeology*, edited by C. Krammer, pp. 102–138. Columbia University Press, New York.

Dougenik, J. A., and D. E. Sheehan
    1975   *SYMAP user's reference manual.* Laboratory for Computer Graphics and Spatial Analysis, Harvard University, Cambridge.

Dunnell, Robert C.
    1962   A general survey of Fort Ancient in the Kentucky—West Virginia area. Manuscript on file, Museum of Anthropology, University of Kentucky.
    1966a   Archaeological reconnaissances in Fishtrap Reservoir, Kentucky, 1966. Manuscript on file, Department of Anthropology, Yale University.
    1966b   1965 excavations in the Fishtrap Reservoir, Pike County, Kentucky (mimeo). National Park Service, Southeast Region, Richmond.
    1967   The prehistory of Fishtrap, Kentucky: archaeological interpretation in marginal areas. Ph.D. dissertation, Yale University. University Microfilms, Ann Arbor.
    1972   Prehistory of Fishtrap Kentucky. *Yale University Publications in Anthropology* 75.
    1978a   Archaeological potential of anthropological and scientific models of function. In *Archaeological essays in honor of Irving B. Rouse*, edited by R. C. Dunnell and E. S. Hall, Jr., pp. 41–73. Mouton, The Hague.
    1978b   Style and function: a fundamental dichotomy. *American Antiquity* 43:192–202.

Dunnell, R. C., L. H. Hanson, Jr., and D. L. Hardesty
    1971   The Woodside component of the Slone site, Pike County, Kentucky. *Southeastern Archaeological Conference Bulletin* 14.

Evans, C.
    1955   A ceramic study of Virginia archaeology. *Bureau of American Ethnology, Bulletin* 160.

Hanson, L. H., Jr.
  1966 The Hardin village site. *University of Kentucky, Studies in Anthropology* 4.
  1975 The Buffalo site—a late 17th century Indian village site in Putnam County, West Virginia. *West Virginia Geological and Economic Survey, Report of Archaeological Investigations* 5.
Hanson, L. H., Jr., R. C. Dunnell, and D. L. Hardesty
  1964 The Slone site, Pike County, Kentucky (mimeo). National Park Service, Southeast Region, Richmond.
Heilman, J. M.
  1975 Ceramic and spatial patterning at the Incinerator site (33 My 57). Paper presented at the 40th Annual Meeting of the Society for American Archaeology, Dallas.
Heilman, J. M., and R. R. Hoefer
  1980 Astronomical alignments in a Fort Ancient settlement at the Incinerator site in Dayton, Ohio. Paper presented at the 45th Annual Meeting of the Society for American Archaeology, Philadelphia.
Hietala, H. J., and D. S. Stevens
  1977 Spatial analysis: multiple procedures in pattern recognition studies. *American Antiquity* 42:539–559.
Hill, J. N.
  1966 A prehistoric community in eastern Arizona. *Southwestern Journal of Anthropology* 22:9–30.
  1970 Broken K Pueblo: prehistoric social organization in the American Southwest. *University of Arizona, Anthropological Papers* 18.
Hodder, I.
  1979 Economic and social stress and material culture patterning. *American Antiquity* 44:446–454.
Hodder, I., and C. Orton
  1976 *Spatial analyses in archaeology.* University of Cambridge Press, Cambridge.
Holley, G. A., and T. A. Del Bene
  1981 An evaluation of Keeley's microwear approach. *Journal of Archaeological Science* 8:337–349.
Jelinek, A. J.
  1976 Form, function and style in lithic analysis. In *Cultural change and continuity*, edited by C. E. Cleland, pp. 19–33. Academic Press, New York.
Jermann, J. V.
  1973 A consideration of computer methods in the study of prehistoric community pattern structure. Paper presented at the 38th Annual Meeting of the Society for American Archaeology, San Francisco.
Jermann, J. V., and R. C. Dunnell
  1979 Some limitations of isoplethic mapping in archaeology. *Arizona State University, Publications in Anthropology* 16.
Johnson, W. C., J. M. Adovasio, and J. P. Marwitt
  1980 Fort Ancient on the frontier: a view from Bluestone Lake, West Virginia. Paper presented at the 45th Annual Meeting of the Society for American Archaeology, Philadelphia.
Keeley, L. H.
  1980 *Experimental determination of stone tool uses.* University of Chicago Press, Chicago.
Keeley, L. H., and M. H. Newcomer
  1977 Microwear analysis of experimental flint tools: a test case. *Journal of Archaeological Science* 4:29–62.
LeBlanc, S. A.
  1971 An addition to Naroll's suggested floor area and settlement population relationship. *American Antiquity* 36:210–211.

Lewarch, D. E., and M. J. O'Brien
   1981   Effect of short term tillage on aggregate provenience surface pattern. *Vanderbilt University Papers in Anthropology* 27:7–49.

Longacre, W. A.
   1964   Archaeology as anthropology. *Science* 144:1454–1455.
   1970   Archaeology as anthropology: a case study. *University of Arizona, Anthropological Papers* 18.

Lukesh, S. S.
   1981   A non-classificatory arrangement of early Bronze Age south Italian sites: results of cluster analysis. In *Manejos de datos y methodes matemáticos de arqueología*, edited by G. L. Cowgill, R. Whallon, and B. S. Ottaway, pp. 41–64. Union Internacional de Ciencias Prehistóricas y Protohistóricas, México, D.F.

McDonald, H. P., and R. L. Blevins
   1965   Reconnaissance soil survey of fourteen counties in eastern Kentucky. *USDA Soil Conservation Service, Series 1962*, 1.

Mahalanobis, P. C.
   1936   On the generalized distance in statistics. *Proceedings of the National Institute of Sciences of India* 2:49–55.

Matson, R. G., and D. L. True
   1974   Site relationships at Quebrada Toraoaca, Chile: a comparison of clustering and scaling techniques. *American Antiquity* 39:51–74.

Naroll, R.
   1962   Floor area and settlement population. *American Antiquity* 27:587–589.

Odell, G. H., and F. Odell-Vereecken
   1980   Verifying the reliability of lithic use-wear assessments by 'blind tests': the low power approach. *Journal of Field Archaeology* 7:87–120.

Purrington, B. I.
   1967   Prehistoric horizons and traditions in the eastern mountains of Kentucky. Unpublished M.A. thesis, Department of Anthropology, University of Kentucky.

Ritter, D. F.
   1978   *Process geomorphology*. W. H. Freeman, San Francisco.

Robinson, W. S.
   1951   A method for chronologically ordering archaeological deposits. *American Antiquity* 16:293–301.

Schiffer, M. B.
   1972   Archaeological context and systemic context. *American Antiquity* 37:156–165.
   1976   *Behavioral archaeology*. Academic Press, New York.

Schwartz, D. W.
   1962   An archaeological survey of the Fishtrap reservoir (mimeo). National Park Service, Region 1, Richmond.
   1967   Conceptions of Kentucky prehistory. *University of Kentucky, Studies in Anthropology* 6.

Sokal, R. R., and F. J. Rohlf
   1969   *Biometry*. W. H. Freeman, San Francisco.

Sokal, R. R., and P. H. A. Sneath
   1963   *Principles of numerical taxonomy*. W. H. Freeman, San Francisco.

Solecki, R.
   1949   An archaeological survey of two rivers in West Virginia: the Bluestone reservation. *West Virginia History* 10:319–432.

Stiles, D.
   1979   Paleolithic culture and culture change: experiment in theory and method. *Current Anthropology* 20:1–21.

Thomas, D. H.
   1972   The use and abuse of numerical taxonomy in archaeology. *Archaeology and Physical Anthropology in Oceania* 7:31–49.

Thompson, G. T.
   1978   Prehistoric settlement changes in the southern Northwest Coast: a functional approach. *University of Washington, Reports in Archaeology* 5.
Ward, J. H.
   1963   Hierarchical grouping to optimize an objective function. *American Statistical Association Journal* 58:236–244.
Watanabe, N.
   1950   The preservation of boney substances in the soil of prehistoric sites. *Journal of the Anthropological Society of Nippon* 61:183–190.
Watson, P. J.
   1979   *Archaeological ethnography in western Iran.* University of Arizona Press, Tucson.
Webb, W. S., W. G. Haag, and C. E. Snow
   1942   The C and O mounds at Paintsville. *University of Kentucky Reports in Anthropology and Archaeology* 5(4).
Whallon, R.
   1973a   Spatial analysis of occupation floors: the application of dimensional analysis of variance. In *The explanation of culture change: models in prehistory*, edited by C. Renfrew, pp. 115–130. Gerald Duckworth, London.
   1973b   Spatial analysis of occupation floors I: application of dimensional analysis of variance. *American Antiquity* 38:266–278.
   1974   Spatial analysis of occupation floors II: application of nearest neighbor analysis. *American Antiquity* 39:16–34.
   1979   Unconstrained clustering for analysis of spatial distributions in archaeology. Paper presented at the 44th Annual Meeting of the Society for American Archaeology, 23–25 April, Vancouver, B.C.
Wishart, D.
   1978   CLUSTAN user's manual (third ed.). *Edinburgh University, Program Library Unit, University/Research Council's Series, Reports* 47.

MISSISSIPPIAN SEEN FROM LA TÈNE: ON COMPARISONS OF PREHISTORIC SOCIAL DISORGANIZATIONS[1]

Carl-Axel Moberg

My purpose in writing on Mississippian archaeology, an area in which I have but modest background, is to attempt to provide a different perspective on this important cultural development, one that draws upon my experience in European approaches and materials. To accomplish this goal, I have made comparisons, looking for similarities and differences between Mississippian culture and a field somewhat more familiar to me, La Tène culture. I use "Mississippian" in the broad sense of the term (cf. Smith 1975) rather than as a specific cultural unit. Similarly, La Tène should be understood to encompass an area in Europe, mainly outside the Mediterranean world, and comprising the La Tène period proper as well as the periods immediately before and after it.

Many archaeologists, both European and American, might not regard these two units as at all comparable, and with good reason. First you must imagine La Tène lacking cattle, iron, bronze, silver, gold, swords, cavalry, and war chariots. Then you must appreciate the important differences between maize and the European cereals. Last, but not least, you must recognize the differences between the entirely inland and riverine area of the Mississippian system and the central and eastern parts of Europe where La Tène is at home. With two seacoasts never farther away than the distance between Moundville and the Mississippi delta; with mountain chains separating the plains; and many islands and peninsulas, the La Tène area is certainly quite different geographically. Taking all these differences into account, the prospects for fertile comparisons might not seem very bright.

On the other hand, one might argue like this: we have two areas, both within somewhat comparable climatic ranges; both have food production or—not the least important—combined food-collection and food-production as the economic basis; and both display a broadly parallel north-south zonation. Other similarities include hierarchic settlement patterns with urban-like, often fortified, central places as foci; the obvious importance of warfare; and finally, rather complex symbolic systems and other indications of important, intricate ceremonialism performed by some kind of "priesthood." To these kinds of similarities ought to be added the broadly parallel historical situations of the two traditions. Both were situated north of an area with more sophisticated political organization, writing, monumental stone architecture, and complex art—the Mediterranean civilizations and Mesoamerica. Accordingly, both areas have significant contact situations where reports by Caesar and DeSoto must be read with the same kind of textual criticism.[2] Also parallel is the conflicting evidence supplied by the archaeologically visible realities when compared with either Classical and Medieval descriptions of the societies in Gaul and Ireland or missionary and explorer accounts of aboriginal southeastern United States (Moberg 1975).

LA TÈNE

This is not the place for a systematic presentation of the European "La Tène" culture, since basic information is relatively accessible to American students. However, a few points may be made within the broad usage of La Tène in this paper, especially insofar as this usage differs from the usual view (Filip 1962; Piggot 1965; Powell 1958).

The concept of "La Tène" originates with the Swiss discoveries at La Tène, the real character of which is still somewhat controversial. At that site there were strong indications of warfare, such as the many swords, spears, and a special art style. From the original site, the idea of a "La Tène culture" was generated. As the application of the notion expanded, severe discrepancies appeared. Table 1 summarizes roughly these discrepancies.

Distribution
Monothetically, the nuclear La Tène area is a zone from Burgundy into Czechoslovakia; polythetically, the Marne and southeast England areas might be included. If the distinctive art style is taken as the deciding criterion, La Tène encompasses a much broader area. However, none of these areas coincides geographically with either the historically documented distribution of people named "Celts" (including linguistically

TABLE 1
VARIABILITY IN THE USE OF LA TÈNE,
WESTERN AND CENTRAL EUROPE

Trait	Southeastern England	Marne Northeastern France	Eastern France to Switzerland	East-Central Europe
Warfare				
Arms	X	X	X	X
Forts	X	X	X	X
Chariots	X	X	X	
Art style	X	X	X	X
Graves				
Cemeteries with rank differences	X	X	X	X
Single high rank burials	X		X	

equivalent names), or the distribution of Celtic languages, with which the La Tène culture is often said to be associated.

One should also remember that an even broader perspective can be taken. Areas much farther east display analogous traits. I refer here to what is often called "Scyths" in handbooks, a term which is used as extensively but rather more doubtfully from an archaeological point of view than "Celts." Also one ought to remember the important Dyakovo and Ananyino groups in eastern Europe with their emphasis on fortified settlements. Beyond the Urals there are the southwest Siberian Tagar and Tashtyk groups as well. To sum up, there are La Tène-like patterns in terms of settlement hierarchies, warfare importance, and symbolic systems (often including asymmetrical curvilinearity, human faces, and animals) within one giant zone from the Atlantic to beyond the Yenisei. This distance is considerably greater than that from coast to coast in North America.

Economy

Quite essential aspects of the economic basis will not be discussed here. In fact, it would be pointless to do so because of the gross differences in ecology. In the nuclear La Tène area, comparatively little is known on this subject, too little to apply the concepts of Clay (1976) for instance. Continued analysis will show what the enormous amount of osteological data at the Bavarian fortified site of Manching will tell. There has been much research carried out on agricultural history in England, Denmark, and the island of Gotland in the Baltic; however, the results are too localized for the present comparative purpose. One quite interesting facet, however, is the La Tène preference for ecological "frontier" locations that provide ready access to multiple resources. The environmental mosaic characteristic of Europe offers many more opportunities of this sort than is true of the American Southeast.

Monumental, planned, collective works could suggest redistribution, including "monumental" burial programs even if there is no actual monument, in the usual sense of the word, erected. These works relate to an argument expressed by Peebles and Kus (1977) in their paper on archaeological correlates of ranked societies. In the present state of La Tène research, their requirements for "refinements to the model of chiefdom" can hardly be met. In the case of ceremonial structures, it could be noted that rectangular or quadratic enclosures, certainly ceremonial in nature, which occur in southern Germany seem to have counterparts as far northwest as the English hillforts and cemeteries (Cunliffe 1974). It is likely that there were at least the beginnings of a market economy within the La Tène nuclear area. Coinage is important in this context, although the relative importance of a market economy should not be exaggerated. Of interest here is the obvious importance of salt as a staple ware in Europe long before the La Tène. It is often mentioned, along with iron, in this context and with good justification.

Warfare and "Art"

The coincidence between La Tène "art" and arms or warfare is quite evident as is the central importance of fortifications. Warfare seems to define the La Tène.

Change

Like Mississippian, the La Tène is not internally synchronous. Change is mainly seen as territorial expansion (e.g., Filip 1962). It is obvious why expansion in La Tène is generally interpreted as "migration"—ancient authors described migrations. But did they really know? There has been and will continue to be argument on this issue, but the important thing to consider is that the origin of migrationist interpretations was not archaeological. The general belief in migrations is waning in Europe in recent years. Even the "Battle Axe Peoples" are beginning to disappear from some accounts (e.g., Moberg 1978). Basic questions of continuity and discontinuity are involved. Many years ago I tried to explore this problem (Moberg 1941). This research necessitated an attempt to analyze the idea of gaps in occupation, an issue taken up more recently by Williams (1977). Can the archaeologist know that a region was unoccupied or does the "gap" remain an untestable explanation? In La Tène, as everywhere, we arrive at a common stumbling block. The key we need is demography. But how much demographic data do we have in archaeology?

Change: Displacement of Centers of Gravity

The distribution of La Tène art at opposite ends of its times range is paradoxical. First, around 400 B.C., it is found only in the inner Danube-Rhine area of central Europe—not, for instance, in western France. By A.D. 400 it is no longer found in the Danube-Rhine area; instead it flourishes in southeastern England. By A.D. 1100, the art style is still going strong but now it is found only in Ireland and possibly in the adjacent areas of Scotland and Wales.

These mutually exclusive distributions of La Tène art at different times can be compared with the location of Celtic languages as witnessed by inscriptions (including names in coin inscriptions) and, later, in manuscripts. Initially, the Celtic language is attested only in central Europe. On the other hand, today Gaelic languages are alive only around the Irish Sea and in western France. Again, the distributions are exclusive.

Both distributions could point toward a displacement of centers of gravity from southeast to northwest. But do they, really? Or do they, just as a negative imprint, reflect the expansion of the Roman empire and thus represent survival of relics in marginal areas? The answer is not easy and straightforward.

MISSISSIPPIAN

The nature of my background, especially my concern with European La Tène, has influenced my general view of the Mississippian culture. To identify this influence, the main outline of my understanding of Mississippian is presented first before taking up specific issues.

Mississippian culture does not exist as such in reality apart from the archaeological literature. There does exist, however, an enormous complex of archaeological and ecological data, some portions of which share at least partially common denominators. In broadest outline, this complex consists of one geographically central area and several peripheral or eccentric areas. The Central Area lies within the broad Mississippi alluvial valley from Cairo, Illinois, southward. Treating this region as an area does not preclude important internal differentiation (Brain 1971). The Eccentric Areas lie both within and beyond the Mississippi river system, but outside the Central Area. Included in the Eccentric Area are, for example, Cahokia, Aztalan, Spiro, Moundville, and Etowah. There are several other Eccentric Areas of considerable importance, but the argument has come to focus very much on these five cases. Others, such as the Tennessee-Cumberland area, have been omitted because of my lack of knowledge. In this paper, the Illinois Valley Mississippian is seen as an annex to the Cahokia area.

The overall size of the Mississippian area, between latitudinal and longitudinal extremes such as Belle Pass, Louisiana, and Trempealeau, Wisconsin (Griffin 1960), and between Mount Royal, Florida, and Spiro, Oklahoma, is comparable to a European area from Prague to western Ireland and from the Mediterranean Gulf of Lions to the Baltic Sea. Cultural differentiation over this area is considerable: (1) the "typical" ecological situation of the more central areas seems not to be present in areas such as Etowah (cf. Clay 1976); (2) monumental complexity (i.e., mounds and plazas) is greater at Moundville than in the other areas except for Cahokia where monumental complexity reaches extreme development; (3) mortuary differentiation reaches its highest levels of sophistication at Spiro, Moundville, and Etowah, but seemingly not to the same extent in the Central Area; (4) local "site hierarchy"—so far studied only in a few areas—is present in the Powers phase (Smith 1975: App. D) and in the Moundville phase (Peebles 1971, 1976.) Between these two, there seems to be considerable variability, caused not only by investigatory differences, but also by actual prehistoric differentiation; and (5) fortifications are not uniformly distributed. In this context, and in others, "St. Francis type" sites in the northern portion of the Central Area present special problems. Clay's (1976) suggestion that Mississippian in this area represents a disturbed-reactive situation may be applicable.

In the symbolic realm, one gets the impression that the Long-Nosed God of Early Mississippian[3] is better known from the Eccentric Areas than it is in the Central Area. It is difficult to get a clear impression as to how the Middle Mississippian "Southern Cult" symbols are distributed over the different parts of the Mississippian area. Are they less frequent in the Central Area than in some of the Eccentric Areas (Phillips 1970; Phillips, Ford, and Griffin 1951)?

The history of investigation has created special problems of a kind well known in the archaeological world. Early field research was very much concentrated on the large monuments, the mounds. As a consequence of such biased investigation, considerable parts of the area are virtually "Mesopotamian" in their data base. The concentration on mounds, as on Near Eastern tells, has caused potentially great pitfalls in the interpretation of social organization. This situation is not unknown in the La Tène area either. Traditional emphasis on Late La Tène *oppida* has certainly created erroneous impressions (for Late La Tène, see Crumley 1974; for

Marne, see Rowlett and Pollnac 1971). In the Mississippian area from the 1930s on, the situation began to be counterbalanced in part by the large scale salvage projects. Nonetheless, it is only in those few areas noted above that more reliable settlement studies have been carried out to date.

This spatial variability in Mississippian can be summarized in a matrix (Table 2) and shows that the differences among the several subareas are considerable.

TABLE 2
SPATIAL VARIABILITY IN MISSISSIPPIAN

Trait	Central Area	Powers Phase	Cahokia	Spiro	Mound-ville	Etowah
Ecology	Typical	Typical	Typical?	?	Typical	?
Monumentality	Present	Present	*Maximal*	Present	Maximal	Present
Mortuary differentiation	?	?	Maximal	Maximal	Maximal	Maximal
Settlement hierarchy	Probably	Present	Probably	?	Present	?

THE MAIN PROBLEM: DIACHRONIC KEYWORDS

Diachronic questions are a focal point of this discussion as they were in the 1974 seminar. *Change*, *development*, and *dynamics* are the key terms. This kind of analytic emphasis cannot be pursued for Mississippian as a whole, but only in special situations and from certain points of view. Variability in the kind and quality of the complex data limit this approach. However, in some cases, arguments might be made on possible changes within Mississippian culture. Although important from a theoretical point of view, the origin of Mississippian culture is not considered. Not only would it have greatly expanded the temporal and spatial boundaries of this essay, but its resolution seemingly requires data and approaches not now available.

Transition from Early to Middle Mississippian

A possible change of major importance can be seen in the transition (at least in some of the most important Eccentric Areas) from Early Mississippian, characterized by the Long-Nosed God symbolism, to Middle Mississippian with its traditional "Southern Cult" symbolism, which is closely tied to increased mortuary differentiation. From the special point of view of this observer, this change might be analogous with the emergence of La Tène symbolism with its corresponding ties to mortuary and military differentiation. One gets the impression that major problems in this transition have a differential spatial distribution as suggested by the weaker presence of Middle Mississippian in the Central Area[4] (Phillips 1970; Phillips, Ford, and Griffin 1951).

Disorganization: From Mississippian to its Successors

As interesting as the earlier changes are, major attention here will be concentrated on a third change complex—the one that can be characterized as the decline of the Mississippian and represented by the change from DeSoto's Natchez to the Natchez of the full historic period and the change from Spiro, Cahokia, Moundville, and Etowah to post-Spiro, post-Moundville, post-Etowah, etc. To some extent, this change could represent a process initiated by European contact. On the other hand, in some areas it is clearly initiated before contact, and in other areas there seems to be no evidence of historic contact whatsoever during the entire change.

This is the change characterized by Peebles (1976:46): "...large ceremonial towns surrounded by agricultural villages were replaced by rural communities centered around village square ground.... There was a major change in the spatial distribution of cultural groups.... The occupations along the Tennessee River changed from permanent villages on river islands to semi-permanent villages and camps of transient groups." For the Caddoan area in Texas, Oklahoma, and Arkansas, Woodall (1972:81ff.) discusses the problem of "disappearance of a relatively complex social organization in favor of a simpler one." For the southern portion of the Central Area, Brain (1971) speaks of a "...final period of major displacements, with a broader pattern of a phenomenon, that pulsed at irregular intervals, in different fashions"; whereas further north in the Central Area the decline of the "Ramey State" had already occurred. Perhaps the end of the Powers phase can also be seen as a case in point, despite its narrow time span (Price and Griffin 1979). Such "disorganizatory" changes are the focus of the remainder of this discussion. Disorganization, as used here, does not imply confusion, only restructuring. One kind of organization is replaced by another. I view these changes in Mississippian culture as a set which could be of major and more general interest.

ON GENERALIZING TERMINOLOGIES: LEVELS

To make broad-scale comparisons, a common generalizing language, a system of nomenclature that can be applied to the actual prehistoric societies, must be used. Nomenclatures of this sort, intended to be useful for both anthropologists and archaeologists, are those used by the neo-evolutionists such as Service (1962), Fried (1960, 1967), and Mochon (1972). These concepts have been used sparingly by Mississippian archaeologists. The most important development along these lines (Peebles and Kus 1977) cannot be applied to La Tène culture because the La Tène data lack sufficient detail.

"State" in the Mississippian Area

A real "state" level of social organization is usually only inferred or suggested for Cahokia. Beyond this area a state level of organization is inferred cautiously and sporadically. For example, Sears (1968) interprets not only Cahokia, but also Spiro and other portions of the Caddoan area, Moundville, and Etowah as "states" (cf. Price 1973:143ff.). Peebles 1974:32-37) has analyzed Sears's ideas in a critical way. One could add that *if* there really had been state level social integration within the Mississippian area, then this area might have been one of the few examples of a "pristine state" in Fried's sense, provided one does not see this development as caused by influence from Mesoamerica.

Rank, Stratified, and Chiefdom Levels in the Mississippian Area

The importance of ranking and/or stratification in the different subareas of the Mississippian is more generally appreciated (e.g., Brown 1971; Larson 1971; Toth 1973). For Brown (1971) the "great stratification" of Spiro seems to be the distinctive difference separating pre-Spiro and Spiro. Peebles and Kus (1977) attempt a more thorough analysis of the questions of ranking and/or stratification at Moundville. As a consequence, there seems to be rather clear agreement that Mississippian culture can be identified with the term "chiefdom." Hatch (1974, as quoted in Peebles 1974:54), for example, characterizes the Dallas phase in these terms. Flannery (1972:401) sees Natchez society as chiefdom level.

Societal Terms in Europe: West and East

In recent years, such concepts have been applied with increasing frequency in Old World prehistory, although not in entirely identical ways. For example, in the Aegean world, Renfrew (1972) uses "tribe,"/"chiefdom," and "principality." For Scandinavia, similar terminologies have been used by Clark (1975), Gjessing (1973, 1975), Moberg (1974), Odner (1972, 1973), and Randsborg (1973). The same approach has been used in Southwest Asia (e.g., Hole 1968; Johnson 1973). Of special interest in the present context is the partial application to La Tène by Crumley (1974) and Clarke's (1972) and Cunliffe's (1974) approaches in pre-Roman southwest England.

Other European prehistorians have used different nomenclatures. Even so, these may be seen as clearly evolutionary, with sequences from Savagery through Barbarism to Civilization (e.g., Childe 1942; Clark and Piggott 1965; Piggott 1965). Thus, the corresponding levels in Hallstatt and La Tène with that discussed for Mississippian culture would be within what Piggott (1965) characterized as "barbarian stratified societies" where there is an "office of the king or chieftain." This is the same type of society which is not only "highly stratified," but even "a primitive state" to Crumley (1974). There can be no doubt that these societies were distinctly nonegalitarian (Moberg 1977).

Childe's scheme provides a link to the eastern European, Marxist terminology. However, here one encounters different expressions—the "Primitive-Communal Societal Order" proceeds through "Band" and "Gens" levels. The Gens level has substages. Of these, the last is a level of "Dissolution of the Primitive-Communal Society," regularly comprising traits of a Military Democracy (Avdusin 1977; Otto 1955, 1961; Radig 1955; Sellnow 1961). This terminology has been severely criticized by Maenchen-Helfen (1973). These concepts may seem irrelevant, especially to American archaeologists, but the point is that the inclusion of Eurasia east of Hamburg requires command of this terminology.

A Kinship System of Terminologies

These seemingly different evolutionary terminologies have a common background. All of them can be traced back to Lewis H. Morgan (1877), who is a remote, but not entirely mythical, ancestor. The history of these concepts before Morgan and Darwin is outside the scope of this paper. Common descent of these terminologies opens the possibility of general parallelisms between them. The results of such a comparison can then be checked by comparing their references to ethnographically known societies (e.g., Sellnow 1961; Service 1962). As a result of this analysis, one is entitled to compare evaluations of western and eastern European prehistoric societies with prehistoric societies in America. For example, Service (1962) and Flannery (1972) see Tongan, Hawaiian, Kwakiutl, and Nootka societies as integrated on a chiefdom level. Sellnow (1961) assigns these same societies to the "Period of Decay of the Primitive-Communal Social Order."

The crucial point is that we have a warrant to equate Fried's transition from egalitarian to nonegalitarian societies with Service's tribe to chiefdom transition with the Period of Dissolution of the Primitive-Communal Social Order. As this equation brings a number of archaeologically and ethnographically-known societies together as a single set, its usefulness for comparative studies ought to be investigated. Certainly, one has to be aware that grave concerns may arise at this point among

CHANGE FROM LESS TO MORE EGALITARIAN SOCIETY

Individual Cases

The change from an egalitarian, nonranked, nonstratified level of social integration to the nonegalitarian, ranked and/or stratified level characteristic of Mississippian, essentially the origin of Mississippian, has not been treated. The changes in Final Mississippian do, however, represent a return to the antecedent conditions, a "re-egalitarization" of Mississippian, and it is interesting to compare this change with changes in the same direction in European societies. Certainly, one first thinks of earlier and later periods than the Hallstatt-La Tène. The "Dark Ages" of Western Europe, the "Migration Period" of central and eastern Europe are considered in traditional historical perspectives as standard examples of such social and political disorganization.

Also, to the extent that there are more or less strong tendencies toward a chiefdom organizational level (corresponding to "Military Democracy") in the Bronze Age of northern Europe (a traditional concept recently revitalized by Randsborg with profoundly different techniques) and for the Unetice "culture" in central Europe (Otto 1955), it is also reasonable to expect a certain amount of disorganization after A.D. 1, before the trend is reversed. There are similar indications in the European Iron Age. The dissolution of the Hunsrück-Eifel culture, the society represented by the earlier La Tène cemeteries at Marne, and the eventual decline of central European *oppida* are cases in point (Filip 1956).

This perception again introduces the question of ethnological comparisons. It is interesting to ask if there are cases of transitions from more to less egalitarian levels of social integration known from the ethnographic literature. This kind of "disorganization" seems to have occurred as a reorganization among the Maori when adapting to conditions in the northern areas of New Zealand (Service 1962:137). Thus, in this specific case, an explanation has been suggested which could then be applied in cases where a population had had to adapt to a new environment either as a result of migration (as supposed in the Maori case) or environmental change.

A Digression on Migration

Some remarks on migration hypotheses seem appropriate here in order to explain why migrations are considered outside the scope of this paper.

If our problem is to determine why a change (C_1) occurred in an area (A_1) within a given population (P_1), and it is answered that the change occurred because A_1 was occupied by another population, P_2, then the question has gone unanswered. The problem remains for P_2, the organization of which must have changed in some other area, A_2, to result in the organization they had when they occupied A_1. The question of why this second reorganization took place is beyond the temporal and spatial scope of this paper where isolation of the main problem by eliminating cases with complicating events of this kind is a goal.

In the present perspective—Mississippian as seen from La Tène—meaningful comparisons cannot be made as far as unique events like migrations are involved. Deliberately, I refrain from arguing the applicability, if any, of the "Law of Evolutionary Potential" (Sahlins and Service 1960:93ff.) and keep to factors which promote other general conclusions. No attempt is made either to study possible Mississippian migrations along with traditionally depicted "Celtic Invasions" nor to look at mechanisms possibly causing such migrations.

The Moundville Case

For his special subarea, Peebles (1976:47ff.) discussed four models with differential involvement of ecological and contact factors. For our problem, an especially interesting material implication of one of his models is that "changes in the demographic profile of human populations should precede the introduction of European trade goods" (Peebles 1976:50).

The Caddoan Case

For the Caddoan area, Woodall (1972:87–93) rejects a "cultural exhaustion" theory as untestable and thus considers it unscientific and not useful as an explanatory device. Instead, he discusses three different hypotheses: military defeat, disease, and soil exhaustion. His attempts to test each results in the rejection of both military defeat and disease. He concludes that environmental and demographic pressures caused dispersion into smaller tracts which could not support a managerial elite.

Change from More to Less Egalitarian Levels: A Generalizing View?

Apart from such specific analyses, more general theories of disorganization can be discussed. A claim of special interest for Mississippian culture seems to be one made by Fried (1967:225). He speaks of inherent "great pressures," within stratified society "for its own dissolution and for return to a simple kind of organization." Also, the special role of warfare has to be considered in such a context (e.g., Gibson 1974; Larson 1972). Does Mississippian not provide useful starting points for a closer investigation of Fried's view together with the more special explanations submitted by Peebles and Woodall?

THE IMPORTANCE OF MISSISSIPPIAN CULTURE IN A ONE WORLD ARCHAEOLOGICAL PERSPECTIVE

More than once in these pages there has been good reason to be aware that the very idea of cross-spatial and cross-temporal comparisons is not generally accepted in archaeology. In fact, many European archaeologists may react quite negatively. To these readers, such juxtapositions as those between Mississippian and La Tène are appalling. A long list of negative assessments of this approach could be cited, extending from long before Merhart's famous declaration in 1931, up to Hogarth (1972), Waterbolk (1974), and Jankuhn (1969).

We are on the division between archaeology with anthropological ambitions and ideographic, particularizing archaeologies. The view taken here is that if it is unacceptable to attempt to apply universal concepts, then *archaeology* does not exist, only *archaeologies* do. But if such attempts are to be acceptable, then we need generalizing concepts and terminologies as vehicles for comparison and critical argument.

The types of concepts and terminologies mainly discussed and used in this paper are generally considered to be closely related to evolutionary concepts by their authors. This is not necessarily and exclusively so. They can be useful even without the implications of evolutionary mechanisms determining transitions. The acceptance of typologies current among neo-evolutionists—as they have been used in this paper—does not imply acceptance of their evolutionary explanatory concepts as well.

In traditional archaeology, not the least in Europe, there are clear tendencies to believe in some sort of evolutionism without, however, a corresponding belief in the value of generalization. On the other side, one can find instances of a positive attitude toward generalization linked with a negative view of evolution in archaeology (e.g., Rouse 1972:191–236). The view taken in the preceding pages is that one ought to attempt to use the "level" terminology insofar as it seems, useful and then test the underlying evolutionary concepts in a critical way.

If the so-called "reverse" transitions such as those discussed here are regarded as acceptable by the neo-evolutionists (cf. Fried 1967:115), then it seems that the situations noted for the Mississippian culture could offer important analytic opportunities for evolutionary ideas in general. After all, it can be seen as something of a paradox that our discipline, which is conceptually better equipped to study declines and even collapses, should be expected to explain origins, beginnings, and genesis. The study of "reverse" movements is especially important for arguments about evolution today because of the recent transformations in biological concepts.

The idea of a broadly-conceived Mississippian tradition should have an enormously important place in the development of regional American archaeology. But the latent importance of the concept in a more general perspective should not be underrated. I have tried to emphasize one possible element of Mississippian, changing levels of integration, where Mississippian seems to provide very good fuel for constructive debate. This outsider has not only become spellbound by this fascinating complex, but also has been convinced that scholars studying other cultural units, such as La Tène, should watch the continuing research on Mississippian because it can be expected to contribute to general insight in patterns of mutual interest, even for temporally and spatially distant prehistoric populations. It seems to me that energetic pursuit of research on the Mississippian culture, especially in view of the emergency situation caused by rapid site destruction, is a desideratum of high priority for a One World Archaeology.

Notes

1. This article is based on a paper of the same title presented at the Advanced Seminar, "Reviewing Mississippian Development: A Study in the Dynamics of Cultural Growth in the Eastern United States," held at the School of American Research, Santa Fe, NM, November 10–16, 1974. I am indebted to the School of American Research and its Director, Dr. Douglas W. Schwartz and the symposium chair, Dr. Stephen Williams. Appreciation is also extended to the University of Alabama, especially Professor David L. DeJarnette and Dr. Paul H. Nesbitt. The northern European research for this manuscript was carried out for the program "Forms of Society in Northern Europe 1500 B.C.–A.D. 500" in the Department of Archaeology, University of Gothenberg. Since the original presentation, this paper has been revised twice, once in 1978 and again in preparation for this publication. Over this period of time, several changes have taken place in the understanding of La Tène. Except for critical points, I have not attempted to revise the presentation of La Tène here. I am anxious to emphasize that were I to review anew La Tène for an American audience, it would not be identical with the one presented in Santa Fe and, in large part, published here. Sincere thanks are due to Professor Robert C. Dunnell, for his much appreciated revision and editing.

2. It might even be suggested that one ought to look for possible indirect influences from Caesar's account of the Gaulish war on the accounts of the DeSoto expedition. Did these authors know "The Gaulish War?" Was their image of a Cacique masked by their image of a Vercingetorix?

3. I use "Early Mississippian" for that period prior to A.D. 1200, "Middle Mississippian" for the period A.D. 1200 to A.D. 1300, and "Final Mississippian" for fifteenth century manifestations, roughly corresponding to the "Pan-Southern Iconographic System" periods I-III of the 1974 Sante Fe conference.

4. At least, this is the impression I have formed as an "outsider" in Mississippian archaeology.

REFERENCES

Avdusin, D. A.
   1977   *Arkheologija SSSR* (second ed.). Vysshaya shkola, Moskva.

Brain, J. P.
   1971   *The Lower Mississippi Valley in North American prehistory*. National Park Service, Southeast Region, Atlanta.

Brown, J. A.
   1971   The dimensions of status in the burials at Spiro. In Approaches to the social dimensions of mortuary practices, edited by J.A. Brown, pp. 92–112. *Society for American Archaeology, Memoir* 25.

Childe, V. G.
   1942   *What happened in history*. Penguin, Harmondsworth.

Clarke, D. L.
   1972   A provisional model of an Iron Age society and its settlement system. In *Models in archaeology*, edited by D. L. Clarke, pp. 801–869. Methuen, London.

Clark, G.
   1975   *The earlier Stone Age settlement of Scandinavia*. Cambridge University Press, Cambridge.

Clark, G., and S. Piggott
   1965   *Prehistoric societies*. Hutchinson, London.

Clay, R. B.
   1976   Tactics, strategy, and operations: the Mississippian system responds to its environment. *Mid-Continental Journal of Archaeology* 1:137–162.

Crumley, C. L.
   1974   Celtic social structure: the generation of archaeologically testable hypotheses from literary evidence. *University of Michigan, Museum of Anthropology, Anthropological Papers* 54.

Cunliffe, B.
   1974   *Iron Age communities in Britain. An account of England, Scotland and Wales from the seventh century B.C. until the Roman conquest*. Routledge and Kegan Paul, London.

Filip, J.
   1956   Keltové v střední Evropě. Zusammenfassung: Die Kelten in Mitteleuropa. *Monumenta Archaeologica* 5.
   1962   *Celtic civilisation and its heritage*. Academia, Prague.

Flannery, K. V.
   1972   The cultural evolution of civilizations. *Annual Review of Ecology and Systematics* 3:399–426.

Fried, M. H.
   1960   On the evolution of social stratification and the state. In *Culture in history, essays in honor of Paul Radin*, edited by S. Diamond, pp. 713–731. Columbia University Press, New York.
   1967   *The evolution of political society*. Random House, New York.

Gibson, J. L.
   1974   Aboriginal warfare in the protohistoric Southeast: an alternative perspective. *American Antiquity* 39:130–133.

Gjessing, G.
   1973   *Norge i Sameland*. H. Aschehoug, Oslo.
   1975   Socio-archaeology. *Current Anthropology* 16:323–341.

Griffin, J. B.
   1960   A hypothesis for the prehistory of the Winnebago. In *Culture in history, essays in honor of Paul Radin*, edited by S. Diamond, pp. 809–865. Columbia University Press, New York.

Hogarth, G. A.
   1972   Common sense in archaeology. *Antiquity* 46:301–304.

Jankuhn, H.
1969   Vor- und frühgeschichte vom neolithikum bis zur völkerwanderungszeit. *Deutsche agrargeschichte*, Vol. 1, edited by G. Franz. Ulmer, Stuttgart.

Johnson, G. A.
1973   Local exchange and early state development in southeastern Iran. *University of Michigan, Museum of Anthropology, Anthropological Papers* 51.

Hole, F.
1968   Evidence of social organization from western Iran, 8000–4000 B.C. In *New perspectives in archeology*, edited by S. R. Binford and L. R. Binford, pp. 245–265. Aldine, Chicago.

Larson, L. H., Jr.
1971   Archaeological implications of social stratification at the Etowah site, Georgia. In Approaches to the social dimensions of mortuary practices, edited by J. A. Brown, pp. 58–67. *Society for American Archaeology, Memoir* 25.
1972   Functional considerations of warfare in the Southeast during the Mississippi period. *American Antiquity* 37:383–392.

Maenchen-Helfen, J. O.
1973   *The world of the Huns: studies in their history and culture.* University of California Press, Berkeley.

Merhart von Bernegg, G.
1931   Urgeschichte als geschichtswissenschaft. *Mitteilungen Universitätsbund Marburg* (1931):1–9.

Moberg, C. -A.
1941   *Zonengliederungen der vorchristlichen eisenzeit in Nordeuropa.* Gleerup, Lund.
1974   Comments on economic structures in the Iron Age. *Norwegian Archaeological Review* 7:117–121.
1975   Anthropologists on archaeology. *Ethnos* 40:360–364.
1977   La Tène and types of society in Scandinavia. In *Ancient Europe and the Mediterranean. Studies presented in honour of Hugh Hencken*, edited by V. Markotic, pp. 115–120. Aris and Phillips, Warminster.
1978   Some developments in north European prehistory in the period 1968–1976. *Norwegian Archaeological Review* 11:6–16.

Mochon, M. J.
1972   Language, history and prehistory: Mississippian lexico-reconstruction. *American Antiquity* 37:478–503.

Morgan, L. H.
1877   *Ancient society or researches in the lines of human progress from savagery through barbarism to civilization.* Holt, New York.

Odner, K.
1972   Ethno-historic and ecological settings for economic and social models of an Iron Age society: Valldalen, Norway. In *Models in archaeology*, edited by D. L. Clarke, pp. 623–651. Methuen, London.
1973   Økonomiske strukturer på Vestlandet i eldre jernalder. Summary. (mimeo). Historisk Museum, Universitetet i Bergen, Bergen.

Otto, K. -H.
1955   Die sozial-ökonomischen verhältnisse bei den stämmen der leubinger kultur in mitteldeutschland. *Ethnographisch-archäologische Forschungen* 3(1).
1961   *Deutschland in der epoche der urgesellschaft.* Deutscher Verlag der Wissenschaften, Berlin.

Peebles, C. S.
1971   Moundville and surrounding sites: some structural considerations of mortuary practices. In Approaches to the social dimensions of mortuary practices, edited by J. A. Brown, pp. 68–91. *Society for American Archaeology, Memoir* 25.
1974   Moundville: the organization of a prehistoric community and culture. Ph.D. Dissertation, Department of Anthropology, University of California, Santa Barbara.
1976   Untitled manuscript on file with the University of Michigan, Ann Arbor.

Peebles, C. S., and S. Kus
　1977　Some archaeological correlates of ranked societies. *American Antiquity* 42:421–443.
Phillips, P.
　1970　Archaeological survey in Lower Yazoo Basin, Mississippi, 1949–1955. *Papers of the Peabody Museum of Archaeology and Ethnology* 60.
Phillips, P., J. A. Ford, and J. B. Griffin
　1951　Archaeological survey in the Lower Mississippi alluvial valley, 1940–1947. *Papers of the Peabody Museum of American Archaeology and Ethnology* 25.
Piggott, S.
　1965　*Ancient Europe from the beginnings of agriculture to classical antiquity.* University Press, Edinburgh.
Powell, T. G. E.
　1958　*The Celts.* Thames and Hudson, London.
Price, J. E.
　1973　Settlement planning and artifact distribution on the Snodgrass site and their socio-political implications in Powers phase of Southeast Missouri. Ph.D. dissertation, Department of Anthropology, University of Michigan.
Price, J. E., and J. B. Griffin
　1979　The Snodgrass site of the Powers phase of Southeast Missouri. *University of Michigan, Museum of Anthropology, Anthropological Papers* 66.
Radig, W.
　1955　*Die siedlungstypen in Deutschland und ihre frühgeschichtlichen wurzeln.* Henschelverlag, Berlin.
Randsborg, K.
　1973　Wealth and social structure as reflected in the Bronze Age burials—a quantitative approach. In *The explanation of culture change: models in prehistory*, edited by C. Renfrew, pp. 565–570. Duckworth, London.
Renfrew, C.
　1972　*The emergence of civilisation. The Cyclades and the Aegean in the third millennium B.C.* Methuen, London.
Rouse, I.
　1972　*Introduction to prehistory. A systematic approach.* MacGraw-Hill, New York.
Rowlett, R. M., and R. B. Pollnac
　1971　Multivariate analysis of Marnian La Tène cultural groups. In *Mathematics in the archaeological and historical sciences*, edited by F. R. Hodson, D. G. Kendall, and P. Tăutu, pp. 46–58. University Press, Edinburgh.
Sahlins, M. D., and E. R. Service (editors)
　1960　*Evolution and culture.* University of Michigan Press, Ann Arbor.
Sears, W.
　1968　The state and settlement patterns in the New World. In *Settlement archaeology*, edited by K. C. Chang, pp. 134–153. National Press, Palo Alto.
Sellnow, I.
　1961　*Grundprinzipien einer periodisierun der urgeschichte, ein beitrag auf grund ethnographischen materials.* Akademie-Verlag, Berlin.
Service, E. R.
　1962　*Primitive social organization, an evolutionary perspective* (second ed.). Random House, New York.
Smith, B. D.
　1975　Middle Mississippi exploitation of animal populations. *University of Michigan, Museum of Anthropology, Anthropological Papers* 57.
Toth, A.
　1973　Mississippian developments in the Tennessee-Cumberland area. (mimeo).
Waterbolk, H. T.
　1974　L'archéologie en Europe: une réaction contre la "New Archaeology." *Helinium* 14:135–162.

Williams, S.
    1977   Some ruminations on the current strategy of archaeology in the Southeast. Paper presented at the Annual Meeting of the Southeastern Archaeological Conference, 28 October, 1977, Lafayette.
Woodall, J. N.
    1972   *An introduction to modern archaeology.* Schenkman, Cambridge, Massachusetts.

A QUANTITATIVE APPROACH TO CULTURE CHANGE: THE DELAWARE INDIANS AS AN ETHNOHISTORIC CASE STUDY[1]

David A. Baerreis

Culture change is a common focus of concern shared by anthropologists of a variety of persuasions, archaeologists, ethnologists, and even applied anthropologists. From an archaeological perspective where the enumeration and tabulation of items of material culture have fostered a quantitative approach based upon the analysis of gradual change, there has often seemed to be a marked discontinuity between the data of archaeology and ethnology. Ethnology has tended to focus more upon qualitative aspects, an approach which may indeed bias the formulation of a comprehensive body of theory. It is suggested here, however, that in ethnohistoric data one can find information that serves to test the accuracy and reliability of archaeological information pertaining to the historic period and provides a link between archaeology and the ethnological present. To illustrate the potential of this approach and some of the methodological problems, culture change among the Delaware Indians in the early nineteenth century is described. The material providing the archaeology-ethnology link is the records of the trading posts, the lists of sales and purchases that permit one to tabulate the importance of those items of material culture and subsistence procured through such economic transactions.

The Delaware Indians, today resident in Oklahoma and merged with the Cherokee tribe, are the consolidated remnants of a group once occupying portions of the present states of Delaware, Pennsylvania and New York and all of New Jersey. Though not then a unified tribal group, they were the first peoples to become involved in trade with the Swedes and Dutch, transactions which included the noted sale of New York's

Manhattan Island and subsequently the land purchases of William Penn. Continued pressure on their territory and unsuccessful competition with the Iroquois were important factors that drove the Delawares westward. In Ohio, early in the eighteenth century, the Delawares evolved as a political entity. Yet even this development of more complex and unified political institutions did not prevent a repetition of their initial exodus from the east as their ultimate forced removal to the Plains region demonstrates. However, this long period of contact with European and American culture has some positive benefits in that the changes in Delaware culture are recorded in various descriptive accounts and the history of the Delaware people comprises one of the important case studies available to the student of culture change.

One of the most comprehensive studies of culture change among the Delaware Indians is that of W. W. Newcomb, Jr. (1956). Utilizing a diverse series of sources, he described change in terms of four sequent periods beginning with a Contact period initiated in 1524 and terminating with the close of a Decadent period in 1867. While Newcomb based his study on an excellent series of eyewitness accounts, both published and in manuscript, trading post records might have been utilized more intensively. Records of traders and trading posts yield quantifiable data on changing patterns of Indian purchases which would seem to be a useful check on verbal, descriptive accounts. Purchases spanning two of Newcomb's acculturative periods during the nineteenth century are analyzed here. It must be clearly indicated, however, that it is not the intent of the preceding statements to imply that Newcomb's study neglects to consider the impact of the trader or fails to document the kinds of goods the Delawares received. To the contrary, such matters are treated with skill and form an integral part of his analysis. Indeed, it is the very indication of the importance of such factors that justifies a more detailed, quantitative analysis of the trading records. The results of this study only supplement rather than in any way supplant the type of analysis made by Newcomb and seem congruent with his interpretation.

NINETEENTH-CENTURY PHASES OF DELAWARE CULTURE CHANGE

The time span for which we have attempted an analysis of selected trading post records spans the transition between two of the periods of culture change outlined by Newcomb (1956:87–105). Before discussing the trader's records, some background is provided through a summary of the characteristics of the relevant periods in Newcomb's analysis. The first he designates the Nativistic period (1750–1814).

Newcomb describes how the Delawares "... by the opening of this period had risen, Phoenix-like, from the ashes of their subjugations and removal and had forged themselves into a tribe which was able to defy the Six Nations and the Europeans" (1956:87). But while this was a period of militarism, they were notably unsuccessful in their wars in that they aligned themselves with the loser or were themselves defeated in each of these actions. Military defeat was coupled with increasing American pressure aimed toward the alienation of their lands, a pressure which reached a climax after the War of 1812 even though in this affair the Delawares remained neutral.

The Nativistic period was also one of marked social disorganization, accompanying excessive use of alcohol and frequent food shortages. The greater stress on acquisition of fur-bearing animals led to a decline both in gardening and the hunting of food animals such as deer. The inability of the Delawares to resolve their problems in a practical fashion led to the appearance of various prophets from about 1750 to 1812. Preaching various ritual techniques by which the presumed "Golden Age" of former times could be restored, the prophets rejected Christianity and most elements of American culture.

Following the military defeats and unsuccessful religious revivals of the prophets, Newcomb defines another phase of acculturation which he designates the Decadent period (1814–67). In this phase, pressure was placed upon the Delaware to shift to a farming economy and assimilation of American technology was thorough. After the conclusion of the treaty of peace between the United States and England in 1814, the Delawares were dominated politically and militarily by the Americans. Pressure was exerted, not only to become "civilized" Americans but also to sell their land in Indiana and move west of the Mississippi River. The land sale was accomplished by a treaty in 1818 and by 1820 the westward movement had begun, the Indiana Delaware joining relatives who had previously moved to Missouri taking up residence on the headwaters of White River. This earlier faction of the Delaware had moved to this area with the permission of the Spanish government residing on lands assigned to them by the Spanish governor at Saint Louis on January 4, 1793 (Weslager 1972:353). The historian Louis Houck (1980:217–218) indicates the Delaware specifically had villages on White River as early as 1806.

DELAWARE PURCHASES

In an earlier study (Baerreis 1961), a tabulation was made of Delaware purchases and annuity goods selected at the Federal Factory located at Fort Wayne, Indiana, between 1804 and 1806. We may compare these purchases with those made in the years 1829-31 (Table 1). The figures for the latter period are based on a day book, Ledger Book A, of the firm of Menard and Vallé comprising the White River Outfit of the American Fur Company.[2] The ledger indicates the location of the outfit, or trading group, as being on the James Fork of White River. These purchases were made shortly before the last of the groups were to leave Missouri for a new reservation in Kansas.

Some explanation of items in Table 1 is needed. The actual purchase price of all items is not recorded in the ledgers. Often only an unpaid balance, that is the difference between the value of furs turned in to the trader in exchange for the goods selected and the actual cost of an item, is given. One may note that the first purchase listed at White River in 1829-30 is one horse at $7.00. Even though the prices were in many instances below the levels of today, it was not possible to purchase a horse for $7.00 in 1829. At Bertrand's trading post in Michigan, for example, horses were sold to Potawatomi Indians in 1833 and 1834 for from $30.00 to $80.00 each. Such a range in price indicates the difficulty involved if an attempt were made to convert statements of a balance due to the original figure involved, when the ledger records only the amount owed the trader by the individual involved. While an average cost for such an item as a horse could be computed, it has seemed appropriate to retain the partial credits. Presumably a random distribution of partial purchases in each category is preserved even though it is to be expected that many transactions are not recorded at all when sufficient pelts were provided to cover the cost of the goods. To provide a partial check on the reliability of the dollar figures, the number in parentheses following the value of an item is the number of units of a particular item sold when this can be ascertained.

Since the purpose of this paper is more an illustrative treatment of the utility of trading post purchases than an exhaustive analysis of Delaware culture change, comparisons are restricted to these two sets of records pertaining to the Indians. While one may assume that these are a random selection of Indian purchases and that the portion of their income spent for particular categories of goods is fairly shown, one can not assume that this represents the total volume of their participation in a cash economy. For this purpose it would be essential to ascertain whether more than one trader had stationed himself near their permanent villages or whether some purchases were made at greater distances from their home community. Different traders might well have had a slightly different stock of goods available for the Indian also.

One further column in Table 1, Kaskaskia—1830, requires discussion. To properly evaluate the significance of Delaware purchases from the traders, some basis of comparison with non-Indian purchases during the same period must be available. Over any period of time, if only through the action of changing fashion, the pattern of purchases will shift. Without a basis of comparison with non-Indian purchases, how can we evaluate whether changes over time represent a growing accommodation to White patterns or, alternatively, an even greater deviation? Ideally such a comparison would involve non-Indian purchases in the same general region and covering the same time span. Indeed, just as there are indications in Newcomb's study that the time span involved was a critical time period in regard to change for the Delaware, so too it may have been for the non-Indian. Frederick Gerhard in writing his gazetteer of the state of Illinois in 1856 states:

> During the years from 1820 to 1830, a great change took place in the appearance and modes of dressing of the people. The coon-skin cap, the hunting-shift, and leather breeches, the moccasins, and the belt around the waist, to which the butcher-knife and tomahawk were appended, had entirely disappeared before the modern clothing apparel. The women had exchanged their cotton and woolen frocks, manufactured, and striped with blue dye, by themselves, for modern dresses of silk and calico; they had laid aside the cotton handkerchiefs, which formerly covered their heads, and adopted bonnets instead; they would not, as formerly, walk barefooted to church, but would often be seen riding on fine horses to the house of worship. [Gerhard 1847:66]

Finding appropriate records to span the particular time period and in the appropriate place may present some difficulties. Where the Indian groups reside in an area set aside for their exclusive use, no directly comparable records for precisely the same region may exist. Obviously one can only select as close an area as possible and make the selection with some consideration for community size and complexity of the social unit. Use here has been made of a sample of purchases for the year 1830 from Day Book "F" of the firm of Menard & Vallé of Kaskaskia, Illinois.[3] The sample, tabulated from each odd page in the ledger also excludes transactions with Indians and the Indian Department as well as the records of wholesale purchases by the firm. It might be argued that Kaskaskia on the Mississippi River in southern Illinois is a rather distant region for comparison with the White River in Missouri but it does have in its favor that it represents the same firm that is trading with the Delaware and they thus could potentially draw on any item in their stock that would seem useful or was wanted in the Indian trade. Perhaps a greater objection to the use of Kaskaskia than distance is that as one of the more important settlements of the region at this time period, a comparison with settlements of a more frontier character would have been appropriate. Despite these limitations the Kaskaskia purchases serve as a starting point and reminder that a thorough quantitative analysis would include a parallel study of non-Indian as well as Indian sources. Commercial records of general stores are, of course, even more readily available in manuscript collections than are the Indian trader's accounts.

In preparing Table 1, which itemizes the purchases, individual items are grouped into categories such as Horse Complex, Clothing, Food, etc. The intent in such groupings is to secure meaningful cultural categories which might reveal trends as grouped units. Specific items that are purchased might vary on grounds of stylistic preference, fashion trends or technological improvement, while the given category remains stable. Alternatively the total quantity of items within a category might reveal significant trends. How broad or how narrow the categories should be can perhaps best be established by trial and error. The items purchased are listed by the name which appears on the records. The meanings of these are generally self-evident and while in some cases more modern terms could be substituted (e.g., spittoon for spitting box or wallpaper for hanging paper), leaving them in their original form prevents the possible introduction of error at this level of organization. While generally an unabridged dictionary will list obsolete words, an early or contemporary dictionary is often useful. Some entries are not sufficiently explicit for categorization with certainty. Is a "shoe hammer" equipment for the blacksmith working with horseshoes or part of the equipment of a shoemaker? In a few instances, as an aid to the reader, a suggested identification or clarification is inserted in brackets following the original term.

A comparison of the Indian purchases between 1804–06 and 1829–31 reveals some interesting differences. In the horse complex, substantial numbers of horseshoes are purchased in the latter time yet do not appear to have been utilized in the earlier period. The addition of the use of horseshoes by the Indian may be an example of further acculturation in the horse complex bringing Indian techniques of horse utilization closer to White practices. It is possible, however, that the impact of a new environment brought about by the transfer of their residence to Missouri might have made horseshoes more necessary. In the hunting complex an important addition is the large increase in the number of traps. In this instance, as in some other categories, it is clear that the jump from zero to sixty traps requires some qualification. We know from the diaries of the Moravian missionaries in the White River area of Indiana that traps were in use by the Delawares as early as 1803 (Gipson 1938:265). One further problem that arises in relation to the records presented for these two periods is that the Fort Wayne transactions represent purchases or presents given at the time of annuity payments at the Indian agency some distance from the Delaware Indian settlements. No record has been

TABLE 1
DELAWARE PURCHASES AT TRADING POSTS COMPARED WITH NON-INDIAN PURCHASES AT KASKASKIA, ILLINOIS

Purchase Category	DELAWARE			NON-INDIAN
	Ft. Wayne 1804–06	White River 1829–30		Kaskaskia 1830
Horse complex:				
Horses ["balance" at White River]	—	7.00[1] (1)[2]		127.50 (2)
Saddles	22.50 (11)	88.50 (7)		34.00 (2)
Bridles	22.50 (11)	63.50 (16)		7.63 (7)
Surcingles	8.00 (8)	15.00 (10)		1.63 (2)
Spurs, pr.	—	4.50 (2)		—
Stirrups, pr.	1.00 (1)	9.00 (3)		2.63 (2)
Saddle bags, pr.	8.50 (2)	12.00 (3)		—
Horseshoes, pr.	—	28.50 (54)		—
Bells	—	13.75 (8)		8.00 (12)
Shoe rasp	—	—		.25 (1)
Shoe hammer	—	—		.32 (1)
Curry combs	—	—		.25 (2)
Waggon whips	—	—		1.38 (2)
Trace chains, pr.	—	—		7.50 (5)
Cart wheels, pr.	—	—		35.00 (1)
Horse collars	—	—		2.00 (2)
Wheel pins, set	—	—		.31 (1)
Cart boxes, set	—	—		.75 (1)
	$ 62.50	241.75		229.15
Hunting equipment, etc.:				
Rifles	28.00 (2)	218.00 (12)		—
Gun locks	9.75 (4)	18.00 (4)		—
Gun stock	—	5.00 (1)		—

TABLE 1 (continued)

Purchase Category	DELAWARE Ft. Wayne 1804–06	DELAWARE White River 1829–30	NON-INDIAN Kaskaskia 1830
Flints	5.00 (125)	15.00 (720)	—
Powder, lb.	25.00 (25)	335.25 (335)	7.65 (15)
Lead, lb.	18.50 (74)	135.25 (797)	.63
Traps	—	374.88 (60)	—
Beaver baits	—	10.00	—
Ball, box	—	—	—
Shot	—	.50 (9)	8.29
Fish hooks	—	—	.13
	$ 76.25	1,111.88	16.70
Other equipment:			
Knife	.38 (1)	28.50 (43)	2.94 (9)
Butcher knife	—	18.25 (24)	.25 (1)
"Indian skinner" knife	2.00 (6)	42.25 (31)	—
"Damask" knife [Damascus knife]	—	3.75 (4)	—
Pen knives	—	.88 (2)	7.00 (10)
Pocket knives	—	—	1.50 (5)
Shoemaker's knife	—	—	.13 (1)
Drawing knife	—	—	1.00 (1)
Hoes	3.00 (2)	—	1.63 (2)
Small tomahawk	—	4.00 (4)	—
Axes	—	—	23.00 (9)
Axe handles	—	—	.50 (2)
Iron/steel	—	11.00	52.65
Nails, brass	—	.25	—

QUANTITATIVE APPROACH TO CULTURE CHANGE 193

Nails, iron			40.54
Screws			1.30
Log chain			5.00 (1)
Handsaw			1.75 (1)
Files			2.88 (8)
Scythe			3.50 (2)
Oil Stone			.94 (1)
Foot adze			1.25 (1)
Hinges, pr.			1.41 (5)
Bitts			8.88
Shovels			5.00 (5)
Spades			4.00 (4)
Thumb latches			1.75 (3)
Lock		1.00 (1)	12.88 (8)
Bolt			.19 (1)
Augers			3.13
Iron sledge hammer			1.95 (1)
Chisels			8.17
Gimblet			.57
Spikes			.68
Oakum			16.50
Brass latches			1.50 (2)
Planks			26.99
Glass panes			6.88
Bellows			28.00 (1)
Tar			9.25
Rosin			.69
Indigo			3.38
Spanish burnt madder [also for dyeing]			.25
Tacks			.31
Ploughs			73.11
	$ 5.38	109.88	363.23

TABLE 1 (continued)

Purchase Category	DELAWARE Ft. Wayne 1804–06	DELAWARE White River 1829–30	NON-INDIAN Kaskaskia 1830
Household equipment:			
Brass kettles	47.50 (48#)	33.00 (5)	6.50
Tin/iron kettles	10.75 (11)	7.25 (4)	2.50 (2)
Tin cups	1.50 (3)	—	—
Tin pans	1.50 (3)	3.63 (5)	—
Pewter basin	2.50 (1)	—	—
Dipper	—	.38 (1)	—
Large bun box	—	1.00 (1)	—
Bottles	—	1.00 (3)	2.81 (3)
Bag	—	1.00 (1)	—
Trunk	—	13.00 (2)	8.65 (3)
Canteen	.75 (1)	—	—
Coffee pot	—	1.00 (1)	2.63 (3)
Pitcher	—	1.00 (1)	1.88 (2)
Coffee mill	—	—	.32
Cream jug	—	—	—
Salt cellars	—	—	1.00 (4)
Sugar bowl/plates/dishes/ bowls/cups & saucers	—	—	16.55
Glasses/tumblers/mugs	—	—	13.38
Churn	—	—	1.00 (1)
Hanging paper, pc.	—	—	1.31 (3)
Pots & pans	—	—	5.50 (5)
Shovels & tongs, pr.	—	—	4.00 (2)
Snuffer & tongs	—	—	.75 (1)

Brooms/brushes	—	—	4.01 (9)
Skillet	—	—	1.07 (1)
Sieve	—	—	1.25 (1)
Jars	—	—	3.18 (4)
Candle sticks	—	—	.38 (1)
Bed cords	—	—	4.12 (14)
Chamber pot	—	—	.75 (2)
Spitting box	—	—	.50 (1)
Faucet	—	—	.13 (1)
Hand irons, pr. [andirons]	—	—	2.44 (1)
Knives/forks/spoons	—	—	15.50
Tea pots	—	—	2.00 (2)
Oven	—	—	2.38 (1)
Lantern	—	—	.88 (2)
Oil cloth	—	—	.94
	$ 64.50	62.26	107.93
Personal Ornaments, etc.:			
Broaches, clasp	—	29.00 (17)	.50 (1)
Ear bobs	—	49.75 (481)	—
Ear wheels, pr.	—	2.00 (2)	—
Gorget (half moon)	—	12.00 (1)	—
Mending half moon	—	1.13 (1)	—
Head (hat) bands	—	34.00 (7)	—
Arm bands, pr.	—	43.00 (7)	—
Wrist bands, pr.	—	35.00 (14)	—
Rings (box)	—	3.00 (1)	—
Vermillion/"paint"	—	14.75	—
Looking glasses	1.00 (1)	4.25 (10)	—
Combs	—	11.75 (35)	15.51 (42)
Feathers	3.50 (3)	14.50 (25)	—

TABLE 1 (continued)

Purchase Category	DELAWARE Ft. Wayne 1804–06	DELAWARE White River 1829–30	NON-INDIAN Kaskaskia 1830
Wampum	1.50	10.75	—
Beads/necklaces	—	4.50	1.63
Spectacles & case	—	5.75 (1)	.88 (1)
Cologne water	—	—	.38
Watch string	—	—	.50 (1)
Waist buckles	—	—	.75 (1)
Hair broom	—	—	.75 (1)
	$ 6.00	275.13	20.90
Clothing, cloth, etc.:			
Hats	13.00 (4)	15.50 (4)	32.63 (21)
Leggings	13.50 (7)	15.00 (8)	—
Shirts	12.50 (6)	188.75 (151)	3.00
Shirt patterns	21.50 (11)	—	.75 (1)
Handkerchiefs [worn as kerchiefs]	53.75 (54)	38.63 (61)	24.96 (47)
Shawls	29.00 (29)	120.00 (54)	1.00 (1)
Blankets	360.50 (129)	640.44 (122)	37.00 (8)
Moccasins, pr.	5.00 (3)	2.50 (10)	.50 (2)
Shoes/boots	—	42.25 (22)	135.25 (90)
Belts	1.00 (2)	—	2.94 (3)
Breech cloth	—	47.75 (47)	—
Cloth, yard goods	1,038.82	591.82	633.55
Binding/tape/piping	—	1.25	2.64
Ribbon	1.00	54.50	9.44
Needles (doz.)	—	5.50 (22)	.53
Scissors, pr.	—	6.50 (13)	.75 (1)
Thread/silk	.48	9.10	14.60

Stockings/socks	16.25 (7)	1.50 (2)	14.88 (24)
Gloves/mittens	—	—	4.62 (9)
Thimbles	—	—	.44 (3)
Buttons	—	—	9.17
Coat/capes	—	—	13.25 (5)
Dressed skins	1.50 (1)	11.00 (14)	7.15 (10)
Shoe blacking	—	—	1.00
Suspenders, pr.	—	—	1.63 (4)
Parasol	—	—	5.25 (2)
Knitted drawers, pr.	—	—	2.00 (2)
Pins	—	—	.38
Silk cravat	—	—	3.50 (2)
Hooks & eyes	—	—	.63
Knitting pins	—	—	.38
Spun Cotton	—	—	5.50
Awls	—	—	.13
Buffalo robes	—	—	15.00
Making pantaloons	—	—	2.00
Mending coat	—	—	.50
Bobbins, doz.	—	—	.38 (1)
Cotton/wool cards	—	—	1.38
	$1,567.80	1,791.99	988.71
Food, condiments, etc.:			
Coffee (lb.)	1.00 (.5)	2.00 (6)	9.67
Tea (lb.)	.50 (.5)	—	25.63
Sugar (lb.)	1.25 (4.5)	2.00 (14)	143.65
Chocolate	—	—	1.00
Beef	—	—	18.24
Pork	—	—	55.78
Venison	—	—	.38
"Mackrels"	—	—	7.50

TABLE 1 (continued)

Purchase Category	DELAWARE		NON-INDIAN
	Ft. Wayne 1804–06	White River 1829–30	Kaskaskia 1830
Flour (lb.)	—	7.00 (67)	85.38
Rice	—	—	1.38
Cheese	—	—	5.25
Butter	—	—	1.50
Corn/corn meal	—	3.00	3.61
Salt (qt.)	3.50 (14)	22.00 (132)	106.37
Pepper	—	1.25	2.00
Ginger	—	—	.44
Spice	—	.25	—
Allspice	—	.50	.94
Cinnamon	—	—	.75
Nutmeg	—	.25	1.75
Cloves	—	1.25	.19
	$ 6.25	39.50	553.41
Miscellaneous:			
Tobacco/snuff/cigars	1.00	84.65	14.06
Pipe tomahawk	—	61.00 (13)	—
Pipes	—	—	.16
Soap	—	1.50	2.53
Playing cards, deck	—	1.00	—
Jews harps	—	.50 (4)	—
Whiskey	—	—	35.94
Rum	—	—	4.00
Wine	—	—	13.62
Alum	—	—	6.59
Epsom salts	—	—	1.38

Brads			1.25
Asafetida			.13
Tallow		.50	1.00
Castor oil			.06
Camphor			.25
Coal			9.00
Pencils			.13
Cat gut			.50
Copperas			.50
Fiddle			5.00
White lead			1.75
Linseed oil			.88
Bag			4.00 (6)
Box Sus Pills [for Swine?]			.38
Pinchers, pr.			.38 (1)
Tooth brush			.19 (1)
Twine/rope			1.11
Slate pencil			.07
Almanac			.38 (3)
Primer			.13 (2)
Bible			.75 (1)
Spelling book			.75 (4)
Pike's arithmetic			.38 (1)
Snuff box			.25 (1)
Saltpetre			.25
Quills [as pens]			.25
Compasses [dividers]			.25
Canvas			1.00
Paste board			.06
Empty barrels			1.75
	$ 1.00	149.15	111.16

[1] Value in dollars.
[2] Number of transactions.

published that would indicate what the Delawares might have been purchasing from traders closer to their home area in the 1804–06 period and perusal of such records might well substantially modify the picture here presented. Nevertheless, the assumption is here made that since ordinary, utilitarian objects representing a wide range in type of goods were purchased from the Fort Wayne Factory, these do represent a random sample of the type of purchases made in the 1804–06 period and that changes in frequency have some significance.

Another marked shift is the substantial number of silver ornaments that appear on the inventory for 1829–31. Here again we know from the Moravian diaries that silver ornaments were already in use by the earlier period (Gipson 1938:241, 295, 301) but we may postulate an increasing popularity for this type object. Larger numbers of knives are purchased in the 1829–31 period in a diverse series of types including "Indian skinner," "Damask" or Damascus steel knives, pen knives and butcher knives. Since knives can be put to such a diversity of uses, it is difficult to make an assessment as to which of the various complexes is being enhanced but most might well be associated with the hunting complex. The category "Iron/steel" would seem to indicate raw material that is to be fabricated by a blacksmith into some finished form but it is again not specifically identified. On the whole the size and diversity of the Other Equipment category seems to reflect an increase in acculturative trends in material culture.

The category of Clothing, Cloth, etc. compresses a tremendous diversity in kinds of cloth, quality of blankets, handkerchiefs or shawls. The uses of these objects should not be thought of in terms of modern connotations. Blankets, for example, represent primarily an item of clothing rather than of bedding. Handkerchiefs, as we have previously noted, were used in lieu of hats even in non-Indian culture. Sketches and paintings by the early artists are most helpful in the interpretation of clothing, ornaments, and other items of material culture. George Catlin published two portraits of Delaware chiefs (1842, 2: Pls. 197–198) based upon his observations between 1832 and 1839, and he mentions in his text that

> In both of these instances, their dresses were principally of stuffs of civilized manufacture; and their heads were bound with vari-coloured handkerchiefs or shawls, which were tastefully put on like a Turkish turban. [Catlin 1842, 2:103]

The quantity of yard goods seems proportionately high in relation to the quantity of thread and needles but this also holds true for non-Indian purchases at Kaskaskia. Some acculturation is reflected in this category, as in the purchase of shoes and in the succeeding categories with spices, soap, playing cards, and Jew's harps.

It is evident in a comparison with the non-Indian purchases at Kaskaskia that there is clearly an "Indian" pattern in the 1829-30 Delaware purchases. Part of this would seem to be a reflection of economic differences, evident in the importance of hunting in the Delaware pattern. In addition, the Delaware are more self-sufficient in being less dependent on purchased foods. Partly, it is also a difference in dress and personal ornamentation but in all categories there is a much wider range of purchases in the non-Indian column (Kaskaskia). What is of particular interest is the fact that in a number of important ways the 1829-30 Delaware pattern is further from European culture while the 1804-06 pattern might be seen as reflecting greater acculturation. We can see the greater expenditure for silver ornaments, for example as a further acceptance of traits from the White culture and a dependence upon White technology, but it is also the acceptance and utilization of a trait which has become distinctively Indian. Whatever European prototypes the silver ornaments may have had, they certainly do not represent a pattern of decoration or enhancement of dress in which the Indians are copying from White examples. Though dependent upon White technology, the silver represents a distinctive and identifiable "Indian" element in their culture and a trait shared with other contemporary Indian groups. The increase in expenditures for vermillion or paint, for feathers and beads, as well as the prevalence of times of dress such as blankets and breech cloths, suggest a counter trend from that of assimilation. One of the bases of this counter trend is perhaps to be found in the physical location of the Delaware in close proximity to the Plains and in their participation in the activities of the Plains Indians. Washington Irving's *Tour on the Prairies* based on his travels in 1832 states:

> The expeditions of the Delawares, whether of war or hunting, are wide and fearless. A small band of them will penetrate far into these dangerous and hostile wilds, and will push their encampments even to the Rocky Mountains. [Irving 1836:98]

Thus the diverse contacts of the Delawares would have provided them with multiple models for emulation, not just the continued contacts with Americans providing further opportunities for modification in material culture but also wider contacts with Plains tribes whose culture, still unbroken, reflected great vigor. Could it be that the conflicts between these diverse value systems are also responsible for some of the characteristics of the "Decadent Period"?

One can also summarize the trends as in Table 2, which provides a

TABLE 2
PERCENTAGES OF PURCHASES ACCORDING TO MAJOR CATEGORIES

Purchase Category	Delaware 1804–06	Delaware 1829–31	Non-Indian 1830
Horse complex	03.5	06.4	09.6
Hunting complex	04.2	29.4	00.7
Other equipment	00.3	02.9	15.2
Household equipment	03.6	01.6	04.5
Personal ornaments	00.3	07.3	00.9
Clothing, cloth	87.6	47.4	41.3
Food, condiments	00.3	01.0	23.1
Miscellaneous	00.1	03.9	04.6

computation of the percentage of total income spent in each of the categories utilized in Table 1. Table 2 shows quite clearly the increased expenditure of funds for hunting equipment during the 1829–31 period. Reflected in this category is both the increase in expenditure for trapping equipment and probably also an increased dependence upon hunting for subsistence rather than agriculture. The most marked decrease over time is in the percentage of income spent for clothing and cloth. The reader is reminded that the individual purchases can be grouped in a variety of ways, not just those here presented. The kind of tabulation should depend on the hypotheses generated, the problem being investigated, or the theories being tested.

I have illustrated the potentiality of the records in terms of specific purchases but this does not exhaust their possible interpretations. Since the individuals making the purchases are identified on the trading records, one can investigate this facet of the records. Who did make purchases at the stores? Both males and females? Only heads of extended households? Obviously some of these questions require genealogical information, but persons frequently are identified on the records as "son of . . .," "brother of . . .," "wife of . . .," etc. and one obviously has collateral information from other sources. One may also investigate when the purchases were made to see what the frequency of seasonal distribution reveals. This latter point is illustrated in Table 3 where the purchases at the trading post on the White River between 1829 and 1831 are shown.

It will be noted in Table 3 that purchases in 1829 and 1830 show that the traders were inactive during the months of November and December. The year 1831 is not of value in substantiating this cessation of activity in these months since this year marks the termination of Delaware occupation of Missouri and the removal of the group to Kansas. How is this cessation of activity to be explained? Did the traders simply close up shop

TABLE 3
SEASONAL DISTRIBUTION OF DELAWARE PURCHASES
FROM MENARD AND VALLÉ AT JAMES FORK,
WHITE RIVER, MISSOURI

Period	1829	1830	1831	Total
Jan. 1–15	—	11	—	11
Jan. 16–31	—	17	—	17
Feb. 1–15	—	13	2	15
Feb. 16–28	—	8	1	9
Mar. 1–15	—	12	1	13
Mar. 16–31	—	9	4	13
Apr. 1–15	—	29	1	30
Apr. 16–30	—	45	2	47
May 1–15	—	54	1	55
May 16–31	—	36	—	36
June 1–15	—	10	—	10
June 16–30	—	23	—	23
July 1–15	—	44	2	46
July 16–31	—	28	—	28
Aug. 1–15	—	4	—	4
Aug. 16–31	—	15	—	15
Sep. 1–15	—	23	1	24
Sep. 16–30	—	49	—	49
Oct. 1–15	26	41	—	67
Oct. 16–31	19	10	—	29
Nov. 1–15	—	2	—	2
Nov. 16–Dec. 31	—	—	—	0

and return to Kaskaskia for a long Christmas and pre-Christmas holiday? Or alternatively, were the Delawares involved in some kind of activity which might prevent their patronizing the traders? If it is the latter, it could also be a time when the traders returned to their home base since commercial activities would be at a minimum. An incontrovertible answer to these questions is not available, but some suggestions can be made. First, there would appear to be good evidence that the Menard and Vallé trading post on the James Fork of White River was not closed in November and December. In a recapitulation of the accounts that accompanies the ledger, the amount owed by each individual is tabulated. This list is headed by the title "White River Outfit." The first nine names that appear under the heading are: John B. Clark, Silvester Saucier, Anthony L. Diel, John St. Clair, Caswell Beckham, Pascal Boyez, Francois B. Menard, John Hogel, and Louis Michelain. Then the word "Delawares" appears and there follows a list of 162 names representing the individuals we have tabulated to provided the enumerated 1829–30

Indian purchases on the White River. The accounts of the first enumerated individuals were kept in a separate ledger that included other individuals, also clearly not Indians. Some of these individuals would seem to have been employees of Menard and Vallé. Francis C. Lalumandiere, for example, has an account in which he accumulated an indebtedness of $135.87½ (including $20.00 in cash advances) which was discharged by "11 months and 10 days work at $12 per month," for a total of $136.00, leaving Menard and Vallé owing Mr. Lalumandiere 12½ cents for this long period of work. Not all were employees, however, for after John B. Clark's name is the notation "with Delawares." While part of Clark's account was paid by "4 months and 21 days work," the account spans a total period from October 3, 1829 to April 26, 1831, and there is a final notation to the effect, "Gillis says this man is dead & don't believe he left any thing." Clark may have been married to a Delaware, lived with them and occasionally performed some work for the traders. The account of William Gillis which also appears in this ledger would seem to involve purchases far in excess of what an individual could consume, evidently representing the stock of a small trader. Gillis's account is headed "James Fork, March 4th, 1830" when it is initiated so we clearly are dealing with purchases in this same region. The ledger has entries for Nov. 1, Nov. 16, Nov. 19 and Dec. 27, so that if we are correct in assuming that Gillis was a white trader, he, unlike the Delawares, was making purchases during the months of November and December. Silvester Saucier similarly made purchases in 1830 on Nov. 5, Nov. 6, Nov. 18, Dec. 20 and Dec. 27. The point that the trading establishment was active, even though Indian purchases ceased during November and December, would seem sufficiently established not to require further enumeration of this kind. The explanation thus must lie within some activities of the Indian culture. The absence of the Delaware from the trading post during November and December could be explained, for example, if this were a time of great ceremonial activity. The Big House Ceremony of the Delaware (Speck 1931) lasts a total of twelve days, but there is no indication that the ceremony is given exclusively or even primarily in midwinter. In any event, twelve days are not adequate to account for a two-month absence. Lacking specific references to the character of the economic cycle in Missouri, we may fall back upon some of the data available concerning their activities in Indiana prior to removal. In the diaries of the Moravian missionaries (Gipson 1938:195, 261, 389) we find frequent mention of the fact that the Delawares left their villages every year for a winter hunt, the time when this occurred being recorded as Oct. 21, 1802, Oct. 24, 1803, and Nov. 5, 1805, clearly very close to the first of November. In elaborating upon this activity it is stated:

> We saw many Indians hunting, which happens every year at this time so that one meets no Indians in their towns at present, and not until spring, when some come home to plant. [Gipson 1938:195]

> In these days many heathen families passed through our village on their way to the hunting grounds, as is the custom every year about this time. Few of the women come home to plant, so that from now until planting time one meets only a few old women in the Indian towns. [Gipson 1938:261-262]

While the Indiana evidence suggests a more sustained absence from their village community, the shorter period in Missouri could reflect an adjustment to different environmental conditions. In the absence of other evidence, it would seem to be the best explanation of the seasonal pattern. However, the trading post records do contain other information that sheds some light on economic practices. Records of what the Indians sold to the traders not only confirm the cessation of activities during the midwinter period but also further clarify the nature of their economy. By 1830 the Delawares settled most of their accounts for cash, perhaps not so much an indication of the importance of a cash economy as it is a reflection of the fact that their frequent land sales provided substantial annuity payments from the Federal government. There are, however, a variety of other sales of furs and skins which are shown in Table 4 according to the time of the transaction. Unfortunately the bulk of the transactions are listed by the vague term "skins," effectively restricting the precision of any ecological interpretations that might be made. The only additional sale which could be added to the list is one pair of moccasins "with silk" which was purchased by the trader for $1.50. It will be noted on Table 1 that ordinary moccasins sold for 25 cents a pair.

SUMMARY

The trends of change we have discussed above between purchases by the Delawares in 1804-06 and 1829-31 do not seem incompatible with the period characteristics as outlined by W. W. Newcomb, Jr. Though we are dealing with the end of the Nativistic period and the beginning of the Decadent period in these two time units, there is no sharp difference in the kind of purchases nor perhaps should one expect that there would be one. The 1829-31 period seems to mark an increasing dependence upon trapping and hunting, a trend initiated in the earlier period. It is also marked by an increasing pattern of utilization of "Indian" elements at the same time that increasing borrowing of White elements continues. Such contradictory patterns seem appropriate for a Decadent period.

TABLE 4
SALES OF FURS AND SKINS IN 1829–31
BY THE DELAWARES TO MENARD AND VALLÉ
ON THE JAMES FORK OF WHITE RIVER, MISSOURI

Period	"Skins"	Red Deer	Beaver	Otter	Bear	Total
Jan. 1–15	—	—	—	—	—	—
Jan. 16–31	2.00	—	—	—	—	2.00
Feb. 1–15	17.00	—	—	—	—	17.00
Feb. 16–28	7.25	—	—	—	—	7.25
Mar. 1–15	67.69	—	—	—	—	67.69
Mar. 16–31	—	—	119.26	—	—	119.26
Apr. 1–15	—	—	21.50	—	—	21.50
Apr. 16–30	41.50	—	—	2.50	—	44.00
May 1–15	68.50	—	68.00	5.00	4.00	145.00
May 16–31	23.00	—	—	—	—	23.00
June 1–15	11.50	—	—	—	—	11.50
June 16–30	32.00	33.75	8.00	—	—	73.75
Jul. 1–15	360.50	24.00	21.50	—	—	406.00
Jul. 16–31	34.00	32.25	6.00	—	—	72.25
Aug. 1–15	2.50	—	—	—	—	2.50
Aug. 16–31	38.75	7.25	—	—	—	46.00
Sep. 1–15	—	22.00	13.25	—	—	35.25
Sep. 16–30	9.50	11.25	—	—	—	20.75
Oct. 1–15	13.50	—	34.00	—	—	47.50
Oct. 16–31	6.00	—	—	—	—	6.00
Nov. 1–Dec. 31	—	—	—	—	—	—

The analysis of the records of purchases and other transactions appears to be of considerable utility in providing the kind of data from which rates of change might be computed and with a longer series, alternative times for period subdivision might be proposed. Suggestions and illustrations regarding methodological procedures have been provided and one may finally indicate that some of the inferences are testable through archaeological excavation. In regard to the specific Delaware problem, the records presented here have serious limitations, for the two grouped periods of years are not directly comparable, one being from a Federal Factory in the Fort Wayne area of Indiana and the other being from a private trader on the White River in Missouri. Nevertheless such limitations can be overcome by the discovery and analysis of further records of this kind and, of course, we are forced to see culture change among many Indian groups as much a consequence of their repeated spatial removal as of culture contacts.

Notes

1. The writer is indebted to the late Dr. Robert F. Heizer of the University of California, Berkeley, who read an earlier version of the paper and made a number of very useful suggestions that helped improve the text.
2. Ledger Book A is housed in the manuscript collections of the Chicago Historical Society, and the writer is indebted to the Chicago Historical Society for permission to study and utilize material in its Menard Papers.
3. Day Book "F" of the Kaskaskia operations of the firm of Menard & Vallé, together with other of their financial records, is housed in the manuscript collections of the Illinois Historical Society and the materials here tabulated are presented through the courtesy of that institution. To facilitate the rather tedious copying of the transactions, the author was permitted to pay the cost of having a microfilm of the day book made and then allowed to borrow the microfilm for a limited period. The sample, drawn from odd pages in the ledger, was not selected because of the strategy of sample design but because the even pages on the microfilm were not legible, doubtless due to the pattern of lighting at the time of copying for no such distinction between pages was noted when the Day Book was first examined.

REFERENCES

Baerreis, D. A.
    1961   The ethnohistoric approach and archaeology. *Ethnohistory* 8:49–77.
Catlin, G.
    1842   *Letters and notes on the manners, customs, and condition of the North American Indians* (fourth ed.). 2 Vols. London.
Gerhard, F.
    1875   *Illinois as it is.* Chicago.
Gipson, L. H. (editor)
    1938   The Moravian Indian mission on White River. *Indiana Historical Collections* 23.
Houck, L.
    1908   *A history of Missouri*, Vol 1. Chicago.
Irving, W.
    1835   *A tour on the prairies.* Paris.
Newcomb, W. W., Jr.
    1956   The culture and acculturation of the Delaware Indians. *Anthropological Papers, Museum of Anthropology, University of Michigan* 10.
Speck, F. G.
    1931   A study of the Delaware Indian big house ceremony. *Publications of the Pennsylvania Historical Commission* 2.
Weslager, C. A.
    1972   *The Delaware Indians: a history.* Rutgers University Press, New Brunswick, N. J.

RETHINKING THE FRENCH PRESENCE IN THE UPPER GREAT LAKES[1]

David S. Brose

At the present time in the Upper Great Lakes Region there are very few known archaeological sites that belong to the Middle Historic period; therefore, each of them is a precious document for the study of Indian Culture History.

[Quimby 1966b:117]

One of the earliest archaeological experiences I choose to recall is that of sitting at mid-afternoon coffee in the University of Michigan Museum of Anthropology and listening to James B. Griffin and Volney Jones describe George Irving Quimby's summer survey of aboriginal sites in the Upper Great Lakes while the captain of a schooner with an all-female crew.

While never having achieved that high goal, in other ways I have followed Quimby's lead, working at many sites which he first discovered, and sharing some of his concern that we understand that aboriginal significance of the French presence in North America. Certainly no recent student of that historic period has traveled as widely, or to such good purpose, as has Quimby—the twentieth century's Parkman (1879, 1885) with a shovel.

A good part of Quimby's professional career as a field archaeologist can be seen as a distant reflection of the professional careers of René –Robert Cavelier, Sieur de La Salle, and Pierre LeMoyne d'Iberville. As agents of the French Crown they traveled by sail and by canoe from Canada to Louisiana in the late seventeenth and early eighteenth centuries. Their attempt to control the Western Great Lakes, the Mississippi River, and the Gulf Coast drew the French into contact with American Indian societies as diverse as the Huron, Ojibwa, Natchez, and Bayou Goula.

In one of his most widely read books, *Indian Culture and European Trade Goods*, Quimby (1966b) brought together many results of his earlier studies to discuss those two centuries (A.D. 1610–A.D. 1810) which changed many of the diverse aboriginal societies in the heart of the country into a single economically dependent and politically doomed pan-Indian culture. Within those 200-plus years was what Quimby called the Middle Historic period, A.D. 1670–A.D. 1760. Prior to that 90-year period, the future of the Amerindian was uncertain; afterward it was inescapable.

Many historians have seen this issue as one of colonial competition, attributing cultural decline to the triumph of Anglo/American land policies over French trade considerations. Yet, in a review of Quimby's book, I argued that "The seeds of the Pan-Indian culture which Pontiac urged against the English were sown by the French who came bearing gifts. These gifts soon became necessities for the Indians of the Western Great Lakes, thus placing them in economic dependence [to] the Europeans, condemning their 'rebellions' to failure before they had fired a single musket" (Brose 1967:32).

It is my position here that the economic and technological clientism deliberately fostered by the French is far more culpable than the terrestrial acquisitiveness of the soon-to-be embattled farmer for the destruction of the Indian, though the latter surely accelerated the process. Beyond that, I will argue that rather early in the Middle Historic period, French colonial manipulation of the aboriginal societies they encountered was responsible for a large degree of the material homogenization whose results so frustrate the direct historic approach to pre-contact ethnic identification in the mid-continental watersheds. While my hypothesis in no way implies that Quimby would agree with my interpretation, I feel certain that the topic will be one to which he has given some thought. In a trial formulation, Quimby (1942:550) identified an Early Trade period (A.D. 1700–A.D. 1760), noting that, "despite the distance between the Fort St. Joseph site in Michigan and the [Angola Farm, Bayou Goula, and Fatherland] sites in the lower Mississippi Valley, the same types of trade objects occur in both areas."

The aboriginal materials, however, were quite different. The ceramics, later characterized as Lower Valley types and varieties (e.g., Brain 1979; Neitzel 1965; Quimby 1957) are significant, not because they differed in style from the coeval Great Lakes ceramics, but because they occurred at all. For early in this period, aboriginal ceramics had virtually disappeared at aboriginal sites in the Great Lakes; whereas, in the Lower Mississippi Valley, there are French accounts of their manufacture and use from at least A.D. 1718 (Swanton 1946:549–550), and possibly from as late as A.D.

1734 (Brain 1979). Yet it is my impression that by the later part of this period, say by 1740, even in the lower valley, most aboriginal ceramics are found in a mortuary rather than domestic context.

Within the Upper Great Lakes region, few sites yield both ethnically identifiable aboriginal material and European trade goods appropriate for tying the historic documents to the archaeological remains. By following Quimby's lead, I was fortunate enough to excavate such a site at Summer Island (Quimby 1966b:56; Brose 1970), but the ethnolinguistic identity was uncertain (e.g., Brose 1978; Mason 1976). I have been equally fortunate at the Dunn Farm Plateau site (Fig. 1).

THE DUNN FARM PLATEAU SITE

The discovery of the Dunn Farm Plateau (20Lu58) site was fortuitous. During 1974 while engaged in the excavation of a Late Archaic-Early Woodland mortuary site (20Lu22) at the Dunn Farm in Leelanau County, Michigan, I undertook a limited archaeological survey of the Burdickville area, on the eastern shore of Big Glen Lake. Discussions with Mrs. Sarah Johnson, owner of the Dunn Farm property, revealed that in the 1900–1915 period, Ottawa Indians from Traverse Bay, engaged in temporary agricultural work, would often camp at a spring on the higher ground to the east. In the process of locating that twentieth century occupation I chanced to cross a relatively flat plateau about 3 m higher and about 15 m further east than site 20Lu22. In scrambling down a recent erosional gully, I observed a small triangular projectile point on the surface of the gravels. Further inspection of the gully surface yielded a small amount of lithic debitage, six small white opaque hot-tumbled glass seed beads, and a single shell-tempered body sherd. None of these artifacts were *in situ* but shaving of the northern bank revealed a 3 cm to 8 cm thick zone of sandy silt, and charcoal-flecked sandy soil lying below the medium-fine sands and organic A_o upper horizon.

The recovered materials were obviously from late prehistoric times, and I was rather excited. As they appeared to have little relationship either chronologically or spatially to the 800 B.C. cremation or to the A.D. 1900 labor camp, a new USNM site number was obtained from the Michigan State Historic Preservation Office. With the kind permission and continual interest of Mrs. Johnson, the archaeological investigations of the Dunn Farm Plateau site were carried out over several one to two week periods during the summer, from 1975 through 1979 by myself, and Barbara, Robert, and Thomas Brose.

The vegetation of the area, as recorded in an 1839 survey, has been

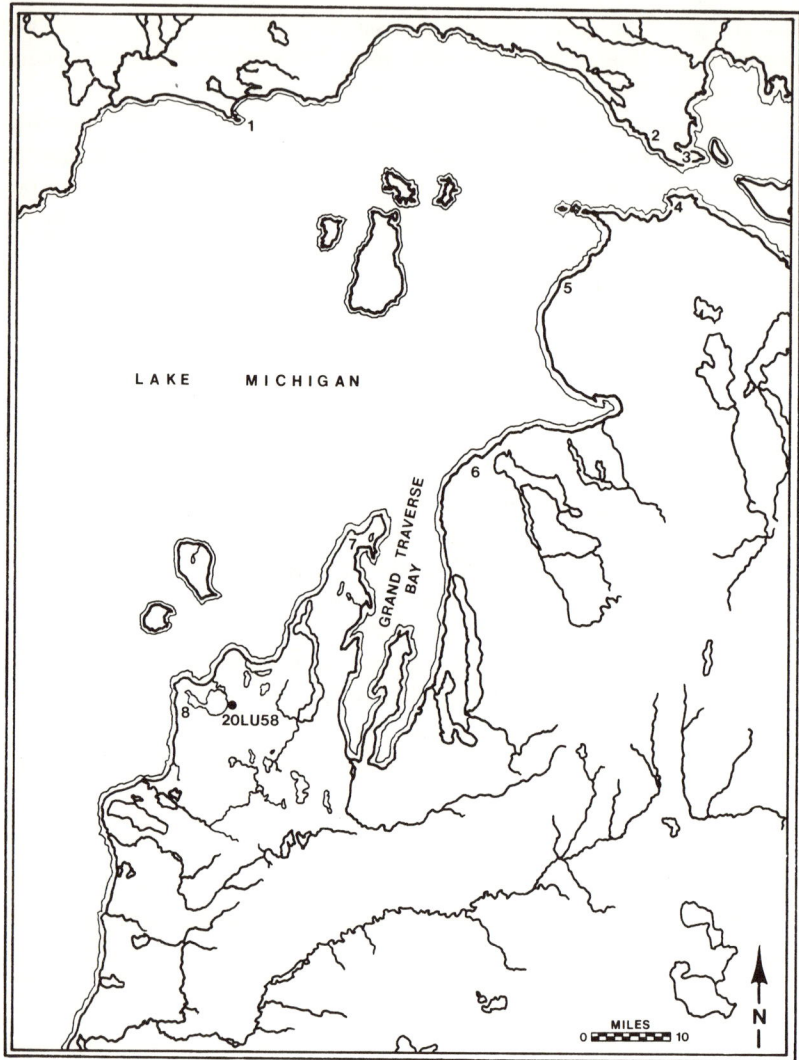

Fig. 1. Map of the northern Lake Michigan basin showing locations mentioned in the text: *1*, Seul Choix Point; *2*, Gros Cap cemetery; *3*, Lassanen site; *4*, Ft. Michilimackinac; *5*, L'Arbre Croche; *6*, O'Neill site; *7*, Cathead Bay site; *8*, Sleeping Bear Dunes, 20Lu58, Dunn Farm Plateau site.

reconstructed by Isleib (cited in Lovis 1973:4-8). This reconstruction shows the areas immediately to the east of the site with a mixed forest of sugar maple, beech, and hemlock with white pine, elm, basswood, birch, ironwood, and cherry. Indeed the upland moraines are so covered today. To the immediate north of the site as far as Brooks Lake, the low Algoma stage lake bottom now represents a drained but still wet field of cottages, cattails, scouring rush, and cedars. The Johnson family who cleared, drained and cultivated the land after 1868, later described it to their heirs as "a beaver swamp." The eastern shore of Glen Lake, prior to development, was predominantly spring-fed wetlands with cedar, tamarack spruce, alder, white pine, and spruce (see also Lovis 1973:8).

The site sits on a relatively high and level terrace, probably an old Nipissing beach, which runs north and south about 100 m behind the modern shoreline at an elevation ranging between 190 m (622 ft.) and 194 m (635 ft.) AMSL. At the site itself this plateau is about 35 m wide, east-west, tapering to the north and abruptly cut approximately 75 m to the south by a deep valley which opens onto Glen Lake. That valley at present contains several gullies which occasionally carry the overflow from a spring-fed intermittent stream. In especially wet years before development, this stream is said to have become a narrow creek flowing west about 2 km from the high moraine to a seasonally reconstituted marsh along the eastern shore of Big Glen Lake (Fig. 2).

ARCHAEOLOGICAL INVESTIGATIONS

Due to the frequently deflated nature of the plateau surface, the initial recovery technique consisted of intensive surface collection. The provenience controls consisted of 2×2 m blocks (Fig. 3). While some aboriginal and European materials were recovered across the entire surface of the plateau, an area of about 30×10 m, none appeared still to be in its original position. There were three zones, each about 10 m², which yielded rather low frequencies of cultural materials. These appeared to be areas in which remnants of the original upper strata had been protected from erosion by vegetation. Within each of those seven protected 2×2 m blocks, the upper 3–8 cm A_o horizons were removed by troweling. The only cultural materials recovered were four more white glass seed beads from the southern edge of Unit 3f. The underlying pale brown (10YR3/4) A_1 podzolic soils varied in thickness from just over 5 cm in Units 1a, 1d, 2a, and 2g, to about 3 cm in Unit 3g. There did not appear to be any obvious intrusions although the thin overburden certainly urges caution. Within this pre-

Fig. 2. Dunn Farm Plateau site (20Lu58): *above*, the view to the east showing the exposed edge of the plateau; *below*, view to the west showing Glen Lake from 20Lu58.

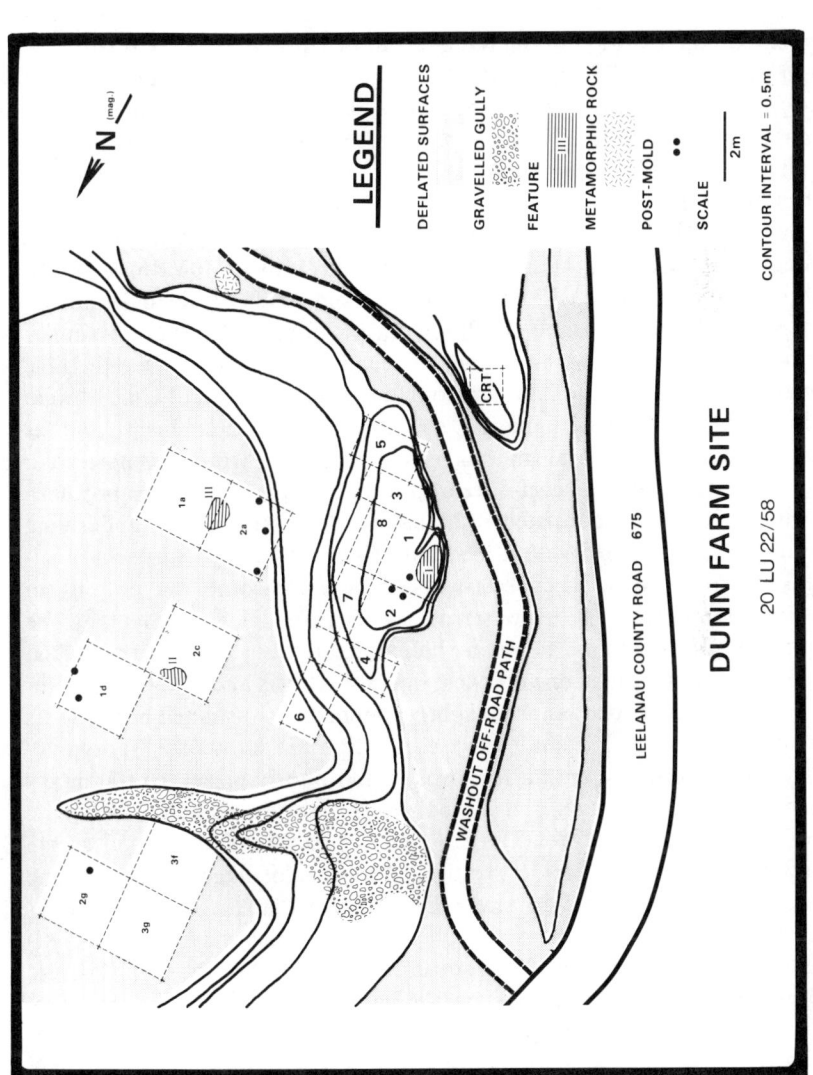

Fig. 3. Dunn Farm (20Lu22) and Plateau (20Lu58) sites: topography and excavation unit locations.

sumptive paleosol level, a reasonably consistent assemblage of late aboriginal and Middle Historic period trade goods were recovered. Neither earlier nor later materials were seen as the troweling and finger screening proceeded by 1×1 m quadrats in each 2×2 m unit with the aid of a child's sand sifter having circular holes about 2 mm in diameter. Most artifacts appeared concentrated in the NE quadrat of Unit 2a, the NW quadrat of Unit 1a, and the SW quadrat of Unit 1d. No cultural materials were encountered from subsurface contexts in Unit 3g nor were artifacts assignable to the Middle Historic period recovered in the excavations of Units 1 through 8 located on those lower portions called the Dunn Farm site (20Lu22).

Several Middle Historic postmolds were noted originating from the paleosol intruding into the underlying light brown (10YR6/4) sands. Three postmolds about 12 cm in diameter and 20–23 cm deep formed an arc along the western and southwestern portions of Unit 2a. A similar postmold was encountered in the NE quadrat of Unit 1d. One possible postmold in Unit 2g and another along the eastern margin of Unit 1d were smaller (about 8 cm in diameter), shallower (about 15 cm deep), and far less distinct. No cultural materials were recovered from any postmold.

Two features at this level were also noted. Feature II, in the northern portion of Unit 2c, consisted of a shallow depression in the underlying sands which was filled with a medium brown (10YR4/4) silty, charcoal-flecked matrix. It was 85 cm east-west, 45 cm north-south, and only 10 cm in maximum depth at its western end. Feature III, located along the centerline of Units 1a/2a, was a shallow hearth filled with fire-cracked rock and burned limestone cobbles. Feature III was about 160 cm north-south, 90 cm east-west, and its slightly rounded basin-shaped bottom was about 18 cm deep. The soil matrix consisted of dark (10YR2/3) organically stained silt-loam with a few broken and poorly preserved fragments of bone, lithic debitage, and a small pale blue glass bead.

The structural interpretations of these remains are as limited as the discontinuous areas of intact stratigraphy. I would suggest that all of the pits and posts encountered at the Dunn Farm Plateau site can be considered to have been part of a single structure which may have approximated the subrectangluar "longhouse" associated with the protohistoric component at the O'Neill site on the east side of Grand Traverse Bay (Lovis 1973). In that case the structure would be between 6 m and 7 m long and about 3 m wide for a floor area of about 20 m^2 (215 sq. ft.). Such a structure might have housed a patrilocal extended family of about eight Middle Historic period Upper Great Lakes Indians (e.g., Brose 1968:267–273; Quimby 1966b:161–164).

MATERIAL RECOVERED

The materials recovered from the Middle Historic period Dunn Farm Plateau site represent three distinct classes: aboriginal artifacts, European trade goods, and biotic environmental remnants. Only four metal artifacts appeared to represent aboriginal modification of European material.

Ceramics

Table 1 shows the distribution of aboriginal ceramics recovered from the site. The 134 sherds were rather evenly divided among grit-tempered, shell-tempered, and mixed tempered wares. As usual, most sherds were from the vessel body, but reconstructions suggest 13 minimal vessels were present, representing 11 types, or variants. Although unwilling to embark on any extended methodological discussion of these eleven ceramic types, some comparative analysis seems appropriate.

Two grit-tempered rimsherds represent a single high-collared vessel (Fig. 4a; Fig. 5a) strongly resembling protohistoric Iroquoian ceramics from southwestern Ontario (e.g., Wintemberg 1939, 1946).[2] Perhaps the most similar ceramics are the Richmond Incised vessels recovered from the Cayuga/Seneca Adams, Broughton Hill, and Dutch Hollow sites in western New York (MacNeish 1952: Pl. XXI, Fig. 3; Ritchie 1954:74, Pl. 22, Fig. 1, Pl. 28, Fig. 1; Schoff 1949). Similar Ontario types are usually found at sites assigned to a period around A.D. 1620–A.D. 1650 (e.g., Kidd 1949; M. J. Wright 1981), while the Hochelaga site and the New York sites may be at least in part as early as A.D. 1590 (MacNeish 1952; Ritchie 1954; Schoff 1949). However, White (1978) has noted that between A.D. 1668 and A.D. 1682 a number of Huron lived in Cayuga villages. Ritchie (1954:70–74) suggests that, through trade, the Adams site potters were responsible for the Richmond Incised vessels with Dutch Hollow burials between A.D. 1615 and A.D. 1630. One of the conclusions reached by Englebrecht (1971) was that between A.D. 1570 and A.D. 1640 among the New York Iroquois there was some significant inter-tribal female exchange which involved the Dutch at Ft. Orange on the eastern end and which (if it did not involve actual movement/ceramics) certainly resulted in an east-to-west movement of ceramic styles and patterning. This may explain the similarity of these high-collared ceramics from the Genessee River, Georgian Bay, and Glen Lake.[3]

A second grit-tempered vessel, represented by four rimsherds and possibly three necksherds may be a low-collared Ontario Iroquois type (Fig. 4b; Fig. 5b). One such rim is attributed to Roebuck low-collared at Hochelaga (Pendergast and Trigger 1972: Pl. IV, Fig. 2).[4] Fitting (1974:

TABLE 1
ABORIGINAL CERAMICS FROM THE DUNN FARM PLATEAU SITE

Provenience	Grit Temper	Mixed Temper	Shell Temper	Total
Surface	5/ 0/ 16[1]	3/ 1/ 14	2/ 0/ 5	10/ 1/ 35
Paleosol	3/ 2/ 9	7/ 2/ 16	12/ 3/ 6	22/ 7/ 31
Features	2/ 3/ 3	0/ 3/ 8	2/ 0/ 7	4/ 6/ 18
Totals:				
Sherds:	10/ 5/ 28	10/ 6/ 38	16/ 3/ 18	36/ 14/ 84
By temper:	43	54	37	134
Minimal number of vessels:	4	4	5	13

[1]Counts of rim, shoulder or neck, and body sherds respectively.

243, 246, Fig. 36j) has documented a vessel with a similar rim at the Beyer site, and Nern and Cleland (1974:46, Fig. 23c) illustrate one from the nearby Gros Cap cemetery, both A.D. 1660–A.D. 1690 Ottawa-Huron occupations. Several vessels of this type were recovered at the Graham-Vogt earthwork northwest of Lake St. Clair from post–A.D. 1400 contexts (Zurel 1980: Pl. 1 Nos. 1040, 1042), and Quimby (1939b: Pl. 11, Fig. 2, lower center) recovered this type of rim from Chippewa Harbor and McCargoe's Cove on Isle Royale. Several of the "push pull" tradition ceramics illustrated from the nearby Michipicoten site, level III, are similar (J.V. Wright 1968b: Pl. VIII, Figs. 8, 9).

The last grit-tempered ceramic type recovered at the Dunn Farm Plateau site is represented by four rimsherds and two necksherds from two vessels of approximately 3 liter and 6 liter capacity (Fig. 4c; Fig. 5c). These vessels, with their vertical sub-lip stamping or tool impressing above seven broad incised horizontal lines above the shoulder, are similar in almost all ways to the latest variety of Reeve Horizontal (South Park phase: A.D. 1590–1640) Whittlesey ceramic type from northeastern Ohio (Brose et al. 1981). Ceramics similar to these have been widely reported from protohistoric contexts in the Upper Lakes and attributed to a number of Iroquoian types.[5] These rims are also quite similar in decoration to a number of shell-tempered ceramics assigned to the protohistoric Upper Mississippian components of the lower Lake Michigan area (Brose 1978; Lovis 1973; Schnell 1974; Slaymaker and Slaymaker 1971: Fig. 93c), or to what I called Garden Incised at Summer Island (Brose 1970: Pl. I f–h).

The blurred significance of ceramic temper can be further illustrated by the four vessels of mixed shell and grit temper. The first is a slightly outflaring jar (Fig. 4d; Fig. 5d) represented by three rimsherds and two bodysherds. Decoration consists of a band of parallel oblique narrow incisions around the neck of the vessel. Temper aside, this is virtually the same as the Bell site type I pottery (Wittry 1963:21–25) assigned to the

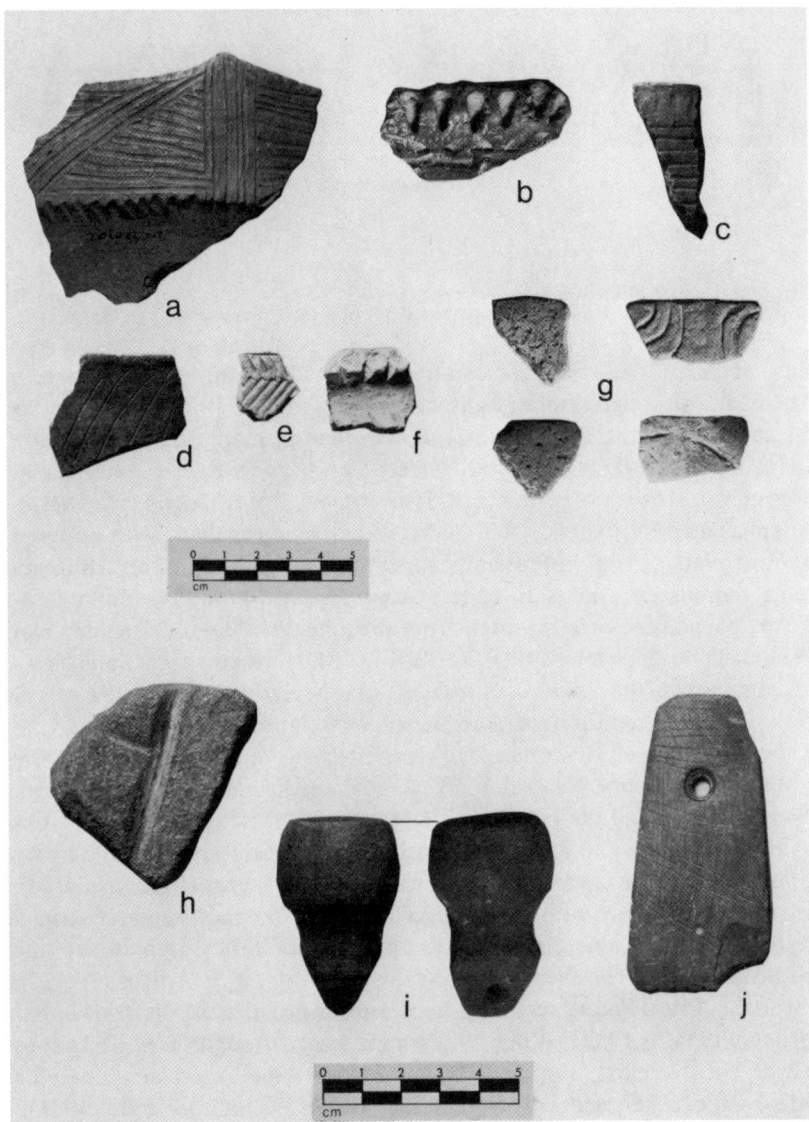

Fig. 4. Dunn Farm Plateau site aboriginal ceramic and groundstone artifacts: *a–c*, grit-tempered rimsherds; *d–f*, mixed shell and grit-tempered rimsherds; *g*, shell-tempered rimsherds; *h*, sandstone abrader; *i*, sandstone "Mic-mac" pipe; and *j*, incised red shale gorget.

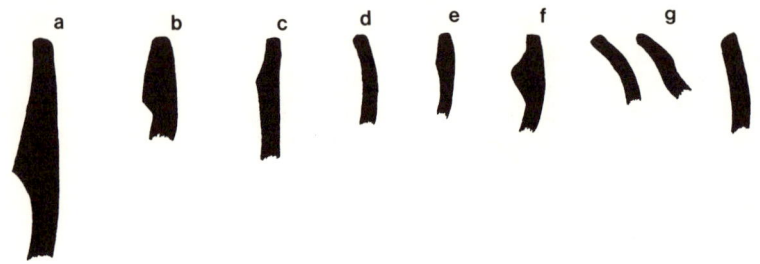

Fig. 5. Dunn Farm Plateau site rimsherd profiles (interiors oriented to the right).

Fox at A.D. 1680. Similar ceramics are widespread in southwestern Michigan (although seldom tightly dated [e.g., Brose 1978]) and occur as far eastward as the Late Historic period Neutral Hamilton site (Lennox 1981: Fig. 39, 7-13) or the 28th Street Cemetery in Erie, Pennsylvania, around A.D. 1640 (Carpenter et al. 1949:Pls. 6a, 7b). A second small vessel is represented by a single shell- and grit-tempered rimsherd with opposed oblique plats of tool impressing or stamping (Fig. 4e; Fig 5e). Although quite reminiscent in design to the earlier Ontario Oblique, similar grit-tempered ceramics are reported from protohistoric "Ojibwa" contexts at Whitefish Bay (Conway 1980:20-22, Fig. 10, third row right) and in an "Algonkian" protohistoric context at Lake Nipigon (Dawson 1976:Pl. I, Nos. 17, 26, 27) and in Georgian Bay (J.V. Wright 1981:47, Fig. 2, No. 3). They are relatively common, with mixed shell- and grit-temper, at the seventeenth-century Neutral Walker Village (M.J. Wright 1981:Fig. 50, Nos. 1-4, 5, 7) and the Hamilton sites (Lennox 1981:Fig. 39,Nos. 1, 4, 6).[6]

The final shell- and grit-tempered sherds, two vessels represented by six rimsherds, four necksherds, and at least six bodysherds (Fig. 4f; Fig. 5f), are from simple jars with an outcurved rim with notched appliqué strip, a style widespread across the Great Lakes/Ohio Valley area in the late prehistoric and protohistoric periods (e.g., Brose 1978; Griffin 1943). In the Lake Erie region, such ceramics are termed Seneca Barbed Collar (Ritchie 1954:53,Pl. 23; White 1978) or are assigned to the Whittlesey type Tuttle Hill Notched (Fitting 1974:240-241) although more similar to the late Fairport Filletted *var.* Painesville (Brose 1980; Brose et al. 1981).[7]

Five shell-tempered vessels were also recovered from the Dunn Farm Plateau. Two open bowls of Mississippi Plain, variety indeterminate (Phillips 1970) are represented by eight and six rimsherds respectively (Fig. 4g, upper and lower left; Fig. 5g, left). Two less fine, shell-tempered bowls, each represented by a single nearly vertical rim (Fig. 4g, upper and lower right; Fig. 5g, left) bear different incised designs. The plain shell-tempered bowls are more similar to the protohistoric Mississippi plain *var.* Pocahontas (Brain 1979:238–240; Phillips 1970) than they are to the shell-tempered plain ceramics from the Bell site (Wittry 1963:26–27) or to the shell-tempered plain rim described from the Beyer site (Fitting 1974:248, Fig. 38) or the associated Richardson (Greenman 1958) or Gros Cap cemeteries (Quimby 1963; Nern and Cleland 1974:45–46, Fig. 23c), all of which are closer to the Oneota types Koshkonong Bold or Grand River plain (cf. Brose 1978; Hall 1962). The two shell-tempered incised jars are not Upper Mississippian either. Neither are they similar to any local Middle Mississippian precedents. Both are reminiscent of variants assigned to odd varieties of Natchez Incised, Fatherland Incised, or Bayou Goula Incised (Brain 1979:242; Neitzel 1965:52, Fig. 19f; Quimby 1957:126–127) now all absorbed in the somewhat coarse paste, deliberately vague, incised super type Leland Incised *var.* Blanchard (Phillips 1970:105). To the extent that I have correctly interpreted Phillips and that this is the incised equivalent of Mississippi Plain *var.* indeterminate, then I feel it is a correct typological attribution for the incised shell-tempered Dunn Farm vessels despite the nearly 2600 km of intervening Mississippi River Valley. There are mitigating circumstances which, to me, argue in favor of such an approach.

Not illustrated in Figure 4 are three red-filmed, fine shell-tempered body sherds which may all have come from the shoulder area of a single wide rim or high-sided open globular bowl or plate. These ceramics were all recovered from Unit 2C at depths of 5–10 cm below the recent leaf litter and A_o soil horizon. A single similar vessel, recovered from the A.D. 1706–13 French period levels at the D'Olive Creek site on the east side of Mobile Bay, was assigned by Jenkins to the type Pensacola Red Filmed (cf. DeJarnette 1976:14, 88–96, 142–152, Pl. Ia; Willey 1949). In these same levels at D'Olive Creek the majority of the ceramics were shell-tempered Pensacola types although several Lower Valley clay/grog-tempered vessels were present along with grit-tempered, cord-impressed sherds of several non-local vessels. Jenkins assumed these represented the post-A.D. 1703 influx of refugee Apalachee from northwest Florida (DeJarnette 1976). The latter are, however, quite unlike any of the Apalachee ceramics recovered *in situ* from that region (e.g., Boyd, Smith, and Griffin 1957; Tesar 1980). The relevant Alachua tradition ceramic types in north central Florida had virtually disappeared by A.D. 1400 (J. Milanich, personal communication, 1981) and there is no evidence of Timucuan populations in the Mobile region at any time (Hamilton 1976).

At least one of those D'Olive Creek site collared, grit-tempered cord-marked and punctate rims seems similar to the punctate over cordmarked collared rim sherd recovered at Dunn Farm in direct association with the shell-tempered red-filmed Pensacola-like plate bodysherds.

An unfortunate, if traditional, pattern has developed among Great Lakes archaeologists reporting upon the non-local shell-tempered ceramics recovered at aboriginal historic sites. Almost invariably these have been assigned to *the closest* major late prehistoric Mississippian complex known to have produced shell-tempered ceramics with vaguely similar vessel modes, or with approximately similar decorative styles (e.g., Brose 1970; J. A. Brown 1961; M. K. Brown 1975; Fenner 1961; Herrick 1958; Lennox 1981; Mainfort 1979; Maxwell 1964; Quimby 1939b, 1963; Ridley 1954; Schnell 1974; Slaymaker and Slaymaker 1971; Smith 1951; Wintemberg 1946). However, north of the Cairo lowlands there is no good evidence that any of these cultural centers continued to be occupied by Middle Mississippian populations after A.D. 1450 (cf., Williams et al. 1982).

Certainly such an apparently economical assumption is demonstrably inappropriate to explain significant portions of the Woodland prehistoric sequence. In addition there is sufficient information available to seriously question this assumption for the Middle Historic period as well. Excavations in the French occupations on Dauphin Island, at the mouth of Mobile Bay, revealed that nearly half of the diagnostic aboriginal ceramics were not local types but rather were: ". . . manufactured largely by Indian women whose homeland and corresponding ceramic tradition were rooted in one or more Indian tribes of the Lower Mississippi River Valley, and who were present on Dauphin Island from about 1701 to about 1725 in services of the few French Canadian settlers and soldiers based there" (Knight 1976:50-67). Knight (1976) noted that copies of the 1715 French Council minutes in the Mississippi Provencial Archives list Arkansas, Tunicas, Chickasaws Chacchoumas, Kastkaskias and Tamaroas, among others; many of these, including the last two groups noted, lived well into the Upper Mississippi Valley. Beyond Indian wives, mistresses, and servants, Hamilton (1976) documents at least two dozen distinct military and trading expeditions from Tonty in 1699 to Bossu in 1749 which moved between the Upper Great Lakes and Mobile with Indians from both areas.

Similar French use of local Indians and/or Canadian voyagers with Indian wives can be seen as early as 1615 (Biggar 1922-36) and as late as 1734 (Brain 1979). They were noted throughout the French records, most commonly during the period between 1680 and 1720 (Brose 1968; Brown 1961; Cleland 1971; Conway 1980; Fitting 1976; Galinee 1903; Greenman 1957, 1958; Hickerson 1960; Hunt 1940; Innis 1962; Joutel 1685; Kidd 1949; Kinietz 1940; La Houtan 1905 [1703]; La Potherie 1911; Mason 1974, 1981; Nern and Cleland 1974; Perrot 1911; Quaife 1962; Quimby 1939a, 1957, 1966b; Radisson 1885; Swanton 1911; Thwaites 1896-1900).

Most of this movement was between Quebec and Montreal via the Upper Great Lakes and the Mississippi River, to the Gulf Coast, tying together the French provinces of Canada and Louisiana with a web of political, military, and economic strands.

It should therefore come as little surprise that the ceramic assemblage recovered at the Dunn Farm Plateau contains so many types and varieties, drawn from such diverse ethnic traditions. Analogous situations occurred at the 1670–1730 level of the Rock Island II site across Lake Michigan (Mason 1981:400–404). That this situation was less frequent in the lowest portions of the Mississippi Valley may have been due in part to the greater ceramic conservatism in those more highly structured and matrilineal societies.

Chipped Stone

The Dunn Farm Plateau investigations recovered a wide range of local and exotic chipped stone artifacts and debris (Table 2). In addition to the 2 gunflints, there were in whole or in part some 34 formal chipped stone tools; 2 bifacial preforms (Fig. 6*t, u*), 6 bifacial knives (Fig. 6*f,g,m,n*), 3 bifacially worked drills (Fig. 6*q–s*), and 18 bifacially worked triangular projectile points (Fig. 6*a–e, h–l*; Table 3). There were also 5 snub-nose unifacially flaked end scrapers (Fig. 6*v–y, bb*), 2 bipolar cores with some suggestion of subsequent utilization (cf., Brose 1968), and 31 unifacially utilized waste flakes. Although some (e.g., Fitting and Cleland 1969) have found uniface to biface ratios suggestive of site function and group demography, I have not (Brose 1968; Brose et. al. 1981). In this case we may have biface to uniface ratios of just under 5:1 for finished formal tools alone; of over 6:1 for all formal (deliberate pre-made) tools; or of 1:1.3 for all tools used, even if we ignore the locally produced spall gunflint. While few of these aboriginal chipped stone tools are of great intrinsic interest, it is worth noting that, unlike the ceramics, they suggest a rather homogeneous assemblage and presumably a conservative tradition (cf., Mason 1981:406; J.V. Wright 1968a, 1971; M.J. Wright 1981).

William Fox has presented data suggesting that there were significant and consistent differences between the Huron/Petun and the Neutral lithic industries in the contact period, the latter distinguished by large ($\bar{x}$ length = 25 mm) equilateral triangle projectile points, large laterally retouched end scrapers, and a high incidence of bipolar core technology (Fox 1970, 1971, 1972). A regional comparison of the rather similar protohistoric period triangular projectile points is of some interest. These projectile points are the most frequent aboriginal artifact class, as well as being those artifacts presumably most directly involved with economic extraction (Brose 1970).

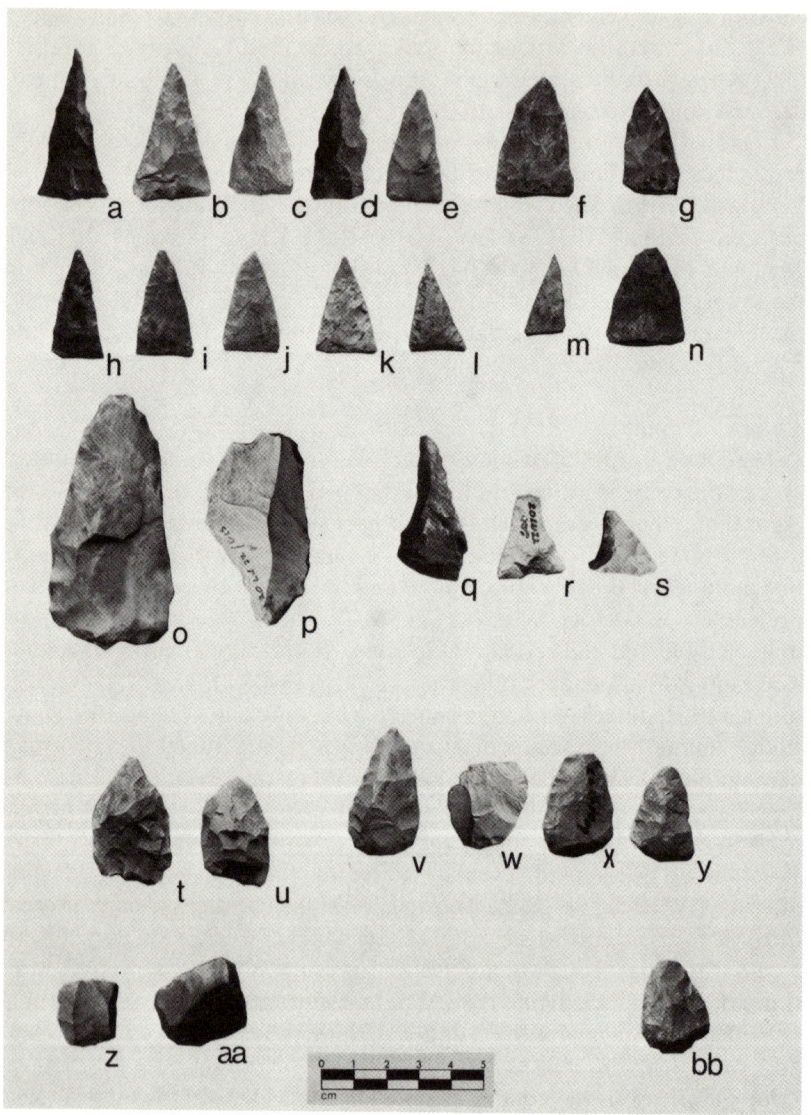

Fig. 6. Dunn Farm Plateau site chipped stone artifacts: *a–e, h–l*, projectile points; *f, g, m, n*, broken tips of bifacial knives; *o–p*, unifacial knives; *q, r, s*, drill and drill fragments, *t–u*, bifacial preforms; *v–y, bb*, snub-nosed end scrapers; *z*, Norwood chert spall gunflint; *aa*, Gran Presigny (France) flint blade gunflint.

TABLE 2
LITHIC DEBITAGE FROM 22Lu58

Class	Material	Unutilized No.	Unutilized %	Utilized No.	Utilized %	Total No.	Total %
Pebble Cores	Local Chert	3	0.7	1	0.2	4	0.9
	Other	—	—	—	—	—	—
Bipolar Cores	Local Chert	4	1.0	2	0.5	6	1.5
	Other	—	—	—	—	—	—
Block Flakes	Local Chert	104	25.2	6	1.5	110	26.7
	Other	69	16.7	7	1.7	76	18.4
Flat Flakes	Local Chert	99	24.0	15	3.6	114	27.7
	Other	46	11.2	8	1.9	54	13.1
Bifacial Thinning Flakes	Local Chert	17	4.1	—	—	17	4.1
	Other	15	3.6	—	—	15	3.6
Other Debris		16	3.9	—	—	16	3.9
TOTALS		373	90.5	39	9.5	412	100.0

Table 4 presents the mean projectile point lengths (L) and widths (W), and W/L ratios for a number of ethnically identified sites. While Fox is correct that Neutral points tend to be larger, their overall morphology as measured by the width/length ratio is not statistically different than the mean for contact period sites whatever the ethnic group ($\bar{x}$ = .6649; s.d. = .0498), the Maurice Village points falling just within the 1 s.d. area for a normal distribution. However, looking at those sites from which there are adequate samples to calculate the coefficient of variation (Table 4B) suggests that there is a highly significant tendency through time for less intrasite control of projectile point thickness. Although the correlation of later time with increasingly variable thickness is very good (r^2 = .763) there are obvious boundary conditions beyond which I suspect the data would sharply curve away from our linear regression. Certainly projectile point thicknesses were not all deviation-free in A.D. 1537.

Although Fox (1970:24) noted that by A.D. 1640 at Huron village sites, edge-retouched tools had been virtually replaced by iron knives, he also (1970:28ff.) suggested that by A.D. 1640 most lithic tools were imported onto their sites as finished bifaces from other groups further west, from which I infer that at least until the Huronian diaspora (A.D. 1649–53) some groups in the northern Great Lakes area may have been producing bifaces for trade. Nevertheless, in this area there is a clear shift in at least one aspect of lithic production. I suggest that those changes, observed during the seventeenth century in the Great Lakes region, are not simply due to the replacement of chipped-stone projectile points by iron or brass points (or by the notoriously inaccurate firearms). If that were so there should be a concomitant increase in variablility in all morphological

TABLE 3
METRIC ATTRIBUTES OF DUNN PLATEAU
CHIPPED STONE PROJECTILE POINTS, KNIVES, AND BIFACES[1]

Field Cat.	Length	Width	Thickness	Material Source	Comments
Triangular projectile points					
22/018	2.47	1.60	0.43	Eastport-Norwood	
22/013	3.16	2.05	1.22	Eastport-Norwood	
22/013	3.59	2.31	1.22	Eastport-Norwood	
22/003	3.92	2.35	0.47	Eastport-Norwood	
22/008	3.09	1.61	0.43	Onondaga/Upper Mercer	
22/009	2.39	2.07	0.48	Bois blanc	
22/009	2.98	2.13	0.58	Bois blanc	
22/009	2.22	1.78	0.31	Bois blanc	
22/007	3.34	2.71	0.71	Flint Ridge?	
22/007	3.62	2.41	0.55	Flint Ridge?	
22/007	3.00	2.35	0.55	Bois blanc	
22/007	2.72	1.98	0.72	Eastport-Norwood	
22/011	2.64	1.74	0.69	Eastport-Norwood	
22/011	2.24	1.65	0.46	Eastport Norwood	
22/011	2.28	×1.26	0.40	Eastport-Norwood	
22/011	2.68	2.08	0.73	Bois blanc	
22/011	2.66	1.86	0.73	Bois blanc	
22/011	2.76	1.67	0.74	Bois blanc	
Mean:	2.876	1.978	0.634		
s.d.:	0.502	0.365	0.251		
Bifacial knives					
22/015	5.84	3.17	0.78	Banded grey and white chert	
22/013	7.62	3.45	1.15	Kaolin Chert?	Heavy gloss on ridges
22/009	×1.65	1.00	0.56	Eastport-Norwood	Tip
22/003	×2.00	1.45	0.65	Eastport-Norwood	Tip
22/009	×1.86	1.23	0.41	Bois blanc	Tip
22/009	×1.28	1.17	0.76	Onondaga/Upper Mercer	Tip
Bifacial Preforms					
22/009	3.54	2.48	1.48	Devonian Chert	
22/009	2.79	1.74	0.86	Eastport-Norwood	

[1] Measurements in cm; × = broken along measured vector.

dimensions. The increased variability in thickness alone seems attributable to changes in earlier reduction stages of lithic technology. That is, the initial flake production becomes increasingly less well controlled after the appearance of the French. It is unknown whether this could be due to a breakdown in traditional inter-generational learning pathways because of social or epidemic demographic changes, or whether the French-mandated relocation of aboriginal groups to areas with differing lithic sources could have resulted in increasing technological imprecision. Both conditions can be documented to have occurred throughout the Middle Historic period (cf., Brose 1970; Mason 1981; Quimby 1966b; J.V. Wright 1965, 1968a).

Of the aboriginal lithic materials recovered from the Dunn Farm Plateau site, it is worth noting that all preforms and nearly 70% of the debitage were from materials which were locally available, while only 35.3% of the finished projectile points were *not* made of imported cherts and flints. The argument that a low frequency of snub-nosed "thumbnail" endscrapers is indicative of an Upper Mississippian affiliation (Hall 1962) seems generally unsupportable in regional terms (cf., Brose 1978). In a contact period site it would seem impossible to determine to what extent this change was due to the introduction of European replacements (e.g., Brose 1970).

Two final chipped stone artifacts merit attention: a single blade gun-flake of beeswax or honey-colored, transluscent flint with opaque white inclusions (Fig. 6aa) and a single spall gunflint of locally available Norwood chert (Fig. 6z). In the terminology provided by Witthoft (1966) and Brain (1979:210), the fine and reworked champfered French gunflake has a side to side length of 2.3 mm, a heel-edge width of 19.7 mm, and a miximum thickness of 6.8 mm. The local chert wedge spall is 17.0 mm in length, 13.5 mm in width, and 5.4 mm thick without champfer. The near 1:1 ratio of both suggests the pre-eighteenth century period (Brain 1979) and thus a French, rather than English source. Both may have been held in a light musket or fowling piece (cf. Blanchette 1973). Similar gunflints of French import and local aboriginal copy are recorded from a number of late seventeenth century occupations in the Great Lakes region such as Summer Island (Brose 1970), Fort St. Joseph (Quimby 1939a, 1942), Auden (Dawson 1976), Pic River (J.V. Wright 1966a), the Beyer site (Fitting 1974), the Bell site (Wittry 1963), Hotel Plaza (Schnell 1974), Zimmerman (M.K. Brown 1975), the Seul Choix site (Brose 1978), the O'Neill site (Lovis 1973), and the Rock Island II site (Mason 1981). They are apparently far less common as grave goods (e.g., Kidd 1953; Quimby 1966a), a point to which I shall return, although they were present at Lasanen (Cleland 1971:60–63).

TABLE 4
SOME SUMMARY STATISTICS FOR CONTACT PERIOD
UPPER GREAT LAKES CHIPPED STONE TRIANGULAR POINTS[1]

Site	Ethnic Affiliation	$\bar{x}$ Length	$\bar{x}$ Width	W/L	Source
A. BASIC MEASUREMENTS					
Summer Island	?	35	21	.600	Brose 1970
Robitaille	Huron	31	19	.613	Fox 1970
Maurice	Huron	28	20	.714	Fox 1971
Walker	Neutral	29	18	.621	M. Wright 1981
Hamilton	Neutral	25	17	.680	Lennox 1981
Beyer	Huron/Ottawa	27	17	.630	Fitting 1974
Dunn Farm Plateau	?	29	20	.690	this paper
Pic River	Algonkian	29	18	.621	J. Wright 1966a
Michipicoten	Ojibwa	22	15	.681	J. Wright 1968a
Bell	Fox	24	15	.625	Wittry 1963
Dumaw Creek	Potawatomi	25	17	.690	Quimby 1966a
South Park	Mascouten?	24	17	.708	Brose 1980

B. COEFFICIENTS OF VARIATION ($\frac{s.d.}{\bar{x}}$)

Site	Length	Width	Thickness	Estimated Date
Dunn Farm Plateau	.175	.184	.396	A.D. 1695–1715
Summer Island	.225	.219	.319	A.D. 1680–1690
Bell	.198	.129	n/a	A.D. 1680
Beyer	.139	.144	.275	A.D. 1650–1655
Hamilton	.180	.157	.259	A.D. 1640–1650
Robitaille	.129	.158	.200	A.D. 1620–1640
Dumaw Creek	.192	.124	.139	A.D. 1605–1620
South Park	.186	.150	.128	A.D. 1575–1640

[1] All measurements in mm.

Ground Stone

Few ground stone artifacts were recovered from the site. A single irregular flat fragment of sandstone 59×42×17 mm in maximum dimension was found near the Feature II depression in the southwest quadrat of Unit 1d (Fig. 4h). Across one face is a large abraded groove about 6.5 mm wide at the surface tapering to a 1 mm wide slot at a depth of 5 mm. Similar "abraders," presumably for sharpening wooden or bone points, needles, or awls, have been recovered at a number of Middle Historic period sites in the general area (Brose 1980; Fitting 1974; Lennox 1981: Fig. 34; Quimby 1966a, 1966b; M.J. Wright 1981: Fig. 49, No.4).

A single red shale gorget was recovered from the sub-A_o podzolic paleosol in Unit 2a just west of the Feature III hearth. Ignoring the two fractured corners, the gorget (Fig. 4j) is 22.5 mm wide at the "poll" and 37 mm wide at the "bit" end. It is 68.5 mm long and was 6.8 mm in maximum thickness just at the hole which was 4.5 mm from one face and 7.8 mm from the other face. Both faces of the gorget carry a series of parallel narrow incised lines in sets of two or three, each set about 7.5 mm wide and 15 mm apart. Execution is sloppy indeed, and over-incising above the hole was common. Below the hole the line sets on both faces gradually become oblique, descending to the right. Transverse parallel incisions on one edge looked like an unsuccessful attempt at wrap-around decoration. All fractures appear to postdate the decorative incising as does the single, small, white pigment-filled pit in the lower center of one face.

This same area of the Dunn Farm Plateau site yielded a sandstone "mic mac" style pipe, a widespread artifact type of the entire contact period. (Quimby 1939a, 1942, 1966a). Indeed, in Granville's 1701 drawing, the "*Sauvage de la Nation Outaouaks*" "is smoking a long-stemmed pipe whose incised bowl is of a 'Mic-Mac' style identical to that recovered at the Dunn Farm plateau (Fig. 4*i*) even to the basal thong tied from the hole in the tapering wedge-shaped base to the apparently detachable stem. Granville's man wears little beyond a necklace of beads, and similar small beaded loops in both ears and in his nose" (Feest and Feest 1978:775, Fig. 3).

European Artifacts

Like most Middle Historic period sites, the Dunn Farm Plateau yielded a number of European artifacts, representing (with the exception of glass beads) a relatively small number of artifacts of any one type. The three iron artifacts included a hand-headed, hand-forged iron spike with a ground broken end (Fig. 7*a*); a cut, beveled, serate-tanged iron projectile point 57 mm in length (Fig. 7*b*); and a corroded podal fragment of a cooking kettle of unascertainable dimensions (Fig. 7*c*). Iron spikes were noted at the Gros Cap Cemetery (Nern and Cleland 1974:9–12). Although a common item of French-Indian trade during the period, they are not commonly reported from non-European fort sites (e.g., Stone 1974). Brain (1979:290) illustrates a similar iron hinge pin noting that several (at 10 shillings) were shipped to LeFel, the blacksmith at Biloxi in 1701. An iron spike, modified in a fashion like that from Dunn Farm was recovered at the Glen site (J.V. Wright 1981:51). Brain (1979:291) also recorded that 1800 ferruled iron arrowheads like that recovered at 20Lu58 were a part of the trade goods shipped to Sieur Daniaud at Biloxi on the *l'Enflammé* in September 1701. Several similar iron points have been recovered from contexts as early as A.D. 1630 at Great Lakes aboriginal sites such as Walker (M.J. Wright 1981:Fig. 61, Nos. 1–2). They are common from 1650–90 (Fitting 1974:262; Wittry 1963) and occur as late as A.D. 1734–46 at Fort St. Joseph (Quimby 1942:547) and Trudeau (Brain 1979). Iron kettles and fragments occur on most Middle Historic period European sites (DeJarnette et al. 1976; Knight 1976; Stone 1974). Their use by both French and Indians is fully described in numerous documents of the late seventeenth century (Greenman 1957; Hamilton 1976; Joutel 1685; La Hontan 1905 [1703]; LaPotherie 1911; Quaife 1962), and they are recovered on both French and Indian sites from the Great Lakes to the Gulf (Brain 1979; Carpenter et al. 1949; Kidd 1949, 1953; Knight 1976; Mason 1981; Quimby 1939a, 1942, 1966b; Stone 1974).

Three pewter or German silver artifacts were also encountered in excavations at the Dunn Farm Plateau site: a single rolled pewter ferrule-like bead (?) (Fig. 7e); a pewter annular brooch (Fig. 7f); and a plain slightly convex pewter button with a broken cast button hole shank (Fig. 7g). Although neither pewter nor silver are presumed to be French in origin or Middle Historic period in time (e.g., Quimby 1942, 1966b), pewter dishes are reported from the ca. 1690 Gros Cap Cemetery (Nern and Cleland 1974:12ff; Quimby 1963). Rolled beads of brass similar to the Dunn Farm rolled pewter bead are common on Early and Middle Historic sites (e.g., Brose 1970; Greenman 1958; Mason 1981; Ritchie 1954:44; J.V. Wright 1981; M.J. Wright 1981; Wittry 1963:18). The Lasanen site yielded a pewter button (Cleland 1971: 25–27) and Stone (1974:53) illustrated a brass button similar to the Dunn Farm Plateau pewter button. Not only are English silver and German silver ear bobs similar to the Dunn Farm pewter annular brooch, they are widespread in the area by 1740, and there is unambiguous documentation that English traders were in the Upper Great Lakes as early as 1687 (Perrot 1911, 2:250–251).

The seven lead balls recovered from various subsurface areas within Units 3f and 2c were all about 8.5 mm in diameter (Fig. 7h). These are equivalent in caliber to today's .38 or #1 shot. All are flattened on one side and at least four are "dimpled" with some faint evidence of clamp mold-making on the others. Again, relying on Brain's compilation (1979:206–208, 291) this should indicate an approximate manufacturing date between A.D. 1665 and A.D. 1769. Within the Indian trade goods shipped to Mssr. Audran at Biloxi in 1701 were 22£ worth of "Goose shot" at 10s/cwt. Similar lead shot is reported from Ft. Michilimackinac (Stone 1974). Whether from aboriginal or European context is uncertain, although Maxwell (1964) recovered lead balls (caliber unspecified) from what he felt were aboriginal contexts and numerous Middle Historic period, unquestionably aboriginal, sites have yielded lead balls of almost every conceivable caliber (Brain 1979; Brose 1970; Conway 1980; Herrick 1958; Quimby 1942, 1957, 1966b; Wittry 1963). They should also be expected at any site yielding gunflints or gun parts.

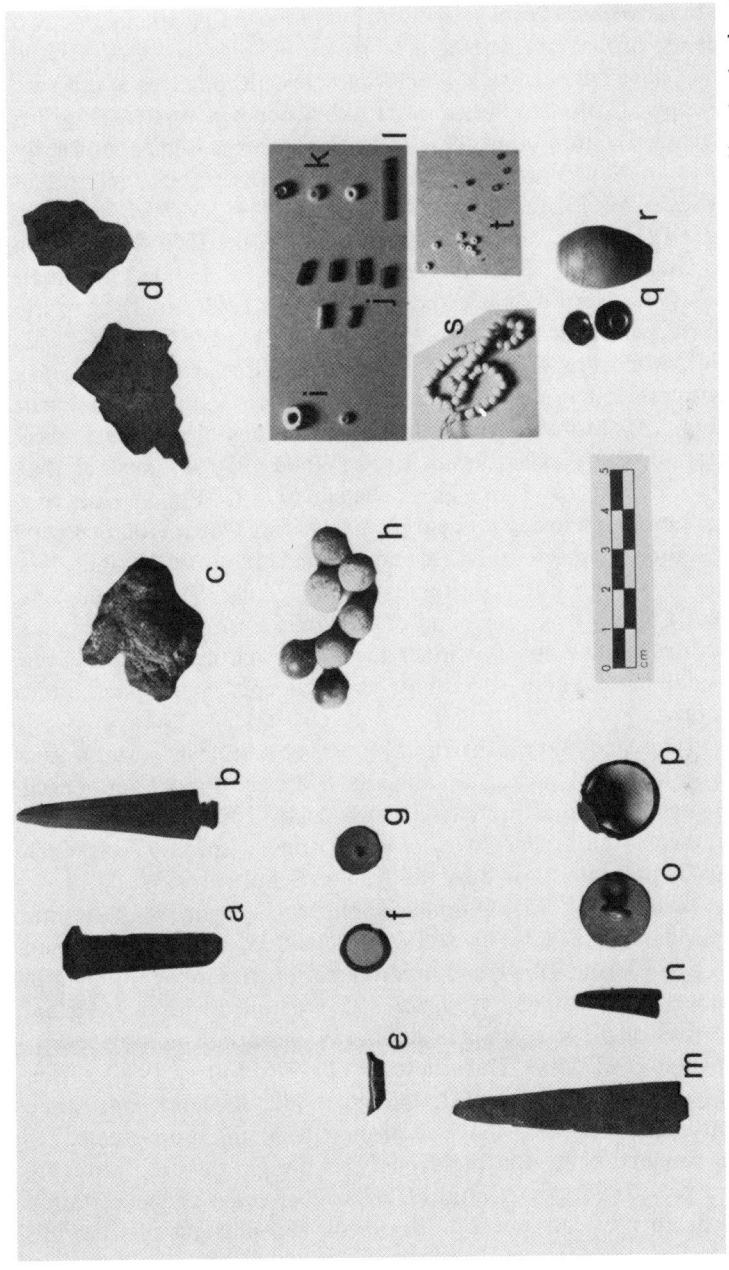

Fig. 7. Dunn Farm Plateau site European trade goods: *a*, proximal end of iron spike; *b*, iron projectile point; *c*, podal fragment of iron kettle; *d*, cut brass (kettle?) scraps; *e*, pewter ferrule (?); *f*, pewter annular brooch; *g*, pewter button with loop shank; *h*, clamp-made lead balls; *i*, disc shell beads; *j*, drilled shell wampum; *k*, *l*, and *q-t*, glass beads described in text; *m*, brass projectile point; *n*, brass tinkling cone; *o*, brass button with cast loop; and *p*, brass ring.

The six brass artifacts recovered at the Dunn Farm Plateau include two flat fragments, probably cut from a worn kettle (Fig. 7d). Few Middle Historic sites have failed to yield similar remains, although, as at this site, the brass scraps are often modified into tinkling cones or tinklers (Fig. 7n) and, less frequently, into points (Fig. 7m). Such materials may be as early as A.D. 1615 in New York (Ritchie 1954:44); A.D. 1630–50 or later in Ontario (Kidd 1949, 1953; Lennox 1981; Ridley 1954; J.V. Wright 1968b; M.J. Wright 1981). They are common throughout the 1650–80 period in the Upper Great Lakes (Cleland 1971; Fitting 1975a, 1975b; Greenman 1958; Lovis 1973; Nern and Cleland 1974; Wittry 1963), and last to the Late Historic period around A.D. 1760 (Maxwell 1964; Quimby 1942; Stone 1974). Almost as widespread in space and time are flat cast brass buttons with welded loops such as that recovered at the Dunn Farm Plateau (Fig. 7o). More restricted in all dimensions are the cast brass finger rings, popularly called Jesuit rings (Wood 1974:38), such as that from Feature II from the Dunn Farm Plateau (Fig 7p; Fig. 8). This ring has a roped border enclosing an oval plaque bearing Christ crucified with a standing figure at the left and a shrouded female figure at the right. It is an example of Wood's Calvary ring division (1974:88–89). Like the New York Seneca Calvary rings, the band of the Dunn Farm Plateau ring has a curved convex outer and flat inner face, although unlike the Seneca rings this small band, about 18.5 mm in circumference, is not plain but is "double ridged."

In 1970 I suggested that the distribution of such catechism prizes would reflect the influence of particular religious orders in French-influenced aboriginal sites; the conjecture has yet to be tested rigorously. However, the appearance of particular styles of these rings at specific New York Seneca and Cayuga sites visited by the Jesuits (Schoff 1949; Wood 1974), in Huronia (Kidd 1949, 1953; Quimby 1966b; M.J. Wright 1981), at some sites in the Mackinac Straits (Brose 1970; Cleland 1971, 1972; Greenman 1958; Nern and Cleland 1974), and at a number of sites in the Mississippi Valley (Neitzel 1965; Quimby 1939a:26, 1957), coupled with their virtual absence at sites of other periods or at coeval sites not visited by Jesuits (e.g., Carpenter et al. 1949; DeJarnette et al. 1976; Fitting 1974, 1975a, 1975b; Knight 1976; Lennox 1981; Quimby 1942; Ritchie 1954; Stone 1974; Wittry 1963) suggests that the argument is still supportable.

With its rounded bezel and high relief cast design, this ring probably represents a pre-1715 style (Cleland 1972:206, 208) and is almost certainly the actual prototype from which to derive the second stage of Cleland's I.H.S. "A Series" progression of stylistic change (1972:206, Fig. 3). At any rate, both direct dating (Cleland 1971; Nern and Cleland 1974; Wood 1974:100) and seriation (Cleland 1972) suggest that this style would date between A.D. 1650 and A.D. 1710.

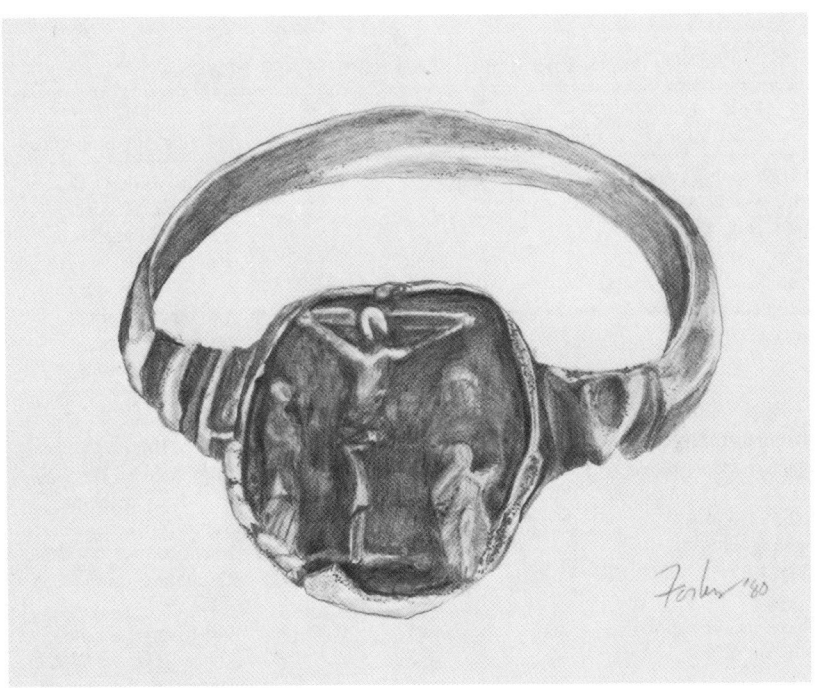

Fig. 8. Cast brass "Jesuit" ring from unit 2c.

The final category of non-aboriginal material recovered at Dunn Farm Plateau consists of 206 glass beads, 2 disc marine Columella beads, one of which was stained red (Fig. 7i, upper), and 19 wampum beads (Table 5).

The shell wampum beads (Fig. 7j) are all apparently iron-tool drilled. Orchard (1929:62ff.) suggests the shift to machine drilling may be as early as A.D. 1650, and had become uniform between A.D. 1714 and A.D. 1750. The colors of the recovered specimens from Dunn Farm Plateau (5 gray, 4 white, 4 purple, 6 black) are the normal range of color to be found in the shell of the hardshell quahog clam (*Venus mercenaria* L.). A number of other Middle Historic sites (all late seventeenth century) have yielded identical wampum beads (Brose 1970; Brown 1961; Cleland 1971; Fitting 1975b:106; Hooten and Willoughby 1922), frequently in large numbers.

In all, the only thing unusual about the assemblage of glass beads seen here is the absence of black or red and blue layered beads, both of which are common not only on Mississippi Valley and Great Lakes Middle Historic period sites (e.g., Brain 1979; Kidd and Kidd 1970; Quimby 1957, 1966b), but are also relatively common on early eighteenth century Overhill Cherokee sites in the Little Tennessee River valley (R. Polhemus, personal communication, 1982). The Middle Historic attribution of the

TABLE 5
DUNN FARM PLATEAU SITE GLASS BEADS

Description (Illustration)	Quantity	Classification[1]	Age	Middle Historic Sites
Large opaque white, wire wound, spun glass (Fig. 8r)	1	WIC 1 C 3	1630–1731	Dutch Hollow; Bell; Ossasane; Trudeau; Ft. Michilimackinac; Richardson
Cobalt blue, translucent (Fig. 8q)	2	IIA 6 a56	1680–1740	Ft. Ligonier; Bell; Summer Island; Kaskaskia; Birch Island; Trudeau
Medium tumbled, opaque white barrel	70	IIIA 2	1630–1835	Dutch Hollow; Gros Cap; Kaskaskia;
		IIIA 2	1630–1835	Ft. Michilimackinac;
Small tumbled, opaque white barrel (Fig. 8s)	96	IIIA 2	1630–1835	Summer Island; Beyer; Michipicoten; Trudeau; Dauphine Island
Red cane or tubular, interior striae (Fig. 8l)	1	IVA 1 a13	1600–1890	Pic River; Lassanen; Dutch Hollow; Walker; Hamilton; Fatherland; 28th Street
Very small white seed (Fig. 8t, left)	14	IIA 1 a14	1640–1820	Ossasane; Ste. Marie; Lassanen; Gros Cap; Richardson; Bell
Small dark blue seed (Fig. 8i, lower)	10	IIA 4 a47	1689–1800	Trudeau; Ft. deBaude; Richardson; Norge Village
Medium green seed (Fig. 8i, lower)	1	IIA15 a27	1680–1890	Bell; Ft. deBaude; Ft. Michilimackinac
Very small green seed (Fig. 8t, right)	9	IIA15 a29	1650–1850	Bell; Ste. Marie
Medium rounded, multicolored "Cornaline d' Aleppo" with abraded surfaces (Fig. 8k, upper center)	2	IIIA 1 a 3	1650–1850	Trudeau; Fatherland; Ft. deBaude; Dutch Hollow; 28th Street

[1]Roman designation from Brain (1979); italic designation from Kidd and Kidd (1970).

Dunn Farm Plateau occupation seems most tightly dated within 1699–1725, based on the chronology from glass beads.

In summary, the Dunn Farm Plateau site yields an assortment of native-made and European traded artifacts, with few aboriginal modifications of the latter. As at coeval sites in the Upper Great Lakes, the durable material culture, although limited in quantity, represents a considerable degree of acculturation. Little more European material has been recovered at any single family non-urban or non-military Colonial occupied site during the seventeenth century (Cotter 1958:57–60, App. F., Table 13; Noel-Hume 1981). Indeed, contemporary historical sources suggest that we would not find much more metal and/or glass in use at any non-elite rural dwelling whether in the Colonies or in Europe itself (Braudel 1981:274–276, 283–285, 303–306; Hamilton 1976; Noel-Hume 1981; Radisson 1885:136ff.).

The aboriginal group (or splinter groups) which occupied the Dunn Farm Plateau in the late seventeenth or early eighteenth century was certainly involved with the French fur trade. It would be most useful, for our study of acculturation, to know who they were and why they were there.

ETHNIC IDENTITIES

A brief inspection of the available Middle Historic period maps from this region of the northern lake Michigan basin reveals that prior to the Middle Historic period almost nothing was directly known of the area. Sanson's map of 1650 shows only the *N. [ation] du Feu* in the Saginaw Valley. However, his 1656 map shows *Ouk[t?]ouararonons* vaguely located somewhere in the northern Lower Peninsula north of the *N. du Feu* in the St. Joseph valley, the *Arratoeronon* along eastern Saginaw Bay, and the *Attinouandarons* in the Upper Peninsula, west of Mackinac (Karpinski 1931). The 1660 Creuxius maps show nothing in the area. Following the exploration of LaSalle, Marquette, and Joliet there is an explosion of detailed knowledge (e.g., Winsor 1884, Vol. 4). The "First Parkman Map," which was probably produced by Jesuits between 1669 and 1673, shows *Ouchikioutoulibik* somewhere south of south Manitou Island and just west of Leelanau County (Winsor 1884, 4:206). The "Third Parkman Map," probably produced after Joliet's 1674 map, shows the tip of the Lower Peninsula inhabited by *Les Tionontateronons* (Winsor 1884, 4:212–216). Of some interest is the Pierre Vander Aa a' Liede map dated 1673, which is based on Marquette's voyage. It describes the St. Ignace area as, "*Missilimakinac mission des Jesuites. Detroit par ou le lac des Illinois communique avec celuy des Hurons par ou passent les sauvages du midy quand ils vont au Montreal chargez de Castors"* (Winsor 1884, 4:216).

Based upon the data provided by Hennepin and correspondence with Du L'Hut, the Bernou 1682 map shows "-tets -[Ou]ntaten" located along the Lake Michigan shore between Frankfort and Leland (Tucker 1942:4, Pl. 8). The Franquelin 1684 map clearly shows and names *Le Traverse* [Bay] showing an unnamed aboriginal village again on the coast between Empire and Leland (Temple 1958:Pl. 59). The 1688 Franquelin map, probably relying on LaSalle's data, more clearly delineated Grand Traverse Bay and Pyramid/Sleeping Bear Point, the latter named *l'O[urs] qui dor[t]*, as it is named *Cape de l'Ours* on the 1688 Coronelli map. By 1690 Coronelli had published a newer map showing an unnamed Indian village near the O'Neill site at Petoskey and an *Outouac* village near Mackinac (Temple 1958:Pl. 61; Tucker 1942:4, Pls. 10, 108).

The 1709 edition of La Houtan's *Nouveaux Voyages* contained a map showing the French mission at St. Ignace associated with villages of Hurons and *Outaouas* while Grand Traverse Bay is called *B[aye] de l [']ours Qui d[ort]*, and a number of small aboriginal villages (spaced across the northern Lower Peninsula from above the Manistee River mouth on Lake Michigan east to Thunder Bay on Lake Huron) are called *Chasse de Cast[or] des amis des fr[ancois]* (Winsor 1884, 4:258). This map almost certainly reflects the period prior to 1702 when La Hontan visited the area.

The 1755 Bellin map (in the William Clements Library, University of Michigan) shows Grand Traverse [Baye] as *L'Ours qui dort* but shows no villages. Thomas Hutchins's 1762 map (Temple 1958:Pl. 71) shows Ft. Michilimakinac and the "Ottawas Town" at Cross Village (*L' Arbe Croche*). While Hutchins still depicts Mission Point in Grand Traverse Bay as an island, both the Leland and Crystal rivers are clearly drawn and no aboriginal villages are located nearby.

The local legend of Sleeping Bear is invariably attributed to the Ottawa or Chippewa (Ojibwa). While the latter occasionally sojourned south into the Lake Michigan area, they did so rarely, and almost never unless accompanied by other Algonkian-speaking groups (Conway 1980; Galinee 1903; Hunt 1940; LaPotherie 1911; Mason 1974, 1981; Radisson 1885; G.A. Wright 1967; J.V. Wright 1965). It would seem that the Grand Traverse Bay/Leelanau County area, when first visited by the French in the 1630–50 period, was occupied by refugee Ontario Iroquois and then by non-Ottawa/Ojibwa Algonkian groups. The Ottawa can only be cartographically inferred to have arrived some time between A.D. 1682 and A.D. 1688.

From my admittedly limited review of the historical reconstructions, it appears that the Ottawa were first encountered by the French in Georgian Bay after 1615. By 1650 they had been driven west (along with numerous other groups in the Great Lakes region) as the result of Iroquoian military adventures; by 1667 the Ottawa villages were located at French posts in Green Bay and at Mackinac. Between 1670 and 1671 the Ottawa were reported living at Green Bay, along with Miami, Mascouten and Potawatomi; at St. Ignace along with the refugee Huron; at Sault Ste. Marie, with some part of the Ojibwa; and on Manitoulin Island (Feest and Feest 1978; Kinietz 1940).

With the 1697 abandonment of the French posts in the Upper Lakes, many of the Ottawa followed Cadillac to Ft. Ponchartrain (Detroit) where from 1702 to 1717 they lived in a small village adjacent (and spatially nearly identical) to a village of Huron. Nearby groups were Fox-Sauk, Ojibwa and Missisauga, and Miami. By 1712 most of the Ottawa were again located in a village at Michilimackinac, along with some Ojibwa (and after 1715 with some Huron). Other Ottawa lived at Saginaw (with some Potawatomi) and along the St. Joseph (with Miami and Potawatomi groups). By 1742 most of the Ottawa had moved to *L' Arbe Croche* (Cross Village), although small groups were still reported at Ft. Michilimackinac and along the western shore of Lake Huron as far south as Saginaw Bay (Feest and Feest 1978; Kinietz 1940).

J.V. Wright (1965) stated explicitly that he subsumed a number of socio-ethnic Algonkian-speakers under his Ojibwa rubic. However, as Mason (1976:352–356) has wryly noted, earlier equations of "Ottawa" with "trader" are inadequate: while in one sense all "Ottawa" are equal, some Ottawa are more equal than others. Furthermore, "care must be taken not to assume that because, say, the Bell site has been identified as Fox, then all Fox sites, or even just contemporaneous ones, must yield the same artifacts, culinary features, or settlement patterns"(Mason 1976:361).

To the extent that these tenuous lines of inference are reliable, it would appear that the pre-1650 occupants of the area were not Ottawa, but rather more closely related to Algonkian speaking groups such as Sauk-Fox, Kickapoo, or Potawatomi. To test this conjecture we may hypothesize that the socio-ethnic style of artifacts from pre-contact sites in this area will look more similar to those from the southern half of lower Michigan, northern Illinois and Indiana than they will to the styles of similar pre-contact artifacts in the region from Mackinac Straits through northern Lake Huron to the Sault. Fortunately, someone else has done the work for me.

Lovis presented evidence showing that this portion of the "Traverse Corridor" saw the juxtaposition of northern and southern ceramic stylistic traditions from the Middle Woodland period through the fifteenth century A.D. He noted earlier suggestions that these may also have represented differing northern and southern economic adaptations, but cautioned that, "with the exception of scattered materials from the Wycamp Creek site [at Cross Village] and the prehistoric component at Fort Michilimackinac, our knowledge of the material culture of the protohistoric inhabitants [of the corridor] is minimal" (Lovis 1973:12). In an effort to address this lacuna, Lovis conducted excavations at the multicomponent O'Neill site. His work revealed the latest levels to be a protohistoric component dated at A.D. 1455 ±100 (uncorrected) without trade goods, and a series of short term Historic period camps. Although Lovis suggested some Early Historic period occupation, he recovered no trade goods which could not equally well (or better) be assigned to a post-1670 horizon (e.g., Lovis 1973:243, 199–207).

According to Lovis (1973), the protohistoric O'Neill component is represented by a small, multi-family longhouse occupied during the spring by a group engaged in quarrying the nearby Norwood chert. The protohistoric ceramic assemblage suggests a homogenization of Late Woodland northern (Jutunen-like) and southern (Peninsular Woodland) traditions, with the exception of two vessels. Although unillustrated, one of these vessels (Lovis 1973:90–91) may be similar to the protohistoric Indian Hills ceramics from the lower Maumee valley in northwestern Ohio (Pratt 1981:150–154). Lovis stated that the second of these vessels "... might well be either the product of trade, movement of people, or an experiment with something new" (Lovis 1973:89, 243 ff.). Indeed, similar ceramics were recovered from post-Jutunen, pre-A.D. 1730 contexts at Whitefish Island in the St. Mary's River (Conway 1980:20–22, Fig. 10, upper 1) where Conway (1980:18), noting that such ceramics co-occur with "Iroquoian" ceramics, said: "In the Sault such Iroquoian-like ceramics include low and high collared vessels with traditional Iroquoian motifs. The pots are castellated with flat plain lips and undecorated bodies. Perhaps a researcher could explain their origin and affinities when more work is devoted to the early historic and late prehistoric Ottawa."

Lovis's historic components at the O'Neill site all seem to have been single-family fall hunting camps. Although Lovis suggests chert quarrying may have been carried out, there was little evidence for post-contact lithic stone working. Middle Historic period trade goods consisted of two iron knives, one clasp, one sheath; four glass beads; three imported gun spalls; a brass coil; two brass tinkling cones; and an armband fragment (Lovis 1973:199–207, 242–245).

In short, the pre-1670 occupations at O'Neill show a developed ceramic assemblage which (weakly) supports my non-Ottawa/Ojibwa ethnic conjecture. The Middle Historic period ceramic styles, while woefully limited, suggest an infusion of northern Algonkian speaking potters (or their wares).

SITE SEASON AND FUNCTION

In his survey of the Sleeping Bear National Lakeshore, Lovis identified several late prehistoric components whose artifact styles, functions, and distributions support the argument that within the region, occupation was seasonal, of low demographic intensity, and environmentally circumscribed to areas of floral and (inferentially) faunal diversity, proximal to shoal water shorelines or well drained spring heads (Lovis et al. 1976:26–45, 90–96).

In looking at late prehistoric sites further north and south in this Lake Michigan basin, Fitting (1969) proposed a general dichotomy of summer fishing and winter hunting sites. The former are large sites on the open lake shore and/or near river mouths, with relatively high frequencies of ceramics and low frequencies of lithic material that had a high ratio of uniface to biface tools. The latter are small, often inland, upland sites with few ceramics and lots of broken bifacial tools and preforms, but little debitage. By these criteria the Dunn Farm Plateau site would be a winter hunting camp while the O'Neill site, the Seul Choix site, and the Late Woodland site at Cat Head Bay (Fig. 1) would be summer fishing villages. This picture is rendered questionable to the extent that few of the lake fish likely to have been heavily exploited spawn in the summer. Rather, from mid-June to late September, they are to be found well offshore below the 150-foot thermocline (cf. Brose 1968:243–248).

Then, if with reasonable confidence we may attribute the Dunn Farm Plateau occupation to a group of late seventeenth century Ottawa, possibly with some associated Huron relatives or friends, we may turn to the historic records for a fuller picture of the demographic, social, and economic aspects of the population. I shall avoid any assumption which fails to distinguish among these aspects, and between these and the ethnolinguistic identity itself. That such an anthropologically self-evident statement is needed at all in this region is due in part to historical accident.

In 1962, Quimby wrote a provocative article that looked to the reports of the Late Historic period for explanation of particular archaeological sites from that period in the Upper Great Lakes. Moving beyond a temporally limited direct historic approach, Fitting and Cleland (1969) looked at the ethnohistoric indications of settlement-subsistence site types, from which they hypothesized several different types of Late Woodland adaptive systems, correlated with environmental zones. Their most critical assumption was that although "the cultural environment was greatly altered during the early historic period by the incorporation of the area into the European economic network ... the technological innovations from outside were superimposed upon existing adaptations which do not appear to have been substantially altered" (1969:291). It was, perhaps, unfortunate that these differing adaptive strategies were named for the ethnolinguistic group which appeared to be practicing such an adaptive pattern in the records of the Middle Historic period. A similar theoretical approach was attempted by Gary Wright (1967:191) with more historical restraints.

Fitting (1969) carried this approach back into the Middle Woodland period, and later distinguished Huron and Ottawa as "ecotypes" whose adaptation to the same central transitional environmental zone differed due to the economic "minimax strategy" of the latter (Fitting 1972:15–16). Stimulating as these post-Quimby (1962) essays may be, I have argued that the assumptions required to apply them to the prehistoric period are entirely unacceptable (Brose 1968:446–450, 1970:29–30). Therefore, my reconstructions of the Dunn Farm Plateau Ottawa, meant to apply to the Middle Historic period only, will rely upon the contemporary documents.

THE MIDDLE HISTORIC OTTAWA

According to La Hontan, firearms were initially introduced to the Ottawa around 1670, despite the fact that as early as 1662 Nicholas Perrot reported that the Ottawa were trading their used and worn European goods to the tribes north of Chequamegon for beaver robes. According to LaPotherie, by 1670 the Ottawa had initiated similar trade with the Green Bay Potawatomi and, at St. Ignace, were engaged in gathering fruit and manufacturing bark canoes to exchange with the French for glass beads and other trade goods (Kinietz 1940:244–246).

La Hontan noted in 1688 that at the "... Mouth of the Illinese Lake [Mackinac] we met the party of Huron that I mentioned before; and four or five hundred [?] Outaouas, who were bound home after having spent the winter in hunting of beavers upon the river of Saguinan..." (La Hontan 1905 [1703]:295–300). He also noted that while those Ottawa would hunt in the Saginaw Valley every other year, prime beaver were only hunted every third winter in the country around Glen Lake by small groups of patrilaterally related families (Kinietz 1940:237). It would be interesting to learn whether these Indians still followed their early practices, described by Le Mercier, who, commenting on Fr. Claude Allouez's journal for 1665, noted that the *Outaouacs* never burned fish bones for fear of offending the Fish Spirits (Thwaites 1898, 51:121).

During the winter of 1675, Père Henri Nouvel traveled throughout the Lower Peninsula, between Ludington on Lake Michigan and the Saginaw Bay region. He was with a hunting party of Huron, Nipissing, Mississagi, and several splinter Algonkian groups later identified as either Chippewa or Ottawa clans. Nouvel mentions that somewhere on the Lake Huron shore, between Thunder Bay and Saginaw Bay, he encountered a hut occupied by *Pennengous* [Abenaki?] married to Algonkian women whom he had previously encountered at Tadoussac and Sillery . . . that is, on the lower St. Lawrence (Greenman 1957:14). Dablon's relation also noted that the Kiskakon (Bear clan or group) of Ottawa who had removed Marquette's bones to St. Ignace had spent the winter of 1676/77 hunting along Lake Michigan in the area between where Marquette died (probably Ludington) and St. Ignace (Thwaites 1900, 59:138).

It was apparently this group of northern Lake Michigan Ottawa who were involved in the two French expeditions against the Iroquois (with de la Barre to the east of Niagara in 1684, and with Denonville into the Seneca-Cayuga County in the winter of 1686/87) where at least one Iroquoian village was looted (LaPotherie 1911:16). Despite these apparently anti-English efforts by the Ottawa, Perrot reported in the late spring of 1687 that Monsieur de la Durantaye had just arrested two parties of 30 English traders near Michilimackinac who had come to trade with the Ottawa. Although the English trade goods were confiscated, they were later given to the Ottawa by the French. More English traders were arrested in 1693 near DuLuth's Fort (near Sarnia), and by 1706 Perrot bemoaned the fact that most of the Great Lakes Indians were dealing with the English who entered the region from the south and southeast rather than trading with the French at Michilimackinac or Detroit (Perrot 1911:250–251, 261).

However, this should not be taken to imply that Ottawa trade with the French had ceased by 1700. From the accounts of Robert-Lionel Seguin, it is apparent that as early as 1689 the Michilimackinac Huron and Ottawa were accustomed to spending a good part of each year traveling from the upper Lakes to La Chine (at the western end of Montreal Island) where they were strongly acculturated. For example, "in the summer of 1690 a flotilla of about 80 canoes, Hurons as well as Outaouais, reached Lachine. Immediately orgies resumed worse than ever . . ." (Seguin 1954 [1709]).

Etienne de Carheil in his argument with Cadillac referred disparagingly to these same Ottawa, noting that at the St. Ignace Mission there was much illicit traffic in brandy and prostitution, both public. He called the Indian village a "mere tavern," stating that the French soldiers "all kept open house in their dwellings for female Indians who now did nothing without bribes due to too many presents having been given to them... The Indian women do chores for French soldiers; they cook, they carry, they cut wood... but mainly they copulate. They are ruined...." (Thwaites 1901, 65:177). Despite his willingness to abandon St. Ignace, Carheil added that although the new establishment at Detroit was not really favored by the Indians (now that they knew the Iroquois were not to be destroyed by the French), they would go to Detroit merely to join in the trade with the English (Thwaites 1901, 65:177).

In arguing for the continuance of Ft. deBaude, Cadillac mentioned that, following the 1697 burning of Ft. St. Joseph by the Spanish, there was no major French post on the Lake other than at the Straits: "This post is the key of all the tribes bordering the north shore of Lake Michigan, for there are no villages along its southern part, on account of the raids of the Iroquois...." (Cadillac, cited in Quaife 1962:71). In his discussion of those Huron and Ottawa at Ft. deBaude and in northern Lake Michigan, Cadillac also mentioned that they generally made war on the tribes in the south beyond the Illini (Cadillac, cited in Quaife 1962:62–63). Perhaps this throws some light on DeLiette's observation in 1700 that, as a dowery custom, the Ottawa and Huron, like the Illinois, gave earthern pots and female slaves from further south (DeLiette, cited in Quaife 1962:117, 131, 151).

In all, the French documents, whether authored by Jesuit missionary or Royal Agent, are unambiguous in their depiction of Ottawa acculturation between A.D. 1667 and A.D. 1715. Although not addressing the issue of differing sexual roles and rates of acculturation during the Middle Historic period (cf. Brose 1970), in his discussion of the role of early French Indian trade, Fitting (1976:331–333) has provided an interesting answer to another rhetorical question I raised in discussion of the seventeenth century occupation on Summer Island: "One would also like to know whether a brass kettle should be considered as a male status symbol or as a female implement" (Brose 1968:446). Fitting suggested that European trade goods initially served a utilitarian purpose until "saturation" of the aboriginal societies shifted them from a sociotechnic to an ideotechnic realm of behavior and they became most useful as status-marking grave goods. While this is an appropriately processual answer, I believe it to be almost entirely incorrect.

As I suggested earlier, there are differences in artifact types between the European trade goods that occur in aboriginal mortuary contexts and in aboriginal domestic contexts. We are often unable to reconstruct the cultural, biological, and pedological pathways by which artifacts are incorporated into domestic site matrices. However, due to numerous eyewitness reports, we are under no such handicap in reconstructing the way artifacts were incorporated in aboriginal mortuary contexts during the Historic period. (e.g., Cleland 1971; Hickerson 1960; Kidd 1953; Neitzel 1965; Quimby 1966a; Swanton 1911, 1946; Thwaites 1900). The ethnohistoric documents relate unambiguously to the archaeological sites. Together they clearly show the sequence of trade good use: the earliest European trade goods were articles of personal adornment (beads, bangles, mirrors); next came items of general domestic use (pots, kettles, thimbles); and last were artifacts of use in direct economic extraction (knives, arrow points, guns, traps). This is exactly the same sequence in which the mortuary offerings occur in coeval aboriginal sites. It appears that the initial aboriginal use of European trade goods was primarily as ideotechnic artifacts, for much of the aboriginal retrading into the western country was of disfunctional items (Brose 1970; Joutel 1685; Radisson 1885). Only after high frequencies of such items had "saturated" socioideological values of the aboriginal group do they cease to appear as grave goods. Thus I expect that any grave goods accompanying the burials of that Ottawa family who occupied the Dunn Farm Plateau site to hunt beaver during the fall between 1693 and 1715 would look very much like those from the Lassanen or Gros Cap or Richardson cemeteries. Indeed, some of those burials may well have *been* occupants of the Dunn Farm Plateau.

THE NATURE OF FRENCH ACCULTURATION

Based on the interpretations offered above, it may be appropriate to rethink the nature of French acculturation and the effects of the French presence in this region of America as opposed to that of the British after A.D. 1760.

In looking at the differences between the purportedly beneficent French and the presumably destructive British economic relationships with the Indians, one historical fact seems all too often overlooked: the only major aboriginal societies in the Eastern Woodlands able to withstand the cultural disintegration of the eighteenth century were the New York Iroquois and the Overhill Cherokee, groups which had been consistently allied with the British.

Indeed, the parochial failure to recognize the changes in material culture between the early seventeenth and the late eighteenth century in Europe itself (e.g., Braudel 1981), has incorrectly suggested a significant difference between the nature of French acculturation of American Indian societies and the nature of British acculturation of those American Indian societies. The major difference, I suspect, is that the British of A.D. 1760 simply had far more durable goods than did the French of A.D. 1670. To the extent possible, the French expansion into the Great Lakes-Mississippi Valley-Gulf Coast area represented a major cultural trauma for the economy and technology of every aboriginal group they encountered from the very beginning. We should not need to be reminded of this cold-blooded effort by Rochefort's 1701 memorandum, adjusting the funds allocated for one partial shipload of trade goods for Biloxi, to insure that "there must be 1500£ worth of Brandy . . . one cannot wage war and travel distances of 3 to 400 leagues without brandy" (cited in Brain 1979:292).

Contrasting the 1680 Tionantate Village at St. Ignace with the 1694–96 Lassanen and Gros Cap cemeteries and the Juntunen site on Bois Blanc Island just off shore, Fitting (1976:323–331) argued that pre-contact aboriginal patterns in subsistence economy were only intensified, not drastically altered: that ritual emphases especially reflect the changed "internal patterning" of society, while the overall social and economic patterns remained conservative until the arrival of the British. I do not agree.

Surely there is nothing in the archaeological record of the late prehistoric period in the Great Lakes (Brose 1978; Mason 1981; White 1978; J.V. Wright 1963, 1965; Wintemberg 1939), the Mississippi Valley (Brain 1979; Phillips 1970; Williams et al. 1982), or along the Gulf Coast (Knight 1976; Tesar 1980) to suggest the rapid alterations in aboriginal cultural geography that are the hallmark of the Historic period. These were French, not British phenomena. There is no evidence for intensive pre-contact inter- and intra-tribal territorial aggrandizement (e.g., Hunt 1940) even in those areas where legend suggests it may have existed (Englebrecht 1971). There is no evidence for any late prehistoric economic exchange system or network which even approaches that inferred for the Middle Woodland period in these same regions (*contra* G.A. Wright 1967).

Perhaps with tongue-in-cheek, Fitting stated that:

> The overall significance of acculturation during the French occupation of the Upper Great Lakes can be understood best by contrasting it with the later British and American occupations. The French occupation was mercantile but not colonial. Local economic and social traditions were supported . . . imported goods were utilized to reinforce and augment economic, social, and ideological components of prehistoric origins. *The French helped the Indians be better Indians with the introduced trade goods.*

> British . . . economic attitudes were more capitalistic than mercantilistic . . . the *local cultures which had been enriched by their dependence on an imported technology* were destroyed as the traditional concepts of gift-giving gave way before their dependence on imported goods. [Fitting 1976:333–334, emphasis added]

What are we to think of this *Ancien Régime* Newspeak? Certainly to the extent that either economic term is applicable, eighteenth century British capitalism is no more than the late manifestation of seventeenth century French mercantilism. This is what Quimby has been telling us for over forty years.

And beyond that devastating economic and technological dependence was the social and political dependence fostered by the French. The internal restructuring of aboriginal societies to support French military adventures, the far-flung geographic resettlement of aboriginal populations to improve French logistics, the alternating rearrangements of aboriginal alliances to facilitate French strategy, all were activities undertaken in a spirit of Colonial *Realpolitik*. They left neither the cynical officials who initiated them nor the frustrated missionaries who opposed them with any illusions as to their ultimate consequences.

Notes

1. There is little question that the work of my long suffering field crew, Barbara, Robert, and Thomas Brose, was appreciated. The support, forbearance, and caution of Mrs. George Johnson was equally valuable. I also thank Dr. John Halsey, State Archaeologist, Michigan Historical Commission for arranging partial support. Thanks are due to Dr. William Lovis, The Museum, Michigan State University, for his freely given (though not always heeded) information. The maps and drawings were produced by Mark Schornak and Mel Forbes, Archaeology Department, Cleveland Museum of Natual History. Ms. Doris Willis typed several versions of this manuscript. All metric analyses and much photographic assistance were provided by Robert M. Brose.

2. Similar ceramics have been assigned to an atypical variant of Lalonde High Collar (J.V. Wright 1966b:73, Pl. XVII, 1; Ridley 1954) or a variant of Lawson Opposed (MacNeish 1952:99, Fig. 4) or Lalond High Collar itself (J.V. Wright 1968b: Pl. IV, Fig. 2; Pl. VI, Fig. 2). Similar vessels attributed to Lawson Opposed were recovered at the 1630–51 Neutral Walker site (M. Wright 1981:84, Fig. 51, No. 4), while several similar vessels from Hochelaga were untyped (Pendergast and Trigger 1972: Pl. VII, Fig. 2).

3. There is one further possibility. Schoff (1949:21–23) notes that the Broughton Hill site is the same St. Jacques mission that was burned by the French in A.D. 1687. The burials were looted for glass beads and metal by Denonville's Ottawa and Ojibwa Indians from Michilimackinac. If those looted burials were similar to the 14 which remained intact on the McMahon Farm portion of the site, the loot could have been carried home in a Richmond Incised pot.

4. Vaguely similar ceramics occur on later Ontario Neutral sites such as Walker (M.J. Wright 1981:Fig. 52, No. 6) or Algonkian sites such as Auden (Dawson 1976:56, Pl. I, Nos. 26 and 27).

5. E. g., as Huron Incised (J.V. Wright 1968b:Pl. IV, Fig. 1; Brose 1970: Pl. I, Fig. L); Round Necked (J. V. Wright 1968b:Pl. VI, Fig. 9; MacNeish 1952:101, Fig. 3); a variant of Middleport Oblique (MacNeish 1952:103, Fig. 8); a variant of Long Point Horizontal

(MacNeish 1952:129, Fig. 2); Copeland Incised (J.V. Wright 1966a:73–74, Pl. XVII, Fig. 2); or simply Huron-like (Fitting 1974:241–244). Wright has also assigned similar ceramics to the protohistoric Stamped Tradition (J.V. Wright 1968a:Pl. IX, Fig. 3; Pl. XIII, Figs. 4–5; Pl. XVI, Figs. 8 and 10), and frequently they are simply illustrated as being present at Isle Royale (Quimby 1939b: Pl. 11, Fig. 1, lower row, first and second sherds).

6. Grit-tempered varieties called Black Necked also occur at the 1690s Ottawa and Huron/Petun Norge Village and Beyer site at St. Ignace (Fitting 1974: 200, Fig. 29a, vessel 1; 240, Fig. 36, i,k). Further east, similar rimsherds are assigned to the Black Necked type (MacNeish 1952:121, Fig. 3) or Copeland Incised (Pendergast and Trigger 1972: Pl. V, No. 6).

7. At the Bell site, these ceramics with shell temper only (?) were called LaSalle Filletted (Wittry 1963:26–27, Fig. 17b). When encountered at protohistoric Illinois sites, the implication is that they are refugee Shawnee (e.g., J. A. Brown 1961; M. K. Brown 1975; Fenner 1961; Schnell 1974). In the general area of northern Lake Michigan, such notched appliqué rim strip vessels are reported for the protohistoric Ada site (Herrick 1958: Fig. 10), from the Beyer site (Fitting 1974:246, Fig. 37e) at Fort Michilimackinac (Maxwell 1964:28) and from cemeteries at Gros Cap (Nern and Cleland 1974:45, Fig. 22; Quimby 1963) and Richardson (Greenman 1958). The shell- and/or grit-tempered appliqué strip ceramics from Historic period Neutral sites (Lennox 1981; M.K. Wright 1981) are not at all similar. They are *not* Whittlesey ceramics, but rather represent trades, raids, or maids from the Indian Hills complex of the lower Maumee valley (Pratt 1981).

REFERENCES

Biggar, H. P. (editor)
    1922–   *The works of Samuel de Champlain.* 6 Vols. The Champlain Society, Toronto.
    1936
Blanchette, J. -F.
    1973   Gunflints from Chicoutimi Indian site (Quebec). *Historical Archaeology* 9:41–54.
Boyd, M. F., H. G. Smith, and J. W. Griffin
    1957   *Here they once stood: the tragic end of the Appalachee missions.* University of Florida Press, Gainesville.
Brain, J.
    1979   Tunica treasure. *Papers of the Peabody Museum of Archaeology and Ethnology* 71.
Braudel, F.
    1981   *The structures of everyday life: the limits of the possible.* Translated by S. Reynolds. Harper and Row, New York.
Brose, D. S.
    1967   Review of "Indian culture and European trade goods" by G. I. Quimby. *Michigan Archaeologist* 13(1):33–34.
    1968   The archaeology of Summer Island: changing settlement systems in the northern Lake Michigan area. Ph.D. dissertation, Department of Anthropology, University of Michigan, Ann Arbor.
    1970   Summer Island III: an early historic site in the Upper Great Lakes. *Historical Archaeology* 6:3–33.
    1978   The late prehistoric period in the Upper Great Lakes. In *Handbook of North American Indians*, edited by B. G. Trigger, 15:569–582. Smithsonian Institution, Washington, D.C.
    1980   The late prehistoric occupations of the south-central Lake Erie area. Paper presented at the 14th Annual Meeting of the Ontario Archaeological Society Symposium, London, Ontario.

Brose, D. S., S. Belovich, M. Brooslin, R. Burns, J. Hall, H. Haller, C. Pierce, and C. Ubbleohde
    1981   Prehistoric and historic archaeological investigations of the Cuyahoga Valley National Recreation Area, Ohio. *Archaeological Research Reports of the Cleveland Museum of Natural History* 30:1–524.

Brown, J. S.
    1961   The Zimmerman site. *Illinois State Museum, Reports of Investigations* 9.

Brown, M. K.
    1975   The Zimmerman site: further excavations at the Grand Village of Kaskaskia. *Illinois State Museum, Reports of Investigations* 32.

Carpenter, E. S., K. R. Pfirman, and H. L. Schoff
    1949   The 28th street site. *Pennsylvania Archaeologist* 19(1–2):3–16.

Cleland, C. E.
    1972   From sacred to profane. *American Antiquity* 37:202–210.

Cleland, C. E. (editor)
    1971   The Lasanen site: an historic burial locality in Mackinac County, Michigan. *Publication of the Museum, Michigan State University, Anthropological Series* 1.

Conway, T. A.
    1980   Heartland of the Ojibway. In Collected archaeological papers, edited by D. S. Melvin, *Ontario Ministry of Culture and Recreation, Historic Planning and Research Branch, Archaeological Research Report* 13:1–28.

Cotter, J. L.
    1958   Archaeological excavations at Jamestown: colonial national historical park and Jamestown national historic site, Virginia. *National Park Service, Archaeological Research Series* 4.

Dawson, K. C. A.
    1976   Algonkians of Lake Nipigon: an archaeological survey. *National Museum of Man, Archaeological Survey of Canada, Mercury Series* 48.

DeJarnette, D. L. (editor), with N. J. Jenkins, V. J. Knight, Jr., C. B. Curren, Jr., K. Shaw, and M. F. DeLeon
    1976   Highway salvage excavations at two French colonial period Indian sites on Mobile Bay, Alabama. Report to the Alabama Highway Department, University of Alabama.

Englebrecht, W. E.
    1971   A stylistic analysis of New York Iroquois pottery. Ph.D. dissertation, Department of Anthropology, University of Michigan, Ann Arbor.

Feest, J. E., and C. Feest
    1978   Ottawa. In *Handbook of North American Indians*, edited by B. G. Trigger, 15:772–786. Smithsonian Institution, Washington, D.C.

Fenner, G. J.
    1961   The Bowmanville site. *Illinois Archaeological Survey, Bulletin* 4:37–56.

Fitting, J. E.
    1969   Settlement analysis in the Great Lakes region. *Southwest Journal of Anthropology* 25:360–377.
    1972   The Huron as an ecotype: the limits of maximization in a western Great Lakes society. *Anthropologica* 14(1):1–18.
    1975a   A late 17th century burial from St. Ignace, Michigan. *Michigan Archaeologist* 21(2):97–104.
    1975b   A middle historic period burial from St. Ignace, Michigan. *Michigan Archaeologist* 21(2):105–108.
    1976   Patterns of acculturation in the Straits of Mackinac. In *Culture change and continuity*, edited by C. E. Cleland, pp. 321–334. Academic Press, New York.

Fitting, J. E. (editor)
    1974   Contributions to the archaeology of the St. Ignace area. *Michigan Archaeologist* 20(3–4):117–286.

Fitting, J. E., and C. E. Cleland
    1969   Late prehistoric settlement patterns in the Upper Great Lakes. *Ethnohistory* 16:289–302.

Fox, W. A.
    1970   Robitaille Village site, BeHa–3: analysis of an historic Huron lithic assemblage. Manuscript on file, University of London, Ontario.
    1971   The Maurice Village site, BeHa–2: lithic analysis. In Palaeoecology and Ontario prehistory, edited by W. Hurley and C. Heindenreich. *University of Toronto, Department of Anthropology, Research Report* 2:137–165.
    1972   Neutral lithics. Paper presented at the 1972 Canadian Archaeological Association Annual Meeting, St. John's, Newfoundland.

Galinee, R. deB.
    1903   A voyage to the Upper Canadian missions. *Proceedings of the Royal Ontario Historical Society*, Vols. 1–11.

Greenman, E. F.
    1957   Wintering in the Lower Peninsula, 1675–1676. With a portion of the "Journal of the Last Winter Mission of Father Henry Nouvel, Superior of the Missions of the Ottawas," translated by M. Guta. *Michigan Archaeologist* 3(3):5–21.
    1958   An early historic cemetery at St. Ignace. *Michigan Archaeologist* 4(2):28–35.

Griffin, J. B.
    1943   *The Fort Ancient aspect.* University of Michigan Press, Ann Arbor.

Hall, R. L.
    1962   *The archaeology of Carcajou Point.* 2 Vols. University of Wisconsin Press, Madison.

Hamilton, P. J.
    1976   *Colonial Mobile.* University of Alabama Press, University.

Herrick, R.
    1958   A report on the Ada site, Kent County, Michigan. *Michigan Archaeologist* 4(1):1–27.

Hickerson, H.
    1960   The feast of the dead among the 17th century Algonkians of the Upper Great Lakes. *American Anthropologist* 62:81:107.

Hooten, E., and C. Willoughby
    1922   Indian village site and cemetery near Madisonville, Ohio. *Papers of the Peabody Museum of American Archaeology and Ethnology* 8(1).

Hunt, G.
    1940   *The wars of the Iroquois.* University of Wisconsin Press, Madison.

Innis, H. A.
    1962   *The fur trade in Canada* (second ed.). Yale University Press, New Haven.

Joutel, H.
    1685   Journal of La Salle's last voyage to discover the River Mississippi, translated and edited by B. F. Frency. *Louisiana Historical Collections* 1:85–193.

Karpinski, L. C.
    1931   *Map bibliography of Michigan and the Great Lakes region.* Michigan Historical Commission, Lansing.

Kidd, K. E.
    1949   *The excavation of Ste. Marie I.* University of Toronto Press, Toronto.
    1953   The excavation and identification of a Huron ossuary. *American Antiquity* 18:359–379.

Kidd, K. E., and M. Kidd
    1970   A classification system for glass beads for the use of field archaeologists. *Canadian Historic Sites, Occasional Papers in Archaeology and History* 1.

Kinietz, V.
    1940   The Indians of the western Great Lakes. *Occasional Contributions from the Museum of Anthropology, University of Michigan* 10.

Knight, V. J., Jr.
  1976 Archaeological investigations on Dauphin Island, Mobile County, Alabama. Report to the National Park Service, Office of Archaeology and Historic Preservation, IAS, Atlanta.
La Hontan, Baron de
  1905 *New voyages to North America* (reprinted from the English edition of 1703, [1703] edited by R. G. Thwaites). 2 Vols. McClurg, Chicago.
LaPotherie, B.
  1911 History of the savage peoples who are allies of New France. In *Indian tribes of the Upper Mississippi Valley and the region of the Great Lakes*, edited by E. H. Blair, Vol. 2:13–136. Arthur H. Clark, Cleveland.
Lennox, P. A.
  1981 Hamilton site: late historic Neutral town. *National Museum of Man, Archaeological Survey of Canada, Mercury Series* 103:211–403.
Lovis, W. A., Jr.
  1973 Late Woodland cultural dynamics in the northern Lower Peninsula of Michigan. Ph.D. dissertation, Department of Anthropology, Michigan State University, East Lansing.
Lovis, W. A., Jr., R. Mainfort, and V. Noble
  1976 An archaeological inventory and evaluation of the Sleeping Bear Dunes National Lakeshore, Leelanau and Benzie counties, Michigan. *Michigan State University Museum, Archaeological Survey Report* 5:1–114.
MacNeish, R. S.
  1952 Iroquois pottery types. A technique for the study of Iroquois prehistory. *National Museum of Canada, Bulletin* 124.
Mainfort, R. C.
  1979 Indian social dynamics in the period of European contact: Fletcher site cemetery, Bay County, Michigan. *Michigan State University Anthropological Series* 1(4).
Mason, R. J.
  1974 Huron Island and the Island of the Poutouatamis. In Aspects of Upper Great Lakes archaeology, papers in honor of Lloyd A. Wilford, edited by E. Johnson. *Minnesota Prehistoric Archaeology Series* 11:149–156.
  1976 Ethnicity and archaeology in the Upper Great Lakes. In *Culture change and continuity*, edited by C. E. Cleland, pp. 349–362. Academic Press, New York.
  1981 *Great Lakes archaeology*. Academic Press, New York.
Maxwell, M. S.
  1964 Indian artifacts at Fort Michilimackinac, Mackinac city, Michigan. *Michigan Archaeologist* 10(2):23–30.
Neitzel, R. S.
  1965 Archaeology of the Fatherland site: the Grand Village of the Natchez. *Anthropological Papers of the American Museum of Natural History* 51(1).
Nern, C. F., and C. E. Cleland
  1974 The Gros Cap cemetery site, St. Ignace, Michigan: a reconsideration of the Greenless collection. *Michigan Archaeologist* 20:1–58.
Noel-Hume, I.
  1981 *Martins Hundred*. Knopf, New York.
Orchard, W. C.
  1929 Beads and beadwork of the American Indian. *Heye Foundation Contributions* 11.
Parkman, F.
  1879 *LaSalle and the discovery of the Great West*. Little, Brown, Boston.
  1885 *The conspiracy of Pontiac*. Little, Brown, Boston.
Pendergast, J. F., and B. G. Trigger
  1972 *Cartier's Hochelaga and the Dawson site*. McGill-Queens University Press, Montreal.

Perrot, N.
1911 Memoir on the manners, customs, and religion of the savages of North America. In *Indian tribes of the Upper Mississippi Valley and the region of the Great Lakes*, edited by E. H. Blair, 2:25-272. Arthur H. Clark, Cleveland.

Phillips, P.
1970 Archaeological survey in the Lower Yazoo Basin, Mississippi, 1949-1955. *Papers of the Peabody Museum of Archaeology and Ethnology* 60.

Pratt, G. M.
1981 The Western Basin tradition: changing settlement-subsistence adaptation in the western Lake Erie Basin region. Ph.D. dissertation, Department of Anthropology, Case Western Reserve University, Cleveland.

Pratt, P. P.
1961 Oneida Iroquois glass trade bead sequence/1585-1745. *Fort Stanwix Museum, Color Guide Series* 1.

Quaife, M. (editor)
1962 *The western country in the 17th century: the memoirs of Antoine Lamothe Cadillac and Pierre Liette*. Citadel Press, New York.

Quimby, G. I.
1938 Dated Indian burials in Michigan. *Papers of the Michigan Academy of Science, Arts, and Letters* 23:67-72.
1939a European trade articles as chronological indicators for the archaeology of the Historic period in Michigan. *Papers of the Michigan Academy of Science, Arts, and Letters* 24(4):25-31.
1939b Aboriginal campsites on Isle Royale Michigan. *American Antiquity* 4:215-223.
1942 Indian trade objects in Michigan and Louisiana. *Papers of the Michigan Academy of Science, Arts, and Letters* 27:542-551.
1957 The Bayou Goula site, Iberville Parish, Louisiana. *Fieldiana: Anthropology* 47:91-170.
1962 A year with a Chippewa family 1763-1764. *Ethnohistory* 9:217-239.
1963 The Gros Cap cemetery in Mackinac County, Michigan. *Michigan Archaeologist* 9(4):50-57.
1966a The Dumaw Creek site, a 17th century prehistoric Indian village and cemetery in Oceana County, Michigan. *Fieldiana: Anthropology* 56:1-91.
1966b *Indian culture and European trade goods*. University of Wisconsin Press, Madison.

Radisson, P. E.
1885 *Voyages of Peter Esprit Radisson, being an account of his travels and experiences among the North American Indians 1652-1684*. The Prince Society, Boston.

Ridley, F.
1954 The Frank Bay site, Lake Nipissing, Ontario. *American Antiquity* 20:40-50.

Ritchie, W. A.
1954 Dutch Hollow, an early historic period Seneca site in Livingston County, New York. *Research Records, Rochester Museum of Arts and Sciences* 10.

Schnell, G. S.
1974 Hotel Plaza: an early historic site with a long prehistory. *Illinois State Museum, Reports of Investigations* 29.

Schoff, H. L.
1949 'Black Robes' among the Seneca and Cayuga. *Pennsylvania Archaeologist* 19(1-2):18-26.

Seguin, R. L.
1954 The behavior of certain inhabitants of Alchine around 1689. *Le Bulletin des*
[1709] *Recherches Historiques* 60(4):187-193 (1954). (1959 translation by M. Guta in manuscript collections, Great Lakes Range Anthropology, University of Michigan Museum of Ann Arbor).

Slaymaker, C. M., III, and C. M. Slaymaker, Jr.
  1971 Au Sagaunashke Village: the Upper Mississippian occupations of the Knoll Springs site, Cook County, Illinois. In Mississippian site archaeology in Illinois, I. Site reports from the St. Louis and Chicago area. *Illinois Archaeological Survey Bulletin* 8:192-250.
Smith, H.G.
  1951 The Crable site, Fulton Co., Illinois. *University of Michigan, Museum of Anthropology, Anthropological Papers* 7.
Stone, L. M.
  1974 Fort Michilimackinac, 1715-1781: an archaeological perspective on the Revolutionary frontier. *Publications of the Museum, Michigan State University, Anthropological Series* 2.
Swanton, J. R.
  1911 Indian tribes of the Lower Mississippi Valley and adjacent coast of the Gulf of Mexico. *Bureau of American Ethnology, Bulletin* 43.
  1946 The Indians of the southeastern United States. *Bureau of American Ethnology, Bulletin* 137.
Temple, W.
  1958 Indian villages of the Illinois country. Part I, Atlas Supplement. *Illinois State Museum, Scientific Papers* 2(2).
Thwaites, R. G. (editor)
  1896–
  1901 *The Jesuit relations and allied documents: travel and explorations of the Jesuit missionaries in New France, 1610-1791; the original French, Latin, and Italian texts, with English translations and notes.* 73 Vols. Burroughs Bros., Cleveland.
Tesar, L. D.
  1980 The Leon County bicentennial survey report: an archaeological survey of selected portions of Leon County, Florida. *Bureau of Historic Sites and Properties, Division of Archives, History and Records Management, Florida Department of State Miscellaneous Project Report Series* 49, Sec. 1 and 2.
Tucker, S. J.
  1942 Indian villages of the Illinois country, Part I, Atlas. *Illinois State Museum, Scientific Papers* 2(1).
White, M. E.
  1978 Neutral and Wenro; Erie. In *Handbook of North American Indians*, edited by B. G. Trigger, 15:407-418. Smithsonian Institution, Washington, D.C.
Williams, S., M. Mehrer, J. Price, J. Muller, F. Schamback, D. Hally, G. Schroedl, C. Munson, D. Brose, V. Steponaitis, and J. Brain
  1982 The vacant quarter hypothesis: a discussion symposium. Symposium at the 39th Annual Meeting of the Southeastern Archaeological Conference, Memphis.
Willey, G. R.
  1949 Archaeology of the Florida Gulf Coast. *Smithsonian Institution, Miscellaneous Contributions* 113:1-547.
Winsor, J. (editor)
  1884 *Narrative and critical history of North America.* Vols. 1-6. Houghton, Mifflin, Boston.
Wintemberg, W. J.
  1939 Lawson prehistoric village site, Middlesex County, Ontario. *National Museum of Canada, Bulletin* 94.
  1946 The Sidey-Mackay village site. *American Antiquity* 11:154-184.
Witthoft, J.
  1966 A history of gunflints. *Pennsylvania Archaeologist* 36:12-49.
Wittry, W. L.
  1963 The Bell site, Wn9, an early historic Fox village. *Wisconsin Archaeologist* 44(1):1-57.

Wood, A. S.
   1974   A catalogue of Jesuit and ornamental rings from western New York State. *Historical Archaeology* 10:83–104.

Wright, G. A.
   1967   Some aspects of early and mid-17th century exchange networks in the western Great Lakes. *Michigan Archaeologist* 13(4):181–197.

Wright, J. V.
   1963   An archaeological survey along the north shore of Lake Superior. *National Museum of Canada, Anthropological Paper* 3.
   1965   A regional examination of Ojibwa culture history. *Anthropologia* 7(2):189–229.
   1966a   The Pic River site. *National Museum of Canada, Bulletin* 206(1):54–99.
   1966b   The Ontario Iroquois tradition. *National Museum of Canada, Bulletin* 210.
   1968a   The application of the direct historical approach to the Iroquois and Ojibwa. *Ethnohistory* 15:96–111.
   1968b   The Michipicoten site, Ontario. *National Museum of Canada, Bulletin* 224(1):1–84.
   1971   The Nodwell site: a mid 14th century Iroquois village. *Archaeological Society Bulletin* 3:1–11.
   1981   The Glen site: an historic Cheveux Releves campsite on Flowerpot Island, Georgian Bay, Ontario. *The Ontario Archaeologist* 35:45–59.

Wright, M. J.
   1981   The Walker site. *National Museum of Man, Archaeological Survey of Canada, Mercury Series* 103:1–209.

Zurel, R.
   1980   Perspectives from southeast Michigan on the late prehistoric and historic Indians' interactions in the western Lake Erie region. Paper presented at the 7th Annual Symposium of the Ontario Archaeological Society, London, Ontario.

THE ROLE OF NATIVE ANIMALS IN THE FOOD ECONOMY OF THE HISTORIC KICKAPOO IN CENTRAL ILLINOIS[1]

Paul W. Parmalee and Walter E. Klippel

Relatively little specific data pertaining to the species of animals hunted and their utilization by early historic Indian tribes in Illinois are available. In the case of the Kickapoo, who periodically occupied various parts of what is now Illinois from about 1685 to 1832, only general mention has been made of their "hunting grounds" and migrations down (from Wisconsin) into the Illinois country to "hunt game" and to "catch beaver" (Temple 1966:158-159). Until now, a study of the faunal materials from a historic Sauk-Fox village located near the mouth of the Rock River, Rock Island County, Illinois (Parmalee 1964), a site probably contemporaneous with the Rhoads site reported here, provided the only information available on the subsistence economy of protohistoric Indians of the period. Generally, the observation made by Quimby (1966:140) over 15 years ago that "with some rare exceptions the archaeology of the Late Historic period has not been studied by professional archaeologists, most of whom chose to work with more ancient cultures and periods" still holds true today.

THE HISTORIC PERIOD IN "ILLINOIS COUNTRY"

The earliest written records that describe the mixed prairie and forest areas of the Prairie Peninsula east of the Mississippi River and the Native Americans who occupied them are provided by French missionaries and traders, beginning with the pioneering voyage of Marquette and Joliet down the Mississippi and up the Illinois rivers in 1673. Earlier in the seventeenth century, i.e., the Early Historic period, 1610-1670 (Quimby

253

1966:102–116), French *coureurs de bois* and *hivernauts* restricted their activities to the north and east (Quimby 1966:3–4). At the beginning of the Middle Historic period (ca. 1670) and the time of the first written records about the Prairie Peninsula, the area east of the Mississippi River was occupied by a confederacy of Algonquian-speaking tribes known collectively as the Illini, which included the Cahokia, Kaskaskia, Michigamea, Moingwena, Peoria, and Tamaroa, among others (Temple 1966:11–56).

During the Middle Historic period (1670–1760; Quimby 1966:117–139), the Illini were drastically reduced in number through disease and conflicts with other tribes such as the Iroquois, Sioux, Chickasaw, Sauk, Fox, Potawatomi, and Kickapoo. By the time the British gained sovereignty over the area (in 1763) much of the "Illinois Country" was occupied by groups partially responsible for the demise of the Illini. The Late Historic period, 1760–1820 (Quimby 1966:140–185), then, witnessed the occupation of the Illinois Country by tribes such as the Kickapoo, Potawatomi, Sauk, and Fox (Klippel 1976:11).

The American settlers were the last alien group to invade the Illinois Country prior to the time that the Indians were deported across the Mississippi River. The influx began less than 15 years after the British took the area from the French. Access for the settlers came with the American capture of Kaskaskia on the Mississippi River and Vincennes on the Wabash River during the mid-1770s. With a foot in the door, the settlers generally moved from the forested south to the mixed prairie and forest in central and northern Illinois.

The Federal government began to apply the American Rectangular Survey System to what is now the State of Illinois around the turn of the nineteenth century to meet the needs of the settlers. The survey, as with the influx of the settlers, began in southern Illinois and gradually extended northward as settlers claimed land in the new areas. As such, the survey records generally reflect the extent and direction of American settlement in Illinois. A map constructed by John Melish in 1818 from the Federal Land Office Surveys shows much of central Illinois unsurveyed and, incidentally, shows the location of two Kickapoo villages. One of these almost certainly represents the Rhoads site (Conway 1972:396; Klippel 1976:12; Temple 1966:167). By the early 1830s, all Native Americans had been expelled from the Illinois Country.

Historic records suggest that groups like the Kickapoo, Sauk, and Fox who inhabited portions of the Prairie Peninsula during the Late Historic period moved from summer to winter villages on an annual basis. One fur trader's account of Sauk between 1773 and 1775, for example, points out that "some of their huts are sixty feet long and contain several families [each] .... In the fall of the year they leave their huts and go into the woods in quest of game and return in the spring to their huts before planting time. The women raise large crops of corn, beans, pumpkins, [and] melons . . . ." (Quimby 1966:142). Wilson (1924:136) also noted that the Kickapoo continued the practice of seasonal movement even after they were pushed out of the Prairie Peninsula. Summer villages were reported to have been the more substantial, containing large rectangular or square bark and reed covered houses. Horticulture was practiced in the vicinity of these villages, in which a considerable portion of the year's harvest was stored in large underground pits while the group was away at winter quarters. These same facilities were occasionally used to cache objects not taken to winter camps. When the storage pits had outlived their usefulness as storage units, they were employed as refuse receptacles.

Quimby notes that:

> in terms of the kinds of classification used by archaeologists when dealing with prehistoric cultures, the cultures of the Late Historic period seem to belong in one category. This was not true of the cultures of the Middle and Early Historic periods, even though the same kinds of acculturational forces were operative then. The tribal cultures were still intact and differentiated. In the Late Historic period the tribal cultures were submerged and subsumed by the Pan-Indian culture of the region. This culture was manifested by various bands and tribes of Indians who made their living by hunting and trapping for European and American commercial interests. Their principal product was beaver fur, which they exchanged for liquor, tools, weapons, utensils, ornaments, food, medicine, and any other thing supplied by traders. [1966:140–141]

Artifacts recovered from the Rhoads site were predominantly of Euro-American manufacture and included rifle and musket parts; iron knives, adzes, hoes, and kettles; copper kettles and ornaments; silver crosses, bracelets, broaches, and ear ornaments; glass beads; and kaolin tobacco pipes (Klippel 1973a, 1973b, 1976). The cultural materials recovered from this site are congruent with Quimby's (1966) characterizaton of those from the Late Historic period and this temporal placement in turn agrees with historic records that suggest Rhoads was occupied during the second decade of the nineteenth century.

THE RHOADS SITE

Excavation of the Rhoads site (11Lo8), situated on the first terrace of Kickapoo Creek approximately 3 km west of Lincoln, Logan County, Illinois, was conducted between October 1972 and August 1973. Investigations at the site were undertaken to mitigate impact of interstate highway construction (I-55) between Chicago and St. Louis.

The preponderance of the faunal materials to be considered here were recovered from refuse pits ranging up to 1.5 m in diameter and 3 m in depth. Pollen analyses of deposits from these features indicate that the site was occupied from spring through fall (King et al. 1975:187). Further information on the site and its content can be found in Klippel (1972, 1973a, 1973b, and 1976). However, it should be mentioned here that in addition to extensive hunting activities carried out by the Kickapoo during their occupation of the Rhoads site, these people engaged in agricultural pursuits as evidenced by the quantities of burned corn cobs and other cultigens recovered from the site.

Processing and Analyses Procedures

Pieces of bone and mollusk shells encountered during excavation and removal of the soil from the various storage pits were placed in bags which were labeled with the appropriate feature number, site designation, date, and level of recovery at the Illinois State Museum. Features (storage/refuse pits) were generally excavated by arbitrary 6-inch (15.2 cm) levels. Soil from each level was water screened through $1/16$-inch (2.4 mm) hardware cloth (Klippel 1972:2); all bone and shell from each pit (water-screened material plus the larger pieces removed during initial excavation) were then combined for each 6-inch level.

Animal remains from each level within each feature were initially identified and recorded separately, although in several instances pieces of a bone from one of the 6-inch levels were found to be part of a particular element recovered in another 6-inch level. In such cases, and after all pieces of a particular bone were fitted (glued) together in order to obtain the maximum degree of completeness, the restored element was recorded for that level which the majority (or largest) pieces were recovered. Before identifications were attempted and counts of the number of fragments recorded, every effort was made to restore all elements within each level and feature. This is always a time consuming but necessary preliminary step, especially in the case of the carapace and plastron of turtles which usually separate along the sutures. However, the more complete an element, the better the possibility of obtaining an accurate determination and a realistic count of the number of pieces in the sample. In the case of some specimens, for example the skull of a white-tailed deer or the carapace of an aquatic turtle which was crushed or rotted and beyond restoration, the numerous sections of these bones were recorded as one element.

Vertebrate remains occurred in 58 features (primarily storage/refuse pits) and varied in number from a single bone to as many as 1782 pieces (Feature 11; see Appendices). All bone recovered from the plow zone, humus zone, backhoe and grader cuts, surface collections, and from other areas lacking provenience was combined and listed under Plow

Zone/Humus Zone (P.Z./H.Z.) in the Appendices. In addition to the species listed in the Appendices, the remains of modern dogs, pigs, sheep?, cattle, domestic cats, a rat (*Rattus* sp.), chickens, a cottontail and an opossum were encountered, the majority as obviously intrusive burials or as discarded carcasses on the surface or in the humus zone. These animals will be discussed briefly in the appropriate sections under "Accounts of Species." Elements of the anterior half of a horse which occurred in Feature 46/70, and the canid fetus or new-born pup found in Feature 75 were not recorded in the Appendices because they represented "complete" carcasses and their inclusion would tend to bias the percentages. They will be considered under the section "Mammals." Taking into account the numbers of elements of modern intrusive species, the two above-mentioned animals, and all other vertebrate remains deposited by the Indian occupants or those occurring as a result of aboriginal habitation of the Rhoads site, a total of approximately 17,500 bones were recovered and examined during this study.

In order to obtain a reasonably accurate estimation of the number of pounds of usable meat and the caloric values derived from those animals which were, in all probability, killed for food, the minimum number of individuals of each species was determined. This was done for each feature (pit) and for the entire faunal sample as a whole. The minimum number of individuals determined for the total sample was considered to provide the most valid and realistic measure of taxonomic abundance, in light of relatively short time span of site occupation, the small area (ca. one acre) of concentrated habitation, and the apparently small number of family groups involved. Although there appears to have been a very minimum of mixing or scattering of remains of a particular animal in two or more pits, it cannot be assumed that some of the elements from those individuals represented in one pit would not occur in other pits. If, for example, one were to consider the remains of gar (in this instance, primarily scales) from each pit as representing at least one individual, there would have been a minimum of 38 fish represented. Examination of all gar remains from all features, however, showed that no more than 5 or possibly 6 fish were represented.

Minimum number of individuals of each species was determined by counting the element (e.g. the right jaw, left astragalus, left tibia) which occurred in the greatest number. In addition, elements from juveniles, aged individuals and/or from animals which were obviously larger or smaller than the ones from which the basic count was determined were considered when arriving at the total. The method presented by Krantz (1968) was generally followed in the case of the white-tailed deer. A count of skulls, jaws and the major postcranial elements of this species showed jaws as representing the largest number of animals. There were 60 left jaws and 48 rights; 10 of these could be paired. Therefore, by adding the 60 lefts and 38 rights (subtracting 10 for the pairs), a total of 98 individuals were represented in the Rhoads site sample. Determination of minimum number of individuals for the turtles (especially the *Pseudemys, Graptemys, Chrysemys* group) was the most difficult because of similarity in structure and/or size and because of the fragmentary condition of the shell; the counts are probably conservative. Minimum number of individuals determined for each species is listed in the Appendices.

Accounts of Species

Numerous remains of modern domestic animals were encountered during excavation of the Rhoads site, the majority being found at the surface and in the humus and plow zones. Bones of domestic pigs, *Sus scrofa* (mostly shoats; at least six individuals), and chickens, *Gallus gallus* (at least seven individuals) were the most numerous. Although isolated elements were recovered, the majority of the shoats and chickens appear to have been originally complete animals that were simply thrown out or buried in the fields or hog lots surrounding the out-buildings. Postcranial elements of possibly two or three cows, *Bos* cf. *taurus*, occurred in the surface areas; sections of one innominate and one ulna had been cut with a meat saw. Four hind limb bones (metatarsal, tarsal, calcaneum, phalanx) of a young sheep, *Ovis aries*, were uncovered by shovel scrapings. Remains of a kitten were found along the north wall of the farmhouse and the lower right jaw of an adult cat, *Felis domesticus*, occurred at the top or surface of Feature 17. Two modern dog burials, one a German shepherd and one which was possibly a chihuahua, were recovered in the humus zone. A complete set of teeth of a large, young adult dog was found in the upper six-inch level of Feature 116; only the enamel surfaces remained and no bone of this animal was recovered. This dog is presumed to have been of recent origin and not part of the aboriginal faunal assemblage.

Three elements of an adult cottontail, including a scapula which appears to have a shot hole in the blade, occurred in surface areas and are also presumed to be modern. Cottontails recorded in Appendix D from Features 22 and 46/70 were very young juveniles and, like the small rodents and amphibians, probably fell into the open pits and were unable to escape. A canine tooth, skull section, and the right humerus of an opossum, *Didelphis marsupialis*, were found in surface and humus zone areas and, like the adult cottontail elements, postdate the Indian occupation.

Animals considered to be part of the aboriginal faunal assemblages may be arbitrarily separated into three categories, depending upon their apparent or probable use by the Rhoads inhabitants or their occurrence at the site: (1) species, such as the white-tailed deer, whose basic use was that of a source of meat; (2) species, such as the hawks and passerine birds, which were probably taken for use in ceremonies or for decorative purposes; (3) animals, such as the small amphibians and rodents, which were present during but incidental to the occupation of this Kickapoo village. Of the approximately 80 species identified from the Rhoads site faunal sample (see Appendices), about 30 species may be classified as food animals, 26 were probably taken for decorative purposes, and about 18 species may be categorized as being of accidental occurrence. It is difficult to evaluate the significance of certain "food" species when only one individual is represented, except to indicate they were of little or no significance in the total food economy (e.g., 1 badger, 1 squirrel, 1 flathead catfish). However, in the case of species such as squirrels (*Sciurus* spp.) and the prairie chicken which should have been available in some abundance in the timbered floodplain of Kickapoo Creek and in the prairie grasslands, respectively, scarcity may reflect the Indian's indifference to certain potential food sources, regardless of availability. Other species may well have served a dual purpose: recovery of only the outer wing bones of a great blue heron suggests that this bird was taken solely for its plumage (or wings as "fans" or decoration), although it is certainly possible that the heron also served as a food animal.

The method presented by White (1953) for determining the approximate percent of usable meat and the actual pounds of usable meat derived from a particular animal was generally followed for most species of birds and mammals. For species not recorded by White, various mammalogy and ornithological references were consulted for estimated live weights. In the case of certain species such as the raccoon and white-tailed deer, which were represented at Rhoads by both adult and juvenile individuals of an approximate known age, the average live weights recorded by White (1953) were adjusted to accommodate the differences. For example, data accumulated by the Illinois Department of Conservation on live weights of yearling deer in central Illinois (Calhoun and Loomis 1974) showed that bucks and does averaged 140 pounds (bucks, 154 lbs.; does, 126 lbs.). White (1953) calculated the amount of usable meat according to body form; e.g., 70% of a raccoon's weight was usable meat and that of a deer only 50%. Instead of using White's estimate of the average live weight of 200 pounds ([91 kg] 50% or 100 lbs. [45.5 kg] of usable meat) for all deer, those individuals in the yearling class (ca. 12–14 mos.) were therefore estimated to have supplied 70 pounds (31.8 kg) of usable meat. Weights of animals in the younger age classes were likewise adjusted.

In the case of fish and turtles, a similar approach was followed in an effort to arrive at relatively accurate meat weights. It is probably more difficult to calculate the pounds of usable meat obtainable from fish and turtles because of individual differences in the rate of growth resulting from variable habitat conditions, food supply, and/or the season collected. The figures in Table 1 of estimated pounds of usable meat are based on 50% of the animals's live weight. This figure is based on data obtained from several species of fish (channel catfish, bowfin, freshwater drum) and turtles (map, painted, snapping turtles) which were processed in the laboratory; their various body parts (skeleton, viscera, meat) were weighed and the percentages of each calculated. Estimated live weights were determined from comparative specimens of known total length/weight (fish) and carapace length/weight (turtle) ratios. In some cases it was necessary to estimate size and weight of animals represented in the Rhoads faunal sample from incomplete elements.

VERTEBRATES

Class: Teleostomi—*Fishes*

Remains of fish, representing approximately 30 individuals and nine species, occurred in 40 of the 58 features (including the Plow Zone/Humus Zone). The actual number of pieces amounted to nearly 28% of the total number of bones from the Rhoads site faunal sample, and 70% were identified to the generic and/or species level. No attempt was made to specifically identify the several hundred fish scales (other than gar) which occurred in several features, and they were not included as part of the count of indeterminate fish bone pieces (1364) listed in Appendix A. Several were, however, recognizable as having come from catostomids and centrarchids. In spite of what appears to have been a substantial utilization of fish in the diet of these people, the total number of individuals represented and the actual pounds of meat contributed (Table 1) tend to relegate fish, as a group, to the role of an occasional dietary supplement. The estimated pounds of fish derived from the individuals identified from the faunal sample was determined by comparing recovered elements with those from specimens of known weight in the osteological reference collections, Department of Anthropology, Zooarchaeology Section, University of Tennessee, Knoxville.

Family Lepisosteidae: gars. As previously mentioned, gars appear to have been taken in considerable numbers because of the quantity of remains and their distribution in a high percentage of the pits. The majority of these remains were scales, however, and because of their hard, enameled bone structure they preserve well. Skull elements were concentrated primarily in Features 11, 46/70, 75, 128 and 141; only a few pieces of maxillae and lower jaws were recovered, making specific identi-

TABLE 1
ESTIMATED POUNDS OF MEAT AND CALORIC VALUES FOR RHOADS SITE

Species	Minimum Number of Individuals	Estimated Pounds of Meat	%	Calories (100 g. raw)[1]
FISHES	(30)	(83)	(0.86)	
Gar, *Lepisosteus* sp.	5	16	0.17	?
Buffalo, *Ictiobus* sp.	1	3	0.03	113
Redhorse, *Moxostoma* spp.	8	20	0.21	98
Channel catfish, *Ictalurus punctatus*	1	7	0.07	103?
Flathead catfish, *Pylodictis olivaris*	1	10	0.10	103?
Rock bass, *Ambloplites rupestris*	6	2	0.02	104?
Bass, *Micropterus* sp.	6	11	0.11	104
Freshwater drum, *Aplodinotus grunniens*	2	14	0.15	121
TURTLES	(55)	(47)	(0.49)	
Snapping turtle, *Chelydra serpentina*	1	4	0.04	89?
Blanding's turtle, *Emydoidea blandingi*	2	1	0.01	"
Box turtle, *Terrapene* sp.	2	1	0.01	"
Painted turtle, *Chrysemys picta*	12	3	0.03	"
Red-eared turtle, *Pseudemys scripta*	12	12	0.13	"
Map turtle, *Graptemys* spp.	16	16	0.17	"
Softshell, *Trionyx* sp.	10	10	0.10	"
BIRDS	(21)	(93)	(0.97)	
Great blue heron, *Ardea herodias*	1	3	0.03	?
Canada goose, *Branta canadensis*	1	5	0.05	354?
Duck sp.	1	1	0.01	233
Hooded merganser, *Lophodytes cucullatus*	1	1	0.01	233?
Greater prairie chicken, *Tympanuchus cupido*	1	1	0.01	117?
Turkey, *Meleagris gallopavo*	12	80	0.83	218
Woodcock/shorebirds	2	1	0.01	?
Passenger pigeon, *Ectopistes migratorius*	2	1	0.01	279?
MAMMALS	(140)	(9401)	(97.68)	
Black bear, *Ursus americanus*	2	420	4.36	?
Raccoon, *Procyon lotor*	23	227	2.36	?
Striped skunk, *Mephitis mephitis*	3	15	0.16	?
Badger, *Taxidea taxus*	1	12	0.12	?
Gray wolf, *Canis lupus*	1	30	0.31	?
Dog, *Canis familiaris*	4	30	0.31	?
Bobcat, *Lynx* cf. *rufus*	2	30	0.31	?
Squirrel, *Sciurus* sp.	1	1	0.01	?
Beaver, *Castor canadensis*	2	52	0.54	248 (cooked)
Muskrat, *Ondatra zibethica*	2	4	0.04	153 (cooked)
Elk, *Cervus elaphus*	1	350	3.64	126?
White-tailed deer, *Odocoileus virginianus*	98	8230	85.52	126
Total	246	9624	99.99	

[1] Watt & Merrill 1963.

fication from other skull elements questionable. However, cleithra from two individuals compare fairly well with identified specimens (and descriptions provided by Quertermus 1967) of longnose gar, *Lepisosteus osseus*, and may be referable to that species. Gilmore (1932:40, 44, 46) noted "gar pike" skins in three of the Arikara sacred bundles which he examined.

Family Catostomidae: suckers. One species (and one individual) of a buffalo, probably the smallmouth buffalo, *Ictiobus bubalus*, and two species of redhorse were determined. At least four individuals each of the golden redhorse and probably the northern redhorse are represented. One individual of *Moxostoma* cf. *macrolepidotum* from Feature 127 weighed approximately 12 to 14 pounds (5.5–6.4 kg); the buffalo and a golden redhorse from Feature 128 weighed about 5 pounds (2.3 kg), while the remaining suckers fell within the 1½- to 3-pound (0.7–1.4 kg) range. These catostomids still occur today in the streams and/or lakes of Logan County (Rogers 1968).

The only fish bone artifact consisted of a fragmented opercular, possibly from one of the larger catostomids, which had been cut and drilled. This worked piece was found in Feature 54; it may have been fashioned as a pendant.

Family Ictaluridae: catfishes and bullheads. Skull elements of a large flathead catfish (ca. 15 pounds [6.8 kg]) from Feature 105 and those of probably a channel catfish, *Ictalurus* cf. *punctatus*, comprise the only remains of representatives of this family. Possibly more than one channel catfish is represented, but the five bones from Features 11, 54, and 128 were from a fish (or fishes?) weighing approximately 6 pounds (2.7 kg) and conceivably could have come from the same individual.

Family Centrarchidae: sunfishes. At least six rock bass and six smallmouth bass, *Micropterus* sp., were represented in the sample. All of the rock bass weighed less than 1 pound (.45 kg) each while individuals of the latter species varied from 2 to 4 pounds (0.9 to 1.8 kg). It is surprising that remains of other representatives of this family such as crappie, *Pomoxis* spp., and some of the sunfishes, *Lepomis* spp., were not encountered. Rogers (1968:30) records both the black and white crappies and five species of *Lepomis* as occurring in Logan County streams and ponds today. He describes Kickapoo Creek (Rogers 1968:19) as being "a series of riffles and pools with a predominantly gravel bottom. There are numerous gravel bars, undercut banks, and brush piles. The banks are lined with trees of which willows, cottonwood, sycamore, and silver maples are most numerous." Undoubtedly Kickapoo Creek was a much "cleaner" stream during the time of aboriginal occupation of the Rhoads site than it is today, and the fish fauna theoretically should have been more abundant and varied.

Family Sciaenidae: drums. Bones of the freshwater drum occurred in seven features, although remains of this fish in four of the pits consisted only of isolated pharyngeal teeth. The two individuals represented were large and weighed between 10 and 12 pounds (4.5 to 5.5 kg).

Class: Amphibia—*Salamanders, Toads, Frogs*
Order Caudata: salamanders. An incomplete innominate of an unidentifed species of salamander occurred in Feature 11; no other remains of species comprising this group of amphibians was encountered at the site.

Order Salientia: toads and frogs. Remains of toads (*Bufo* sp.: Family Bufonidae) and frogs (*Rana* sp.: Family Ranidae) were numerous and occurred in 21 of the 58 features. The approximately 650 toad and frog elements (at least 41 individuals) amounted to nearly 4% of all the bone pieces recovered at the Rhoads site. With few exceptions, these amphibians were subadults and their occurrence in the storage/refuse pits may be attributed to falling or jumping accidentally into the pits while empty (or partially empty); they were unable to climb or jump back out due to the depth and/or the gradual sloping outward of the pit walls from the top. Entrapment of small amphibians and rodents in open excavations is commonplace and familiar to all field archaeologists. Depending on the location of a particular site (e.g., a floodplain terrace), open trenches or test squares 30 cm or more in depth will serve as an efficient natural trap.

Although some remains of toads and frogs were recovered from the upper levels of the pits, the greatest concentration occurred below the 1½-foot level. It may be argued that loose soil and debris in the pits would have provided very suitable matrix for burrowing at the onset of fall hibernation. However, the concentration of remains of these small amphibians within these pits, some to over a depth of 2 m, and the occurrence of mice and shrews (which do not hibernate) in similar context with the frogs and toads, suggests strongly of entrapment during the time the pits were completely or partially empty. If our interpretation is correct and the pits were filled by the Kickapoo inhabitants with food stores during the late fall and winter months and opened in late spring upon their return to the village, these open or partially debris-filled pits would then serve to trap amphibians, rodents and shrews during the summer. In any case, the evidence suggests that their occurrence in the storage/refuse pits is accidental and that they are not part of the fauna purposely accumulated by the inhabitants.

Class: Reptilia—*Turtles, Lizards, Snakes*
Approximately 935 pieces of turtle bone and shell, representing a

minimum of 57 individuals, were recovered at the Rhoads site. The predominance of aquatic species is noteworthy and implies a decided effort by the Rhoads inhabitants to capture these forms. There is no reason to believe that the terrestrial box turtles (*Terrapene* spp.) were any less abundant in the area ca. A.D. 1800 than now. Their capture simply involves picking them up, yet only 2 of the 57 individuals represented were box turtles. The difficulty in capturing certain aquatic species, especially the map and softshell turtles, is well known (Smith 1961:153, 158), yet the apparent preference for these turtles by the Kickapoo justified the effort in hunting them. Both young juveniles and adults were represented, so it was not a matter of obtaining large individuals which prompted what appears to have been selective hunting. No turtle shell artifacts were found; probably they were prized strictly as food animals.

Family Chelydridae: snapping turtles. The common snapping turtle, *Chelydra serpentina*, occurs in almost every pond and stream in Illinois today (Smith 1961:120) and, like the box turtles, was also probably not uncommon in the vicinity of the Rhoads village during its occupation. However, only one individual was represented (by two elements: an ilium from Feature 127, and a claw from Feature 141). Either this turtle was uncommon to rare in Kickapoo Creek and adjoining floodplain or prairie marshes or, for some reason, the inhabitants would not collect it. In contrast, 90 pieces of shell and bone of the snapping turtle were found at the Crawford Farm site, a contemporaneous Sauk-Fox village in Rock Island County (Parmalee 1964:168).

Family Testudinidae: Eighteen shell and limb elements of Blanding's turtle, *Emydoidea blandingi*, representing no more than two individuals, occurred in seven features. The complete plastron from a large adult (plastron max. length 200 mm; max. width 105 mm) found in Feature 44 represents a turtle that closely approaches the largest specimen recorded for Illinois (carapace length 240 mm, [Smith 1961:131]). Logan County represents the southernmost limit of this turtle's range in central Illinois. Although Blanding's turtle now occurs only as scattered colonies, Smith (1961:133) suggests that it was probably abundant on the central prairies before the marshes were drained. Floodplain sloughs along Kickapoo Creek and/or prairie marshes would have provided suitable habitat from which the Indians might have collected them. Scored marks on the interior of a section of carapace from Feature 71 was the only evidence of butchering of this species.

It has already been suggested that the Rhoads site inhabitants did not use box turtles to any extent even though the species should have been common in the vicinity. A similar situation was encountered in the faunal materials from the historic Sauk-Fox (Crawford Farm) site in Rock

Island county: of the nearly 1400 pieces of turtle shell/bone recorded (seven species), none were those of *Terrapene* (Parmalee 1964:171). As at Rhoads, none of the turtle shell from the Crawford Farm site had been modified.

Four other species of turtles in the Family Testudinidae, all represented at the Rhoads site, include the painted, red-eared, map, and false map. The painted and red-eared turtles are common throughout much of Illinois today. They occur in a variety of aquatic habitats, preferring ponds, lakes and river sloughs to fast-running streams (Smith 1961:141, 145). The map turtle, *Graptemys geographica*, "shows preference for large rivers, backwater sloughs, and large lakes" (Smith 1961:153). On the other hand, the false map turtle, *G. pseudogeographica*, is characteristic of swift rivers although it may also be found in other aquatic habitats. Only one false map turtle was represented in the Rhoads site fauna, while there were at least 12 individuals each of the painted and red-eared turtles and 15 map turtles. Although inconclusive in itself, the prevalence of painted, red-eared and map turtle remains—plus the occurrence of Blanding's turtle—suggest the presence of former permanent backwater sloughs and/or lakes along Kickapoo Creek as the principal habitat exploited by Indians for turtles.

Depending upon climatic conditions (water and air temperatures), the majority of these turtles become active in April and enter hibernation in October in central Illinois. Their presence at the Rhoads site verifies at least a late spring, summer, and/or early fall occupation by the Kickapoo. The difficulty in capturing large adults of most aquatic species, because of their wariness and speed in swimming, has been mentioned. How they were taken by these people is unknown, although most were probably caught by hand while wading; possibly some females were picked up on land at the time of egg-laying. Athough turtles appear to have been a preferred food, the total estimated pounds of meat (47) contributed to the diet was, as in the case of fish, small and served only as an occasional supplement to daily subsistence.

Family Trionychidae: softshell turtles. Remains of at least ten softshell turtles, two of which were determined as the spiny softshell, *Trionyx spinifer*, on the basis of plastron configuration as illustrated by Webb (1962:474), occurred in about one-third of the pits. Butchering cuts, absent on elements of the above-mentioned species except the one Blanding's turtle carapace, were noted on several *Trionyx* bone and shell pieces. Scored marks occurred on the pelvis (ischium) and paired precoracoids of a large individual from Feature 127, the neck of a scapula from Feature 41, the interior surface of the hypoplastron extremities from Feature 46/70, and the exterior surface of the hyoplastron/hypoplastron extremities from Feature 1. In addition, deep transverse cuts occurred on the inner surface at mid-point on a hyoplastron/hypoplastron from Feature 11. The broad, compact structure of softshells probably made processing difficult. Cuts on the distal projections of the plastron resulted while attempting to separate it from the carapace, while those on the limb elements occurred during removal of the animal from its shell.

Smith (1961:158) states that the spiny softshell is found most abundantly in sand-bottomed rivers, although it is adaptable to a variety of other aquatic habitats. These turtles, because of their alertness and speed at both running and swimming, are difficult to capture. However, their habit of burrowing themselves at the margin of a stream, often leaving a telltale depression in the sand above, makes them more susceptible to capture. It is of interest to note that remains of softshells at the Crawford Farm site were the most numerous (768 pieces of a total of 1361 [56%]; see Parmalee 1964:170) of all the turtles represented. Softshell turtles—and all aquatic turtles in general—appear to have been a preferred food by the inhabitants of these two historic sites and a special effort was made to hunt them.

Family Colubridae: snakes. Six snake vertebrae, each from a different feature and possibly representing two or three individuals (and species?), were not specifically determined. One of the more complete vertebrae from Feature 152 has been very tentatively identified as belonging to the genus *Elaphe* (black snake?). It is apparent from the recovery of only six snake vertebrae, all from non-poisonous species, that these reptiles were of little, if any, significance to the inhabitants. Their presence may well have been incidental to the human occupation of the Rhoads site.

Class: Aves—*Birds*

Approximately 34 species of birds were identified to the generic and/or species level from about 190 bone remains. In addition, 275 elements were recognizable as those of various species of birds belonging to other Order Passeriformes. However, because of osteological similarities among many of the closely related forms in this large order of perching birds (e.g., warblers, sparrows) and the preponderance of non-diagnostic and/or fragmentary elements in the sample, specific determinations were uncertain or impossible. Most of the 435 indeterminate bird bone pieces listed in Appendix C were from large birds, in all probability the turkey. About 55% of the identified species were woodpeckers, raptors and passerine birds. The turkey appears to have been the only avian species to provide a supplement of any significant value to the food economy of the Rhoads site inhabitants.

It is difficult to categorize many of the species of birds identified from the Rhoads site faunal assemblage as having been taken either primarily for food or for some other purpose. Although turkey feathers may have played a role in the ceremonial and/or decorative aspects of the Kickapoo culture, it is safe to assume the flesh of this bird was valued for subsistence by these people. Without specific ethnohistoric or ethnozoological reference to a particular species, however, there is a tendency to interpret utilization based on modern standards. The inclusion of an occasional duck, prairie chicken, shorebird, or passenger pigeon in the diet seems apparent, but does the same hold true for a marsh hawk, red-headed woodpecker, or indigo bunting? Some birds served a dual function (food and plumage). There are specific data relative to the use of birds such as the cardinal and bluebird for decorative purposes (e.g., Swanton 1946:253), but the number of named or identified species is small. Recovery of only certain parts (e.g., wing or leg elements) of "non-edible" birds such as marsh hawk suggests utilization other than for food, although in reality the occurrence of only such apparent decorative parts (wing "fans," claws) does not preclude the possibility that the animal was also eaten. Nevertheless, as an attempt to provide at least a relative comparison of the estimated pounds of meat contributed by the various groups of vertebrates to the diet, only those species of groups considered "edible" are listed in Table 1.

Family Ardeidae: herons and bitterns. A right carpometacarpus, phalanx I, and a pollex of the great blue heron, *Ardea herodias*, were recovered in Feature 40. These elements support the primary flight feathers and their occurrence suggests that the wing of this large heron functioned as a fan or some form of decoration. A cut mark at the base of the inner surface of the metacarpal I process indicates its removal from the distal ends of the radius/ulna. The distal two-thirds of a right humerus shaft, possibly referable to the common egret, *Casmerodius albus*, occurred in Feature 41. No other elements of these birds were found at the site.

Family Anatidae: ducks, geese, swans. Only four bones of ducks were encountered in the pits; two of these from Feature 127 (sections of a tibiotarsus and tarsometatarsus) may be those of a wood duck, *Aix sponsa*. The distal end of a lower mandible of the hooded merganser, *Lophodytes cucullatus*, also occurred in Feature 127. Although both ends were broken off, a left humerus shaft of a large goose found in Feature 40 is probably that of the Canada goose, *Branta canadensis*. Butchering cuts occurred at the proximal end. The proximal shaft end of a left humerus, also with scored marks, found in Feature 128, and the distal shaft end of a left humerus from Feature 40, may also be referable to this species although both are too incomplete to be specifically identified.

Unless the Kickapoo had journeyed to the Sangamon and/or Illinois rivers during the spring or fall migrations, they would have had little opportunity to obtain waterfowl locally. Little can be inferred concerning season of site occupation from such a paucity of duck and geese remains. The wood duck could have been taken along Kickapoo Creek from April through October, while it is not unusual to encounter hooded mergansers along small streams such as Kickapoo Creek during migration. Ridgway (1895) mentions several species of waterfowl that formerly nested in the prairie marshes of northern and central Illinois, but if breeding ducks and geese were present locally during the period of site occupation, the Kickapoo made no effort to exploit this food resource.

Family Accipitridae: hawks, kites, harriers. One of the most interesting avian species to be recorded from the Rhoads site fauna was the swallow-tailed kite, *Elanoides forficatus*, now considered a very rare vagrant in Illinois (Bohlen 1978:37), but in former years "common throughout the State" (Ridgway 1889:445). A complete left ulna, exhibiting deep scored marks encircling the shaft three-fourths of an inch (.64 cm) from the proximal end, and the distal end of a left humerus were recovered in Feature 46/70. The incomplete proximal end of a tibiotarsus shaft from this feature may also be referable to *E. forficatus*. The proximal end of a right humerus, the shaft having been "shaved" or cut away (removal of the wing?), occurred in Feature 2. Remains of this bird have been previously reported from Mississippian sites (Cahokia site, St. Clair Co.; Jasper Newman site, Moultrie Co.) in central Illinois (Parmalee 1967:155). The Indians were probably attracted to this kite because of its size and beauty; the cut wing elements from the Rhoads site suggest that the bird was prized for its plumage.

A phalanx I from Feature 141 and the proximal end of a right ulna from Feature 10 have been tentatively identified as *Buteo* sp. and possibly may be referrable to the broad-winged hawk and red-shouldered hawk, respectively. Because of the nature of the elements involved (incomplete or specifically non-diagnostic), these determinations are unsubstantiated. The right carpometacarpus and phalanx I of a marsh hawk, *Circus cyaneus*, from Feature 118 again suggest the probable desirability and use of raptorial birds for wing and/or plumage decoration.

A complete left tarsometatarsus and a right carpometacarpus of a sparrow hawk, *Falco sparverius*, were found in Feature 54. Bird skins and parts carried by members of several tribes of Plains Indians are well documented; Gilmore (1932:40, 44), for example, identifies several species of birds from Arikara bundles, one of which was "a sparrow-hawk skin with small shell beads for eyes . . . ." Early accounts by James (1823, 1:293) include mention of medicine bundles of the Omaha which almost always included skins of sparrow hawks. Possibly these outer wing and leg elements of a sparrow hawk which occurred in Feature 54 were from a discarded skin which had been part of a medicine bundle. However, Mandelbaum (1940:199) includes the sparrow hawk, as well as the chicken hawk, owl, and eagle (species?), in the list of birds eaten by the Plains Cree; birds that were not eaten included the "crane." In any case, wing and/or leg elements (including indeterminate claws of a hawk from Feature 40) from raptorial birds and the great blue heron were very possibly worn or displayed as decorative or ceremonial objects.

Family Tetraonidae: grouse, ptarmigan. Only four elements of a native grouse, in all probability those of the greater prairie chicken, *Tympanuchus cupido*, were encountered in the avian remains. The former abundance and wide distribution of the bird throughout the prairie regions of Illinois is well known (Cory 1909:440), and remains of the prairie chicken have been reported from numerous prehistoric sites in the state (e.g., the Cahokia site [Parmalee 1957]). This bird should have been common in the prairie within the vicinity of the Rhoads village, yet this abundant and easily accessible food species was not exploited by the Kickapoo.

Family Meleagrididae: turkeys. The turkey, *Meleagris gallopavo*, was the one bird species which appears to have been of some significance in the food economy of the Rhoads site inhabitants. Remains of at least 12 individuals were found in approximately 38% of the pits and contributed an estimated 80 pounds (36.4 kg) of meat (Table 1). Compared with the total estimated pounds of meat determined for all "food" species represented in the sample, however, the 80 pounds of turkey amounted to less than 1%. Nevertheless, the turkey appears to have been a desired game species and, like the fish, turtles, and a few other bird and mammal species, served as an occasional supplement to the basic meat diet provided by the white-tailed deer.

Butchering cuts were noted on a number of turkey elements. The external condyle and ectepicondylar prominence of a humerus from Feature 105 display cuts that resulted from removal of the outer wing at the elbow (proximal end of radius/ulna). Cuts along the edge of the glenoid facet and on the brachial tuberosity of a Feature 40 coracoid indicate disarticulation of the entire wing at the proximal end of the humerus; scored marks near the sternal facet (on the inner surface) of a Feature 118 coracoid may have resulted from an attempt to detach the pectorial girdle assembly from the sternum. Possible hack or chop marks at the distal ends of two or three tibiotarsi indicate removal of the lower leg (tarsometatarsus).

Although prehistoric aboriginal peoples often modified certain compact elements of the turkey for use as tools, especially the lower leg (tarsometatarsus fashioned into awls), no turkey bone artifacts were encountered at the Rhoads site. The one possible exception noted is a 2¾-inch (7.0 cm) bone tube cut from the center of a radius shaft of a large bird; the overall proportions and location of the nutrient foramen and intermuscular line suggest turkey. At least three individuals were adult toms (presence of tarsometatarsal spurs) and two birds appeared, based on fragmentary wing bones, to have been juveniles of the season when killed. An interesting form of bone pathology was noted in an ulna shaft section (probably turkey?) from Feature 118. The outer surface was roughened, the papillae greatly enlarged into "ridges," and the shaft walls thickened, reducing the inner diameter to ca. 2.5 mm (versus the ca. 7.0 mm diameter of a normal element of comparable size).

Family Scolopacidae: woodcock, snipe, sandpipers. The distal end of a right carpometacarpus of a woodcock, *Philohela minor*, occurred in Feature 127. Several elements (carpometacarpals) of a sandpiper, *Erolia melanotos*, were found in Feature 2; an indeterminate sandpiper (?) ulna fragment occurred in Feature 75; and a right carpometacarpus and phalanx I of a sandpiper (pectoral?) was recovered from Feature 141. The paucity of shorebird remains is not unexpected, given that the Rhoads village was not situated within the main route of the Mississippi and Illinois river flyways traveled by migrating waterfowl and other aqautic and semi-aquatic birds. Bones of shorebirds have been found to be uncommon to rare in prehistoric sites in Illinois, even in those situated along the major rivers.

Family Columbidae: pigeons, doves. With reference to certain tribes in the Southeast, Swanton (1946:298) states that "second in importance [to the wild turkey] was the passenger pigeon, whose roosts were gathering places for Indian hunters at certain seasons." Bones of this now extinct pigeon were found in five features and the plow zone, but no more than two individuals were represented. Eight elements, probably from one bird, occurred in Feature 46/70; a faint butchering(?) cut appears near the proximal end of the tarsometatarsus from this feature. In spite of the bird's former tremendous abundance and its utilization by some aboriginal groups in eastern North America, remains of the passenger pigeon from sites in the Midwest are typically uncommon to rare.

Family Picidae: woodpeckers. Remains of five, and possibly six, species of woodpeckers were recovered from eight of the pits; these included the flicker, red-headed, red-bellied(?), downy, pileated, and ivory-billed woodpecker. Moorehead (1932:57–58) summarized the significance of this group of birds to various prehistoric aboriginal groups:

> The woodpecker occupied a prominent place in the ceremonies and symbolism of many tribes in the central and southern portions of the United States. This bird's

head or tail appears incised on no less than six water bottles from Moundville, Alabama, a group closely related to Etowah. Its head also appears on a shell gorget from Moundville. A similar combination of woodpecker heads and the sun or world symbols appear on shell gorgets from Tennessee. In the Peabody Museum at Cambridge, are two very old calumets, on the upper side of the stems of which are fastened several upper mandibles are turned backward over the scalp which is tightly bound to the pipestem.

Maximilian's account (1907:108, 131) of the Blackfoot Indians includes some noteworthy comments on the use of woodpeckers:

The handsomest are the large medicine pipes, the *calumets* of the French. They are adorned with the red heads of the woodpecker, bills, and a large fan made of feathers, and are used in all the solemn treaties and festivals of the North American tribes, more or less ornamented, but, on the whole, always in the same manner.... Mr. Bodmer had undertaken to paint Mehkskéhmé-Sukahs in full dress, with his face painted black and red, a leather shirt ornamented with slips of otter skin and ermine, a large bunch of the feathers of birds of prey, woodpeckers' bills, ermine and pieces of red cloth in his hand—a remarkably colossal figure.

With reference to the Mandans, Maximilian (1907:319–320) stated that:

the Indians cannot obtain such pipes but at a considerable expense: many of the necessary ornaments are not to be procured among them, such as the upper bill and the red crown of a species of woodpecker (*Picus pileatus*, Linn.) [pileated woodpecker, *Dryocopus pileatus*], a bird which is not found so high up the Missouri. For the head of one of these woodpeckers, which was brought from St. Louis, they gave a large handsome buffalo robe, worth six or eight dollars.

Remains of woodpeckers from the Rhoads site were not especially numerous (21 bones), but the variety of species is somewhat indicative of the significance of these birds to the Kickapoo. Eleven elements of the red-headed woodpecker, *Melanerpes erythrocephalus*, probably from one individual, occurred in Feature 118; no more than two bones of woodpeckers were recovered in any of the other pits. An incomplete lower mandible of the pileated woodpecker was found in Feature 2, while a complete radius and ulna of this large bird occurred in Feature 17. The ivory-billed woodpecker, *Campephilus principalis*, was represented by a distal end section of the upper bill from Feature 128; it was from a slightly larger bird than the one in the collections of the National Museum of Natural History with which it was compared.

All of the other species of woodpeckers represented at the Rhoads site could have been taken locally, but whether the ivory-billed woodpecker ever extended its range northward into central Illinois is questionable. In light of the ethnological evidence of the esteem in which many historic tribes held these birds, it is conceivable that this woodpecker originally represented a trade item or had been collected by these Kickapoo while they were living along the Wabash River—if, in fact, it was this band—in southeastern Illinois. The only authenticated records of living birds in the state are presented by Ridgway (1889:375) who refers to sightings by Audubon at the confluence of the Ohio and Mississippi rivers and ". . . along the latter as far up as the mouth of the Missouri," and to his own sighting 40 miles south of Mount Carmel (in White County, bordering the Wabash River). Parts of one upper and two lower jaw sections of this now apparently extinct woodpecker were recovered at the Crawford Farm site (Parmalee 1964). It was suggested, because this Sauk-Fox village was considerably north of the birds' known range in western Illinois, that ". . . these remains of bills had been part of a headdress or pipe decoration, or had been used as another type of ornament, in which case the birds could well have been obtained elsewhere" (Parmalee 1964:172).

Order Passeriformes: This order of birds is comprised of numerous families, many of which include a large number of species. Representatives of at least eight families of passerine or perching birds were identified from the Rhoads site faunal sample; their remains (all elements determined as being passerine) occurred in 38 (65%) of the 58 features. Although certain bones of many of these birds are diagnostic, at least to the generic level, many more are not, primarily because of close osteological similarities among species, genera, and even families. For this reason several determinations listed in Appendix C are recorded as tentative.

The number and variety of passerine bird remains encountered in the storage refuse pits are especially noteworthy. Birds such as flycatchers, chickadees, wrens, kinglets, vireos, wood warblers, and buntings could conceivably be considered as food species, but because of their extremely small size and especially because of their colorful plumage, these birds were doubtlessly taken by the Kickapoo for the purpose of decoration or body adornment. There are numerous ethnohistoric accounts of small birds—complete "skins" or parts such as the head and wings—being included in personal or medicine bundles, worn in the hair or attached to clothing, or carried as a fetish. Swanton (1946:251–252) mentions the use of down for decorating the hair and the wearing of wings of small species such as the redbird (cardinal?) in the headdress. Some of these birds were of symbolic significance, such as the goldfinch to the Dakota (Gilmore 1932:46).

A late spring, summer, and/or early fall season of occupation of the Rhoads site can be inferred by the presence of the ?least flycatcher (*Empidonax* cf. *minimus*), house wren (cf. *Troglodytes aedon*), kinglet

(*Regulus* sp.), warblers (*Vermivora* sp. and *Dendroica* sp.), redstart (cf. *Setophage ruticilla*), redwinged blackbird (cf. *Agelaius phoeniceus*), rose-breasted grosbeak? (*Pheucticus ludovicianus*) and the indigo bunting (*Passerina cyanea*). These species are summer residents in central Illinois, the majority of which arrive in early May and depart in mid-September. Approximately 25 to 30 individuals were represented by the 312 passerine elements from all features. Remains of the indigo bunting were the most numerous (16 bones, at least 8 individuals) of the identified passerines; the male of this species is one of the most beautifully colored of all the small perching birds and could have been especially favored by the Kickapoo for adornment.

Bird Bone Artifacts: All recognizable bird elements altered in any manner had been fashioned into bone tubes of one sort or another. The largest of these, from Feature 54, consisted of a thoroughly scraped and polished 5¾-inch (14.6 cm) long ulna shaft (Fig. 1*G*) of a large bird, possibly a swan. Both articular ends had been removed and a small inscribed triangle occurred near the broken end. The presence of this inscribed triangle suggests a stage in the manufacture of a whistle. Similar bone tube artifacts, most of which were cut from the humeri of swans, were numerous at the Crawford Farm site (Parmalee 1964:171).

In addition to the cut turkey(?) radius shaft from Feature 118 already mentioned, three other similar bone "tubes" were recovered, broken sections from Features 40 and 118 and a complete 4½-inch (11.4 cm) (radius?) shaft from Feature 1 (Fig. 1*F*). Another but larger cut bird bone (humerus?) section also occurred in Feature 40, and a cut off discarded(?) end of a small bird ulna(?) was found in Feature 4. The inscribed and drilled piece illustrated in Figure 1*D*, fashioned from probably a large bird bone, may have been used as a pendant or possibly some type of barrette. Two other engraved bone fragments from Feature 17 and one from Feature 6 may have been part of similar objects.

Two especially interesting worked bird bones occurred in Feature 118. In both cases, each end had been cut off perpendicular to the shaft, entirely removing the impression of the brachialis anticus and leaving only a small portion of the deltoid crest. Removal of the diagnostic portions of these two right humeri, one of which was inscribed near both ends of the shaft (Fig. 1*E*), made specific determination impossible. However, the general size and curvature of the shafts resemble those of a mallard duck. These humeri may have been fashioned for use as beads, or they may have served as medicine objects.

Class: Mammalia—*Mammals*

In addition to the species of mammals (pig, cow, sheep, cat, rat, dog, opossum, cottontail) and the domestic chicken from the Rhoads site

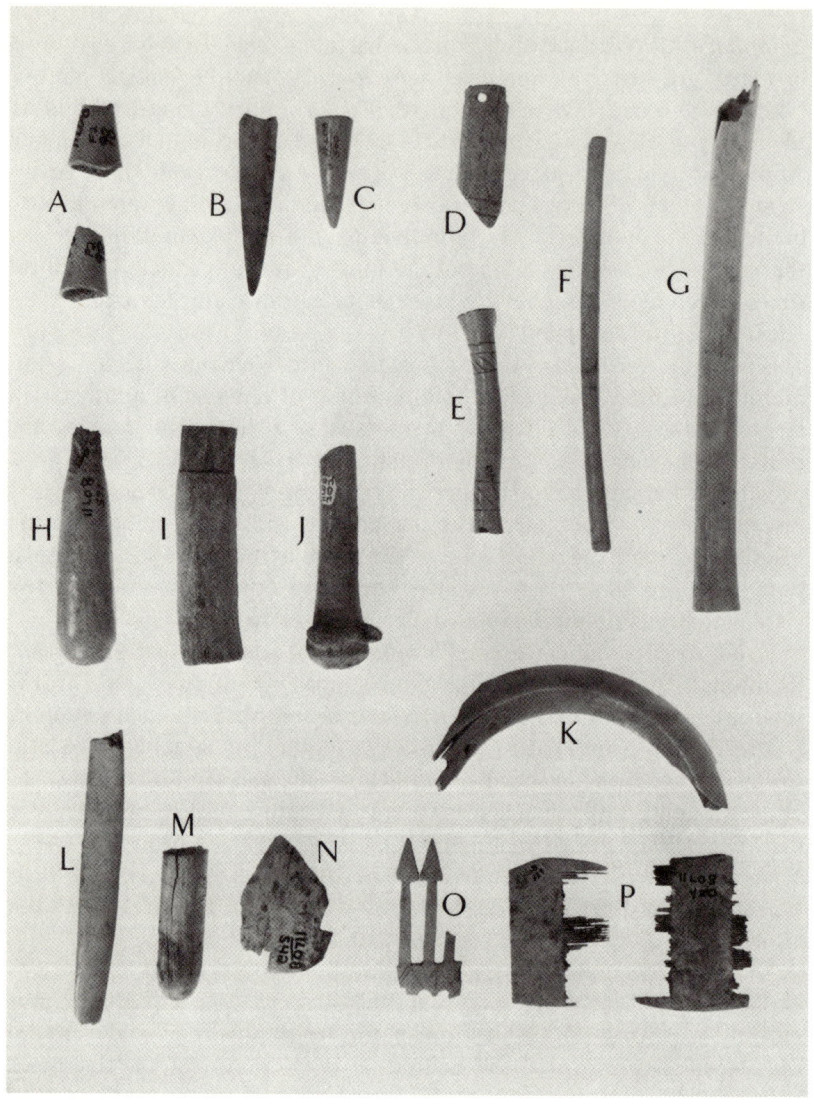

Fig. 1. Examples of bone and tooth artifacts. Objects are identified in the text.

which were briefly discussed earlier in this paper as being intrusive and not a part of the aboriginal faunal complex, remains of approximately 25 other mammalian species were identified from the sample. Several of these animals, although indirectly associated with the Kickapoo during their occupation of the village, were not an integral part of their subsistence. As a group, mammals contributed an estimated 97% of all the meat consumed, based on the recovered bone sample. Of the total estimated pounds of usable meat calculated for the species/number of individuals represented in the faunal sample, that of the white-tailed deer constituted 85% (see Table 1).

The problem of whether an apparently edible animal represented at an aboriginal site by only one or by a very few elements actually constituted a food resource is not easily resolved, especially when the bones are not part of the main appendicular or axial skeleton. To illustrate, the only remains of the gray wolf (*Canis* cf. *lupus*) and the elk (*Cervus elaphus*) encountered in the storage/refuse pits at the Rhoads site consisted of two and four metapodials, respectively. Except for sections of a tibia and fibula from Feature 118 and an ulna from Feature 105, remains of the black bear (*Ursus americanus*) also consisted of metapodials (representing two individuals, compared with one based on the leg bones). It is possible that the wolf and elk metapodials (and decorative bear paws?) had been taken from animals killed at other locations and carried to and finally disposed of at the Rhoads village; such a possibility appears more plausible when no other elements of these animals are in evidence. Nevertheless, these animals are represented in the faunal sample and are known to have been taken by prehistoric and other historic groups for food and/or hides, so they have been included as a food animal in Table 1.

Silverberg (1957:62) has expressed a probably valid point when he states, "By linking together disparate scraps of [Kickapoo] cultural information gathered through three centuries and in a variety of locations, the functional interrelationships of the component parts of a tribe's culture cannot be assessed—a trait from 1640 does not functionally interrelate with traits from 1940." Such a viewpoint is also probably applicable when attempting to interpret faunal information based on animal remains from a site such as Rhoads. The methods and techniques employed by the Kickapoo in exploiting animal resources of the Illinois prairie in ca. A.D. 1800 would not be expected to coincide with those of their ancestors still living today in Oklahoma and Mexico. More accurate interpretations of animal usage by the early Kickapoo (about which there is little specific information) might be arrived at through occasionally detailed ethnohistoric accounts of related contemporaneous tribes. However, in spite of the lapse in time, references such as Wallace (1964) provide interesting accounts of cultural traits, including the utilization of animals for food and other purposes, which appear to have been established over a long period of time. The descriptions by Wallace (1964) involving hunting procedures and the significance of various species, especially certain mammals, to the Oklahoma Kickapoo appear relevant to the following discussion of the Rhoads site mammalian fauna.

Family Talpidae: moles. Remains of the eastern mole, *Scalopus aquaticus*, are often encountered during aboriginal site excavations, especially in the surface and upper humus zones. Thus far there has been no evidence to suggest that moles were used by either the prehistoric or historic Indians of Illinois. The occurrence of two individuals at the Rhoads site (seven elements from five features) was, because of the animals' fossorial habits, probably incidental to the human occupation.

Family Soricidae: shrews. Two soricids, the least shrew, *Cryptotis parva*, and the short-tailed shrew, *Blarina brevicauda*, were represented in the faunal sample. The least shrew is found most often in dry grasslands and weedy fields but, although it may also occur in brushy, weedy, or marshy situations near woods, it is rarely encountered in forests (Hoffmeister and Mohr 1957:62). On the other hand, the short-tailed shrew is an animal principally of forest floors and forest edges and is rarely encountered far from a wooded habitat. Although remains of neither animal were numerous (a total of 14 elements), there were four individuals of *C. parva* represented and only one short-tailed shrew. This difference at least suggests the village was situated on an open tract of prairie. As is probably the case with mice and amphibians, the presence of insectivore remains in the pits may be attributed to the animals having fallen in and having been unable to escape.

Family Vespertilionidae: bats. The presence of bat elements in an open village site is somewhat unusual. Two species were determined from lower jaws: a probable red bat, *Lasiurus* cf. *borealis*, from Feature 152, and a big-eared bat, *Plecotus* sp., from Feature 40. The distal end of a bat humerus was found in Features 125 and 140, as well as postcranial elements in Features 40 and 152 which may be those of the identified species. Based on humeri, at least three individuals are represented. Although the red bat is an early spring and late fall migrant and a common summer resident in Illinois (Hoffmeister and Mohr 1957:81), little is known of the life history and habits of the big-eared bat in the state. The use of bats by the Kickapoo is questionable; it is quite possible that these bats were encountered roosting (or flying) in the houses, killed by the occupants, and simply discarded.

Family Ursidae: bears. Black bears, *Ursus americanus*, were once common in the forested regions of Illinois, but by the late 1800s the animal had been exterminated in the state. The bear has had a long history of veneration and its ceremonial and religious significance to aboriginal man is well documented (Hallowell 1926). Because of special treatment and disposal of bear remains by prehistoric groups, elements other than drilled canine teeth and cut jaws and skulls are rarely encountered in prehistoric sites in the Midwest. After European contact in eastern North America, however, the cultural significance of the bear appears to have lessened somewhat. Swanton (1946:249) indicates the bear was probably second in importance to the deer and it was hunted for its flesh, fat, and hide. Remains of this animal are commonly found in refuse pits and middens at historic sites; bones appear to have been discarded in the trash, like the remains of any other food animal.

In addition to the 15 metapodials found in eight separate features, a left tibia (the proximal end broken away; butchering cuts circling the distal shaft end) and fibula shaft occurred in Feature 118 and a complete left ulna (scored marks on the styloid process for removal of the foot) in Feature 105. Except for the timbered floodplain along Kickapoo Creek, there were few extensive forested areas within the vicinity of the village to support a large population of black bear. Assuming the two individuals represented at Rhoads were killed locally and eaten (at the village), the amount of meat realized would have been considerable (ca. 400–500 lbs. [182–227 kg]). Unless the remains of other bears (if any) were disposed of elsewhere, it is apparent that these Kickapoo rarely encountered or killed this animal, one that would have provided a significant quantity of meat in the diet.

Family Procyonidae: raccoons. A minimum of 23 raccoons, *Procyon lotor*, was represented in the Rhoads site faunal sample, 9 of which were juveniles. Judging from the unfused epiphyses of limb elements, the presence of deciduous teeth, and/or early stages in the eruption of the permanent dentition, at least three or four of the juveniles had been killed in June or July. In Illinois young raccoons are born usually in March or April.

Butchering cuts were noted on the following elements: the posterior ventral edge of the horizontal ramus (two examples from Feature 2 and one from Feature 118; part of the condyle and angle of this latter jaw appears to have been cut off); the distal end of two humeri—to separate the forelimb at the elbow; three proximal ends of femora—cut across the trochlear area/neck/head—to disarticulate the hind limb (or thigh) from the acetabulum (pelvis); the distal end of a femur, "hacked" externally and cut on the face of the lateral condyle—to separate the lower leg (tibia) from the thigh at the knee; the distal end of a tibia shaft—skinning cuts and/or removal of the foot. A perfectly circular hole (3 mm in diameter) occurred in the masseteric fossa of a right jaw from Feature 127, but it is impossible to determine if this hole was caused by some form of pointed instrument (weapon?) or by lead shot.

Taking into account differences in size (weight) between juvenile and adult animals, the estimated weight of meat of all raccoons was determined to be 227 pounds (103 kg), approximately 2.5% of the total for all species. Although this amount of meat is not especially large compared with that of the white-tailed deer, the animal evidently formed one of the more constant and valued meat supplements in the diet. Timbered floodplain along Kickapoo Creek would have provided ideal habitat for this animal.

Family Mustelidae: mink, weasels, skunks, badger, otter. Use of the striped skunk, *Mephitis mephitis*, for food was a common practice of prehistoric peoples in eastern North America. For example, remains of this animal were especially numerous (377 pieces) at the Late Archaic/Early Woodland Tick Creek Cave rockshelter site in Missouri (Parmalee 1965:18); at least 88 individuals were represented. In the case of historic groups in the Southeast, Swanton (1946:250) mentions that "Polecats [skunks] were eaten, at least by some of the Indians . . . ." Mandelbaum (1940:199) lists skunk as a food animal of the Plains Cree. Skunks and other mustelids, however, appear to have been particularly esteemed for inclusion in or serving as personal or sacred medicine bundles; parts of these animals were also worn or carried on the person. Usually the skull, and occasionally foot bones, were left in the skins. If the bundle was interred with its dead owner, it is the skull (and foot bones) recovered in the grave that serves to indicate the animals' former significance (e.g., Bass et al. 1971; Ubelaker and Wedel 1975). Whether or not the particular animal whose skin was prepared as a bundle was also eaten is a matter of speculation.

Remains of the striped skunk from the Rhoads village were not numerous and no more than three individuals were represented. Two tibia sections were recovered in the humus zone, an ulna in Feature 127, a humerus in Feature 140, a lower left jaw section in Feature 17, and a complete skull occurred in Feature 54. The most noteworthy find of *M. mephitis* consisted of a complete skull and lower jaw, plus the lower left jaw and an incomplete skull (probably complete when discarded) of another individual, in the 3½- to 4-foot BT level of Feature 41. In addition, a skunk calcaneum and 23 metapodials were recovered in this level. The foramen magnum and basioccipital area of the more complete skull had been cut away. The presence of this modified skull (and possibly the incomplete one) and foot bones are indicative of a skunk skin that may have once been part of a personal or medicine bundle.

From the paucity of striped skunk remains at the Rhoads site, it is apparent that this common mustelid seldom if ever formed even an occasional supplement in the diet of these Kickapoo.

Remains of badger, *Taxidea taxus*, consisted of four elements: an astragalus from Feature 46/70, the distal half of a fibula from Feature 127, and two ulnae sections (possibly paired) from Features 41 and 114. The shafts of both ulnae had been deeply scored, one just below the semilunar notch and the other at about mid-point. Badgers are associated with open grasslands and prairies and today they are encountered most frequently in the central and western parts of the state. They were probably never a common mustelid in Illinois and, as in the case of the Rhoads site, when badger remains do occur in aboriginal middens, they are few in number.

Family Canidae: wolves, coyotes, dogs, foxes. The gray or timber wolf, *Canis lupus*, was reported to have been common in both the timbered and prairie regions of Illinois prior to the mid-1800s, but by 1900 it had been extirpated in the state (Hoffmeister and Mohr 1957:120). Although this canid was apparently seldom taken by Indian groups occupying the region that is now Illinois, postcranial remains are occasionally found at sites while worked jaw and/or skull sections of the gray wolf are one of the most often encountered artifacts (of this type) found with human burials (Parmalee 1959:91). The flesh of wolves was eaten and the hides used for various purposes. The animal symbolized strength and cunning and it appears to have featured significantly in rituals and ceremonies preformed by certain prehistoric cultural groups (Webb and Baby 1957:61-71). The Kickapoo who occupied the Rhoads site, however, either rarely encountered wolves or were not interested in hunting them. The tentative identification of *C. lupus* was based on two metatarsals from Feature 118 and a section of a right ulna from Feature 37. It is surprising that neither the red fox nor the gray fox was represented in the faunal sample.

The relative scarcity of canid remains referable to the domestic (Indian) dog, *Canis familiaris*, is also somewhat surprising. The dog has been associated with aboriginal man in eastern North America since the Archaic period and has been used as a food animal, guards, a beast of burden, for hunting, and/or simply as a tolerated pet. Ethnohistoric references to dogs owned by various Plains tribes are often detailed. Mandelbaum (1940:197-198), in discussing dogs of the Plains Cree, mentions their value as draught animals and their importance in ceremonial practices, including the serving of dog meat to honored guests or for other special occasions. Wilson (1924:197) quotes Brackenridge concerning dogs of the Arikara: "The dogs, of which each family has thirty or forty, pretend to make a show of fierceness, but on the least threat, run off. They are of different sizes and colors. A number are fattened on purpose to eat, others are used for drawing their baggage. It is nothing more than the domesticated wolf." Wilson (1924:197) also notes Maximilian's (1906) observation that "the Indian dogs are worked very hard, have hard blows, and hard fare . . . ."

No complete Indian dog burials were encountered in the Rhoads site pits and only four postcranial elements (cf. *C. familiaris*) were found. The only butchering cuts noted occurred on the dorsolateral surface of a third cervical vertebra from Feature 2 (inflicted during removal of the head?). Paired lower jaws of a large puppy (total length, 107 mm; length of deciduous carnassial, 13 mm) were recovered at the 4- to 4½-foot level in Feature 2; incomplete skull sections occurred in Features 4, 54 (total length of carnassial of this animal and the one from Fea. 4:19 mm), and 114. In addition, the remains of a fetus or newborn canid pup (dog?) was found in Feature 75, plus deciduous canid teeth in Features 11, 17, and 46/70. It cannot be assumed that these "puppy" teeth are all from different animals, but there are at least four pups and probably four adults represented in the Rhoads site fauna.

From the relatively little canid material recovered at this village, it is difficult to interpret the significance of the dog to these people except to suggest it was minimal. Dogs appeared have been somewhat more numerous at the Crawford Farm site village, judging from the recovery of 36 isolated elements, as well as one partial and two complete burials (Parmalee 1964:169). Comments by Wallace (1964:40–41) on the status of the dog in ceremonies of the Oklahoma Kickapoo may be appropriate in light of the puppies represented at the Rhoads site:

> During Kickapoo ceremonies, practically all food available to them was eaten. The two foods held in highest veneration, however, were the deer and the young dog.
> The use of a puppy in a Kickapoo ceremony followed a set procedure. About three months before the ceremony was to be held, a first-born puppy was selected and given special attention. It was considered sacred, kept in the house, and fed only what the people themselves ate. It was never fed scraps. The following statement of one informant explains why the Kickapoo considered the puppy holy.

> They eat small puppies in these ceremonies. That's in one of those prophecies. Who ever instructed them on this religious ceremony said that they would sooner or later lose all wild game. They told them that there would be a day when all wild game would be gone. They told them that they should use a small dog—a puppy. Use a puppy instead of a bear or a deer. The dog and the puppy will be with them until the end of time. It will be with them until the end of the world.

> Just before the ceremony, the puppy was taken away from the village and killed by breaking its neck with a pole. The hair was then singed off the animal and it was cleaned and dressed. It was then cooked in a kettle.

Family Felidae: cats. A total of 14 elements of the bobcat, *Lynx* cf. *rufus*, were recovered from the refuse pits. All but three claws from Feature 11, the distal three-quarter of a right tibia from Feature 40 (butchering cuts at the distal end), and a complete lower right jaw from Feature 46/70 (skinning cuts on the lateral surface near the symphysis), occurred in Features 26 and 41. The pubis of the right innominate had been cut near the acetabulum (removal of the thigh or hind limb) and both the left calcaneum and astragalus from Feature 26 were scored (removal of the foot). It is possible that the three claws from Feature 11 originally had been left in the skin of one of these cats.

Bobcats were formerly numerous in the wooded regions of Illinois. The heavily forested hill country of the northwestern and southern parts of the state and the timbered floodplains along streams and rivers provided the most suitable habitat. The bobcats represented at the Rhoads site could have been taken locally along Kickapoo Creek. One of the two examples of bone pathology noted in the faunal materials involved the distal end of a right tibia of a bobcat. This bone had been broken about 1 inch (2.5 cm) below the medial malleolus and, during the healing process, the fibula (also broken?) fused to the tibia shaft (Fig. 2A). The healed break probably caused little or no interference of movement in the joint. The distal end of this broken right tibia and that of the normal left (both from Feature 41) had been scored during the Indian's attempt to remove the hind feet.

Family Sciuridae: squirrels. Remains of three species of rodents included in this family occurred in the refuse pits. One, the 13-lined ground squirrel, *Spermophilus tridecemlineatus*, is a common mammal in pastures and other short grass areas in the northern two-thirds of the state. Although possible, it is doubtful that the Kickapoo ate or otherwise used this small ground squirrel. Less than a dozen elements (three individuals) from six features were recovered; its presence was probably incidental to the human occupation. On the other hand, the occurrence of the eastern chipmunk, *Tamias striatus*, at the Rhoads site may have been the result of intentional collecting by the Indian. The chipmunk is an inhabitant of brushy woods and forested ravines; they could have been found along the wooded banks of Kickapoo Creek and in the forest-prairie ecotone. A concentration of 58 elements from seven individuals in Feature 128 appears to be something more than chance accumulation. Mandelbaum (1940:199) mentions that the Cree ate chipmunks as well as other small rodents such as "gopher" (a name often used to denote ground squirrel) and squirrel.

Exploitation of gray and/or fox squirrels, *Sciurus* sp., as an important supplemental food resource by prehistoric peoples in Illinois is well

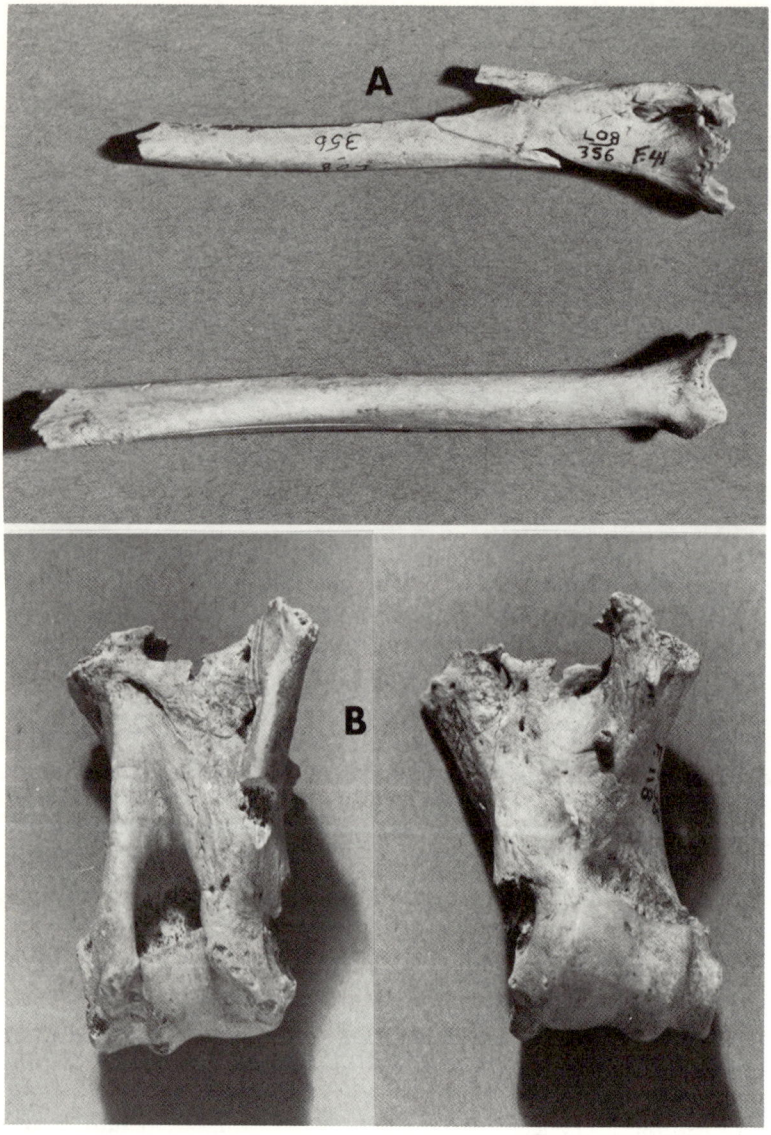

Fig. 2. Examples of bone pathology: *A*, broken and healed distal end of a bobcat tibia compared with a normal element; *B*, two views of a broken and healed distal end of a white-tailed deer humerus.

documented (e.g., Parmalee 1957:239). Although natural habitat requirements vary somewhat for the two species, both may occur together and both are common locally throughout Illinois. It is surprising, therefore, that the Kickapoo made no attempt (or a very minimal one: a total of four *Sciurus* elements, one individual) to hunt these rodents which could have served as an important meat supplement in their diet. Although remains of squirrels found at the Crawford Farm site were somewhat more numerous (22 bones; Parmalee 1964:169), these Sauk and Fox likewise made little use of this food resource.

Family Geomyidae: pocket gophers. The Plains pocket gopher, *Geomys bursarius*, is a fossorial rodent which spends most of its life in underground burrows. Its range in Illinois extends as a diagonal belt from the northeast to the southcentral edge of the state and includes Logan County. There is no evidence to suggest that the few elements (eight pieces, two individuals) of this rodent found in the pits represent anything more than animals which naturally inhabited the village area and died there.

Family Castoridae: beavers. Kickapoo Creek and associated backwater areas, questionable as to size and extent, appear to have been unsuitable habitat for the establishment of a large population of beaver, *Castor canadensis*. Remains of only two animals in the Rhoads site faunal sample reflect these conditions. A single vertebra occurred in Feature 40 and the incomplete (rotted) skull of a juvenile in Feature 55. These and the other elements, 58 in Feature 127, and 13 in Feature 118, represented two individuals, a large mature adult and a juvenile. There appears to have been a mixing of bones (originally carcass sections?) from these two animals between Features 127 and 118. The paired scapulae of the juvenile occurred in Feature 127, all the rest of the elements from this feature being those of the adult beaver. The left humerus of the adult occurred in Feature 127 and the right in Feature 127. One clavicle of the adult occurred in Feature 127 and the other in Feature 118.

Butchering cuts were noted on the following elements: the necks of the two left femora; the distal ends of both tibiae and fibulae of the adult; all of the ribs, 21 from Feature 127 and 1 from Feature 118—still possessing the proximal or vertebral articular ends—were scored at their proximal ends; the clavicle from Feature 127. These scored-marks suggest the animals were disarticulated by separating the hind limb from the pelvis at the acetabulum, the hind feet were cut off at the "heel," the front limb(s) was removed by separating the clavicle at its point of vertebral articulation, and the rib cage was apparently separated from the carcass at its vertebral attachment. All remains of the beaver from Feature 127, a pit 4½ feet in depth, occurred within the ½- to 1-foot level. The concentration of all elements in this 6-inch level suggests immediate disposal of the carcass after the meat was stripped off, or after it was cooked.

Beaver remains ranked third, numerically, of all mammal bones recovered at the Crawford Farm site (Parmalee 1964:169) and second at the Bell site, Winnebago County, Wisconsin, a protohistoric Fox village thought to have been occupied most intensively ca. 1716–30 (Parmalee 1963:59). This large rodent appears to have been an important food animal at both sites, and the suggestion was made (Parmalee 1964:173) that "... it is reasonable to assume (based on early historic accounts, for example, Thwaites, 1911 [The Fur Trade in Wisconsin 1812–1825; Coll. State Hist. Soc. Wis. 20]) that the pelts were bartered to the whites for trade goods. The quantity of beaver remains (28% of the total) found at an historic Fox site (Bell site) in Wisconsin ... also suggested a beginning of intensified fur trapping activity." It is apparent, however, that the Kickapoo occupying the Rhoads village only occasionally obtained beaver because, as has been suggested, the local habitat was unsuitable for the establishment of an abundant population. Remains of a juvenile beaver, in addition to other faunal evidence, found at the site are indicative of summer occupation; pelts would then not have been in prime condition. Wallace (1964:17) states, "Skunks, fox, and beaver were also killed but only for their fur as the pelts of these animals were traded for food, clothing, and in some cases, for money." If the Rhoads Kickapoo did trap beaver and exchange their pelts for European trade goods or other items, the animals were probably taken elsewhere and processed at winter trapping/hunting camps.

Family Cricetidae: native mice and rats. Probably only one of four or five species of rodents in this family that were represented at Rhoads occurred as a direct result of the Indians' hunting activities. Remains of the muskrat, *Ondatra zibethica*, an animal occurring commonly in almost every type of aquatic habitat in the state, were surprising few (ten pieces, two individuals). This aquatic species was often heavily exploited by prehistoric groups, but the historic Sauk and Fox (Crawford Farm site) and the Kickapoo made little use of it. In view of the direct effort made by both groups to collect aquatic turtles, the paucity of muskrat elements at both village sites seems unusual unless, for some reason, it was locally rare. Six of the ten muskrat elements from Rhoads occurred in Feature 127; the only evidence noted of butchering was the scored marks on the distal end of a radius (removal of the foot) from this feature. Combined, muskrat and beaver provided an estimated 56 pounds (25.5 kg) of meat—less than one percent of the total.

Bones of the white-footed and/or deer mouse, *Peromyscus* sp., prairie vole or meadow vole, *Microtus* sp., and the bog lemming, *Synaptomys* cf.

cooperi, along with indeterminate mouse elements (mostly postcranial), were encountered in 32 of the 58 features (pits). Identification of the bog lemming, an inhabitant of marshes and wet meadows having thick stands of grass and other herbaceous plants, was based on the recovery of two diagnostic grooved upper incisors. No cheek teeth, skulls, or jaws were found. Hoffmeister and Mohr (1957:177) indicate the prairie vole, *Microtus ochrogaster*, is most abundant in central and southern Illinois, and it is probably this species rather than the more northern meadow vole, *M. pennsylvanicus*, that occurred at the Rhoads site. Osteological differences between the deer mouse, *Peromyscus maniculatus*, and the white-footed mouse, *P. leucopus*, are usually very subtle, if at all discernible, and it was not possible to separate with certainty the two on the material from Rhoads. The former is an inhabitant of grassland habitats and weedy fields, while the latter is most often found in forested areas and brushlands. At least 66 *Peromyscus* were represented in the faunal sample, and probably most of the indeterminate postcranial mouse bones were from one or both species belonging to this genus.

Family Zapodidae: jumping mice. Five orange-colored, grooved upper incisors characteristic of the meadow jumping mouse, *Zapus hudsonius*, were encountered in three pits; they represented four individuals. No diagnostic cheek teeth, skulls, or jaws were found. Hoffmeister and Mohr (1957:187) state that a grassy or vine-covered bank of a stream or pond where there are a few trees forms the most suitable habitat for this small mouse. The banks of Kickapoo Creek and its terraces would have provided such a habitat, so remains of the meadow jumping mouse at the Rhoads site are not unexpected. The reason why the remains of these mice, shrews and/or small toads and frogs occurred in over half of the pits has already been considered.

Family Leporidae: hares, rabbits. Remains of one, or possibly two, very young cottontails, *Sylvilagus floridanus*, occurred in Features 22 (5½- to 6-foot level) and 46/70 (lens 2A & 3). Since no other remains of the cottontail were found in association with the Kickapoo occupation, and because these juveniles were so young as to have been relatively helpless, it may be assumed their presence (like the rodents and amphibians) was the result of their having fallen into the pits.

Family Cervidae: elk, deer. The matter of whether or not the elk, *Cervus elaphus*, was a food animal of the Kickapoo while they were occupying the Rhoads site village has been discussed. Assuming the one animal that was represented (by metapodials) at the site was killed locally, it would have contributed an estimated 350 pounds (159 kg) of meat or approximately 3.6% of the total of all species comprising the faunal sample. Elk were never as numerous as the white-tailed deer in

Illinois, apparently even during prehistoric times. Except at the Upper Mississippian Noble-Wieting village near Bloomington (Parmalee and Bogan 1981), reported remains of it are typically uncommon to rare in faunal samples from aboriginal sites.

The white-tailed deer, *Odocoileus virginianus*, on the other hand, provided the basic meat staple in the diet of all aboriginal groups in Illinois from the Archaic period to the Historic. The significance of this animal to the Rhoads site Kickapoo is apparent from the number of individuals represented in the faunal sample (98) and the estimated amount of meat (8230 pounds [3741 kg], 85.5%) that was obtained. In his discussion of subsistence of the Oklahoma Kickapoo for the period 1874-94, Wallace (1964:40) states, "The most prized wild animal utilized by the Kickapoo was the deer and, under normal circumstances, all edible parts of the animal were consumed." Moreover, Ritzenthaler and Peterson (1956:37) indicate that "by far the most important animal hunted [by the Mexican Kickapoo] is the deer." They quote (Ritzenthaler and Peterson 1956:38) an informant as saying, "The deer is considered to be the Indian's special food. There is none better. Without deer, we will lose everything: our habits, customs, traditions, and ceremonies."

Remains of the white-tailed deer from the Rhoads site, which totaled 3422 pieces (ca. 20%), were of interest from several different aspects. In addition to forming the basis for determining the number of animals represented in the sample, other data involving deer age ratios (Table 2), evidence for the season of site occupation, processing or butchering procedures, bone and antler tool manufacturing, and pathology were obtained. At the time when the basic identification and the analytic work were being carried out, an effort was made to determine if there was any consistency in the deposition of a particular element or set of elements in any given feature (pit). The presence of only one element, or those elements comprising a particular body region or limb (e.g., the scapula/humerus/radius/ulna:the forelimb), might suggest a specific division of parts of the deer carcass among individuals or families, but such was not the case. A pit might contain parts of a skull, phalanges, elements of both fore- and hind limbs, and vertebrae from one to several regions of the spinal column.

Few postcranial elements (e.g., humeri, femora) from a particular pit, or among pits, could be paired with complete certainty, primarily because of breakage. It was possible, however, to pair the lower jaws of ten individuals; these may have been discarded while still joined at the symphysis. In the case of one of these pairs, the right jaw occurred in Feature 40 and the left in Feature 41. In a few instances two or three consecutive vertebrae (six thoracics in Feature 105) were recovered in the same pit, suggesting they had been discarded while still articulated. With one exception, the distal half of a metatarsal and all associated phalanges from Feature 75, no articulated limb elements were encountered. Several incomplete or fragmentary bone pieces, some of which are illustrated in Figure 3, contained puncture marks which were probably the result of having been chewed, perhaps by dogs?

Age Distribution of Deer: The method of aging white-tailed deer based on tooth eruption and wear in the lower jaw, a technique developed by Severinghaus (1949), has proved especially useful in the study of archaeologically-derived material. This procedure is most accurate up to the time the animal is about two years of age. Although the degree of wear on the permanent teeth after this time progresses at a fairly uniform rate, the rapidity of wear varies depending upon the region (e.g. the Edwards Plateau of Texas compared with central Illinois) and type of forage consumed. However, by comparing the figures and descriptions of tooth development, replacement and wear provided by Severinghaus (1949) and a series of aged jaws obtained from Illinois deer with the Rhoads site specimens (98 jaws), it was possible to obtain relatively accurate ages for the animals represented.

Obviously there is no way of determining the exact date of birth for any of the Rhoads deer and a fawn could conceivably have been born on any date between ca. May 1 and June 30. However, the majority of fawns born in Illinois are dropped in late May or early June (Hoffmeister and Mohr 1957:203; Calhoun and Loomis 1974). For the purpose of estimating the time (months) when deer were killed by the Kickapoo, June 1 has been selected as an "average" birth date for central Illinois fawns. Approximately 30% of the deer taken by the Kickapoo were fawns (an animal is considered a "fawn" until it reaches about 1 year of age). Five of these fawns were less than 6 months old when taken; three, from Features 46/70, 41 and the plow zone, were 1 to 3 weeks of age; while two (Feature 2, plow zone) were 40 to 50 days old. The high percentage of fawns at this site and at others (e.g., Tick Creek Cave, ca. 17% fawns; Parmalee 1965:27) lends little credence to Elder's opinion (1965:369) that the Indian "... was practicing a voluntary and effective conservation measure—sparing the fawns to grow into better hides and more meat."

The 14 individuals falling into the third age group in Table 2 are especially significant. All of these individuals fell within a 5 to 7 month age group, with most probably 6 to 7 months old when killed. This would place the time of death for some, even if they had been born early in the season (early to mid May), in November, thus indicating that at least some Kickapoo were occupying the village into late fall. The 8 individuals in the 12 to 18 month age category were all ca. 12 to 14 months of age,

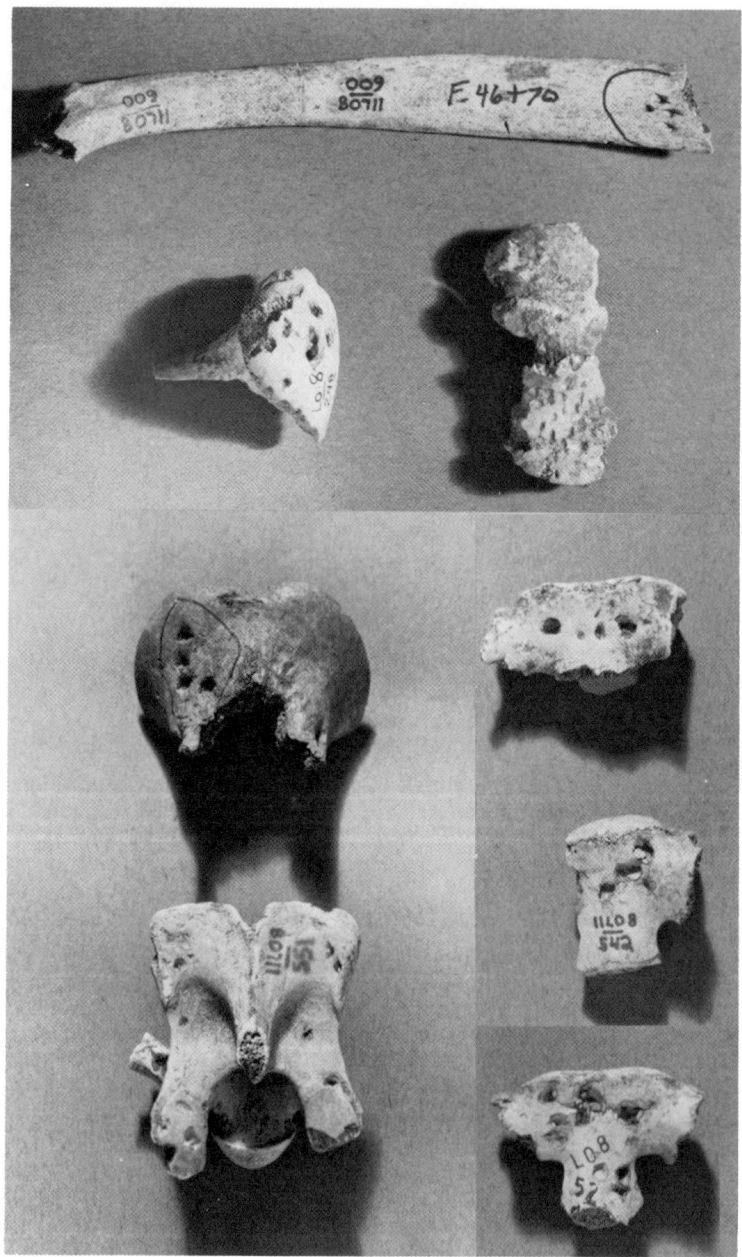

Fig. 3. Bone fragments exhibiting puncture marks from chewing, probably by dogs.

TABLE 2
AGE DISTRIBUTION OF DEER (PERCENTAGE OF EACH GROUPING) FROM THE RHOADS SITE

Feature	Approximate Age										
	Months					Years					
	0–1	2–6	6–12	12–18	18–24	2½–3½	3½–4½	4½–5½	5½–6½	6½–7½	7½–8½
1			2			1					1
2		1	2		3	4	1	1			
4			2			1					
6					1	1					
11				1							
17										1	1
22						1					
29				1							
37										1	
40					1	1	1				
41	1		2	2	3	3	5	3			
46/70	1		1	1	1		1		1	1	
54				1							
55			1		1	1					
73					1						
75					1			1			
105			1		2	1					
114				1							
116						1					
118			1		1	1	3	1	1		1
127			1	1			2				1
128									1		
130			1				3				
141						1					
152						1					
163					1	1					
H.Z./P.Z.	1	1				1	1	2			
TOTALS	3	2	14	8	16	17	20	8	3	3	4
%	3.06	2.04	14.28	8.16	16.32	17.34	20.40	8.16	3.06	3.06	4.08

while the 16 animals listed in the 18 to 24 month age group were approximately 2 years old when killed. All of these deer were probably taken in the months of June and July. About 54% of the deer killed by the Rhoads site Kickapoo were two years or less in age, while nearly 30% fell within the 2½ to 4½ year age range. The pressure of modern-day hunting on Illinois deer herds is such that few animals survive to old age. It would be impossible to assess the actual hunting pressure exerted by the Kickapoo on the deer populations in the vicinity of the village or in their extended hunting territory. However, in view of the animal's somewhat restricted habitat (timbered floodplains and forest-prairie ecotone) and the high percentage of young animals and the low percentage (only 10% of the deer were over 5 to 5½ years of age) of mature-to-old deer, it was probably considerable.

Butchering Procedures: The methods of skinning and butchering large herbivores such as the white-tailed deer by aboriginal peoples in eastern North America underwent little change since the Archaic period. The procedure employed in processing a carcass after removal of the skin was to separate the limbs and various body sections at their points of articulation. It is during this operation that some bones were inflicted with lasting cut or scored marks, and those elements comprising the more compact joints such as the "elbow" (distal end of the humerus, proximal ends of the radius and ulna) and the "heel" or hock (distal end of the tibia, calcaneum, astragalus) are the ones which most often bear these marks. Guilday, Parmalee, and Tanner (1962:63) have pointed out that skinning and butchering marks may be identical in appearance and that they differ mainly in position. To illustrate, the light cuts across the nasal bones of three deer from the Rhoads site resulted as the hide was being cut free from the skull at the nose, while scored marks on or near the glenoid fossa of the scapula occurred during separation of the shoulder from the proximal end of the humerus. Table 3 is a list of the deer elements found with butchering cuts and the approximate percent of each which had been scored.

With reference to the Oklahoma Kickapoo, Wallace (1964:18-19) states that

> after the deer were killed, they were skinned, quarter sectioned, and hung up to dry. Before the women stopped going on the deer hunt, the meat was immediately cut into strips and dried, always leaving the ribs intact to be used later for ceremonial purposes. Without the women to aid them, the men preserved the meat as best they could until they returned to the village at which time it was turned over to the women.

In the case of the Mexican Kickapoo, Ritzenthaler and Peterson (1956:38-39) relate the following observations:

> When the game [deer] is shot, the animal is skinned, cut up, and divided among the hunters. The person shooting the animal gets the hide and the tongue, while the meat is equally divided. The raw liver is usually eaten immediately. If the party is mounted, the meat is tied onto the saddle. If the party is afoot, the animal may be fastened to a pole and carried back to the village on the hunters' shoulders. When alone, a hunter will split open the deer, insert his head in the rib cage with the rest of the animal slung over his back, or carried on the back with the aid of a tump line across the chest, and carry it to the village.

TABLE 3
RHOADS SITE DEER ELEMENTS, NUMBER OF PIECES, AND
APPROXIMATE PERCENTAGE OF EACH WITH CUTS

Element	No. of Pieces	No. Cut	Approx. %
Antler	20	14	70.0
Lower Jaw	182	11	6.0
Hyoid	61	3	4.9
Atlas	23	9	39.1
Axis	19	3	13.0
Cervical vertebrae (other than axis, atlas)	116	12	10.3
Thoracic vertebrae	110	4	3.6
Lumbar vertebrae	77	17	22.0
Sacrum	10	2	20.0
Ribs	604	227	37.5
Scapula	96	27	28.1
Humerus (proximal end)	11	1	9.0
Humerus (distal end)	62	35	58.4
Humerus (shaft sections)	22	5	22.7
Radius (proximal end)	48	24	50.0
Radius (distal end)	26	2	7.6
Radius (shaft sections)	19	3	15.7
Ulna (proximal end)	56	9	16.0
Metacarpal (proximal end)	35	7	20.0
Metacarpal (distal end)	17	6	35.2
Metacarpal (shaft sections)	22	4	18.1
Femur (proximal end)	18	6	33.3
Femur (distal end)	7	2	28.5
Femur (shaft sections)	20	8	40.0
Tibia (proximal end)	11	1	9.0
Tibia (distal end)	35	14	25.4
Tibia (shaft sections)	14	5	35.7
Metatarsal (proximal end)	35	1	2.8
Metatarsal (distal end)	14	4	28.5
Metatarsal (shaft section)	61	6	9.8
Calcaneum	36	10	27.7
Astragalus	28	15	53.5
Tibia tarsal	28	9	31.1
Pelvis (acetabulum area)	149	23	15.4
Pelvis (iliosacral joint)	149	4	2.6

From these descriptions it is apparent that some animals were fleshed out at the point of kill and only the meat (and some bones) were brought back to the village, while in other cases the complete carcass was carried back. Although all elements of the deer were represented in the Rhoads site faunal sample, indicating whole carcasses were processed at the village, there is no way of knowing how many animals may have been butchered at the point of kill with only the meat having been brought back.

Deer bones from the Rhoads site exhibited two types of butchering marks, those inflicted with a knife and those resulting from heavy blows probably made with axes. The use of an ax was especially apparent on sections of antler beam from which tines had been chopped off. At least seven skulls were either split open or a dorsal portion of the frontals and parietals cut away (for removal of the brains?) with a heavy knife or ax (see Fig. 4). Antlers from at least five individuals had been cut off immediately above or below the burr by the use of an ax and/or possibly a knife. Although the general pattern followed by the Kickapoo in butchering deer was not unlike that of most prehistoric groups, the availability of iron tools appears to have changed the precision of work somewhat, e.g., more hacking or chopping and less careful cutting with a knife.

The deer skinning process practiced at Rhoads was probably not unlike the one described for deer from the Eschelman site, a Susquehannock village dating A.D. 1600–1625 in Pennsylvania (Guilday et al. 1962:72–75). Skinning cuts occurred consistently at only two locations on deer bones from the Rhoads site (vs. four from Eschelman), however. These were at the proximal and distal ends of the metacarpals and metatarsals. In the majority of cases, the hide was cut from the legs at the distal ends of these cannon bones; the skin adheres tightly to these elements and the scored marks observed on numerous shaft sections, as well as the articular ends, resulted from the attempts to free the skin as it was being pulled toward the feet. Skinning marks noted on the nasal bones of three individuals and on the premaxilla of a fourth are indicative of the fact that the hide was cut free of the skull. Final removal was accomplished by freeing the skin at the tip of the nose (premaxillae) and the lower jaws. One lower left jaw from Feature 37 exhibited a series of transverse cuts on the dorsolateral surface of the diastema, while a right jaw from Feature 127 was scored in several places at and foreward of the mental foramen. The anterior end of a right jaw from Feature 118 had been severed from the horizontal ramus just posterior to the mental foramen by a downward and backward slicing, or chopping, blow. Another right jaw from this feature had been cut perpendicularly through the diastema. These cuts probably resulted during the final step of removing the hide from the skull. Only one maxilla section (from Feature 105) was recovered that had been cut along the gum line and none of the skulls recovered bore scored marks. It is surprising that the Kickapoo were able to cut away the skin from the top of the skulls, and in the case of bucks from around the antler bases, without leaving a mark.

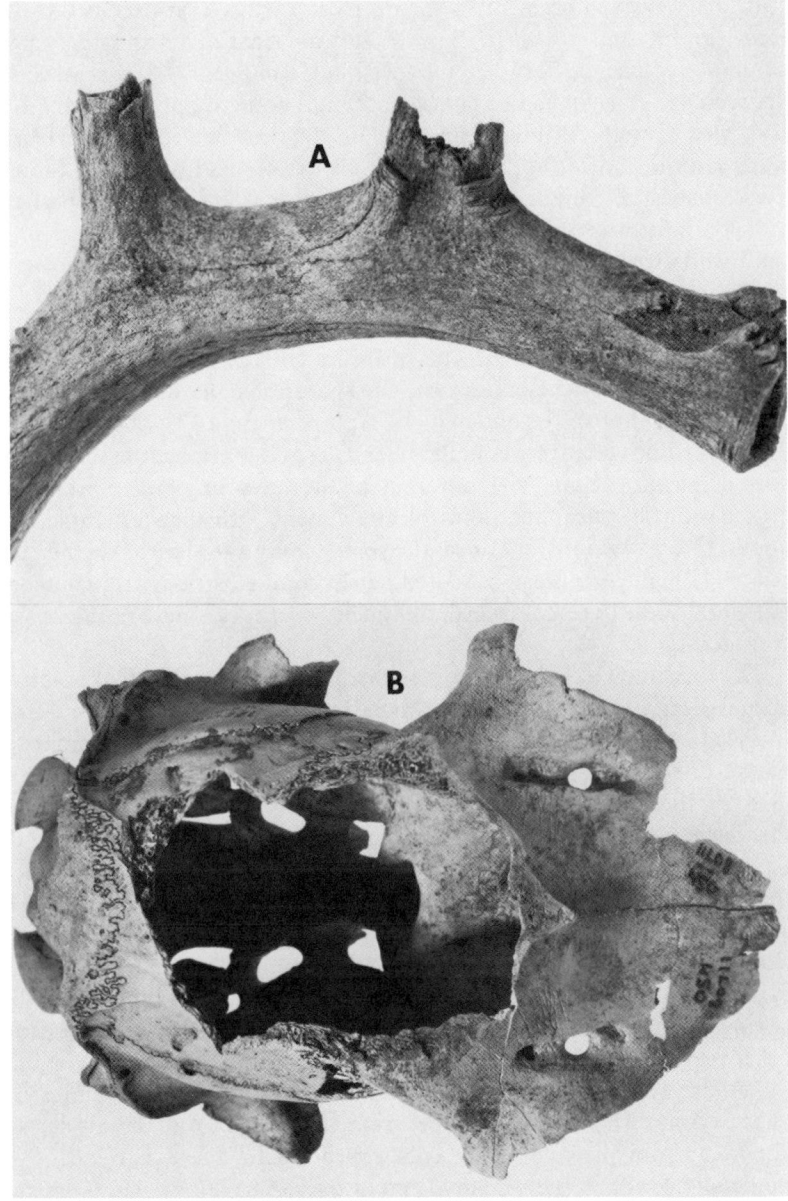

Fig. 4. Examples of cut marks on white-tailed deer antler and skull sections: *A*, chop/cut marks inflicted during the removal of tines; *B*, frontals and parietals cut away for extraction of brains.

Primary dismemberment of the deer carcass involved removal of the head, limbs, and rib cage. The head was separated from the spinal column by cutting between the occipital condyles and the atlas, or between the atlas and axis. The basioccipital bone of only one individual had been scored. All butchering cuts on the first two cervical vertebrae were ventral, indicating the head was always severed by cutting though the throat. The tongue was known to have been a prized part of the animal and it was undoubtedly always removed, but only five percent of the hyoids were cut. Typically this element is scored during removal of the tongue.

Wallace (1964:40) states that "during certain ceremonies . . . only the ribs of the deer were eaten. The ribs were cooked in a kettle that hung from a chain inside the house since the Kickapoo believed the ribs to be a preferred food of spirits and deities." Approximately 37% of the deer ribs (including both relatively complete elements and shaft sections) contained scored marks. About 15% were cut at the head or point of vertebral articulation, 8% near the point of attachment with the sternabrae, and about 13% at various intermediate points along the shaft. Whether this relatively high percentage of scored marks resulted strictly from butchering or is indicative of special treatment or processing are interesting considerations.

The forelimbs of a deer were separated at the three principal points of articulation: (1) the "shoulder," which involved freeing the scapula from the head or proximal end of the humerus; (2) the "elbow" joint, comprised of the distal end of the humerus and proximal ends of the radius and ulna; (3) the "wrist," consisting of the proximal end of the metacarpal and the distal ends of the radius and ulna. Twenty-eight percent of the scapulae were scored; these cuts were located on the neck and on or near the rim of the glenoid fossa. As Guilday et al. (1962:73) pointed out, "The scapula may have been cooked as a separate unit, or have been left on the rib cage." The spine and the dorsal edge of the glenoid border of a scapula from Feature 125 had been chopped or "shaved" away, possibly during the act of defleshing the upper forelimb. The distal ends of four other scapula blades had been cut off perpendicular to the spine and the three bore defleshing(?) marks on the blade parallel to and on either side of the spine. The difficulty of severing the forelimb at the elbow was apparent from the number of cuts appearing on the distal end of the humerus (58%) and the proximal end of the radius (50%). Although only 20% of the proximal metacarpal ends and 7% of the distal radii ends were scored, removal of the metatarsal was probably a standard butchering procedure.

The hind limb was separated from the pelvis either by cutting the round ligament and muscles which aid in holding the head of the femur in the acetabulum, or by severing the pelvis from the sacrum at the iliosacral joint. The former procedure was the only one usually followed. One innominate had been cut along the rim of the acetabulum as well as at the iliosacral joint, while the entire length of the ischiatic spine of another (Feature 152) had been chopped. Approximately 28% of the distal ends (condyles) of femora were scored and 9% of the proximal ends of tibiae. Apparently the thigh was severed from the lower leg by cutting from the underside of the knee joint. It is difficult to explain why only five patellae were recovered in the entire faunal sample. The third or heel joint of the hind limb, and the one causing the most difficulty, involved the separation of the distal end of the tibia (25% cut) from or at the major foot bones—the calcaneum (27% cut), the astragalus (53% cut), and the tibia tarsal (32% cut). The distal end of a tibia from Feature 17 had been almost entirely chopped through from two sides.

Combined, approximately 10% of the cervical (other than atlas, axis), thoracic, and lumbar vertebrae had been chopped or scored with a knife, but there was no apparent consistency in the way the spinal column was sectioned. One cervical vertebra from Feature 11 had been chopped in half transversely while a lumbar from Feature 40 had been similarly split. Another lumbar vertebra from Feature 46/70 had the dorsal (neural) spine and intervertebral disc cut away, probably as a result of transverse knife cuts across the centrum with a few cuts on neural spines and the dorsal surfaces of the transverse processes (removal of the "tenderloin"?). Two sacra, of ten recovered, had been cut posterioventrally, possibly during separation of the innominates along the iliosacral joint. The vertebral column appears to have been divided into at least two, and quite possibly three or more sections. The sacrum and innominates were removed as a unit, the neck as another, and the remaining thoracic and lumbar region was further divided.

Family Equidae: horses. One of the most interesting and perhaps least understood aspects of the Rhoads site faunal complex involved a horse, *Equus caballus*, which occurred in Feature 46/70. Remains of only the anterior half of the animal were present. These included both forelimbs, the skull and jaws, all seven cervical vertebrae, and 16 thoracic vertebrae with the associated ribs. All four tushes had erupted and were fully developed, indicating the animal was a male. Judging from the wear on the occlusal surface of the incisors and the absence of Galvayne's groove (which begins showing at about nine to ten years) on the dorsal surface of the third upper incisors, the horse was estimated to have been around five to seven years of age. The animal was still hobbled when it was deposited—rib cage down, head up—and had not been dismembered or butchered. No other horse elements were encountered at the Rhoads site.

The reason or reasons why "half" a horse was deposited in such a fashion, still articulated, hobbled, and without having been butchered, invokes some interesting speculation. Sixteen elements (one individual?) of a horse were recovered at the Crawford Farm site Sauk-Fox village (Parmalee 1964:173), but these were isolated bones found at various locales in the midden. The one animal represented at the Rhoads site may have accidentally died or was killed and, as simply a matter of expedient disposal, was sectioned into two halves and deposited in one of the storage/refuse pits. The intriguing question, however, is what happened to the posterior half of the horse.

Mammal bone artifacts: All of the mammal bone artifacts recovered at the Rhoads site, which were few in number, had been fashioned from antler, deer bones, and bones of an indeterminate large mammal—probably those of the white-tailed deer. They were manufactured for use as tools (knife or awl handles?), weapons (projectile points), decoration, or gaming pieces. Two bone combs, one from the humus zone and one from Feature 41 (Fig. 1*P*), probably represent European trade items. The availability of other European trade goods, including items such as iron knives, axes, and adzes, probably lessened the need of the Kickapoo to produce their own tools and utensils from bone and other materials. Brief descriptions by features of the worked pieces (probably all fashioned by the Kickapoo) are as follows:

Profile Cleanup: A 2¼ inch (5.7 cm) antler handle (Fig. 1*J*). This small antler section (from a spike buck?) had been cut from the skull below the burr; the piece of frontal bone and burr had then been cut and rounded. The distal end, part of which was broken away during excavation, had been hollowed out for insertion of a knife(?) base.

Feature 3: A 2 inch (5.1 cm) section of deer(?) rib; cut, polished, and rounded at one end and ground along the edges of the other end, exposing the inner latticework (Fig. 1*L*). Function uncertain.

Two cut and hollowed-out bone pieces (Fig. 1*A*). These were probably fashioned from the phalanges of deer and were pieces used in the cup-and-pin game (Guilday 1963).

Feature 40: A ¾ inch (1.9 cm) antler tine. The tip of this small, cut off section appears worn from use. Function uncertain.

Feature 41: A fragmented section of deer antler. The cut end of one of the pieces suggests the finished artifact had originally been cut from a tine; the object had been scraped and polished and one edge serrated.

This latter piece contained five shallow notches, while a smaller fragment appears to have been drilled. Possibly a pendant?

A 4 inch (10.2 cm) section of a pig tusk from this feature contained two completed holes, and the start of a third, drilled at the root end of the tooth (Fig. 1*K*). It may have been worn as a pendant or on a necklace. There is no evidence to suggest these Kickapoo were raising hogs, so this unique tooth artifact may represent a trade item or one extracted from a hog raised or obtained elsewhere.

Feature 118: A well fashioned 2 inch (5.1 cm) antler projectile point was recovered in this feature (Fig. 1*B*). It had been beveled to produce four flattened surfaces, diamond shaped in cross-section, and hollowed out to received an arrow(?) shaft.

Two cut, flattened, and roughly circular bone pieces were also found in Feature 118. One, approximately 1 inch (2.5 cm) in diameter, appears to have been in the preliminary stages of manufacture (as a disc pendant?) when discarded. The second piece, a somewhat heart-shaped section of bone (incomplete section illustrated in Fig. 1*N*) approximately 1½×1½ inches (3.8×3.8 cm) had been notched on either side and two holes drilled at the top center. This artifact was undoubtedly a pendant; it may have been cut from a deer scapula blade.

Feature 128: Circular antler tine projectile point (Fig. 1*C*), approximately 1¼ inches (3.2 cm) in length, hollowed out at the base for insertion of the arrow shaft.

Probably the most unusual piece of worked bone recovered at the Rhoads site was the section of a pendant (or comb?) illustrated in Figure 1 (*O*). The "base" had been drilled and its outer surface decorated with an incised design. Projecting from this base was a series (original number unknown) of arrows, each about 1½ inches (3.8 cm) long. Considering the types of tools then available and the fact that this unique object was carved from a single piece of bone, the individual who created it was a skillful artist.

Feature 140: All three bone artifacts from this feature (Fig. 1*H, I, M*), at least two of which were cut from antler, were fashioned as handles for knives or another type of tool. One (*H*) was a solid, ca. 2½-inch (6.4 cm) polished section of antler, narrowed at one end for possible attachment or insertion of a blade or awl? The second (*I*), also 2½ inches (6.4 cm) long with an interior diameter of ½ inch (1.3 cm), had one end indented for probable attachment of a band for securing the instrument after its insertion into the handle. Only half of this handle was recovered. The third piece (*M*), about 1¾ inches (4.5 cm) in length, was rounded at one end, cut off transversely at the other, and hollowed out for half its length.

The outside surface was polished and beveled, forming four surfaces (diamond-shaped in cross-section).

INVERTEBRATES

Family Unionidae: freshwater mussels. Formerly abundant in eastern North America, freshwater mussels were commonly exploited by aboriginal groups in this area. (e.g., Morrison 1942; Parmalee 1969). Vast quantitites of discarded mussel valves formed the "shell mounds" of the Archaic and Woodland peoples of the lower Ohio, Mississippi, and Tennessee River valleys, and throughout this region shells occur in great abundance in most prehistoric midden deposits. This shell refuse appears indicative of the Indians' dependence on the freshwater mussel as a basic food supplement.

In spite of the tremendous number of freshwater mussels consumed, however, their caloric value is low and it has recently been suggested (Parmalee and Klippel 1974) that they represented only a supplemental food in the diet. Few data are available relative to the significance of freshwater mussels in the food economy of historic Indians of the Midwest. In discussing the vertebrate remains from a historic Fox village (Bell site) in Wisconsin, Parmalee (1963:69) mentions that "mollusks were of little or no value and, like many of the vertebrate species whose remains occurred in limited numbers, served as an occasional supplement to the basic meat diet of deer, beaver, bear and fish."

A total of 64 mussle valves, representing 62 individuals of 14 species, was recovered in the Rhoads site refuse pits (Table 4). All 14 species may be encountered today in one or more of the rivers and streams of Illinois, but quite possibly several recorded from Rhoads no longer occur in Kickapoo Creek. Five species accounted for 80% of the valves recovered; these were the three-ridge, fat mucket, pocketbook, black sandshell, and mucket. In a survey of the freshwater mussels of Kickapoo Creek and Salt Creek, Shier (1962) failed to collect shells of the latter two species as well as those of the spike, sheepnose and monkey-face. It is possible that Shier (1962) would have encountered valves of one or more of the five species had additional collection locales been surveyed, but in all probability these forms were extirpated in recent times as a result of pollution and silting.

The paucity of mussel valves at the Rhoads site is indicative of only occasional efforts by the Kickapoo to gather these mollusks. Mussels could have been collected from about April through September or October, depending upon seasonal variation in water temperatures. The

TABLE 4
SPECIES, NUMBERS, AND ESTIMATED MEAT WEIGHTS OF RHOADS SITE FRESHWATER MUSSELS

Species	No. of Valves	No. of Individuals	Mean[1] Weight	Estimated Weights	%[2]
Three-ridge, *Amblema plicata*	17	16	36	576	17.79
Spike, *Ellipto dilatata*	1	1	12	12	0.37
Wabash pig-toe, *Fusconaia flava*	1	1	16	16	0.49
Sheepnose, *Plethobasus cyphyus*	1	1	37	37	1.14
Monkey-face, *Quadrula metanerva*	1	1	22	22	0.68
Pimple-back, *Q. pustulosa*	2	2	18	36	1.11
Quadrula sp.	1	1	—	—	—
Buckhorn, *Tritogonia verrucosa*	1	1	80	80	2.47
Floater, *Anodonta* cf. *grandis*	1	1	94	94	2.90
Mucket, *Actinonaias ligamentina carinata*	7	7	45	315	9.73
Yellow sandshell, *Lampsilis teres anodontoides*	2	2	82	164	5.07
Slough sandshell, *L. teres fallaciosa*	2	2	26	52	1.61
Fat mucket, *L. radiata siliquoidea*	7	7	55	385	11.89
Pocketbook, *L. ventricosa*	11	11	80	880	27.19
Black sandshell, *Ligumia recta*	7	6	76	456	14.09
Pink heel-splitter, *Potamilus alatus*	2	2	56	112	3.46
TOTALS	64	62		3237	99.99

[1] Mean weight of soft parts for species (Parmalee and Klippel 1974); all weights in grams.
[2] Based on estimated weights.

most opportune time would have been in late summer and early fall when the water level is usually at its lowest and warm temperatures still prevail. By using the mean ($\bar{Y}$) weight of soft parts listed by Parmalee and Klippel (1974:424) for the 15 species recorded from the Rhoads site, an estimated 3237 g (ca. 7 lbs.) of meat is represented by the 62 individuals. Without consuming any other food, the number of calories provided by these mussels would have been sufficient to sustain an adult individual for one, or possibly two, days at most.

Not counting those shells from the plow and humus zones, identifiable mussel valves were recovered from 21 separate features, while indeterminate shell fragments occurred in 7 others. It is apparent that the gathering of mussels was probably done by many individuals or families and was not an activity of a limited few. As a group, however, freshwater mussels contributed little to the total food economy of the Kickapoo. In addition to the 64 valves of unionids, 9 indeterminate shells of small "fingernail" clams (Family Sphaeriidae) were found in six pits, but these were probably picked up accidentally with mussels or other aquatic animals. None of the freshwater mussel valves recovered at the Rhoads site had been modified.

SUMMARY

The discovery and excavation of an early nineteenth century Kickapoo village in central Illinois provided a rare opportunity to study the remains of an endemic fauna that played a major role in the subsistence of this group of Native Americans. The Rhoads site (11Lo8) was situated on the first terrace of Kickapoo Creek, ca. 3 km west of Lincoln, Logan County, Illinois, and covered an area of approximately 2.5 ha.

Approximately 17,500 bones were recovered from 58 features, primarily storage/refuse pits, that were concentrated in five general groupings which may reflect the former location of house structures. At least 9 species of fish (MNI-30), 3 amphibians (MNI-42), 2-3? snakes (MNI-2-3), 8 turtles (MNI-57), 34 birds (MNI-57), and 25 species of mammals (MNI-202) were identified from the Rhoads site faunal assemblage. Although the white-tailed deer provided most of the meat consumed by this band of Kickapoo, a variety of other animals, including certain species of fish and aquatic turtles, the turkey, raccoon, striped skunk, beaver, and others, were taken when available and provided a valued addition to their dietary fare. Data from the interpretation of tooth wear and eruption in the lower jaws of white-tailed deer recovered at the site, coupled with the remains of certain species (e.g. passerines) whose presence is indicative of special seasonal periods, suggest that Rhoads was probably occupied throughout the year except during the winter months. Additional evidence in the form of large subterranean storage pits, known from ethnographic accounts of prairie and plains Indian groups to have been used to keep food stores during winter months while the inhabitants were away on hunting and trapping expeditions, were numerous at Rhoads.

Josiah Gregg (1905:317), in his *Journal* of 1831–39, provided the following observation: "Though the Shawnees, Delawares, and Kickapoos, are among the most agricultural of the northern Indians, yet a few of these spend the greater portion of their time on the Prairies in hunting and trading with the wild tribes." The faunal assemblage from Rhoads provides ample evidence that, although these Kickapoo were now horticulturalists and had become acculturated at least to the extent of substituting native ceramic and lithic artifacts for Euro-American made metal and glass counterparts characterized by Quimby (1966:141) as the "Pan-Indian culture" of the Historic period, they continued to rely on their hunting and gathering prowess. Dependence on and utilization of the native fauna by the Kickapoo in central Illinois differed little from that of prehistoric groups who occupied the Illinois Country for many millennia prior to the onset of Euro-American influence.

Notes

1. We would like to acknowledge with appreciation the Illinois Department of Transportation under whose auspices excavation of the Rhoads site was made possible. Special thanks are due the following individuals: Marion J. Mengel, Adjunct Curator, and associates, Museum of Natural History, The University of Kansas, Lawrence, for verification of a preliminary determination of a swallow-tailed kite element; Dr. Richard L. Zusi, Research Scientist, Division of Birds, National Museum of Natural History, Washington, D.C., for permitting use of the Museum's avian osteological collection; John E. Guilday, Associate Curator of Comparative Anatomy, Carnegie Museum, Pittsburgh, Pennsylvania, for identification of several deciduous canid teeth and the fetal skeleton from Feature 75; Forrest D. Loomis, Wildlife Biologist, Illinois Department of Conservation, Monmouth, for supplying aged jaws of the white-tailed deer and related data; and Marlin Roos, Museum Photographer, Illinois State Museum, for the photographs used in this paper.

APPENDIX A. FISHES IDENTIFIED FROM THE RHOADS SITE: FEATURES 1-37

Species	1	2	4	6	10	11	16	17	22	25	26	29	31	35	36	37
Gar, *Lepisosteus* sp.	1	78	—	3	—	959	—	16	6	—	—	8	1	—	—	7
Smallmouth or black buffalo, *Ictiobus bubalus* or *I. niger*	—	—	—	—	—	—	—	—	—	—	—	—	—	—	—	—
Northern redhorse, *Moxostoma macrolepidotum*	—	—	—	—	—	10	—	—	—	—	—	—	—	—	—	—
Golden redhorse, *Moxostoma erythrurum*	—	—	—	—	—	29	—	—	—	—	—	—	—	—	—	—
Redhorse, *Moxostoma* spp.	—	—	—	—	—	28	—	—	—	—	—	—	—	—	—	—
Suckers/buffalo: Fm. Catostomidae	—	—	—	—	—	2	—	—	—	—	—	—	—	—	—	—
cf. Channel catfish, *Ictalurus punctatus*	—	—	—	—	—	—	—	—	—	—	—	—	—	—	—	—
Flathead catfish, *Pylodictis olivaris*	—	—	—	—	—	—	—	—	—	—	—	—	—	—	—	—
Rock bass, *Ambloplites rupestris*	—	—	—	—	—	2	—	—	—	—	—	—	—	—	—	—
Bass, *Micropterus* sp.	—	—	—	—	—	—	—	—	—	—	—	—	—	—	—	—
Sunfishes: Fm. Centrarchidae	—	1	—	—	—	—	—	—	—	—	—	—	—	—	—	—
Freshwater drum, *Aplodinotus grunniens*	—	—	—	—	—	—	—	7	—	—	—	—	—	—	—	—
Indet. fish	—	11	2	—	—	268	—	—	—	—	—	—	—	—	—	—

APPENDIX A. FISHES IDENTIFIED FROM THE RHOADS SITE: FEATURES 39–71

Species	Number of Identified Specimens by Feature															
	39	40	41	43	44	46	46 & 70	47	48	54	55	58	61	69	70	71
Gar, *Lepisosteus* sp.	3	40	16	1	—	94	183	6	—	6	3	—	—	—	2	3
Smallmouth or black buffalo, *Ictiobus bubalus* or *I. niger*	—	—	—	—	—	—	—	—	—	—	—	—	—	—	1	—
Northern redhorse, *Moxostoma macrolepidotum*	—	—	—	—	—	7	2	—	—	—	—	—	—	—	—	—
Golden redhorse, *Moxostoma erythrurum*	—	—	—	—	—	—	2	—	—	3	—	—	—	—	—	—
Redhorse, *Moxostoma* spp.	—	—	—	—	—	1	—	—	—	—	—	—	—	—	—	—
Suckers/buffalo: Fm. Catostomidae	—	—	—	—	—	1	4	—	—	—	—	—	—	—	—	—
cf. Channel catfish, *Ictalurus punctatus*	—	—	—	—	—	—	—	—	—	2	—	—	—	—	—	—
Flathead catfish, *Pylodictis olivaris*	—	—	—	—	—	—	—	—	—	2	—	—	—	—	—	—
Rock bass, *Ambloplites rupestris*	—	—	—	—	—	—	—	—	—	—	—	—	—	—	—	—
Bass, *Micropterus* sp.	—	—	—	—	—	—	—	—	—	4	—	—	—	—	—	—
Sunfishes: Fm. Centrarchidae	—	—	—	—	—	—	—	—	—	—	—	—	—	—	—	—
Freshwater drum, *Aplodinotus grunniens*	2	1	—	—	—	8	15	—	—	1	—	—	—	—	—	—
Indet. fish	—	1	9	—	—	24	97	—	—	23	—	—	—	—	—	6

APPENDIX A. FISHES IDENTIFIED FROM THE RHOADS SITE: FEATURES 73–128

Species	73	74	75	79	84	86	96	105	114	116	118	119	122	125	127	128
Gar, *Lepisosteus* sp.	1	3	58	19	1	—	5	13	1	3	25	—	—	3	4	136
Smallmouth or black buffalo, *Ictiobus bubalus* or *I. niger*	—	—	—	—	—	—	—	—	—	—	—	—	—	—	—	—
Northern redhorse, *Moxostoma macrolepidotum*	—	—	—	—	—	—	—	—	—	—	1	—	—	—	10	9
Golden redhorse, *Moxostoma erythrurum*	—	—	—	—	—	—	—	—	—	—	—	—	—	—	—	—
Redhorse, *Moxostoma* spp.	—	—	—	—	—	—	—	—	—	—	3	—	—	3	14	24
Suckers/buffalo: Fm. Catostomidae	—	—	1	—	—	—	—	—	—	1	—	—	—	—	—	1
cf. Channel catfish, *Ictalurus punctatus*	—	—	—	—	—	—	—	4	—	—	—	—	—	—	—	—
Flathead catfish, *Pylodictis olivaris*	—	—	1	—	1	—	—	—	—	—	1	—	—	14	—	18
Rock bass, *Ambloplites rupestris*	—	—	—	—	—	—	—	—	—	—	—	—	—	—	18	22
Bass, *Micropterus* sp.	—	—	1	—	—	—	—	—	—	—	—	—	—	34	—	—
Sunfishes: Fm. Centrarchidae	—	—	—	—	—	—	—	—	—	—	—	—	—	2	—	—
Freshwater drum, *Aplodinotus grunniens*	—	—	—	7	8	—	—	—	4	16	73	—	—	154	136	345
Indet. fish	—	—	17	—	—	—	—	—	—	—	—	—	—	—	—	—

APPENDIX A. FISHES IDENTIFIED FROM THE RHOADS SITE: FEATURES 130–163 AND SUMMARY DATA

Species	Number of Identified Specimens by Feature										P.Z. H.Z.	NISP	% NISP	MNI	% of Identified Species
	130	140	141	142	143	146	150	151	152	163					
Gar, *Lepisosteus* sp.	5	7	1361	—	—	—	—	—	—	—	—	4,771	27.78	30	33.37
Smallmouth or black buffalo, *Ictiobus bubalus* or *I. niger*	—	—	—	—	—	—	—	—	9	—	1	3,091	18.03	5	30.33
Northern redhorse, *Moxostoma macrolepidotum*	—	—	1	—	—	—	—	—	—	—	—	3	.01	1	.02
Golden redhorse, *Moxostoma erythrurum*	—	—	—	—	—	—	—	—	—	—	—	24	.14	4	.23
Redhorse, *Moxostoma* spp.	—	—	—	—	—	—	—	—	—	—	—	19	.11	4	.18
Suckers/buffalo: Fm. Catostomidae	—	—	—	—	—	—	—	—	—	—	—	71	.41	—	.69
cf. Channel catfish, *Ictalurus punctatus*	—	—	—	—	—	—	—	—	—	—	—	40	.23	1	.39
Flathead catfish, *Pylodictis olivaris*	—	—	—	—	—	—	—	—	—	—	—	5	.02	1	.04
Rock bass, *Ambloplites rupestris*	—	—	—	—	—	—	—	—	—	—	—	4	.02	—	.03
Bass, *Micropterus* sp.	—	—	—	—	—	—	—	—	2	—	—	34	.19	1	.33
Sunfishes: Fm. Centrarchidae	—	—	1	—	—	—	—	—	—	—	—	48	.28	6	.47
Freshwater drum, *Aplodinotus grunniens*	—	—	—	—	—	—	—	—	—	—	—	38	.22	6	.37
Indet. fish	—	19	99	—	—	—	—	—	—	38	—	1,364	7.95	2	.29

APPENDIX B. AMPHIBIANS AND REPTILES IDENTIFIED FROM THE RHOADS SITE: FEATURES 1-37

Species	1	2	4	6	10	11	16	17	22	25	26	29	31	35	36	37
AMPHIBIANS																
Salamander sp.	—	—	—	—	—	1	—	—	—	—	—	—	—	—	—	—
Toad, *Bufo* spp.	—	—	11	1	—	1	—	11	7	—	—	—	—	—	—	—
Frog, *Rana* spp.	—	3	31	2	—	156	—	17	4	—	—	—	—	—	—	—
Indet. frog/toad	—	—	7	—	—	4	—	19	—	—	—	—	—	—	—	1
REPTILES: SNAKES																
Snake spp.: Fm. Colubridae	—	—	—	—	—	1	—	—	—	—	—	—	—	—	—	—
REPTILES: TURTLES																
Snapping turtle, *Chelydra serpentina*	—	—	—	—	—	—	—	—	—	—	—	—	—	—	—	—
Blanding's turtle, *Emydoidea blandingi*	—	—	2	—	—	1	—	—	—	—	—	—	—	—	—	—
Box turtle, *Terrapene* sp.	—	6	—	—	—	—	—	—	—	—	1	—	—	—	—	—
Painted turtle, *Chrysemys picta*	—	2	—	—	—	—	—	—	—	—	—	1	—	3	—	—
Red-eared turtle, *Pseudemys scripta*	—	2	3	—	—	5	—	—	—	—	—	—	—	—	—	—
False map turtle, *Graptemys pseudogeographica*	—	—	8	—	—	—	—	—	—	—	—	—	—	—	—	—
Map turtle, *Graptemys geographica*	—	1	9	4	—	16	—	5	—	—	2	1	—	3	1	1
Turtle: *Chrysemys, Pseudemys, Graptemys* group	—	—	—	—	—	1	—	—	—	—	—	—	—	—	—	—
Spiny softshell, *Trionyx spinifer*	—	3	—	1	—	21	—	6	—	—	—	—	—	—	—	—
Softshell, *Trionyx* sp.	2	—	—	—	—	—	—	—	1	—	—	1	—	—	—	—
Indet. turtle bone/shell	—	1	1	—	—	—	—	—	—	—	—	—	—	—	—	—

APPENDIX B. AMPHIBIANS AND REPTILES IDENTIFIED FROM THE RHOADS SITE: FEATURES 39-71

Species	39	40	41	43	44	46	46 & 70	47	48	54	55	58	61	69	70	71
AMPHIBIANS																
Salamander sp.	—	—	—	—	—	—	—	—	—	—	—	—	—	—	—	—
Toad, *Bufo* spp.	—	13	2	—	—	—	34	—	—	—	—	—	—	—	—	80
Frog, *Rana* spp.	—	13	—	—	—	11	31	40	—	—	—	—	—	—	—	23
Indet. frog/toad	—	2	—	—	—	—	12	—	—	—	—	—	—	—	—	85
REPTILES: SNAKES																
Snake spp.: Fm. Colubridae	—	—	—	—	—	—	—	—	—	—	—	—	—	—	—	—
REPTILES: TURTLES																
Snapping turtle, *Chelydra serpentina*	—	1	—	—	—	—	—	—	—	2	—	—	—	—	—	5
Blanding's turtle, *Emydoidea blandingi*	—	2	—	—	5	—	—	—	—	—	—	—	—	—	—	—
Box turtle, *Terrapene* sp.	—	1	—	—	—	—	—	—	—	2	—	—	—	—	—	—
Painted turtle, *Chrysemys picta*	—	—	—	—	3	—	5	—	—	16	—	—	—	—	—	—
Red-eared turtle, *Pseudemys scripta*	—	1	5	—	—	1	3	—	—	—	—	—	—	—	—	—
False map turtle, *Graptemys pseudogeographica*	—	—	—	—	—	—	—	—	—	—	—	—	—	—	—	—
Map turtle, *Graptemys geographica*	—	12	—	—	—	—	1	—	—	5	—	—	—	—	1	11
Turtle: *Chrysemys, Pseudemys, Graptemys* group	1	45	13	1	—	17	16	—	9	29	8	—	—	—	—	—
Spiny softshell, *Trionyx spinifer*	—	—	—	—	—	—	1	—	—	—	1	—	—	—	—	—
Softshell, *Trionyx* sp.	—	—	4	—	—	4	1	—	7	—	—	—	—	—	—	—
Indet. turtle bone/shell	—	1	—	—	—	2	—	—	2	11	—	—	—	—	—	—

APPENDIX B. AMPHIBIANS AND REPTILES IDENTIFIED FROM THE RHOADS SITE: FEATURES 73–128

Species	Number of Identified Specimens by Feature															
	73	74	75	79	84	86	96	105	114	116	118	119	122	125	127	128
AMPHIBIANS																
Salamander sp.	—	—	—	—	—	—	—	—	—	—	—	—	—	—	—	—
Toad, *Bufo* spp.	—	3	2	—	—	—	—	—	—	—	—	—	—	—	2	—
Frog, *Rana* spp.	—	—	—	—	—	—	—	—	—	—	3	—	—	—	—	—
Indet. frog/toad	—	—	10	—	—	—	—	—	—	—	—	—	—	—	—	—
REPTILES: SNAKES																
Snake spp.: Fm. Colubridae	—	—	—	—	—	—	1	—	1	—	—	—	—	—	1	1
REPTILES: TURTLES																
Snapping turtle, *Chelydra serpentina*	—	—	—	—	—	—	—	—	—	—	—	—	—	—	1	—
Blanding's turtle, *Emydoidea blandingi*	—	—	—	—	—	—	—	—	—	—	—	—	—	—	2	—
Box turtle, *Terrapene* sp.	—	—	—	—	—	—	—	—	—	—	—	—	—	—	—	—
Painted turtle, *Chrysemys picta*	—	—	3	1	—	—	—	—	—	—	—	1	—	—	—	—
Red-eared turtle, *Pseudemys scripta*	—	5	40	—	—	—	—	—	2	1	10	—	—	—	5	4
False map turtle, *Graptemys pseudogeographica*	—	—	—	—	—	—	—	—	—	—	1	—	—	—	—	—
Map turtle, *Graptemys geographica*	—	3	9	1	—	—	—	—	1	—	33	—	—	—	17	—
Turtle: *Chrysemys, Pseudemys, Graptemys* group	1	9	25	7	—	—	2	—	9	—	107	—	—	6	56	4
Spiny softshell, *Trionyx spinifer*	—	—	—	—	—	—	—	—	—	—	—	—	—	—	—	—
Softshell, *Trionyx* sp.	—	—	4	—	—	—	—	—	—	—	16	—	—	1	9	—
Indet. turtle bone/shell	—	4	9	1	—	—	2	—	3	—	6	—	—	—	—	—

APPENDIX B. AMPHIBIANS AND REPTILES IDENTIFIED FROM THE RHOADS SITE: FEATURES 130-163 AND SUMMARY DATA

Species	Number of Identified Specimens by Feature											P.Z. H.Z.	NISP	% NISP	MNI	% of Identified Species
	130	140	141	142	143	146	150	151	152	163					
AMPHIBIANS												649	3.83	41	6.35
Salamander sp.	—	—	—	—	—	—	—	—	—	—	—	1	.00	1	.00
Toad, *Bufo* spp.	—	1	3	—	—	—	—	—	—	—	—	157	.91	14	1.54
Frog, *Rana* spp.	—	—	10	—	—	—	—	—	—	—	—	347	2.02	26	3.40
Indet. frog/toad	1	—	3	—	—	—	—	—	—	—	—	144	.84	—	1.41
REPTILES: SNAKES												6	.03	2	.05
Snake spp.: Fm. Colubridae	—	1	—	—	—	—	—	—	—	—	—	6	.03	2	.05
REPTILES: TURTLES												935	5.41	57	8.57
Snapping turtle, *Chelydra serpentina*	—	—	1	—	—	—	—	—	—	—	—	2	.01	1	.01
Blanding's turtle, *Emydoidea blandingi*	—	—	—	—	—	—	—	—	—	—	—	18	.10	2	.17
Box turtle, *Terrapene* sp.	—	—	—	—	—	—	—	—	—	—	—	9	.05	2	.08
Painted turtle, *Chrysemys picta*	—	—	—	—	—	—	—	—	1	—	—	30	.17	12	.29
Red-eared turtle, *Pseudemys scripta*	—	—	2	—	—	—	—	1	6	1	3	112	.65	12	1.09
False map turtle, *Graptemys pseudogeographica*	—	—	—	—	—	—	—	—	—	—	—	1	.00	1	.00
Map turtle, *Graptemys geographica*	2	—	6	—	—	—	—	—	1	3	—	102	.59	75	1.00
Turtle: *Chrysemys, Pseudemys, Graptemys* group	2	7	30	—	—	1	—	—	7	20	15	503	2.93	—	4.93
Spiny softshell, *Trionyx spinifer*	—	—	—	—	—	—	—	—	—	—	—	2	.01	2	.01
Softshell, *Trionyx* sp.	—	—	2	—	—	—	—	—	15	—	—	101	.58	10	.99
Indet. turtle bone/shell	1	9	—	—	—	—	—	—	—	—	—	55	.32	—	—

APPENDIX C. BIRDS IDENTIFIED FROM THE RHOADS SITE: FEATURES 1-37

Species	Number of Identified Specimens by Feature															
	1	2	4	6	10	11	16	17	22	25	26	29	31	35	36	37
Great blue heron, *Ardea herodias*	—	—	—	—	—	—	—	—	—	—	—	—	—	—	—	—
? Common egret, *Casmerodius albus*	—	—	—	—	—	—	—	—	—	—	—	—	—	—	—	—
cf. Canada goose, *Branta canadensis*	—	—	—	—	—	—	—	—	—	—	—	—	—	—	—	—
? Wood duck, *Aix sponsa*	—	—	—	—	—	—	—	—	—	—	—	—	—	—	—	—
Duck sp.	—	—	—	—	—	—	—	—	—	—	—	—	—	—	—	—
Hooded Merganser, *Lophodytes cucullatus*	—	1	—	—	—	—	—	—	—	—	—	—	—	—	—	—
Swallow-tailed kite, *Elanoides forficatus*	—	—	—	—	—	—	—	—	—	—	—	—	—	—	—	—
? Red-shouldered hawk, *Buteo* cf. *lineatus*	—	—	—	—	1	—	—	—	—	—	—	—	—	—	—	—
? Broad-winged hawk, *Buteo* cf. *platypterus*	—	—	—	—	—	—	—	—	—	—	—	—	—	—	—	—
Marsh hawk, *Circus cyaneus*	—	—	—	—	—	—	—	—	—	—	—	—	—	—	—	—
Sparrow hawk, *Falco sparverius*	—	—	—	—	—	—	—	—	—	—	—	—	—	—	—	—
Hawk/kite sp.	—	—	—	—	—	1	—	—	—	—	—	—	—	—	—	—
Greater prairie chicken, *Tympanuchus cupido*	—	—	—	—	—	—	—	—	—	—	—	—	—	—	—	—
Turkey, *Meleagris gallopavo*	—	4	2	—	—	1	—	2	—	—	1	—	—	6	—	—
Woodcock, *Philohela minor*	—	—	—	—	—	—	—	—	—	—	—	—	—	—	—	—
cf. Pectoral sandpiper, *Erolia melanotos*	—	6	—	—	—	—	—	—	—	—	—	—	—	—	—	—
Sandpiper/plover sp.	—	—	—	—	—	—	—	—	—	—	—	—	—	—	—	—
cf. Mourning dove, *Zenaidura macroura*	—	—	—	—	—	—	—	—	—	—	—	—	—	—	—	—
Passenger pigeon, *Ectopistes migratorius*	—	1	—	—	—	—	—	2	—	—	—	—	—	—	—	—
Flicker, *Colaptes auratus*	—	1	—	—	—	—	—	—	—	—	—	—	—	—	—	—
Pileated woodpecker, *Dryocopus pileatus*	—	—	—	—	—	—	—	—	—	—	—	—	—	—	—	—
? Red-bellied woodpecker, *Centurus carolinus*	—	—	—	—	—	—	—	—	—	—	—	—	—	—	—	—
Red-headed woodpecker, *Melanerpes erythrocephalus*	—	1	—	—	—	—	—	—	—	—	—	—	—	—	—	—

cf. Downy woodpecker, *Dendrocopos pubescens*	—	—	—	—	—	—	—	—	—	—
Ivory-billed woodpecker, *Campephilus principalis*	—	—	—	—	—	—	—	—	—	—
Flycatcher, *Empidonax* sp.	—	—	—	—	—	—	—	—	—	—
cf. Chickadee, *Parus* sp.	—	—	—	—	—	—	—	—	—	—
cf. House wren, *Troglodytes aedon*	—	—	—	1	—	—	—	—	—	—
cf. Kinglet, *Regulus* sp.	—	—	—	—	—	—	—	—	—	—
Vireo, *Vireo* sp.	—	—	—	—	—	—	—	—	—	—
Warbler, *Vermivora* sp.	—	—	—	—	—	—	—	—	—	—
Warbler, *Dendroica* sp.	—	6	—	—	—	—	—	—	—	—
cf. American redstart, *Setophaga ruticilla*	—	1	—	—	—	—	—	—	—	—
Meadowlark, *Sturnella* sp.	—	—	—	—	—	—	—	—	—	—
cf. Redwinged blackbird, *Agelaius phoeniceus*	—	—	—	—	—	—	—	—	—	—
? Rose-breasted grosbeak, *Pheucticus ludovicianus*	—	26	21	—	1	8	—	—	—	—
cf. Indigo bunting, *Passerina cyanea*	3	21	1	—	2	4	1	—	1	—
Indet. bird	—	—	—	—	—	—	—	—	4	10	1
Passerine Birds: Indet. Species	—	—	—	—	—	—	—	—	—	—

APPENDIX C. BIRDS IDENTIFIED FROM THE RHOADS SITE: FEATURES 39–71

Number of Identified Specimens by Feature

Species	39	40	41	43	44	46	46 & 70	47	48	54	55	58	61	69	70	71
Great blue heron, *Ardea herodias*	—	3	—	—	—	—	—	—	—	—	—	—	—	—	—	—
? Common egret, *Casmerodius albus*	—	—	1	—	—	—	—	—	—	—	—	—	—	—	—	—
cf. Canada goose, *Branta canadensis*	—	1	—	—	—	—	—	—	—	—	—	—	—	—	—	—
? Wood duck, *Aix sponsa*	—	—	—	—	—	—	—	—	—	—	—	—	—	—	—	—
Duck sp.	—	—	—	—	—	—	—	—	—	—	—	—	—	—	—	—
Hooded Merganser, *Lophodytes cucullatus*	—	—	—	—	—	—	—	—	—	—	—	—	—	—	—	—
Swallow-tailed kite, *Elanoides forficatus*	—	—	—	—	—	—	2	—	—	—	—	—	—	—	—	—
? Red-shouldered hawk, *Buteo* cf. *lineatus*	—	—	—	—	—	—	—	—	—	—	—	—	—	—	—	—
? Broad-winged hawk, *Buteo* cf. *platypterus*	—	—	—	—	—	—	—	—	—	—	—	—	—	—	—	—
Marsh hawk, *Circus cyaneus*	—	—	—	—	—	—	—	—	—	—	—	—	—	—	—	—
Sparrow hawk, *Falco sparverius*	—	2	—	—	—	—	—	—	—	—	—	—	—	—	—	—
Hawk/kite sp.	—	—	—	—	—	—	—	—	—	2	—	—	—	—	—	—
Greater prairie chicken, *Tympanuchus cupido*	—	—	—	—	—	—	—	—	—	—	—	—	—	—	—	—
Turkey, *Meleagris gallopavo*	—	5	1	—	—	—	11	2	—	1	—	—	—	—	—	1
Woodcock, *Philohela minor*	—	—	—	—	—	—	—	—	—	—	—	—	—	—	—	1
cf. Pectoral sandpiper, *Erolia melanotos*	—	—	—	—	—	—	—	—	—	—	—	—	—	—	—	—
Sandpiper/plover sp.	—	—	—	—	—	—	—	—	—	—	—	—	—	—	—	—
cf. Mourning dove, *Zenaidura macroura*	—	—	—	—	—	—	—	—	—	—	—	—	—	—	—	—
Passenger pigeon, *Ectopistes migratorius*	—	—	—	—	—	—	8	—	—	—	—	—	—	—	—	—
Flicker, *Colaptes auratus*	—	—	—	—	—	—	—	—	—	—	—	—	—	—	—	—
Pileated woodpecker, *Dryocopus pileatus*	—	—	—	—	—	—	—	—	—	—	—	—	—	—	—	—
? Red-bellied woodpecker, *Centurus carolinus*	—	1	—	—	—	—	—	—	—	—	—	—	—	—	—	—
Red-headed woodpecker, *Melanerpes erythrocephalus*	—	—	—	—	—	—	—	—	—	—	—	—	—	—	—	—
cf. Downy woodpecker, *Dendrocopos pubescens*	—	—	—	—	—	—	—	—	—	—	—	—	—	—	—	1

FOOD ECONOMY OF THE HISTORIC KICKAPOO

Species																	
Ivory-billed woodpecker, *Campephilus principalis*	—	—	—	—	—	—	—	—	—	—	—	—	—	—	—	—	—
Flycatcher, *Empidonax* sp.	—	—	—	—	—	—	—	—	—	—	—	—	—	—	—	—	—
cf. Chickadee, *Parus* sp.	—	—	—	—	—	—	—	—	—	—	—	—	—	—	—	—	—
cf. House wren, *Troglodytes aedon*	—	—	—	—	—	—	—	—	—	—	—	—	—	—	—	—	—
cf. Kinglet, *Regulus* sp.	—	—	—	—	—	—	—	—	—	—	—	—	—	—	—	—	—
Vireo, *Vireo* sp.	—	—	—	—	—	1	—	—	—	—	—	—	—	—	—	—	—
Warbler, *Vermivora* sp.	—	—	—	—	—	—	—	—	—	—	—	—	—	—	—	—	—
Warbler, *Dendroica* sp.	—	—	—	—	—	—	—	—	—	—	—	—	—	—	—	—	—
cf. American redstart, *Setophaga ruticilla*	—	—	—	—	—	—	—	—	—	—	—	—	—	—	—	—	—
Meadowlark, *Sturnella* sp.	—	—	—	—	—	—	—	—	—	—	—	—	—	—	—	—	—
cf. Redwinged blackbird, *Agelaius phoeniceus*	—	—	—	—	—	—	1	—	—	—	—	—	—	—	—	—	—
? Rose-breasted grosbeak, *Pheucticus ludovicianus*	—	—	—	—	—	—	—	1	—	—	—	—	—	—	—	—	—
cf. Indigo bunting, *Passerina cyanea*	44	—	6	18	1	5	—	1	—	—	—	—	—	—	—	—	4
Indet. bird	44	10	—	18	2	3	7	3	—	—	—	—	—	—	—	1	4
Passerine Birds: Indet. Species	2	—	—	11	2	3	—	1	—	—	—	—	—	—	—	—	4

APPENDIX C. BIRDS IDENTIFIED FROM THE RHOADS SITE: FEATURES 73-128

Number of Identified Specimens by Feature

Species	73	74	75	79	84	86	96	105	114	116	118	119	122	125	127	128
Great blue heron, *Ardea herodias*	—	—	—	—	—	—	—	—	—	—	—	—	—	—	—	—
? Common egret, *Casmerodius albus*	—	—	—	—	—	—	—	—	—	—	—	—	—	—	—	1
cf. Canada goose, *Branta canadensis*	—	—	—	—	—	—	—	—	—	—	—	—	—	—	—	—
? Wood duck, *Aix sponsa*	—	—	—	—	—	—	—	—	—	—	—	—	—	—	2	—
Duck sp.	—	—	—	—	—	—	—	—	—	—	—	—	—	—	—	—
Hooded Merganser, *Lophodytes cucullatus*	—	—	—	—	—	—	—	—	—	—	—	—	—	—	1	—
Swallow-tailed kite, *Elanoides forficatus*	—	—	—	—	—	—	—	—	—	—	—	—	—	—	—	—
? Red-shouldered hawk, *Buteo* cf. *lineatus*	—	—	—	—	—	—	—	—	—	—	—	—	—	—	—	—
? Broad-winged hawk, *Buteo* cf. *platypterus*	—	—	—	—	—	—	—	—	—	—	—	—	—	—	—	—
Marsh hawk, *Circus cyaneus*	—	—	—	—	—	—	—	—	—	—	2	—	—	—	—	—
Sparrow hawk, *Falco sparverius*	—	—	—	—	—	—	—	—	—	—	—	—	—	—	—	—
Hawk/kite sp.	—	—	—	—	—	—	—	—	—	—	—	—	—	—	—	—
Greater prairie chicken, *Tympanuchus cupido*	—	—	—	—	—	—	—	—	—	—	1	—	—	—	2	2
Turkey, *Meleagris gallopavo*	—	1	4	—	—	—	—	1	—	—	21	—	—	1	10	—
Woodcock, *Philohela minor*	—	—	—	—	—	—	—	—	—	—	—	—	—	—	1	—
cf. Pectoral sandpiper, *Erolia melanotos*	—	—	—	—	—	—	—	—	—	—	—	—	—	—	—	—
Sandpiper/plover sp.	—	—	1	—	—	—	—	—	—	—	—	—	—	—	—	—
cf. Mourning dove, *Zenaidura macroura*	—	—	—	—	—	—	—	—	—	—	—	—	—	—	—	—
Passenger pigeon, *Ectopistes migratorius*	—	—	—	—	—	—	—	—	—	—	2	—	—	1	2	1
Flicker, *Colaptes auratus*	—	—	—	—	—	—	—	—	—	—	—	—	—	—	—	—
Pileated woodpecker, *Dryocopus pileatus*	—	—	—	—	—	—	—	—	—	—	—	—	—	—	—	—
? Red-bellied woodpecker, *Centurus carolinus*	—	—	—	—	—	—	—	—	—	—	—	—	—	—	—	1
Red-headed woodpecker, *Melanerpes erythrocephalus*	—	—	—	—	—	—	—	—	—	—	10	—	—	—	—	—
cf. Downy woodpecker, *Dendrocopos pubescens*	—	—	—	—	—	—	—	—	—	—	—	—	—	—	—	—

Taxon													
Ivory-billed woodpecker, *Campephilus principalis*	—	—	—	—	—	—	—	—	—	—	—	—	1
Flycatcher, *Empidonax sp.*	—	—	—	—	—	—	—	—	—	—	—	—	—
cf. Chickadee, *Parus sp.*	—	—	—	—	—	—	—	—	—	—	1	—	1
cf. House wren, *Troglodytes aedon*	—	—	—	—	—	—	—	—	—	—	—	—	—
cf. Kinglet, *Regulus sp.*	—	—	—	—	—	—	—	—	—	—	—	—	—
Vireo, *Vireo sp.*	—	—	—	—	—	—	—	—	—	—	—	—	—
Warbler, *Vermivora sp.*	—	—	1	—	—	—	—	—	—	—	1	—	—
Warbler, *Dendroica sp.*	—	—	—	—	—	—	—	—	—	—	—	—	—
cf. American redstart, *Setophaga ruticilla*	—	—	—	—	—	—	—	—	—	—	—	2	—
Meadowlark, *Sturnella sp.*	—	—	—	—	—	—	—	—	—	—	—	—	—
cf. Redwinged blackbird, *Agelaius phoeniceus*	—	—	—	—	—	—	—	—	—	—	—	—	1
? Rose-breasted grosbeak, *Pheucticus ludovicianus*	—	—	—	—	—	—	—	—	—	—	—	—	—
cf. Indigo bunting, *Passerina cyanea*	—	—	—	1	—	2	10	—	86	1	—	20	41	9
Indet. bird	2	10	6	—	—	—	—	—	21	—	—	7	21	1
Passerine Birds: Indet. Species	1	2	7											

APPENDIX C. BIRDS IDENTIFIED FROM THE RHOADS SITE: FEATURES 130-163 AND SUMMARY DATA

Species	130	140	141	142	143	146	150	151	152	163	P.Z. H.Z.	NISP	% NISP	MNI	% of Identified Species
Great blue heron, *Ardea herodias*	—	—	—	—	—	—	—	—	—	—	—	906	5.10	57	4.27
? Common egret, *Casmerodius albus*	—	—	—	—	—	—	—	—	—	—	—	3	.01	1	.02
cf. Canada goose, *Branta canadensis*	—	—	—	—	—	—	—	—	—	—	—	1	.00	1	.00
? Wood duck, *Aix sponsa*	—	—	—	—	—	—	—	—	—	—	—	2	.01	1	.01
Duck sp.	—	1	—	—	—	—	—	—	—	—	—	2	.01	1	.01
Hooded Merganser, *Lophodytes cucullatus*	—	—	—	—	—	—	—	—	—	—	—	2	.01	1	.01
Swallow-tailed kite, *Elanoides forficatus*	—	—	—	—	—	—	—	—	—	—	—	1	.00	1	.00
? Red-shouldered hawk, *Buteo* cf. *lineatus*	—	—	—	—	—	—	—	—	—	—	—	3	.01	1	.02
? Broad-winged hawk, *Buteo* cf. *platypterus*	—	—	1	—	—	—	—	—	—	—	—	1	.00	1	.00
Marsh hawk, *Circus cyaneus*	—	—	—	—	—	—	—	—	—	—	—	2	.01	1	.01
Sparrow hawk, *Falco sparverius*	—	—	—	—	—	—	—	—	—	—	—	2	.01	1	.01
Hawk/kite sp.	—	—	—	—	—	—	—	—	—	—	—	3	.01	—	.02
Greater prairie chicken, *Tympanuchus cupido*	—	—	—	—	—	—	—	—	—	—	—	4	.02	1	.03
Turkey, *Meleagris gallopavo*	2	—	1	—	—	—	—	—	—	—	5	85	.49	12	.83
Woodcock, *Philohela minor*	—	—	—	—	—	—	—	—	—	—	—	1	.00	1	.00
cf. Pectoral sandpiper, *Erolia melanotos*	—	—	—	—	—	—	—	—	—	—	—	6	.03	1	.05
Sandpiper/plover sp.	—	—	2	—	—	—	—	—	—	—	—	3	.01	2	.02
cf. Mourning dove, *Zenaidura macroura*	—	1	1	—	—	—	—	—	—	—	—	1	.00	1	.00
Passenger pigeon, *Ectopistes migratorius*	—	—	—	—	—	—	—	—	—	—	1	14	.08	2	.13
Flicker, *Colaptes auratus*	—	—	—	—	—	—	—	—	1	—	—	5	.02	2	.04
Pileated woodpecker, *Dryocopus pileatus*	—	—	—	—	—	—	—	—	—	—	—	3	.01	1	.02
? Red-bellied woodpecker, *Centurus carolinus*	—	—	—	—	—	—	—	—	—	—	—	1	.00	1	.00
Red-headed woodpecker, *Melanerpes erythrocephalus*	—	—	—	—	—	—	—	—	—	—	—	11	.06	1	.10
cf. Downy woodpecker, *Dendrocopos pubescens*	—	—	—	1	—	—	—	—	—	—	—	1	.00	1	.00

FOOD ECONOMY OF THE HISTORIC KICKAPOO   317

Species												
Ivory-billed woodpecker, *Campephilus principalis*	—	—	—	—	—	—	—	—	1	.00	—	.00
Flycatcher, *Empidonax* sp.	—	2	—	—	—	—	—	—	2	.01	—	.01
cf. Chickadee, *Parus* sp.	1	—	—	—	—	—	—	—	1	.00	—	.00
cf. House wren, *Troglodytes aedon*	—	—	—	—	—	—	—	—	2	.01	—	.01
cf. Kinglet, *Regulus* sp.	—	1	—	—	—	—	—	—	2	.01	—	.01
Vireo, *Vireo* sp.	—	—	—	—	—	—	—	—	—	.00	—	.00
Warbler, *Vermivora* sp.	—	—	—	—	—	—	—	—	1	.00	—	.00
Warbler, *Dendroica* sp.	—	—	—	—	—	—	—	—	1	.00	—	.00
cf. American redstart, *Setophaga ruticilla*	—	—	—	—	—	—	—	—	2	.01	—	.01
Meadowlark, *Sturnella* sp.	—	—	—	—	—	—	—	—	6	.03	—	.05
cf. Redwinged blackbird, *Agelaius phoeniceus*	—	—	—	—	—	—	—	—	2	.01	—	.01
? Rose-breasted grosbeak, *Pheucticus ludovicianus*	—	—	—	—	—	—	—	—	1	.00	—	.00
cf. Indigo bunting, *Passerina cyanea*	—	—	—	—	—	—	—	1	16	.09	1	.15
Indet. bird	13	14	—	—	—	—	5	1	12	435	2.53	8	—
Passerine Birds: Indet. Species	9	125	18	—	—	—	4	5	2	275	1.60	—	2.69

APPENDIX D. MAMMALS IDENTIFIED FROM THE RHOADS SITE: FEATURES 1-37

Species	Number of Identified Specimens by Feature															
	1	2	4	6	10	11	16	17	22	25	26	29	31	35	36	37
Eastern mole, *Scalopus aquaticus*	—	—	—	—	—	—	—	—	—	—	—	—	—	—	—	—
Short-tailed shrew, *Blarina brevicauda*	—	—	1	—	—	—	—	—	—	—	—	—	—	—	—	—
Least shrew, *Cryptotis parva*	—	—	—	—	—	—	—	—	—	—	—	—	—	—	—	—
Bat, Genus and species indet.	—	—	1	—	—	2	—	—	—	—	—	—	—	—	—	—
cf. Big-eared bat, *Plecotus* sp.	—	—	—	—	—	—	—	—	—	—	—	—	—	—	—	—
cf. Red bat, *Lasiurus borealis*	—	—	—	—	—	—	—	—	—	—	—	—	—	—	—	—
Black bear, *Ursus americanus*	—	—	—	—	—	—	—	1	—	—	—	—	—	1	—	1
Raccoon, *Procyon lotor*	—	38	3	—	—	3	—	8	1	—	6	—	—	—	1	—
Striped skunk, *Mephitis mephitis*	—	—	—	—	—	—	—	1	—	—	—	—	—	1	—	—
Badger, *Taxidea taxus*	—	—	—	—	—	—	—	—	—	—	—	—	—	—	—	—
cf. Gray wolf, *Canis lupus*	—	—	—	—	—	—	—	1	—	—	—	—	—	—	—	1
Domestic (Indian) dog, *Canis familiaris*	—	5	2	1	—	1	—	—	5	—	—	—	—	—	—	—
Bobcat, *Lynx* cf. *rufus*	—	—	—	—	—	3	—	—	—	—	4	—	—	—	—	—
13-lined ground squirrel, *Spermophilus tridecemlineatus*	—	—	—	—	—	—	—	—	—	—	—	—	—	—	—	—
Eastern chipmunk, *Tamias striatus*	—	—	—	—	—	2	—	—	—	—	—	—	—	—	—	—
Squirrel, *Sciurus* sp.	—	—	—	—	—	—	—	—	—	—	—	—	—	—	—	—
Plains pocket gopher, *Geomys bursarius*	1	2	1	—	1	—	—	—	—	—	—	—	—	—	—	—
Beaver, *Castor canadensis*	—	—	—	—	—	—	—	—	—	—	—	—	—	—	—	—
Deer/white-footed mouse, *Peromyscus* sp.	—	10	12	—	—	4	—	25	—	—	—	—	—	—	—	—
Bog lemming, *Synaptomys* cf. *cooperi*	—	—	—	—	—	—	—	—	—	—	—	—	—	—	—	—
Prairie/meadow vole, *Microtus* sp.	—	—	—	—	—	3	—	—	—	—	—	—	—	—	—	—
Indet. mouse elements: most cf. Fm. Cricetidae	—	25	50	1	1	58	—	182	3	—	—	—	—	—	—	—
Muskrat, *Ondatra zibethica*	—	—	—	—	—	1	—	—	—	—	—	—	—	—	—	—
cf. Meadow jumping mouse, *Zapus hudsonius*	—	—	—	—	—	—	—	—	—	—	—	—	—	—	—	—
Eastern cottontail, *Sylvilagus floridanus*	—	—	—	—	—	—	—	—	3	—	—	—	—	—	—	—
Elk, *Cervus elaphus*	—	—	—	—	—	—	—	—	—	—	—	—	—	—	—	—
White-tailed deer, *Odocoileus virginianus*	44	399	74	21	14	129	1	147	9	—	49	17	6	23	24	18
Indet. mammal	39	627	86	33	15	68	2	233	16	1	55	28	3	23	20	5
Totals, All Taxa	90	1,282	328	67	32	1,782	3	695	57	1	118	57	10	63	56	35

APPENDIX D. MAMMALS IDENTIFIED FROM THE RHOADS SITE: FEATURES 39–71

	Number of Identified Specimens by Feature															
Species	39	40	41	43	44	46	46 & 70	47	48	54	55	58	61	69	70	71
Eastern mole, *Scalopus aquaticus*	—	1	3	—	—	—	—	—	—	—	—	—	—	—	—	—
Short-tailed shrew, *Blarina brevicauda*	—	—	—	—	—	—	1	—	—	—	—	—	—	—	—	—
Least shrew, *Cryptotis parva*	—	—	—	—	—	—	5	—	—	—	—	—	—	—	—	—
Bat, Genus and species indet.	—	1	—	—	—	—	—	—	—	—	—	—	—	—	—	—
cf. Big-eared bat, *Plecotus* sp.	—	1	—	—	—	—	—	—	—	—	—	—	—	—	—	—
cf. Red bat, *Lasiurus borealis*	—	—	—	—	—	—	—	—	—	—	—	—	—	—	—	—
Black bear, *Ursus americanus*	—	—	—	—	—	—	—	—	1	—	—	—	1	2	—	1
Raccoon, *Procyon lotor*	—	3	19	—	—	1	2	—	—	2	—	—	—	—	—	—
Striped skunk, *Mephitis mephitis*	—	—	6	—	—	—	—	—	—	3	—	—	—	—	—	—
Badger, *Taxidea taxus*	—	—	1	—	—	—	1	—	—	1	—	—	—	—	—	—
cf. Gray wolf, *Canis lupus*	—	2	—	—	—	—	3*	—	—	—	—	—	—	—	—	—
Domestic (Indian) dog, *Canis familiaris*	—	1	—	1	—	—	1	—	—	1	1	—	—	—	—	—
Bobcat, *Lynx* cf. *rufus*	—	—	6	—	—	—	—	—	—	—	—	—	—	—	—	—
13-lined ground squirrel, *Spermophilus tridecemlineatus*	—	—	—	—	—	—	—	—	—	—	—	—	—	—	—	—
Eastern chipmunk, *Tamias striatus*	—	—	—	—	—	—	—	—	—	1	—	—	—	—	—	—
Squirrel, *Sciurus* sp.	—	—	—	—	—	—	—	—	—	—	—	—	—	—	—	—
Plains pocket gopher, *Geomys bursarius*	—	—	—	1	—	—	—	—	—	—	—	—	—	—	—	—
Beaver, *Castor canadensis*	—	1	—	—	—	—	—	—	—	—	1	—	—	—	—	—
Deer/white-footed mouse, *Peromyscus* sp.	—	19	—	—	—	2	20	3	—	5	—	—	—	—	—	14
Bog lemming, *Synaptomys* cf. *cooperi*	—	—	—	—	—	—	—	—	—	—	—	—	—	—	—	—
Prairie/meadow vole, *Microtus* sp.	—	—	—	—	—	—	1	—	—	—	—	—	—	—	—	—
Indet. mouse elements: most cf. Fm. Cricetidae	—	20	6	—	—	10	63	1	1	14	—	—	—	—	—	43
Muskrat, *Ondatra zibethica*	—	1	—	—	—	—	3	—	—	—	—	—	—	—	—	—
cf. Meadow jumping mouse, *Zapus hudsonius*	—	—	—	—	—	—	3	—	—	—	—	—	—	—	—	—
Eastern cottontail, *Sylvilagus floridanus*	—	—	—	—	—	—	—	—	—	—	—	—	—	3	—	—
Elk, *Cervus elaphus*	—	—	4	—	—	—	—	—	—	—	—	2	—	1	4	26
White-tailed deer, *Odocoileus virginianus*	—	220	385	2	2	33	176	21	25	68	36	3	1	4	—	53
Indet. mammal	3	500	363	4	1	71	366	20	76	75	48	—	—	8	9	—
Totals, All Taxa	9	948	854	11	11	293	1,104	96	130	292	103	5	2	8	9	363

*pup

APPENDIX D. MAMMALS IDENTIFIED FROM THE RHOADS SITE: FEATURES 73-128

Species	73	74	75	79	84	86	96	105	114	116	118	119	122	125	127	128
Eastern mole, *Scalopus aquaticus*	—	—	—	—	—	—	—	—	—	—	—	—	—	—	—	—
Short-tailed shrew, *Blarina brevicauda*	—	—	—	—	—	—	—	—	—	—	—	—	—	—	—	—
Least shrew, *Cryptotis parva*	—	—	1	—	—	—	—	—	—	—	—	—	—	1	—	—
Bat, Genus and species indet.	—	—	—	—	—	—	—	—	—	—	—	—	—	—	—	—
cf. Big-eared bat, *Plecotus* sp.	—	—	—	—	—	—	—	—	—	—	—	—	—	—	—	—
cf. Red bat, *Lasiurus borealis*	—	—	—	—	—	—	—	—	—	—	—	—	—	—	—	—
Black bear, *Ursus americanus*	—	—	—	2	—	—	—	—	—	—	3	—	—	1	7	—
Raccoon, *Procyon lotor*	—	2	—	5	—	—	1	1	—	—	10	—	—	—	18	3
Striped skunk, *Mephitis mephitis*	—	—	—	—	—	—	—	—	—	—	—	—	—	—	1	—
Badger, *Taxidea taxus*	—	—	—	—	—	—	—	—	—	—	—	—	—	—	1	—
cf. Gray wolf, *Canis lupus*	—	—	—	—	—	—	—	—	1	—	2	—	—	—	—	—
Domestic (Indian) dog, *Canis familiaris*	—	—	1	—	—	—	—	—	1	—	—	—	—	—	—	—
Bobcat, *Lynx* cf. *rufus*	—	—	—	—	—	—	—	—	—	—	—	—	—	—	—	—
13-lined ground squirrel, *Spermophilus tridecemlineatus*	—	—	1	—	—	—	—	—	—	—	—	—	—	4	—	1
Eastern chipmunk, *Tamias striatus*	—	—	—	—	—	—	—	—	—	—	—	—	—	—	1	58
Squirrel, *Sciurus* sp.	—	—	—	1	—	—	—	—	—	—	—	—	—	—	—	1
Plains pocket gopher, *Geomys bursarius*	—	—	—	—	—	—	—	—	—	—	—	—	—	—	—	—
Beaver, *Castor canadensis*	—	—	—	—	—	—	—	—	—	—	13	—	—	—	58	—
Deer/white-footed mouse, *Peromyscus* sp.	1	—	40	4	—	—	2	—	—	1	7	—	—	3	—	1
Bog lemming, *Synaptomys* cf. *cooperi*	—	—	—	1	—	—	—	—	—	—	—	—	—	1	—	—
Prairie/meadow vole, *Microtus* sp.	—	—	—	—	—	—	—	—	—	—	—	—	—	—	—	—
Indet. mouse elements: most cf. Fm. Cricetidae	6	—	104	15	—	—	1	—	—	13	24	—	—	19	3	7
Muskrat, *Ondatra zibethica*	—	—	—	1	—	—	1	—	—	—	—	—	—	1	6	—
cf. Meadow jumping mouse, *Zapus hudsonius*	—	—	—	—	—	—	—	—	—	—	—	—	—	—	—	—
Eastern cottontail, *Sylvilagus floridanus*	—	—	—	—	—	—	—	—	—	—	—	—	—	—	—	—
Elk, *Cervus elaphus*	—	—	1	—	—	—	—	—	—	—	—	—	—	—	—	—
White-tailed deer, *Odocoileus virginianus*	4	25	76	24	—	—	13	57	52	25	246	—	—	42	177	84
Indet. mammal	2	33	83	28	—	2	19	13	75	19	388	5	1	123	153	52
Totals, All Taxa	15	89	506	131	10	2	49	93	163	80	1,117	7	1	442	784	790

APPENDIX D. MAMMALS IDENTIFIED FROM THE RHOADS SITE: FEATURES 130–163 AND SUMMARY DATA

Species	130	140	141	142	143	146	150	151	152	163	P.Z. H.Z.	NISP	% NISP	MNI	% of Identified Species
Eastern mole, *Scalopus aquaticus*	—	—	—	—	—	—	—	—	—	—	—	9871	57.45	202	46.67
Short-tailed shrew, *Blarina brevicauda*	—	—	—	—	—	—	—	—	—	—	—	7	.04	2	.06
Least shrew, *Cryptotis parva*	—	—	—	—	—	—	—	—	—	—	—	4	.02	1	.03
Bat, Genus and species indet.	—	—	—	—	—	—	—	—	—	—	—	10	.05	4	.09
cf. Big-eared bat, *Plecotus* sp.	—	1	—	—	—	—	—	—	3	—	—	6	.03	1	.05
cf. Red bat, *Lasiurus borealis*	—	—	—	—	—	—	—	—	—	—	—	1	.00	1	.00
Black bear, *Ursus americanus*	—	—	—	—	—	—	—	—	1	—	—	1	.00	1	.00
Raccoon, *Procyon lotor*	1	1	—	—	—	—	—	—	—	1	—	19	.11	2	.18
Striped skunk, *Mephitis mephitis*	—	—	2	1	—	1	—	1	2	3	10	156	.91	23	1.53
Badger, *Taxidea taxus*	—	—	—	—	—	—	—	—	—	—	2	12	.07	3	.11
cf. Gray wolf, *Canis lupus*	—	—	—	—	—	—	—	—	—	—	—	4	.02	1	.03
Domestic (Indian) dog, *Canis familiaris*	—	—	—	—	—	—	—	—	—	—	—	3	.01	—	.02
Bobcat, *Lynx* cf. *rufus*	—	—	1	—	—	—	—	—	—	—	—	22	.12	8	.21
13-lined ground squirrel, *Spermophilus tridecemlineatus*	—	—	—	—	—	—	—	—	—	—	—	15	.08	2	.14
Eastern chipmunk, *Tamias striatus*	—	1	—	—	—	—	—	—	1	—	—	9	.05	3	.08
Squirrel, *Sciurus* sp.	1	1	—	—	—	—	—	—	—	—	—	63	.36	7	.61
Plains pocket gopher, *Geomys bursarius*	—	—	—	—	—	—	—	—	—	—	—	4	.02	2	.03
Beaver, *Castor canadensis*	—	—	—	—	—	—	—	—	—	—	—	8	.04	2	.07
Deer/white-footed mouse, *Peromyscus* sp.	3	2	4	—	—	—	—	—	—	1	—	73	.42	2	.71
Bog lemming, *Synaptomys* cf. *cooperi*	—	—	1	—	—	—	1	—	—	—	—	188	1.09	66	1.84
Prairie/meadow vole, *Microtus* sp.	—	—	—	—	—	—	—	—	—	—	—	2	.01	2	.01
Indet. mouse elements: most cf. Fm. Cricetidae	14	15	6	—	—	—	—	—	2	10	—	3	.01	—	.02
Muskrat, *Ondatra zibethica*	—	—	—	—	—	—	—	—	—	—	—	719	4.19	—	7.05
cf. Meadow jumping mouse, *Zapus hudsonius*	—	—	—	—	—	—	—	—	1	—	—	10	.05	2	.09
Eastern cottontail, *Sylvilagus floridanus*	—	—	—	—	—	—	—	—	—	—	—	5	.02	4	.04
Elk, *Cervus elaphus*	—	—	—	—	—	—	—	—	—	—	—	6	.03	2	.05
White-tailed deer, *Odocoileus virginianus*	67	78	65	7	6	2	—	2	118	17	259	3,422	19.96	98	33.58
Indet. mammal	62	73	108	4	1	3	—	8	472	16	509	5,094	29.72	—	—
Totals, All Taxa	184	394	1,738	12	7	7	1	12	651	117	822	17,138	99.60	389	99.28

REFERENCES

Bass, W. M., D. R. Evans, and R. L. Jantz
   1971   The Leavenworth site cemetery: archaeology and physical anthropology. *University of Kansas Publications in Anthropology* 2.

Bohlen, H. D.
   1978   An annotated check-list of the birds of Illinois. *Illinois State Museum Popular Science Series* 9.

Calhoun, J., and F. Loomis
   1974   *Prairie whitetails*. Division of Wildlife Resources, Illinois Department of Conservation.

Conway, T. G.
   1972   Potawatomi politics. *Journal of the Illinois State Historical Society* 65:395–418.

Cory, C. B.
   1909   Birds of Illinois and Wisconsin. *Field Museum of Natural History (Zoology Series)* Publication 131, Vol. 9.

Elder, W. H.
   1965   Primeval deer hunting pressures revealed by remains from American Indian middens. *Journal of Wildlife Management* 29:366–370.

Gilmore, M. R.
   1932   The sacred bundles of the Arikara. *Papers of the Michigan Academy of Science, Arts, and Letters* 31:33–50.

Gregg, J.
   1905   Commerce of the prairies, or the journal of a Santa Fe trader—1831–1839, Part 2. In *Early western travels 1748–1846*, edited by R. G. Thwaites, Vol. 10. A. H. Clark, Cleveland.

Guilday, J. E.
   1963   The cup-and-pin game. *Pennsylvania Archaeologist* 33:159–163.

Guilday, J. E., P. W. Parmalee, and D. P. Tanner
   1962   Aboriginal butchering techniques at the Eschelman site (36La12), Lancaster County, Pennsylvania. *Pennsylvania Archaeologist* 32:59–83.

Hallowell, A. I.
   1926   Bear ceremonialism in the northern hemisphere. *American Anthropologist* 28:1–175.

Hoffmeister, D. F., and C. O. Mohr
   1957   Fieldbook of Illinois mammals. *Illinois Natural History Survey Manual* 4.

James, E.
   1823   *Account of an expedition from Pittsburgh to the Rocky Mountains, performed in the years 1819–20 . . . under the command of Major Stephen H. Long*. 2 Vols. Philadelphia.

King, J. E., W. E. Klippel, and R. Duffield
   1975   Pollen preservation and archaeology in eastern North America. *American Antiquity* 40:180–190.

Klippel, W. E.
   1972   Report on preliminary site examination undertaken at the Rhoads site, Lo-8, on FAI 55, Logan County, Illinois (mimeo). Manuscript on file, Illinois Department of Transportation, Springfield.
   1973a Archaeological salvage stage 3 Rhoads site, 11 Lo-8, on FAI 55, Logan County, Illinois (mimeo). Manuscript on file, Illinois Department of Transportation, Springfield.
   1973b Recent native heritage of central Illinois. *The Living Museum* 35:206–208.
   1976   Euroamericans and the Kickapoo in the Illinois Prairie. *The Explorer* 18:9–13.

Krantz, G. S.
   1968   A new method of counting mammal bones. *American Journal of Archaeology* 72:286–288.

Mandelbaum, D. G.
    1940   The Plains Cree. *American Museum of Natural History Anthropological Papers* 37(2):189–286.
Maximilian, Prince of Wied-Neuwied
    1907   Travels in the interior of North America. In *Early Western Travels, 1748–1846*, edited by R. G. Thwaites, Vol. 23. A. H. Clark, Cleveland.
Moorehead, W. K.
    1932   *Exploration of the Etowah site in Georgia.* Yale University Press, New Haven.
Morrison, J. P. E.
    1942   Preliminary report on mollusks found in the shell mounds of the Pickwick Landing Basin in the Tennessee River Valley. In An archaeological survey of Pickwick Basin in the adjacent portions of the states of Alabama, Mississippi and Tennessee, edited by W. S. Webb and D. L. DeJarnette, pp. 341–392. *Bureau of American Ethnology, Bulletin* 129.
Parmalee, P. W.
    1957   Vertebrate remains from the Cahokia site, Illinois. *Transactions of the Illinois State Academy of Science* 50:235–242.
    1959   Use of mammalian skulls and mandibles by prehistoric Indians of Illinois. *Transactions of the Illinois State Academy of Science* 52:85–95.
    1963   Vertebrate remains from the Bell site, Winnebago County, Wisconsin. *Wisconsin Archaeologist* 44:58–69.
    1964   Vertebrate remains from an historic archaeological site in Rock Island County, Illinois. *Transactions of the Illinois State Academy of Science* 57:167–174.
    1965   The food economy of Archaic and Woodland peoples at the Tick Creek Cave site, Missouri. *Missouri Archaeologist* 27:1–34.
    1967   Additional noteworthy records of birds from archaeological sites. *Wilson Bulletin* 79:155–162.
    1969   Animal remains from the Archaic Riverton, Swan Island, and Robeson Hills sites, Illinois. In The Riverton culture, by H. D. Winters, pp. 139–144. *Illinois State Museum Reports of Investigations* 13 and *Illinois Archaeological Survey Monograph* 1.
Parmalee, P. W., and A. E. Bogan
    1981   A summary of the animal remains from the Noble-Wieting site (11ML28), McLean County, Illinois. *Transactions of the Illinois State Academy of Science* 73(4):1–6.
Parmalee, P. W., and W. E. Klippel
    1974   Freshwater mussels as a prehistoric food resource. *American Antiquity* 39:421–434.
Quertermus, C.
    1967   A key to the North American species of *Lepisosteus* (Class Pisces) based on the cleithrum. *Transactions of the Illinois State Academy of Science* 60:45–48.
Quimby, G. I.
    1966   *Indian culture and European trade goods.* University of Wisconsin Press, Madison.
Ridgway, R.
    1889   *The ornithology of Illinois.* Vol. I, Pt. I. State Laboratory of Natural History, Springfield.
    1895   *The ornithology of Illinois.* Vol. II, Pt. I. State Laboratory of Natural History, Springfield.
Ritzenthaler, R. E., and F. A. Peterson
    1956   The Mexican Kickapoo Indians. *Milwaukee Public Museum Publications in Anthropology* 2.
Rogers, R. A.
    1968   *Logan County surface water resources.* Illinois Department of Conservation, Division of Fisheries.

Severinghaus, C. W.
    1949   Tooth development and wear as criteria of age in white-tailed deer. *Journal of Wildlife Management* 13:195–216.
Shier, Q. V.
    1962   Distribution and ecology of fresh-water mussels of Kickapoo Creek–Salt Creek Systems. M.S. thesis, Department of Zoology, University of Illinois, Urbana.
Silverberg, J.
    1957   The Kickapoo Indians: first one hundred years of white contact in Wisconsin. *Wisconsin Archaeologist* 38:61–181.
Smith, P. W.
    1961   The amphibians and reptiles of Illinois. *Illinois Natural History Survey Bulletin* 28(1).
Swanton, J. R.
    1946   The Indians of the southeastern United States. *Bureau of American Ethnology, Bulletin* 137.
Temple, W. C.
    1966   Indian villages of the Illinois country (revised ed.). *Illinois State Museum Scientific Papers* 2(2).
Thwaites, R. G. (editor)
    1911   The fur trade in Wisconsin 1812–1825. *Wisconsin State Historical Society Collections* 20.
Ubelaker, D., and W. R. Wedel
    1975   Bird bones, burials and bundles in Plains archaeology. *American Antiquity* 40:444–452.
Voegelin, E. W.
    1941   The place of agriculture in the subsistence economy of the Shawnee. *Papers of the Michigan Academy of Science, Arts, and Letters* 26:513–520.
Wallace, B. J.
    1964   The Oklahoma Kickapoo: an ethnographic reconstruction. *Wisconsin Archaeologist* 45:1–69.
Watt, B. K., and A. L. Merrill
    1963   Composition of foods. *United States Department of Agriculture Agricultural Handbook* 8.
Webb, R. G.
    1962   North American recent soft-shell turtles (Family Trionychidae). *University of Kansas Publications, Museum of Natural History* 13(10):429–611.
Webb, W. S., and R. S. Baby
    1957   *The Adena People. No. 2.* Ohio State University Press, Columbus.
White, T.
    1953   A method of calculating the dietary percentage of various food animals utilized by aboriginal peoples. *American Antiquity* 18:396–398.
Wilson, G. L.
    1924   The horse and the dog in Hidatsa culture. *American Museum of Natural History Anthropological Papers* 15(2):124–311.

THE HOLLY OAK SHELL GAME:
AN HISTORIC ARCHAEOLOGICAL FRAUD[1]

David J. Meltzer and William C. Sturtevant

The contemporaneity of humans with extinct mammoths and mastodons is now taken for granted in American archaeology. But this was not always so. In the early years, evidence for the association included Naskapi and other Indian and Eskimo traditions sometimes interpreted as referring to these animals (Mercer 1885:12–20). These traditions had been reported by Thomas Jefferson and others (Strong 1934; Speck 1935; Michelson 1936; Siebert 1937; Ashley-Montagu 1944; Eiseley 1945), and included Iroquois tales identified by the Tuscarora historian David Cusick as describing mammoths (1827:25; also in Bullock 1827:150). Examination of the evidence from the fossil record began with the work of Robert Koch in Missouri in 1838 (McMillan 1976) and continued for the rest of the nineteenth century. Several notorious archaeological frauds, recognized or suspected as such, attempted to settle the matter (see, for example, Henshaw [1883] and McKusick [1971] on the elephant pipes and elephant mounds of Iowa). The question was part of the fierce debate among American archaeologists and geologists regarding the antiquity of the peopling of America, a debate only resolved with the Folsom discoveries of this century (Hart 1976; Meltzer 1983).

This controversy often involved the validity of parallels with Europe, where the Paleolithic had become well accepted since the 1860s. A key piece of evidence in the earlier European arguments was a beautifully clear representation of a woolly mammoth engraved on a fragment of mammoth tusk (see various depictions in Fig. 1 [bottom] and Fig. 2), discovered in 1864 in excavations supervised by Édouard Lartet at the La Madeleine rock shelter in the Périgord, the Magdalenian type site that Lartet and Christy began to excavate in 1863. "Cette découverte confirma la contemporanéité de l'homme et du mammouth," according to the present exhibit label for this treasure of French prehistory in the Muséum National d'Histoire Naturelle. The artifact, first described by Lartet in 1865 (Lartet 1865), was included in the epochal display of recent French discoveries at the 1867 Éxposition Universelle in Paris (Mortillet 1867:26) which, with the Congrès Internationale Préhistorique de Paris of the same year, marked "a turning point in the study of prehistory" (Bibby 1956:46). A translation of the announcement appeared with an illustration in the final monograph on the Lartet-Christy discoveries (Lartet and Christy 1875:206–208, Pl. 28, in fascicles first issued in 1874 and 1873) (see our Fig. 2). A fine lithograph depicting the engraving was prominently placed in all but the 1865 British first edition of Sir John Lubbock's bestseller *Prehistoric Times* (the second British edition appeared in 1869; all the American editions, beginning in 1872, contain the plate and it also appears in Lubbock 1870:Pl. 1) (see our Fig. 2).

An equivalent specimen would have just as neatly resolved the question of the contemporaneity of humans and extinct mammals in North America. Such an artifact came to light in 1889, at the height of the American debate, although it was claimed to have been discovered in 1864, perhaps not coincidentally the same year as Lartet's find. The artifact was suspected as soon as it was announced, but its validity was not disproven nor even clearly attacked in the contemporary literature. It remained in limbo until the reputation of its purported discoverer was forgotten and the association of man and mammoth in North America had been well established by other evidence. It then reappeared, to take an undeserved place in the archaeological literature of the 1970s.

The artifact in question is the Holly Oak pendant, a section of whelk shell (*Busycon sinistrum*) bearing an engraving of a woolly mammoth (*Mammuthus primigenius*). Alleged to have been discovered by Hilborne T. Cresson in 1864 near the Holly Oak station in northern Delaware, the pendant was brought forth only in December 1889, and then shown publicly in February 1890 at a meeting of the Boston Society of Natural History (Putnam 1890a). In the early 1890s it was displayed at the Harvard Peabody Museum, the Smithsonian Institution, and the international expositions at Madrid and Chicago; it then settled into relative anonymity in a specimen drawer at the United States National Museum.

The obscurity of this artifact in the early literature is evidence that contemporary archaeologists did not take it seriously. Even the Lenape Stone (Mercer 1885) with its far more suspicious engraving (including a mammoth; Fig. 3) had greater prominence in the debates over Pleistocene man. The pendant was almost never cited in the many discussions of the evidence for human antiquity in North America (e.g., it is not cited in Wright 1892, Wright 1893 or Moorehead 1910), and published denunciations of it are few and brief (Brinton 1892, 1893a, 1893b; Mercer 1897:21). The oral tradition that must have surrounded the artifact and its promoter died with his contemporaries, leaving traces only in scattered letters and diary entries.

THE HOLLY OAK PENDANT

> What are your opinions in regard to the shell? Our people are anxious to hear your reply as it was out of the hands of the family, for seven or eight years, in M. Surault's care, they want to feel that it is all right, and not a copy of the original. I told them that no man living, at the present day, could copy that shell, and its ornamentation, nor could anyone place a deposit of dendrites over it. [Cresson to Putnam, January 21, 1890, Peabody Museum Archives, HU]

Frederick Ward Putnam of the Peabody Museum, who exhibited the pendant for Cresson at the February meeting of the Boston Society of Natural History, was obviously struck by the remarkable similarity between the engraving of the mammoth on the Holly Oak pendant and the engraving on the La Madeleine tusk. In March of 1890 Putnam sent Cresson a photograph taken of a drawing and photograph of the Holly Oak pendant placed adjacent to a drawing of the La Madeleine tusk and one of the Lenape stone (Fig. 3). In reply, Cresson observed that it was "strange how faithfully all the copies represent the mammoth" (Cresson to Putnam, March 28, 1890, Peabody Museum Archives, HU).[2]

Daniel Brinton of the University of Pennsylvania also thought this coincidence peculiar. In discussing the La Madeleine tusk he observed:

> In the United States two such delineations [of prehistoric animals] have been brought forward. They are both strikingly similar to this French original, which has long been made familiar to American readers through various publications. [Brinton 1893a:75]

For Brinton the implication was clear, and he went on to conclude that "from the vagueness which surrounds the finding of both [and] for purely technical reasons I believe both to be recent [manufactures]" (Brinton 1893a:75).

Thomas Wilson, Curator at the United States National Museum, who was more willing to believe that humans and mammoths had co-existed in North America and accepted the authenticity of the shell, duly called attention to the resemblance between the Holly Oak pendant and the La Madeleine tusk (Wilson 1898:381).

However, a detailed stylistic comparison between the Holly Oak and La Madeleine engravings has never been published. In making this long-overdue critical investigation we have not, of course, laid the objects side by side (neither did Cresson or anyone else). We have handled and carefully examined both the originals separately (probably no one else has done this except possibly Cresson), and we have directly compared the Holly Oak pendant in its present condition with several photographs and drawings of the same specimen and with several depictions of the La Madeleine mammoth.

Our drawing of the Holly Oak engraving (Fig. 1) is based on a careful tracing of a good recent photograph of the object, taken before it was fragmented and partly shattered in the head region during 30X microscopic examination in 1969 by the Conservation-Analytical Laboratory of the Smithsonian (Organ 1969). This tracing was reworked by Sturtevant from direct comparison with the artifact and with two earlier photographs, one of them made in December 1889 or January 1890 (Kraft and Thomas [1976:Fig. 2] reproduce this photograph, but somewhat cut apart and rearranged [see below]). Our reworking is necessary for two reasons. Firstly, some engraved lines were evidently slightly modified or obscured by minor restoration work conducted after the 1889/90 photograph was made. Secondly, the shell has surface features not readily distinguishable, in a photograph, from the engraved lines: irregular spots and patches of discoloration, and small fissures and flaking in many places (a small amount of which occurred between the making of the second and third photographs we use). The shell is soft and friable, and the engraved lines are crude, of varying widths and depths, mostly unstained. Other interpretations of the depiction can be seen in Kraft and Thomas (1976:757 and issue cover), Meggers (1972:14), Weslager (1941:12; 1944:32), Wilson (1898:Pl. 16; 1901:322), Dragoo (1980:207) and our Figure 3.

The La Madeleine engraving is clearer and less subject to distortion in an interpretive drawing. It is much more skillfully done than the Holly Oak engraving and on a hard, non-friable surface without confusing natural cracks and fissures. It was in five or six pieces when first found; the joins were filled in evidently soon after the discovery, but this repair or restoration does not seriously affect the depiction. The original is on a slightly convex fragment of a tusk—not a piece with circular cross-section but a "plaque" some 1 to 2 cm thick broken off in prehistoric times, on which the engraved lines for the feet run off the edge.

Published reproductions are adequate for comparison with the Holly Oak pendant. Figure 2 (top) is a good representation of the entire design by the Abbé Breuil, an artist of undeniable experience and authority. Figure 2 (center) is a version of the first and best known reproduction, an excellent lithograph that evidently served as the basis for more widely diffused nineteenth century depictions such as the one published in the Lubbock volumes (Lubbock 1869:Pl. 2; 1870:Pl. 1; our Fig. 2 bottom). Among the early derivative depictions of the La Madeleine engraving is a crude and inaccurate one published by Charles Rau (1876:59), our Figure 1 (bottom), in a volume with which Cresson was familiar (he compared the Holly Oak engraving to other illustrations in this book that show a mammoth skeleton and a ludicrous reconstruction of a living mammoth [Cresson to Putnam, January 21, 1890, Peabody Museum Archives, HU]).

Rau's illustration differs from the better reproductions of the La Madeleine engraving in several respects to which the Holly Oak engraving conforms. It is likely that Rau's engraving was the Holly Oak author's model, although it is also possible that he used another depiction such as Lubbock's or a sketch of the original which he could have made while studying art and archaeology in Paris during the 1870s (Cresson 1890a:116).

The best evidence for the copying is visual (Figs. 1 and 2): when one examines the placement and the shapes of the lines, they are too similar to be independent. Such similaries are difficult to express precisely in words, and probably impossible to quantify. The judgment that one is derived from the other is necessarily based in part on knowledge and ideas about the range of possible manners of depicting an animal, in general, and in the styles of the Franco-Cantabrian Paleolithic and the North American Pleistocene and post-Pleistocene.

In 1890 very few depictions of mammoths were known. It was not until 1902 that the "parietal" paintings and engravings of France and Spain were generally known and accepted by all prehistorians (Bibby 1956: 66). Before that, only "art mobilier" was well known and not very many such small engraved depictions were available in 1890, of which less than half a dozen showed mammoths. At that time the variety of ways of depicting mammoths was unknown, and the parallel then noticed between the Holly Oak and the La Madeleine engravings could have appeared in a different light: as evidence that what was depicted was indeed a mammoth, rather than that it was the same mammoth.

A modern observer, however, must be aware of the remarkably realistic style of depicting animals in the very large corpus of Franco-Cantabrian Paleolithic art now known—and of the rarity of any such depictions in the prehistoric record from North America (not to mention the oddity, now evident, of a gorget with a design oriented sideways rather than vertically).

When the Holly Oak and La Madeleine depictions are compared with other Paleolithic representations of mammoths (Fig. 4), their close

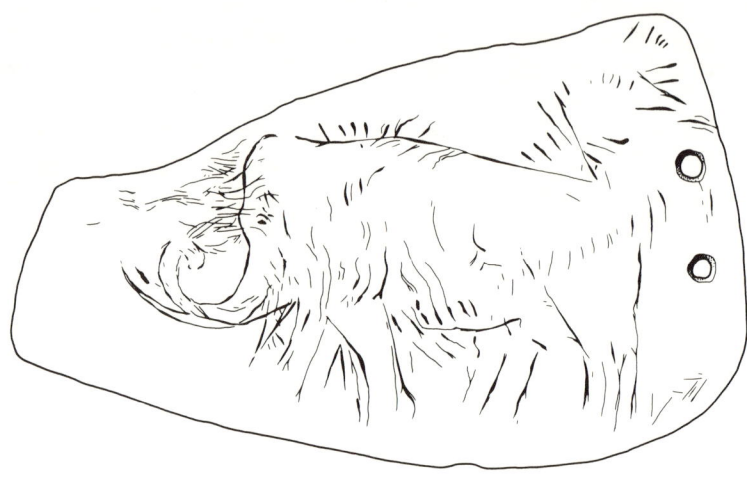

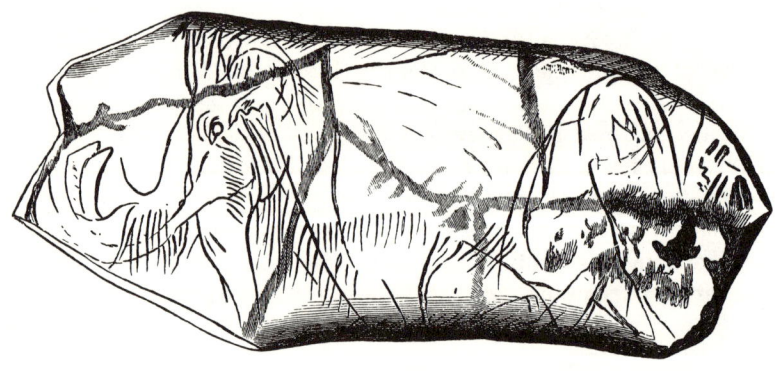

Fig. 1. Engraving on the Holly Oak pendant, drawn in 1982 (*top*); and the La Madeleine engraving as depicted by Rau (1876:59) (*bottom*).

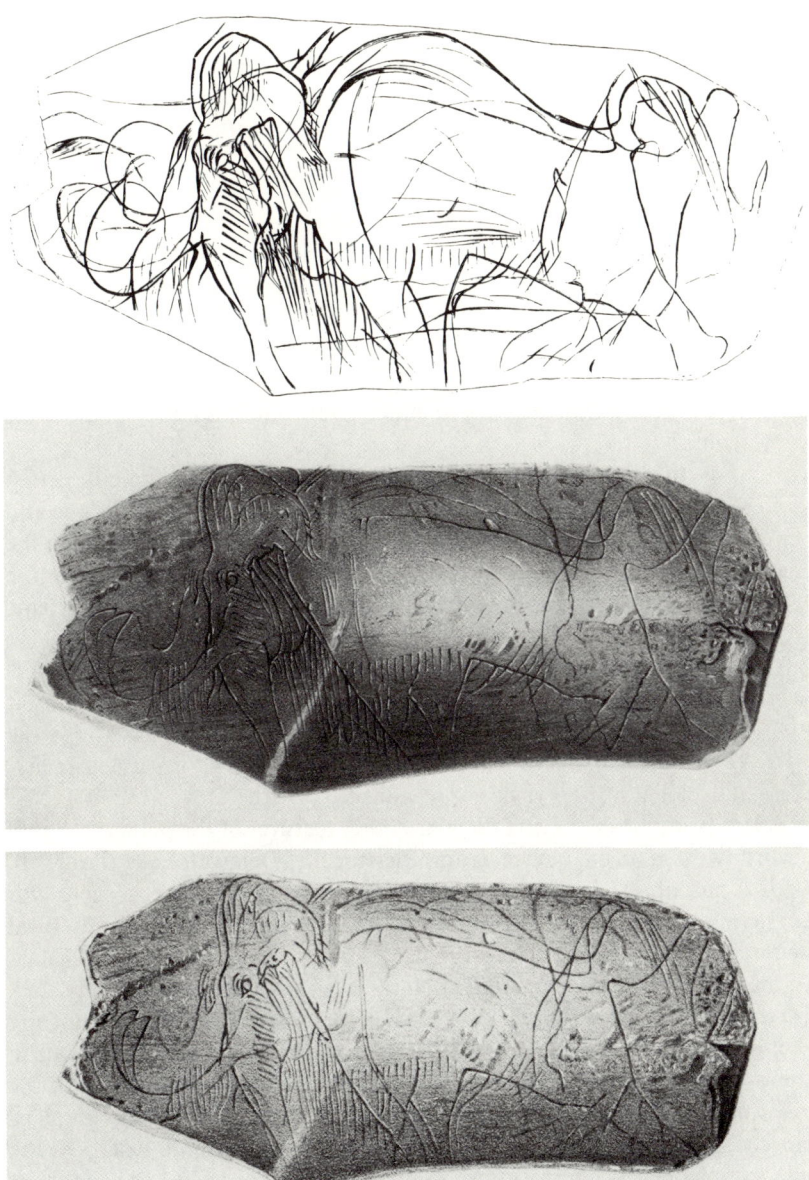

Fig. 2. The La Madeleine engraving as depicted by Breuil (in Capitan, Breuil, and Peyrony 1910:141 (Fig. 110); photo courtesy Bibl. Muséum Hist. Nat. Paris) (*top*); Lartet and Christy (1875:Pl.28) (*center*); and Lubbock (1869:Pl.2) (*bottom*).

similarity is apparent. The two repeatedly chose the same convention among several alternative possibilities. Among the convincing parallels are:

    1) the same orientation and overall posture, especially the leg positions;

    2) the treatment of the feet—most mammoths are shown with bulbous feet, but the La Madeleine feet are cut off by the break in the object (except for part of one hind foot recognized only by Breuil), and the Holly Oak legs terminate in the same way even though there is space where feet could have been drawn;

    3) the raised tail of the La Madeleine animal is somewhat ambiguous, especially in Rau's copy, and was evidently misunderstood by the Holly Oak artist, who added a few random marks in the same region;

    4) the contour of the back, where the La Madeleine artist sketched several lines, but the Holly Oak artist copied only one and that the one resembling a modern elephant's profile rather than the typical mammoth hump; Rau's artist also drew only one line for the back and this is the clearest evidence that Rau's La Madeleine illustration was the one copied by Cresson;[3]

    5) the trunk and tusks, which seem also to have been misinterpreted: here the engraved lines on the Holly Oak pendant are a bit harder to distinguish from other marks, but it looks as though the La Madeleine upcurved tusks were taken for an upturned trunk, and elephant-like tusks were added.

Apart from the engraving there are other features of the pendant that ill accord with a provenience from Pleistocene Delaware. As James B. Griffin has observed (personal communication, 1982), the gorget, *sans* engraving, is of a type commonly found among Fort Ancient cultural materials (although examples are also known from Late Archaic Glacial Kame assemblages discovered after the manufacture of the Holly Oak pendant—see Cunningham 1948). Shell ornaments typical of this late prehistoric occupation are "made from local shells as well as from ocean shells, such as *Busycon perversum* and *Busycon carica*. Examples of the disk-shaped gorget with a large central perforation and two smaller, closely spaced, marginal perforations were found. In some instances the disk has the central perforation only; in other instances it has a *single or double marginal hole*" (Griffin 1943:128, emphasis ours). A later summary of the traits characteristic of Fort Ancient in the Upper Ohio Valley mentions that "circular gorgets of marine [*Busycon*] shell, some with a central hole and some with one or two marginal perforations were used. A few of these bear decorations such as crosses, circles and spiders" (Morgan 1952:95).

When the assemblage from Holly Oak was presented to the Peabody Museum in early 1890, it included some 275 other specimens.[4] Included in this collection were human bones showing evidence of copper staining, various stone tools, broken animal bones, a fragment of wood chopped by a stone axe and, apparently, a mastodon tooth (Cresson to Putnam, January 30 and February 20, 1890, Peabody Museum Archives, HU). No complete listings exist of the collection, but a photograph taken at the Smithsonian in 1889 or 1890 records some of the assemblage. However, this photograph (Fig. 5; compare this with the cut version in Kraft and Thomas 1976:Fig. 2; their Fig. 1 is a later photograph of the pendant) shows an assemblage that, beyond the purportedly Late Pleistocene Holly Oak pendant, incorporates Archaic projectile points and bone beads and tools of an unknown age (but likely later—Woodland—materials).

This association makes little sense archaeologically, but according to Cresson it reflects the manner in which the materials were found.[5] Cresson wrote to Putnam on January 2, 1890, to say that "the shell *and its other objects* are being photographed by Smithsonian" (Cresson to Putnam, January 2, 1890, Peabody Museum Archives, HU, emphasis ours). When he received copies of the photograph he forwarded one to Putnam (who by then had the entire Holly Oak collection), and instructed him to use the photograph to check on the completeness of the assemblage:

> Do me the favor of comparing the various objects with the photograph—I went over the lot and found everything complete. [Cresson to Putnam, January 10, 1890; see also Cresson to Putnam, January 2 and January 30, 1890, Peabody Museum Archives, HU]

The ambiguity and incongruity of the assemblage are said to result from the lack of detail recorded by Cresson (Kraft and Thomas 1976:760). Certainly the report on the Holly Oak material given in the primary source (Putnam 1890a) is not detailed by today's standards, although it does equal most other late nineteenth century field descriptions. More to the point, the description given in Putnam (1890a) is only a partial account; the most complete report is in an unpublished letter from Cresson to Putnam. At the top of that letter, Cresson cautioned Putnam that "I do not wish this published verbatim—you must take notes from it and file it away among our papers" (Cresson to Putnam, January 30, 1890, Peabody Museum Archives, HU). The relevant text of this letter is as follows:

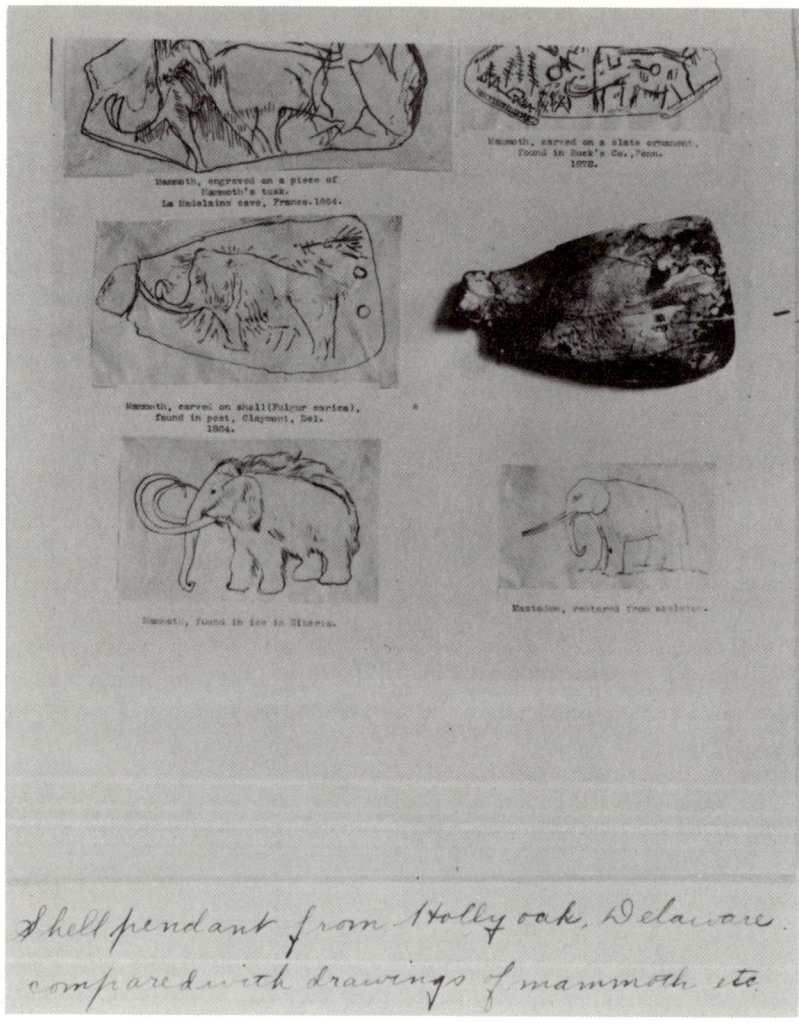

Fig. 3. Photograph prepared by F. W. Putnam in 1890. *Left to right, top row first*: La Madeleine engraving; Lenape stone; Holly Oak pendant drawn; Holly Oak pendant photographed (cf. Fig. 5); "Mammoth found in ice in Siberia"; "Mastodon, restored from skeleton" (Peabody Museum, Harvard University, H692).

Fig. 4. The Holly Oak and La Madeleine mammoths (*upper left*) compared with other French Paleolithic depictions. The drawings are by Sturtevant. The following list specifies for each the site of origin, the interpretaton copied (in parentheses), and those instances here laterally reversed (marked "R"). Original drawings and tracings by the Abbé Breuil preserved in the Bibliothèque Centrale, Muséum National d'Histoire Naturelle, Paris, are identified by their six-digit catalog numbers. We thank Yves Laissus, Conservateur of the library, for allowing Sturtevant to examine and copy these last. *Top row*, left to right: Holly Oak (our Figure 1); La Madeleine (our Figure 1); Bernifal R (Breuil 1952:291). *Row 2*: pair, Font-de-Gaume (541919); Font-de-Gaume R (541918); Les Combarelles R (542883). *Row 3*: Font-de-Gaume (541920); Font-de-Gaume (541908); Les Combarelles R (542224). *Row 4*: Rouffignac (Ucko and Rosenfeld 1967:59); Font-de-Gaume (543135, 1–2); Font-de-Gaume (541908). *Row 5*: Font-de-Gaume (543132); Les Combarelles (542841); Rouffignac (Ucko and Rosenfeld 1967:40). *Row 6*; Font-de-Gaume (541908); Les Combarelles (Breuil in Capitan, Breuil, and Peyrony 1924:36); Font-de-Gaume R (543137). Berdin (1970) enumerates 446 depictions of mammoths in French and Spanish caves, reproducing line drawings of 106 of them (many after Breuil). Barriere (1970) includes careful line drawings of 40 not illustrated by Berdin. Unfortunately, these sources were not located until Figure 4 had been completed.

> The shell pendant, owned by Mrs Fred Spencer of New York, was discovered in 1864 while digging in the "Peat and Fallen Forest Layer". It is a bastard peat, intermixed in places, with rich, decomposed organic material, called Muck. The muck is used as a fertilizer, and in the case referred to was intended to enrich the soil of my father's place at Naaman's Creek (now Claymont). Michael Finclin [cf. Putnam 1890a:469] and Timothy Leary, two laborers, had removed the overlying layers of river mud, yellow glacial clay, sand, etc., reaching the "Peat and Fallen Forest Layer", proceeding with their work for several days. At last stones were reached and some of them, were thrown into the cart & carried thence to our place and dumped on the ground in a field alongside of which was a lane or roadway leading from our residence to the Baltimore Pike. A gentlemen who gave my brother and self, French lessons, was in the habit of coming down from Philadelphia each week. It chanced that on his way from the station he happened to pass near the piles of peat and muck, that had been dumped on our ground. Noticing a stone which indicated that it had been exposed to the action of fire he picked it up, along with several rude flakes & fragments of bone. M. Surault, in his country, had known Lartet and had studied with that well known savant. In the New World this love for research did not abate and the first archaeological excursions I can recall, were made with him in quest of arrowheads, and the usual aboriginal remains that one finds scattered over the fields. So as soon as lessons were over, you can readily imagine, we were off to examine the locality from which the flakes & hearth stone had been excavated by the laborers at the Muck pit. We discovered just what M. Surault suggested, an aboriginal hearth and other traces of early mans presence. M. Surault preserved the specimens and made at the time a plan of the place according to Lartet's methods, a copy of which I have preserved [which still survives in the Peabody Museum Archives, HU; the pendant is not shown on the plan]. Many of these specimens were given to my brother and self, and were boxed away in the cellar of my mother's house. A portion were destroyed by fire, when the house was burned (this took place I think in '67 . . .). Luckily some of the specimens from the hearth were preserved, and others came into our hands before M. Suraults death. [Cresson to Putnam, January 30, 1890, Peabody Museum Archives, HU]

From this account it is not clear whether the pendant was found *in situ* or as part of the deposit spread on the field. The plan, in two parts, shows the stratigraphic profile of a pit and a map of a hearth. No artifacts, except the hearth stones, are noted. However, it is apparent that the collection came from the "Peat and Fallen Forest Layer" (see also Cresson to Putnam, December 13, 1889, Peabody Museum Archives, HU; and Putnam 1890a). This has some interesting implications. When, in 1890, Cresson described the "Peat and Fallen Forest Layer" to Putnam, he observed that in some areas it appeared on the surface, while in others it was "deep down, under postglacial deposits" (Cresson to Putnam, February 20, 1890, Peabody Museum Archives, HU; Cresson to G. F. Wright, July 22, 1889, Wright Papers, OC). In most instances the stratum was interspersed between the "Philadelphia Brick Clay" and "Red Gravel" deposits, so-called "aqueous deposits" that dated to either full glacial times or much earlier (Cresson 1891). At one time Cresson thought the stratum might date "between the 1st and 2nd ice movement" (Cresson to G. F. Wright, July 29, 1889, Wright Papers, OC).

Yet scarcely one year later Cresson (1891, 1892) argued that the "old

Fig. 5. The assemblage purportedly from the Holly Oak site as photographed in 1889 or 1890 (Department of Anthropology, Smithsonian Institution, Negative 5280).

aqueous deposits" showed evidence of considerable *recent* disturbance. The evidence for that disturbance was the "Peat and Fallen Forest Layer" for, as Cresson asked W. H. Holmes rhetorically:

> If they are not [recently disturbed] "how do you account for *organic* remains beneath the Columbian of McGee—at Claymont? *Leaves* of *trees* and peat—branches of Sycamore etc." [Cresson to Holmes, January 15, 1894, Holmes Papers, SIA; emphasis in original]

Cresson therefore concluded that the "'Ancient Forest and Peat Layer' with organic remains do not favor of any great antiquity (i.e. geological time)" (Cresson to G. F. Wright, December 21, 1892, Wright Papers, OC), although his alleged Pleistocene shell came from that deposit.

It is also curious how a shell with pH in the basic range could last for at least 10,000 years in the acidic environment of a peat deposit. An authority on the subfamily Busyconinae has examined the shell, and was struck not only by the preservation of the shell itself but also by the fact that the surface engraving of the mammoth had not been etched off by the acidic deposit (Jerry Harasewych, personal communication, 1982).

Finally, there is no indication that the assemblage as given to the Smithsonian for photographing and ultimately for cataloging is drawn from different strata or different areas. Either the collection as it exists accurately reflects the assemblage found in the "Peat and Fallen Forest Layer" and thus the cultural materials at the site show a great deal of mixing, or the collection is simply a random assortment of archaeological objects Cresson gathered together to give the "discovery" of the pendant some semblance of archaeological context. In his time, this incongruous assemblage of material might well have seemed reasonable. Putnam was apparently not greatly concerned, evidently not recognizing the mixture of archaeological cultures. But given what we now know of eastern North American prehistory, such a collection is suspect, particularly in light of Cresson's assurances that all the items were found together.

The Holly Oak pendant is a fraud. The fundamental evidence is: (1) the engraving is very similar to the La Madeleine engraving—one of the few Paleolithic engravings known at that time; (2) the base is a Fort Ancient gorget, out of place in deposits from Delaware's Pleistocene; (3) the assemblage is contrived; (4) the shell would not have survived its acidic environment; (5) the range of the woolly mammoth did not extend as far south as Delaware (Kurtén and Anderson 1980:353–354), and radiocarbon dates that purportedly demonstrate a late survival for the mammoth in the eastern woodlands are, without exception, unreliable (Meltzer and Mead 1983); (6) the artifact is unique in North America. In listing all these points, some stronger than others, we do not follow

Vayson de Pradenne's sound advice (1932:671–673) on "how to get an error recognized," for we do not expect to be forced into an argument. Furthermore, we are interested in this case as historians as well as scientists. From this point of view it is useful to examine Cresson's biography. Of course we think he was the perpetrator of the fraud, rather than an innocent or knowing collaborator of someone else (such as Surault). But even if Cresson is not the guilty party, his reputation among his contemporaries accounts for the cool reception accorded his championing of the pendant.

HILBORNE T. CRESSON

> Cresson had many good qualities, had large experience and great preparation, but there was a screw loose, a wheel misplaced, cogs broken out, or something broke in his intellectual or his moral nature which incapacitated him from success in this life. [Thomas Wilson to W. K. Moorehead, October 11, 1894, Moorehead Papers, OHS]

Hilborne T. Cresson (Fig. 6) was born Hilborne T. Jones in the late 1840s in New York City to Joseph Hilborne and Elizabeth Delancey Jones. The exact year and date of birth are unknown. The newspaper accounts at the time of his death in 1894 gave his age as between 43 and 48. Strangely, his gravestone in the Cresson family cemetery at Oaks, Pennsylvania shows no year of birth (D. J. Meltzer, fieldnotes, July 10, 1982). However, the 1880 U.S. census returns (National Archives, Record Group 400, 1880 Census, Vol. 64, ED 146, Sheet 15, Line 18) list his age as 32. While a discrepancy does exist in these records, it can be assumed he was born in 1848, and so was 16 years old in the year he later claimed to have made the "discovery."

Some time in the early 1870s, Hilborne Jones married Elizabeth Vaux Cresson, daughter of the wealthy Philadelphian William Penn Cresson. According to the newspaper accounts, Jones changed his name to Cresson either on the occasion of their marriage or in September 1873 on the birth of their first son, William Penn Cresson, Jr. (who later married Margaret Chester French, daughter of the sculptor Daniel Chester French). According to documents in his own handwriting that Cresson left at the Historical Society of Pennsylvania, he changed his name in March, 1875, in the Court of Common Pleas, Philadelphia; perhaps he had forgotten the correct year.

His motives for changing his name are unclear, but (*contra* Weslager 1944:30) it was not because his father-in-law lacked male heirs for the latter already had two sons. Whether he was welcomed by the Cresson family is also not known, although Cresson family descendants (not on

Fig. 6. Hilborne T. Cresson, April 1868 (Chesterwood Museum, a property of the National Trust for Historic Preservation).

Hilborne's line) are quick to observe that he was not a true Cresson (Dr. Samuel L. Cresson, personal communication, 1982). In January, 1875, while Cresson and his family were still residing in Claymont, Delaware, a second son, Emlen Vaux Cresson, was born (as best we have determined, neither of Cresson's sons had children).

Between 1864 (the year Cresson claimed the Holly Oak pendant was discovered) and 1870, Jones/Cresson allegedly excavated a series of sites in and around northern Delaware. These included the Naaman's Creek fish weir (Cresson 1887, 1892) and the Naaman's Creek rockshelter (Cresson 1890b). The results of these investigations were not published until the late 1880s and early 1890s, a pattern of delayed reporting similar to the Holly Oak find.

From the mid 1870s until 1880, Cresson was apparently in France, where he had gone to "pursue studies at the Ecole des Beaux Arts and Ecole d'Anthropologie" (Cresson 1890a:116; Putnam 1888:44). As he observed:

> My early education was artistic rather than scientific—I came in contact with scientific men by illustrating for them with my pencil the primitive endeavors of early man to decorate pottery and chip out his stone implements, and figurines. [Cresson to G. F. Wright, August 26, 1889, Wright Papers, OC]

Cresson first appears on the archaeological scene in 1887, when he is listed as a Field Assistant with the Peabody Museum, Harvard (Peabody Museum 1887). That year he also published his first professional paper (Cresson 1887), in which he claimed to have discovered "pile dwelling" remains. Two years later he changed his interpretation, arguing that the remains were a fish weir. Instead of admitting his change of mind, he attacked the editor of the *American Antiquarian*, accusing him of altering the substance of his 1887 piece. Until December of 1891 Cresson was in the field every summer for the Peabody Museum, working initially in his native Delaware (Cresson 1890b) and later in Indiana (Cresson 1890c), Pennsylvania, and Ohio at the Fort Ancient site of Madisonville, at Turner (Fig. 7), and at the Hopewell site (Putnam 1888:44–46; 1890b:92–97; 1894:8). In the winters he visited the Peabody to work up his collections, but was occupied for the better part of the time pursuing an M.D. degree at the University of Pennsylvania and the Jefferson Medical College. His degree was awarded by the Jefferson Medical College after a two year program of study on April 15, 1891 (Robert Lentz, Jefferson Medical College Archives, personal communication, 1982).

Cresson took an active part in the "Great Paleolithic War" (as he later phrased it—Cresson to Holmes, January 15, 1894, Holmes Papers, SIA) during the late 1880s and early 1890s. His discovery of supposed Paleolithic implements at Claymont, Delaware was hailed by George Frederick Wright—the champion of Paleolithic man and a regular correspondent of Cresson's since 1886—as unfolding a "new chapter in the history of man in America" (Wright 1890:152). These discoveries, made in the so-called "Columbian" deposits that were alleged to be older than the Trenton gravels, appeared to push human presence in North America as far back as 30,000 to 150,000 years ago (Wright 1890:155).

When the government scientists went on the offensive against Paleolithic man, Cresson firmly allied himself with Wright and his "little band." In the late summer of 1889 while visiting the deposits around Claymont, Delaware with Cresson, the Smithsonian archaeologist W. H. Holmes discovered an object that in Cresson's view was a "large sized turtle back of the Babbitt type" (Cresson to G. F. Wright, August 26, 1889, Wright Papers, OC; the reference was to alleged paleoliths found in 1880 by F. E. Babbitt in Minnesota). The USGS geologist W J McGee, who accompanied Holmes and Cresson, determined that the discovery was made in

Fig. 7. In camp at Turner Group, Ohio, 1890. *Left to right*: Ernest Volk, Marshall Saville, Hilborne T. Cresson (Peabody Museum, Harvard University, 1563).

undisturbed gravels, but since neither he nor Holmes felt the specimen was an artifact they dismissed the find. Cresson, however, urged both Putnam and Wright to:

> fight hard for me on this find, *if there is the least thing in my favor*. You can kick up a dust on it, and if we win, the government will be forced to acknowledge that their officials have found chipped implements in Columbian deposits. McGee, however, won't do this—he will dig hard, & so will Holmes, who stands in with him. [Cresson to Putnam, August 25, 1889, Peabody Museum Archives, HU, emphasis in original]

When Putnam became Chief of the Department of Ethnology and Archaeology for the World's Columbian Exposition in Chicago, he appointed Cresson and Warren K. Moorehead Field Assistants. Work began under the direction of Moorehead at the Hopewell site in September of 1891, and Cresson, who was then on his way back east, joined the field party at Moorehead's invitation (Cresson to Putnam, March 14, 1892, Peabody Museum Archives, HU). For three months Cresson worked at the Hopewell site, although judging by Moorehead's diary he didn't work especially hard: "Dr. Cresson is getting so fat and lazy that we can hardly do anything with him" (Moorehead Diaries, October 10, 1891:2773, OHS).

Cresson's affiliation with the World's Columbian Exposition Survey came to an abrupt end when he was fired by Putnam on December 4, 1891. He was fired for theft; while working at the Hopewell site Cresson had been shipping some of the recovered specimens directly to his home in Philadelphia and not to the Peabody Museum. When confronted by Moorehead, Cresson "refused to return the specimens, claiming he had but 15" (Moorehead Diaries, December 16, 1891:2778, OHS).

Perhaps in hopes of recovering the stolen items, Putnam kept Cresson on the Peabody lists until July of 1892, when Cresson resigned (Putnam to Moorehead, February 8 and March 10, 1892, Moorehead Papers, OHS; Putnam 1894:8). Curiously, Cresson showed no apparent remorse over his field dismissal, attributing the incident to having "overstaid" his welcome, but blamed that on Moorehead who "stated that he positively wanted me to stay" (Cresson to Putnam, March 14, 1892, Peabody Museum of Archives, HU). He later effectively dismissed his long association with the Peabody with the wry observation that "when I was with Putnam, I had to work in the Mound region and other localities in which I had no especial interest" (Cresson to Powell, July 8, 1892, BAE Papers, NAA).

His confession to Powell notwithstanding, while employed by the Peabody Cresson was caught up in the debate over man's antiquity and fervently desired to contribute proof of an age that reached into the Pleistocene in North America. But once his connection with Putnam and the Museum was severed, his enthusiasm waned. As he wrote in one of his last letters to G. F. Wright:

> I shall always take a deep interest in paleolithics in spite of all the calumny that has been heaped upon our little band who have earnestly sought for truthful evidence—*even if our endeavors have not been successful* [Cresson to Wright, May 1893, Wright Papers, OC; emphasis supplied]

Cresson's resignation and loss of optimism about the chances for Paleolithic man coincided with the establishment of the De Lanceil Fund, a small endowment offered by a relative of Cresson for the "study of the graphic system of the Ancient Mayas" (Augney 1892). Cresson was named Director of the Fund, and quickly persuaded John Wesley Powell to administer the endowment under the auspices of the Bureau of American Ethnology, to facilitate Cresson's entry into Mexico and Central America. He spent the better part of the next two years on the western Gulf Coast, chiefly in Guatemala and Mexico (Powell 1897:26), and during that time he published at least seven papers on Maya writing. In early 1894 he returned to the United States.

His activities over the next few months are unclear, but from later accounts he moved between Rhode Island, New York, and Philadelphia. Then, on September 6, 1894, he "blew his brains out in a park in New York City" (*Philadelphia Inquirer*, September 8, 1894).

Cresson's suicide was given front page play in the Philadelphia newspapers, and received notice as well in the *New York Times* and *Washington Star*. The headlines in the *Philadelphia Inquirer* (September 8, 1894) were typical:

DR. H. J. [sic] CRESSON TAKES HIS OWN LIFE
A Disordered Mind, the Result of Scientific Study,
Undoubtedly the Cause.
His Body Found in One of the Public Squares in New York.
Friends and Relatives Tell of Strange Hallucinations, and Letters
Left by the Suicide Show That He Was Insane.

Theories of the cause of his insanity abounded, one source attributing the death to an "unbalanced mind due to too close application to the research of esoteric principles" (*Philadelphia Inquirer*, September 8, 1894). A telling note left by Cresson indicated that a manifestation of his mental illness was his conviction that "he was suspected of counterfeiting, and that Secret Service detectives were continually on his track" (*Philadelphia Record*, September 8, 1894).

Cresson's death warranted lines in the annual reports of both the Peabody Museum and Bureau of American Ethnology (Putnam 1894:8; Powell 1897:26), but an obituary only appeared in Warren Moorehead's journal, *The Archaeologist* (Moorehead 1894). Ironically, Moorehead and Putnam were then waging a legal battle over the disposition of the Hopewell site materials, and Moorehead used Cresson's obituary to take a slap at Putnam:

> [Cresson] faithfully served for several years one of the Eastern Professors [Putnam], a man high in Archaeologic matters, and as a reward that man turned the cold shoulder upon him. [Moorehead 1894:308]

Thomas Wilson quickly reminded Moorehead that it was his telling Putnam of Cresson's theft of the Hopewell specimens that precipitated the "cold shoulder" (Wilson to Moorehead, October 11, 1894, Moorehead Papers, OHS).

We have not discovered the smoking gun, a letter or published remark that clearly indicts Cresson as the perpetrator of the Holly Oak pendant fraud. However, the circumstantial evidence in the case is extremely strong. Cresson was a rather unscrupulous and unreliable character, whose contributions to archaeology were viewed by many with marked suspicion. As Henry Mercer observed:

> But as neither this evidence, which at Claymont, according to Professor McGee, would multiply human antiquity by ten, twenty or fifty, nor that, yet more conclusive if true, based on Mr. Cresson's two rock shelters containing "paleolithic" under Indian culture layers, on tributaries of the Delaware near Claymont, or his mammoth drawing on a shell from the same vicinity, or his aboriginal "pile dwelling" or "fish weir", revealing associated traces of evolution in human culture, on Naaman's Creek, Delaware, have been on the whole seriously cited in arguments by students, I refrain, after two visits to Claymont, from discussing the almost purely personal question. [Mercer 1897:21]

What is perhaps most perplexing about these finds is that, despite the questionable circumstances and the controversy surrounding the rockshelter and the fishweir/pile dwellings, George Frederick Wright discussed each in his massive compendia on evidences for man's antiquity in North America (Wright 1892, 1893), yet never referred to the Holly Oak pendant. Furthermore, Cresson wrote many letters to Wright during the period when the shell was made public, but in none of them did he mention the Holly Oak pendant. On January 2, 1890, for instance, shortly after Cresson had revealed the existence of the pendant to Putnam, he mailed four letters. Three of them—to Putnam, Thomas Wilson, and William H. Dall—dealt exclusively with the shell pendant; the letter to Wright of the same day only wished him a Happy New Year (Cresson to Wright, January 2, 1890, Wright Papers, OC). Why he did not tell Wright anything about the shell, despite his previous and continued discussion of all other kinds of evidence related to man's antiquity, remains a mystery. Given Wright's close relationship with Putnam and his central role in the Paleolithic debate, he certainly knew of the pendant's existence despite Cresson's avoidance of the subject. In this light Wright's silence about the find takes on some significance. Wright was willing to accept some questionable evidence on behalf of Paleolithic man (he supported the dubious Nampa Image, a clay figurine allegedly blasted out of an Idaho artesian well shaft), but he shied away from known frauds.

Suspicion surrounded many of Cresson's discoveries, and it was often due to the time lapses between the actual date of discovery and the report of the find (Mercer 1897). In the case of the Naaman's Creek fish weir or pile dwelling and the Naaman's Creek rockshelter, two dozen years elapsed before the finds were made known to Cresson's scientific correspondents, and in both instances, as with the Holly Oak pendant, an examination of the circumstances of the finds was therefore impossible. The rockshelter had been destroyed by the Baltimore and Ohio Railroad and the fish weir or pile dwelling by dredging. The Holly Oak pendant was discovered in a "muck pit" at an unknown location.

Cresson attributed his long silences following his discoveries to various factors, including his stay in France and his lack of appreciation for the importance of the finds. But if in the years before leaving for France when he was as archaeologically astute as he later implied, then he could not have been so naive as to not recognize almost immediately the significance of the finds. Certainly M. Surault would have seen their importance. It strains the bounds of credulity to believe that only after Cresson learned in Europe of mammoth engravings on tusks in French caves and pile dwellings in Swiss lakes, did he return to the United States to announce that he had already discovered these very archaeological features on this continent.

In any case, the announcement of the Holly Oak pendant was also held back, according to Cresson, by his family, who were unwilling to risk a controversy such as the one that surrounded the fraudulent mastodon pipes (in the late 1880s, long after the alleged discovery of the Holly Oak pendant; Cresson to Putnam, January 10, 1890, Peabody Museum Archives, HU; see also McKusick 1971). In fact, throughout 1890-91 while the Peabody Museum and the Smithsonian waited, Cresson reported to Putnam that his family was haggling over where the shell should ultimately be deposited. Putnam must have been somewhat bewildered by Cresson identifying the main force in the family, "Mrs. Spencer" (whose name accompanies the accession records for the pendant at the Smithsonian), alternately as his mother, his sister, or his friend (Cresson to Putnam, December 13, 1889; January 10, 1890; March 30, 1890, Peabody Museum Archives, HU).

From the evidence that exists a scenario can be reconstructed in which Cresson, anxious to make his mark in science and archaeology (he was frequently asking Wright and McGee to nominate him for various scientific societies), and well aware of the evidence necessary to prove human existence in America in Pleistocene times, manufactured a piece of Upper Paleolithic art from a section of *Busycon* shell. The shell would have been readily available from the Fort Ancient sites where he worked and whose collections were accessible to him at the Peabody Museum. The model for the design was obvious: the La Madeleine engraving that Cresson had likely examined while studying art and archaeology in Paris, and that was reproduced in a publication he knew.

In a show of chutzpah, Cresson even observed that the Holly Oak pendant "is quite as valuable as the mammoth engraved on bone"[the La

Madeleine tusk] (Cresson to Putnam, January 21, 1890, Peabody Museum Archives, HU).

CONCLUSIONS

> Conscious fraud is probably rare in science. It is also not very interesting, for it tells us little about the nature of scientific activity. Liars, if discovered, are excommunicated; scientists declare that their profession has properly policed itself, and they return to work, mythology unimpaired, and objectivity vindicated. [Gould 1981:54-55]

As Vayson de Pradenne (1932) has clearly demonstrated, skillful archaeological frauds, especially artistic ones, characteristically only seem obvious later, when the fund of knowledge and experience of the subject has improved. With so few examples of engraved Pleistocene art in both Europe and America in the late nineteenth century, the uniqueness of the Holly Oak pendant was not a strike against it. Now, with the increased number of examples of European Paleolithic art, and the lack of an increase in examples of North American "Paleolithic" art, the singularity of the Holly Oak pendant is particularly suspect. If the pendant did *not* look like one of the comparatively few pieces of European Paleolithic art to have been discovered prior to 1890, then its authenticity might seem more plausible. But a good fraud addressed to a question of current interest and controversy often becomes obvious only after the question has been settled and the structure of the relevant archaeological data set has been outlined. And in North America the Holly Oak pendant is now out of place.

The similarities with the La Madeleine tusk and the widespread existence of forgeries were certainly recognized in the 1890s, with the result that those who might have been inclined to use the pendant as evidence of man's antiquity shied away from it. Even in the midst of the intense debate on the antiquity of man, when any and all testimony was being gathered in support of the American Paleolithic, the Holly Oak pendant was rarely cited. Certainly the proponents of Paleolithic man, all correspondents of Cresson's, were aware that the pendant existed, but few chose to use it to further their cause.

Yet the recognition of the artifact's similarity to the La Madeleine tusk was probably not the only factor that determined the silence with which Cresson's contemporaries greeted the pendant. In all likelihood his reputation among the small and rather closed archaeological community played a role as well. The structure of the archaeological profession in the 1890s was significantly different from its modern state. Unlike the mature sciences with mechanisms for exposing conscious fraud—to which Gould's comment applies—the archaeology of the previous century lacked rigorous means of data evaluation. It was the credibility and integrity of the discoverer that was as important in determining the acceptance of a discovery as any inherent properties of the artifact itself. The Reverend George Frederick Wright was at least given a hearing when he innocently proclaimed that the Nampa Image—certainly a more obvious forgery then and now than the Holly Oak pendant—was proof of human existence in North America during the Pleistocene. Cresson and his Holly Oak pendant were merely ignored. In fact, Frederick Ward Putnam, Cresson's employer who stood by so much of Cresson's questionable work, was so steadfastly silent about the shell after 1890 that one has to remind oneself that it was he who first exhibited the pendant at the meeting of the Boston Society of Natural History. And Putnam spent a lifetime in the search for proof of early man.

It is risky at best to guess the motivations of scientists long dead, but the fact that Cresson's contemporaries chose to ignore the pendant rather than examine it critically and publicly, as the Nampa Image ultimately was, warrants some comment. Perhaps it was misplaced loyalty on the part of those closest to Cresson or, more likely, it was because it was generally known in the community that the pendant was a fraud so that condemnation of the forgery was perceived as unnecessary. This deduction is supported by the fact that it was largely scientists outside of the immediate Peabody Museum/Bureau of American Ethnology axis of archaeologists who felt compelled to suggest that the pendant was a fraud (e.g. Brinton 1892, 1893a, 1893b; Mercer 1897). Apparently, everyone more closely involved knew already.

But these scattered voices were not loud enough and, after the passage of 90 years, their message is barely audible. Thus the artifact became ripe for rediscovery by later generations. Now that the contemporaneity in North America of human beings and the extinct Pleistocene fauna is firmly established, the Holly Oak pendant has been innocently resurrected as further evidence of the association of early man and the mammoth (Weslager [1941, 1944] was the likely source of the rediscovery, followed by others, e.g., Meggers [1972:13]; Kraft and Thomas [1976]; Kraft [1977]; Dragoo [1979:207]). Since the case of the contemporaneity is proven without the Holly Oak pendant as evidence, it should be easy to purge this fraud from the record.

Evidence collected in another era can be of immense value, but its validity should be critically evaluated both from our own perspective and in terms of the methods, theories and debates of its own period. If the data turn out to be unacceptable as scientific evidence, the investigation may nevertheless contribute to the historiography of science.

Notes

1. We offer these pages to commemorate a course taught by George Quimby under the title "Mastodons and Cross-cousin Marriage." It is also a cautionary tale: would that Cresson (or Putnam) had had Quimby's (1978) concern to record contemporary handiwork that might otherwise confuse the archaeological record.

This paper was planned and written, and the Holly Oak pendant examined by both of us, during Meltzer's tenure as a Research Fellow at the Smithsonian Institution. The support of that Institution and a grant to Meltzer from Sigma-Xi, The Scientific Research Society, are gratefully acknowledged. Most of the research and the writing of the first draft was by Meltzer, who conducted all the archival investigations and nearly all the search of the published literature. Sturtevant's main contribution is the stylistic comparison of the engravings. The final draft is a product of both our efforts.

For useful comments and leads to sources, we would like to thank Donald K. Grayson, Curtis M. Hinsley, Jr., Stephen Williams, and especially James B. Griffin (who also suggested the title). Joseph Rosewater and Jerry Harasewych provided the taxonomic identification of the shell of the pendant and offered valuable observations on its condition. Léonard Ginsburg, Institut de Paléontologie, Paris, facilitated Sturtevant's examination of the original La Madeleine specimen at the Muséum National d'Histoire Naturelle and kindly provided us with a new photograph of it. George R. Lewis (who also did the drawing for Kraft and Thomas 1976:Fig. 1) traced and inked out Figure 1, top. Finally, Samuel L. Cresson, M.D. and Susan Frisch Lehrer, Curator of the Chesterwood Museum, graciously answered our inquiries about Hilborne T. Cresson.

2. In the text we cite unpublished correspondence and the like with abbreviations indicating the following archives: HU = Peabody Museum Archives, Pusey Library, Harvard University, Cambridge, Massachusetts; NAA = National Anthropological Archives, National Museum of Natural History, Smithsonian Institution, Washington, D.C.; OC = Oberlin College Archives, Oberlin College, Oberlin, Ohio; OHS = Ohio Historical Society Archives, Ohio Historical Society, Columbus, Ohio; SIA = Smithsonian Institution Archives, Smithsonian Institution, Washington, D.C.

3. Cresson seems to have realized that something was amiss here, but got it wrong, crudely sketching a comparison, in his January 21, 1890, letter to Putnam, between "the line of the back, in the Elephant . . . [which] is much more horizontal than that of the animal drawn on the shell," and the line of the "mastodon" back that he drew sloping quite sharply down from the neck.

4. Curiously, when the collection was given to the Smithsonian Institution a year later, it contained only 79 specimens (see Wilson 1893).

5. See Kraft and Thomas (1976:Fig. 2 caption) for a contrary view.

REFERENCES

Ashley-Montagu, M. F.
    1944   An Indian tradition relating to the mastodon. *American Anthropologist* 46:568–571.

Augney, W. M.
    1892   The de Lanceil Fund for the study of the Maya language and its graphic system. Manuscript in BAE Letters Received, National Anthropological Archives, Smithsonian Institution, Washington, D.C.

Barriere, C.
    [1970]   Les techniques de la gravure à Rouffignac. *Travaux de l'Institut d'Art Préhistorique* 12:11–153. Toulouse.

Berdin, M.-O.
    [1970]   La répartition des mammouths dans l'art pariétal quaternaire. *Travaux de l'Institut d'Art Préhistorique* 12:181–367. Toulouse.

Bibby, G.
    1956   *The testimony of the spade.* A. A. Knopf, New York.

Brinton, D. G.
   1892   Current notes on anthropology—12. *Science* 20:90–91.
   1893a Current notes on anthropology—22. *Science* 21:75.
   1893b On an "inscribed tablet" from Long Island. *The Archaeologist* 1(11):201–203.
Breuil, H.
   [1952] *Quatre cents siècles d'art pariétal. Les cavernes ornées de l'age du renne.* Centre d'Études et de Documentation préhistoriques, Montignac, Dordogne.
Bullock, W.
   1827   *Sketch of a journey through the western states of North America.* London. (Cited from the partial reprint, *Early western travels*, Vol. 19, edited by R. G. Thwaites, Cleveland, 1905).
Capitan, L., H. Breuil, and D. Peyrony
   1910   *La Caverne de Font-de-Gaume aux Eyzies (Dordogne).* Imprimerie Vve. A. Chêne, Monaco.
   1924   *Les Combarelles aux Eyzies (Dordogne).* Masson, Paris.
Cresson, H. T.
   1887   River dwellings on the mud flats of Delaware River. *American Antiquarian* 9(6):363–365.
   1890a Supposed aboriginal fish-weirs in Naaman's Creek, Delaware. *Science* 15:116–117.
   1890b Early man in the Delaware Valley. *Proceedings of the Boston Society of Natural History* 24:141–150.
   1890c Remarks upon a chipped implement, found in modified drift, on the east fork of the White River, Jackson Co., Indiana. *Proceedings of the Boston Society of Natural History* 24:150–152.
   1891   A fallen forest and peat layer underlying aqueous deposits in Delaware. *Bulletin of the Geological Society of America* 2:640–642.
   1892   Paleolithic man in the southern portion of the Delaware Valley. *Science* 20:304–305.
Cunningham, W. M.
   1948   A study of the Glacial Kame culture. *Occasional Contribution from the Museum of Anthropology, University of Michigan* 12.
Cusick, D.
   1827   *Sketches of ancient history of the Six Nations.* Printed for the author, Lewiston (Cited from the 1961 reprint by the Niagara County Historical Society of the 1848 ed., Lockport, N. Y.).
Dragoo, C. W.
   1979   The Proboscideans and man. *Archaeology of Eastern North America* 7:180–213.
Eiseley, L. C.
   1945   Indian mythology and extinct fossil vertebrates. *American Anthropologist* 47:318–320.
Gould, S. J.
   1981   *The mismeasure of man.* W. W. Norton, New York.
Griffin, J. B.
   1943   *The Fort Ancient aspect, its cultural and chronological position in Mississippi Valley archaeology.* University of Michigan Press, Ann Arbor.
Hart, K. R.
   1976   Government geologists and the early man controversy: The problem of "official" science in America, 1879–1907. Ph.D. dissertation, Department of History, Kansas State University.
Henshaw, H. W.
   1883   Animal carvings from mounds of the Mississippi Valley. *Second Annual Report of the Bureau of [American] Ethnology*, pp. 117–166.
Kraft, J. C.
   1977   Late Quaternary paleogeographic changes in the coastal environments of Delaware, Middle Atlantic Bight, related to archaeologic settings. In Amerinds

and their paleoenvironments in northeastern North America, edited by W. S. Newman and B. Salwen. *Annals of the New York Academy of Sciences* 288:35–69.

Kraft, J. C., and R. A. Thomas
    1976   Early man at Holly Oak, Delaware. *Science* 192:756–761.

Kurtén, B., and E. Anderson
    1980   *Pleistocene mammals of North America*. Columbia University Press, New York.

Lartet, É.
    1865   Une lame d'ivoire fossile trouvée dans un gisemet ossifère du Périgord, et portant des incisions qui paraissent constituer la reproduction d'un Éléphant à longue crinère. *Compte Rendu des Séances de l'Académie des Sciences* 61(8):309–311.

Lartet, É., and H. Christy
    1875   *Reliquiae Aquitanicae: Being contributions to the archaeology and paleontology of Périgord and the adjoining provinces of southern France*, edited by T. Rupert Jones. Williams and Norgate, London.

Lubbock, J.
    1869   *Prehistoric times* (second ed.). Williams and Norgate, London.
    1870   *The origin of civilisation and the primitive condition of man*. Longmans, Green, London.

McKusick, M. B.
    1971   The Davenport conspiracy. *State Archaeologist of Iowa*, Report 1.

McMillan, R. B.
    1976   Man and mastodon: A review of Koch's 1840 Pomme de Terre expeditions. In *Prehistoric man and his environments*, edited by W. Wood and R. B. McMillan, pp. 81–96. Academic Press, New York.

Meggers, B.
    1972   *Prehistoric America*. Aldine, Chicago.

Meltzer, D. J.
    1983   The antiquity of man and the development of American archaeology. In *Advances in archaeological method and theory*, edited by M. B. Schiffer, Vol. 6:1–51. Academic Press, New York.

Meltzer, D. J., and J. I. Mead
    1983   The timing of Late Pleistocene mammalian extinctions in North America. *Quaternary Research* 19:130–135.

Mercer, H. C.
    1885   *The Lenape stone or the Indian and the mammoth*. G. P. Putnam's Sons, New York.
    1897   Researches upon the antiquity of man in the Delaware Valley and the eastern United States. *Publications of the University of Pennsylvania, Series in Philology, Literature and Archaeology* 6.

Michelson, T.
    1936   Mammoth or "stiff-legged bear." *American Anthropologist* 38:141–143.

Moorehead, W. K.
    1894   Dr. Hilborne T. Cresson. *The Archaeologist* 2:308.
    1910   *The stone age in North America*. Houghton Mifflin, Boston.

Morgan, R. G.
    1952   Outline of cultures in the Ohio region. In *Archeology of eastern United States*, edited by J. B. Griffin, pp. 83–98. University of Chicago Press, Chicago.

Mortillet, G. de
    1867   *Promenades préhistoriques à l'Exposition universelle*. C. Reinwald, Paris.

Organ, R. M.
    1969   Examination report. Smithsonian Institution Conservation-Analytical Laboratory, Cal No. 698, 7 February 1969. Manuscript on file, Department of Anthropology, Smithsonian Institution, Washington, D.C.

Peabody Museum of American Archaeology and Ethnology
    1887   Officers of the museum and special assistants. *Annual Reports of the Peabody Museum* 4(1)[21st]:6.
Powell, J. W.
    1897   Report of the director. *16th Annual Report of the Bureau of American Ethnology* [for 1894], pp. xiii–xcix.
Putnam, F. W.
    1888   Report of the curator [for 1888]. *Annual Reports of the Peabody Museum* 4(2)[22nd]:31–52.
    1890a   Untitled Putnam comments, General Meeting, February 5, 1890. *Proceedings of the Boston Society of Natural History* 24:467–469.
    1890b   Report of the curator [for 1890]. *Annual Reports of the Peabody Museum* 4(4)[24th]:87–99.
    1894   The Peabody Museum of American Archaeology and Ethnology. Reprinted from Report of the President of Harvard University, in *28th Annual Report of the Peabody Museum for 1893–1894*, separately paginated.
Quimby, G. I.
    1978   An exotic campsite in east Hudson's Bay. *Historical Archaeology* 10:121–123.
Rau, C.
    1876   *Early man in Europe.* Harper and Brothers, New York.
Siebert, F. T., Jr.
    1937   Mammoth or "stiff-legged bear." *American Anthropologist* 39:721–725.
Speck, F. G.
    1935   Mammoth or "stiff-legged bear." *American Anthropologist* 37:159–163.
Strong, W. D.
    1934   North American Indian traditions suggesting a knowledge of the mammoth. *American Anthropologist* 36:81–88.
Ucko, P. J., and A. Rosenfeld
    1967   *Paleolithic cave art.* Weidenfeld and Nicolson, London.
Vayson de Pradenne, A.
    1932   *Les fraudes en archéologie préhistorique, avec quelques exemples de comparaison en archéologie générale et sciences naturelles.* Émile Nourry, Paris.
Weslager, C. A.
    1941   An incised fulgar shell from Holly Oak, Delaware. *Archaeological Society of Delaware Bulletin* 3(4):10–15.
    1944   *Delaware's buried past: a story of archaeological adventure.* University of Pennsylvania Press, Philadelphia.
Wilson, T.
    1893   Report on the Department of Prehistoric Anthropology in the U.S. National Museum, 1892. *Annual Report of the U.S. National Museum for 1892*:135–142.
    1898   Prehistoric art. *Annual Report of the U.S. National Museum for 1896*:325–664.
    1901   La Haute ancienneté de l'homme dans l'Amérique du Nord. *l'Anthropologie* 12(3–4):297–339.
Wright, G. F.
    1890   The age of the Philadelphia red gravel. *Proceedings of the Boston Society of Natural History* 24:152–157.
    1892   *Man and the glacial period.* D. Appleton, New York.
    1893   *The Ice Age in North America and its bearing upon the antiquity of man* (third ed.). D. Appleton, New York.

CONTRIBUTORS

DAVID A. BAERREIS, Professor Emeritus, Department of Anthropology, University of Wisconsin, Madison, WI 53706.
CHARLOTTE BECK, Graduate Student, Department of Anthropology, University of Washington, Seattle, WA 98195.
LEWIS R. BINFORD, Professor, Department of Anthropology, University of New Mexico, Albuquerque, NM 87131.
DAVID S. BROSE, Curator, Cleveland Museum of Natural History, Wade Oval, University Circle, Cleveland, OH 44106.
ROBERT C. DUNNELL, Professor and Chairman, Department of Anthropology, University of Washington, Seattle, WA 98195 and Adjunct Curator, Burke Memorial Museum, University of Washington.
DONALD K. GRAYSON, Associate Professor, Department of Anthropology, University of Washington, Seattle, WA 98195 and Adjunct Curator, Burke Memorial Museum, University of Washington.
JAMES B. GRIFFIN, Curator Emeritus and Senior Research Scientist, Museum of Anthropology, University Museums Building, University of Michigan, Ann Arbor, MI 48109.
ROBERT L. HALL, Professor, Department of Anthropology, University of Illinois at Chicago Circle, Chicago, IL 60680.
GEORGE T. JONES, Graduate Student, Department of Anthropology, University of Washington, Seattle, WA 98195.
WALTER E. KLIPPEL, Assistant Professor, Department of Anthropology, University of Tennessee, Knoxville, TN 37916.
DAVID J. MELTZER, Graduate Student, Department of Anthropology, University of Washington, Seattle, WA 98195.
CARL-AXEL MOBERG, Professor, Department of Archaeology, Göteborgs Universitet, Göteborg, Sweden.
PAUL W. PARMALEE, Professor, Department of Anthropology, University of Tennessee, Knoxville, TN 37916 and Director, Frank H. McClung Museum, University of Tennessee.

ALBERT C. SPAULDING, Professor, Department of Anthropology, University of California, Santa Barbara, CA 93106.

WILLIAM C. STURTEVANT, Curator, Department of Anthropology, National Museum of Natural History, Smithsonian Institution, Washington, DC 20560.